DOWN AND OUT *in Early America*

# DOWN AND OUT

# *in Early America*

*Edited by* *Billy G. Smith*

THE PENNSYLVANIA STATE UNIVERSITY PRESS    UNIVERSITY PARK, PENNSYLVANIA

LIBRARY OF CONGRESS CATALOGING-IN-PUBLICATION DATA

Down and out in early America/edited by Billy G. Smith.
    p.        cm.
    Three of the eleven papers in this volume were presented at a session
    held at the 1997 Organization of American Historians meeting.
Includes bibliographical references and index.
ISBN 0-271-02316-3 (cloth : alk. paper)
ISBN 0-271-02317-1 (pbk. : alk. paper)
1. Poverty—United States—History.  2. Poor—United States—History.
3. Marginality, Social—United States—History.  4. Charities—United
States—History.  5. Economic assistance, Domestic—United States—
History.  6. United States—History—Colonial period, ca. 1600–1775
I. Smith, Billy Gordon.

HC110 .P6D625 2003
362.5'0973'09033—dc22

                                                        2003022441

Printed in the United States of America
Published by The Pennsylvania State University Press,
University Park, PA 16802–1003

The Pennsylvania State University Press is a member of the Association
of American University Presses.

It is the policy of The Pennsylvania State University Press to use acid-free
paper. Publications on uncoated stock satisfy the minimum requirements of American National Standard for Information Sciences—
Permanence of Paper for Printed Library Materials, ANSI Z39.48–1992.

*Frontispiece:* Almshouse on Spruce Street, Philadelphia. Courtesy of
The Historical Society of Pennsylvania.

*to Michelle Maskiell*

*It is the essence of the poor that they do not appear in history.*
—ANONYMOUS

*Give me neither poverty nor riches.*
—PROVERBS 30:8

*Clothes make the poor invisible. . . . America has the best-dressed poverty the world has ever known.*
—MICHAEL HARRINGTON

*Is it possible that my people live in such awful conditions? If I had to live in conditions like that, I would be a revolutionary myself.*
—KING GEORGE V

*But I, being poor, have only my dreams*
*I have spread my dreams under your feet*
*Tread softly because you tread on my dreams*
—W. B. YEATS

*There are only two families in the world, my old grandmother used to say, The Haves and the Have-Nots.*
—MIGUEL DE CERVANTES

*Two nations; between whom there is no intercourse and no sympathy; who are as ignorant of each other's habits, thoughts, and feelings, as if they were dwellers in different zones, or inhabitants of different planets; who are formed by a different breeding, are fed by a different food, are ordered by different manners, and are not governed by the same laws: the rich and the poor.*
—BENJAMIN DISRAELI

*I am a gentleman. I live by robbing the poor.*
—GEORGE BERNARD SHAW

*Look at me: I worked my way up from nothing to a state of extreme poverty.*
—GROUCHO MARX

# CONTENTS

# ACKNOWLEDGMENTS

Editing this volume has been very enjoyable and satisfying, in part because it provided an opportunity to collaborate with wonderful scholars and compassionate human beings, in part because other people did most of the substantive work. I am now well positioned to claim credit for the book's successes yet blame others for its shortcomings.

I thank all the scholars who cared deeply enough about the topic to write essays for the volume. I especially appreciate the patience of Monique Bourque, Ruth Herndon, and Karin Wulf, all of whom waited a very long time for this project to be complete. (Unfortunately, I too frequently heeded the advice of Douglas Adams, author of the *Hitchhiker's Guide to the Galaxy:* "I love deadlines. I love the whooshing noise they make when rushing past.") Gary B. Nash, Simon Newman, and Jean Soderlund provided valuable comments about many of the essays. John K. Alexander twice read the manuscript thoroughly and improved it greatly with his suggestions. Christine Daniels likewise offered very helpful advice about the entire project. Mary Murphy and Michelle Maskiell also proffered excellent criticism, while Trinette Ross, typically efficient as a research assistant, aided the process in innumerable ways. I am very pleased to once again have worked with Peter Potter, a wonderfully supportive editor, while Eliza Childs served as a very valuable copy editor and improved the book at nearly every point.

I also gratefully acknowledge the help of my colleagues at Montana State University. The Vice President for Research, Tom McCoy, has been very farsighted in generously funding many investigations in the humanities, arts, and social sciences, including this project. While I have not asked most of them to review these essays, my departmental colleagues nonetheless have contributed to the book by making Bozeman such a wonderful place to work and live. Historians Rob Campbell, David Cherry, Tim Lecain, Dale Martin, Michelle Maskiell, Mary Murphy, and Bob Rydell have created an appealing intellectual environment; philosophers Jim Allard, Prasanta Bandyopadhyay, Corky Brittan, Dan Flory, and Sandy Levy have often posed oddly intriguing questions; religious studies scholars Susan Cohen and Lynda Sexson have frequently baffled me in a positive fashion. Diane Cattrell and Sheila Wagner add efficiency and liveliness to the department. My thanks go as well to

Jim Bruggeman for numerous conversations about poverty, class, exploitation, early America, and elementary education. My colleagues David Large, Michael Reidy, and Brett Walker play racquetball less effectively than they write history.

Jack Smith, Carol Smith, Betty Smith, and Barbara Gibson have been, as always, loving and supportive. My wonderful daughter, Sage Adrienne Smith, and my life partner, Michelle Maskiell, to whom this book is dedicated, have deeply enriched my life, reminding me that my heart should leap up when I behold a rainbow in the sky.

# INTRODUCTION

## *"The Best Poor Man's Country"?*

### BILLY G. SMITH

No Observation is more common, and at the same time more
true, than That one half of the world are ignorant [of] how
the other half lives.
                              —Anonymous Philadelphian, 1767

We live in an era of economic apartheid, both nationally and internationally.
During the final decade of the twentieth century, many Americans enjoyed
immense and growing prosperity, yet others suffered continuing, sometimes
intensifying deprivation. The "overclass" of enormously wealthy Americans
expanded considerably. Meanwhile, the size of the "underclass" waxed and
waned, confining millions of people to conditions of destitution from which
few escape. From 1980 to 2000, between 11 and 15 percent (approximately 30
to 40 million people) of United States citizens earned incomes below the fed-
erally defined poverty level, and a similar number teetered on the threshold of
indigence. One of every five children lives in poverty each year, and twice that
many children will live in indigent households by the time of their eighteenth
birthday. Fortunately, the proportion of impoverished Americans declined
slightly during the century's final few years as financial boom times finally benefited some of the needy. Unfortunately, one of every ten American households still suffered food shortages, and 4 million others experienced hunger
on a monthly basis, all at a time when public aid to the disadvantaged
declined. Poverty has increased again during the economic downturn of the
first years of the twenty-first century.[1] On a global scale, the number of poor
throughout the world grew by more than 200 million during the last decade.
Currently, 1.5 billion people earn less than one dollar each day—the world-
wide benchmark for abject poverty—and nearly 800 million people suffer
chronic hunger. One result is that various diseases, many of them preventable
with only small sums of money, run rampant in poorer nations. Millions of
lives consequently are shortened solely because people are destitute.

Inequality in the distribution of wealth in the United States has increased during the past two decades at a rate previously unknown in the nation's history. The richest 1 percent of citizens now possesses more wealth than the poorest 90 percent; even after the recent decline in his fortune in stocks, Bill Gates is still worth more than at least 80 million Americans. In its level of inequality, the United States has grown more similar to preindustrial nations than to the industrial and postindustrial world. The economic gap among various classes of Americans has never been greater. The recent rapid spread of capitalism around the world has further encouraged similar patterns of economic inequality throughout the globe.

Yet, historical studies of American poverty have declined during recent years. World events, such as the dissolution of the Soviet Union, the intensification of global capitalism, and the deindustrialization of wealthy nations (with the concomitant movement of low-wage employment to poorer countries), along with challenges issued by new academic fashions have all undermined an examination of the past (and present) from a national class perspective. In addition, the existence of a substantial number of indigents often has been denied in America, in part because it contradicts our avowed commitment to equality, in part because it is difficult to explain the toleration of widespread destitution in an extremely wealthy society. People in the United States seemingly rediscover the American poor every few generations, it has been observed cynically, as was the case in the Great Depression and again during the 1960s. We are long overdue for a similar rediscovery in a new century. The essays in this volume are a small part of the effort to reconsider the long, often tragic history of poverty and the poor in early America.

For more than a generation, many historians have accepted the phrase "it is the best poor man's country in the world," initially penned by indentured servant William Moraley, as an accurate characterization of early North America. Scholars, however, have ignored the context of Moraley's description, the ambivalence he expressed about opportunities for less affluent people, and the particulars of his life, all of which belie his assessment.[2] More important, historians, in agreement with Adam Smith, have embraced the shibboleth that because the New World contained a great deal of available land (as long as Indians were dispossessed) and relatively few laborers, the law of supply and demand dictated that most early American working people should have enjoyed high wages and a decent material standard of life. Thus, while the poor may always be with every society, their numbers in early America are believed to have been few. The essays in this volume challenge that contention; explore the lives and strategies of people who struggled with destitution; evaluate the changing forms of poor relief; and examine the political, religious, gender, and racial aspects of poverty in early North America.

Many prominent historians believe that privation was not widespread in seventeenth- and eighteenth-century North America. "Poverty and economic deprivation," Gordon Wood baldly declares in his Pulitzer Prize-winning volume, "were not present in colonial America." David Hackett Fischer contends that much of the previous historical analysis of "social structure" and "material processes"—including the study of indigence—have distorted our understanding of early North America by causing us to ignore human contingency and individual choice. Both scholars echo the perspective of Bernard Bailyn who argues that revolutionary Americans did not confront the "predicament of poverty." Two leading economic historians, John McCusker and Russell Menard, at least recognize the existence of indigence, especially among slaves. Yet, they conclude, "the colonies experienced little if any of the abject poverty found in contemporary Europe." In essays in this volume, Philip Morgan summarizes the major arguments supporting these conclusions while Gary Nash provides a powerful alternative interpretation.[3]

This appraisal of the lack of economic distress is flawed, both logically and by its facile dismissal of many of the conditions that historically have produced poverty. Symptomatic of their misinterpretation of the extent and nature of destitution in early North America, most scholars have misunderstood William Moraley's account of "the best poor man's country." He used the expression to praise Mid-Atlantic inhabitants for their generous hospitality to impecunious travelers rather than to paint a rosy portrait of early North America. Instead, he criticized the exploitation of and limited economic opportunities available to people without property. While acknowledging the general "Affluence and Plenty" enjoyed by many land-owning farmers in the Middle Colonies in the 1720s, Moraley recognized that numerous unfree residents did not share this abundance; their labor instead served as a primary source of the wealth for their masters. Purchasing servants and slaves rather than paying wages to free workers enriched farmers, Moraley explained, but it did not benefit bound laborers. As a result, "the Condition of Negroes is very bad," he observed, and that of "Bought servants is very hard." Once having gained his freedom, Moraley struggled to survive financially. Because most of the good land in the area had already been claimed, and since he had little aptitude for farming, Moraley was unable to obtain a foothold or establish economic independence. When his watch making and other occupational skills proved in scant demand in the colonies, he was "reduced to Poverty" and forced to return to Britain. Moraley's story, hardly exceptional for the half of Europeans who migrated to North America as indentured servants in the eighteenth century, does not support an overly optimistic interpretation of the British colonies as a region with limitless possibilities and virtually free of destitution.[4]

In a similar vein, historians often have failed to appreciate the numerous factors that generated widespread indigence in early North America. Gary Nash's essay explains many of these historical forces, but a few others bear discussion here. In preindustrial countries, low productivity (by modern standards) severely curtails the society's total wealth. The grim reality is that under such economic conditions, both today and in the past, limited resources dictate that penury will be extensive and endemic, and that the material lives of many people will be financially nasty and brutish. Because relatively little surplus existed, and since the available wealth was inequitably distributed, a great number of inhabitants of the British colonies necessarily lived close to the fiscal edge. Even in the modern United States, the wealthiest of all nations, approximately one-quarter of citizens are mired in poverty or teeter on the brink of indigence. By contrast, to argue that poverty was virtually nonexistent in a much less prosperous land two centuries ago involves fanciful thinking unsubstantiated by careful analysis.[5]

Overly favorable comparisons between early North America and Europe sometimes have clouded scholars' vision. Poverty certainly was more widespread in preindustrial England, Ireland, Scotland, Germany, and France than in seventeenth- and eighteenth-century North America, at least among white Americans. Conditions in American urban centers, for example, did not match the Hogarthian misery of eighteenth-century London. Yet, that city was an anomaly even within its own country. In terms of the total wealth of both societies, the colonies were not as opulent as Britain, and destitution may not have been much more intense in British towns and rural areas than among white inhabitants of comparable North American regions, as Susan Klepp's demographic study in this volume demonstrates. Most important, it is essential not to confuse relative and absolute degrees of poverty. Merely because fewer white Americans than Western Europeans suffered indigence does not therefore mean that destitution was nonexistent or unimportant in early America. As a Scottish "gentleman" commented in 1774, "I hear it is affirmed by many, that poor People in general are like to be as unhappy in America as at Home."[6]

Quick to endorse the notion of an overall labor shortage in early North America which allegedly ensured that few people suffered destitution, scholars have been slow to understand many circumstances that prevented workers from taking advantage of a seemingly beneficial situation. Early British America was constituted by a number of regional rather than a single national economy, which, in turn, was liable to routine cyclical and seasonal variations. The supply of labor correspondingly varied both regionally and over time. During the harvest in wheat-producing areas, for example, laborers were in great demand, and workers, if free, could find employment at good wages. During the winter, however, when the rhythms of both agriculture and maritime trade slowed and even halted, free workers were unlikely to command the pay essential to maintain financial independence for themselves and their families. In addition, European migration, often chaotic and uneven rather than economically rational from the perspective of American employers, frequently skewed local labor markets, creating shortages in some areas while dumping far too many workers in others. Philadelphia is a prime example: the ebb and flow of migrants contributed to boom and bust periods for the city's economy in general and for laboring people in particular.[7]

Neither impoverished migrants nor penniless colonists could easily benefit from the much-vaunted availability of cheap land by moving to the boundaries of European settlement. It was impossible for many if not most poor people because of the requirements of skill and capital. William Moraley and Benjamin Franklin are instructive on this point. Moraley possessed neither the inclination, nor the expertise, nor the financial resources to begin life anew as a farmer after his servitude was complete. Franklin could not become a successful artisan until he could secure assets for an independent shop—one reason he bargained for a marriage to obtain a dowry to support his ambition. The capital required to establish a farm on the frontier was equally crucial to success and well beyond the means of most laboring people. Of course, even the material successes of Euro-Americans on the borderlands usually came at a high price: the dispossession of Native Americans.[8]

Exaggerating the general shortage of labor and easy availability of land, some scholars have overlooked the social and economic organization established by white settlers that limited the opportunities for most other early Americans. In assessing poverty, historians frequently have disregarded the predicament of slaves and Native Americans, who constituted a significant proportion of the population. This airbrushing of Africans and Indians can hardly be overemphasized. Approximately one of every five Americans during the revolutionary era was held in perpetual bondage, and, as Philip Morgan argues in his essay, material "conditions for the vast majority of slaves were far worse than those experienced by white people." Some Indians became refugees, part of the wandering poor in their own land. Many died from disease or violence or were enslaved by Euro-Americans; others either moved westward to escape the European advance or settled on small tracts of land among the colonists, where they often experienced poverty and dependence. (In this volume, Jean Soderlund explores the Jersey Delaware Indians as they adjusted to new social and economic conditions.) Certainly, the lands of the original inhabitants and the labor of African forced migrants

considerably enhanced the wealth of European colonists. When slaves and
Indians are considered as impoverished people rather than as mere property
or as societal "outsiders," the existence of widespread, permanent poverty in
early North America becomes obvious.

Although it has received scant attention from scholars, the lack of life's
necessities abbreviated the lives of many early Americans, both directly and
indirectly. As Philadelphia's almshouse officials reported, "most" people
admitted to the institution were "naked, helpless and emaciated with Poverty
and Disease to such a Degree, that some have died in a few Days after their
Admission." Lydia Landrum was one such victim. She arrived at the
almshouse "in a state of starvation and nakedness, and brought in a Cart . . .
being so extremely numb with cold that she was entirely helpless." She
expired a few days later. People did die of hunger and exposure in early
North America. New York petitioners in 1766 noted, for instance, that the
city's poor "have been in a starving Condition"; in Rhode Island, the poor
subsisted on a cheap bread made of potatoes and flour; "several poor persons" in Boston "froze even while in bed, being destitute of sufficient covering." Malnutrition and inadequate shelter and clothing claimed a significant
number of lives among the homeless population, especially in New England
and in urban centers during the second half of the eighteenth century. Con-
stables apprehended dozens of vagrants each day in American cities, while
officials perceived beggars to be such a problem that soliciting alms was
legally prohibited. For many among both the wandering poor and those living in more permanent arrangements, the physical toll occurred more slowly
as the continual deficiency of food and shelter weakened their bodies and
increased their vulnerability to the ravages of various diseases—among the
primary causes of death in early America.[9]

The early Americans who expressed fears about poverty, both for their
country and for themselves, have been largely ignored by scholars. It is well
known that revolutionary Americans were alarmed that Britain's policies
threatened to enslave them, but widespread complaints about the possibility
of Britain reducing Americans to poverty and distress are less familiar. For
example, a Bostonian complained that the Stamp Act was not only "unconsti-
tutional," but also that it "must infallibly entail poverty and beggary on us and
our posterity." In 1767, a group of Bostonians cautioned that the British
trade policies "threaten the country with poverty and ruin." Three years later,
Alexander McDougall warned his fellow New Yorkers that "the Poverty of
the Colony" is "occasioned by the Restrictions upon our Trade." In 1774,
"A Philadelphian" complained that because of Parliamentary Acts, "Thousands, accustomed to Affluence, are reduced to the lowest Species of

Poverty." Similar anxieties about the future of the country's economy emerged during the debates surrounding Shays's Rebellion and the ratification of the United States Constitution. "Toryism and Shayism are nearly allied," wrote one newspaper contributor: "They both lead to slavery, poverty, and misery." Another writer exhorted that "nothing but the immediate establishment of the Foederal Government can save us from . . . poverty." (In this volume, Thomas Humphrey analyzes the political struggles of the poor in New York during the revolutionary era.)[10] The personal experiences of laboring Americans and their observations of indigence intensified their awareness and apprehension of economic exploitation. They expressed deep resentment against those who abused the destitute, whether they were usurers who "grind the faces of the poor," "monopolizers" and "engrossers" who drove the price of food and firewood to artificially high prices, or the "Rich" who exercised "exorbitant Influence . . . over the Poor."[11]

Besides worrying about the economic health of their country, early Americans agonized about their personal material well-being, in part because so many of them either knew people who were indigent or experienced destitution themselves. As Philip Morgan notes in his essay, laboring people in preindustrial societies commonly floated in and out of indigence, sometimes bobbing on top of the water, other times slipping beneath the surface. (In this volume, Simon Newman analyzes how working people responded to this continual insecurity.) Officials of the Pennsylvania Hospital for the Sick Poor identified some of the reasons why people suffered poverty in a land of plenty:

> In a City of large Trade, many poorer People must be employed in carrying on a Commerce, which subjects them to frequent terrible Accidents—That in a Country where great Numbers of indigent Foreigners have been but lately imported, and where the common Distresses of Poverty have been much increased, by a most savage and bloody War, there must be many Poor, there must be many sick and Maimed—That poor People are maintained by their Labour, and, if they cannot labour, they cannot live without the Help of the more Fortunate—We all know many Mouths are fed, many Bodies cloathed by one poor Man's Diligence and Industry; should any distemper seize and afflict this Person; should any sudden Hurt happen to him, which should render him incapable to follow the business of his Calling, unfit him to work, disable him to labour, even but for a little Time; or should his Duty to aged and diseased Parents, or his fatherly Tenderness for an afflicted Child, engross his Attention and

Care, how great must be the Calamity of such a Family! how pressing their Wants![12]

Only an extremely thin margin separated those who required assistance from those who were able independently to secure the necessities of life. Many early Americans consequently led lives of continual financial insecurity created by a myriad of factors: seasonal and cyclical unemployment; health problems (in an environment of multiple diseases and poor medical care); alcoholism (in an era of rampant consumption of liquor); insufficient wages (compared to the high cost of necessities); mental illness (where little institutional support existed); a large pool of migrants (including escapees from slavery, Indian refugees from white colonists, and Europeans who fled poverty and oppression); low pay for women (where gender definition limited their earnings); high mortality in some areas (which left destitute the families of household heads); abandoned families (when divorce was nearly impossible); and the inability of many communities to provide much help for the poor except to incarcerate them in workhouses and almshouses. The contingencies that produced poverty and financial despair were simply too numerous for historians to continue to ignore.

In the first chapter of this book, Gary Nash, the premier student of poverty in early North America, summarizes the scholarship published during the past three decades. Because his essay indicates how each of the book's studies relates to his interpretive model, it is not necessary to review the individual essays here. It is, however, important to provide a definition of "poverty" as used by early Americans and the authors in this book. Early Euro-Americans generally agreed that anyone dependent on aid (excepting wives and children) was poor. (As Jean Soderlund discusses in her essay, Native Americans had different notions of wealth and poverty.) The first dictionary printed in Philadelphia defined the word as a description of "those who are in the lowest rank of the community, those who cannot subsist but by the charity of others."[13] Yet, as the initial phrase of that definition indicates, poverty encompassed people other than merely those who relied on outside assistance. "The poor," according to Bostonian John Andrew, "always liv'd from hand to mouth, i.e., depended on one day's labour to supply the wants of another."[14] A Philadelphia newspaper reported that a poor person earned "a living by the work of his hands" and "must either work or starve."[15] Indeed, as discussed previously, the precariousness of life for many laboring people meant that no clear line separated the working poor from the dependent poor. As officials recognized, people were "poor" even if "they do not come under the care of an alms house."[16] In this book, "poverty" and its synonyms are used to describe both types of individuals: aid recipients on the one hand and ordinary laboring people on the other who worked each day for their survival, frequently experienced material standards similar to those who received assistance, and continually risked falling dependent on public or private charity.

## Notes

1. Data on poverty, hunger, and inequality in this and the following two paragraphs are from the U.S. Census Bureau, "Poverty, 2001," "Historical Income Tables," and "Number of Poor and Poverty Rates," all three published in 2001, www.census.gov/hhes/poverty/poverty01/povo1hi.html. Also see reports issued by the U.N. Food and Agriculture Organization (October 13, 1999), the U.S. Department of Agriculture (October 13, 1999), the U.S. Census Bureau (September 29, 1999), and by various studies summarized by the Associated Press (August 16 and 30, 1999).

2. Susan E. Klepp and Billy G. Smith, eds., *The Infortunate: The Voyage and Adventures of William Moraley, an Indentured Servant* (University Park: The Pennsylvania State University Press, 1992), quote on 89. Contemporaries apparently rarely used the phrase to describe early America, since it never appeared in the *Pennsylvania Gazette* (Philadelphia) throughout the eighteenth century. James T. Lemon popularized the description among historians by using the quote in the title of his book, *The Best Poor Man's Country: A Geographical Study of Early Southeastern Pennsylvania* (Baltimore: Johns Hopkins Press, 1972).

3. Wood, *The Radicalism of the American Revolution* (New York: Alfred A. Knopf, 1991), 4; Fischer, *Paul Revere's Ride* (New York: Oxford University Press, 1994), xv; Bailyn, "The Central Themes of the American Revolution: An Interpretation," in Stephen G. Kurtz and James H. Hutson, eds., *Essays on the American Revolution* (Chapel Hill: University of North Carolina Press, 1973), 12; McCusker and Menard, *The Economy of British America, 1607–1789* (Chapel Hill: University of North Carolina Press, 1985), 59. McCusker and Menard's otherwise excellent survey of the economy of early North America contains only one index entry for "poverty," noting the "absence of" (page 478). Other historians drew similar conclusions. See, e.g., James F. Shepherd and Gary M. Walton, "Trade, Distribution, and Economic Growth in Colonial America," *Journal of Economic History* 32 (1972): 128–45; Alice Hanson Jones, "Wealth Estimates for the American Middle Colonies, 1774," *Economic Development and Cultural Change* 18 (1970): 127–40; Jackson Turner Main, *The Social Structure of Revolutionary America* (Princeton: Princeton University Press, 1965), 194, 279; Herman Wellenreuther, "Labor in the Era of the American Revolution: A Discussion of Recent Concepts and Theories," *Labor History* 22 (1981): 573–600.

4. Klepp and Smith, eds., *Infortunate*, quotes on 89, 93, 94, 96, 108. On the limited available land in the Mid-Atlantic during Moraley's time, see Lemon, *Best Poor Man's Country*, 68. More than half a century ago, Abbot E. Smith found that few ex-servants enjoyed much financial success, and his conclusion has been supported by a number of more recent studies. Smith, *Colonists in Bondage: White Servitude and Convict Labor in America, 1607–1776* (Chapel Hill: University of North Carolina Press, 1946), 297–300; Russell Menard, "From Servant to Freeholder: Status Mobility and Property Accumulation in Seventeenth-Century Maryland," *William and Mary Quarterly*, 3d ser., 30 (1973): 37–64; Lois Green Carr and Russell R. Menard, "Immigration and Opportunity: The Freedman in Early Colonial Maryland," in Thad W. Tate and David L. Ammerman, eds., *The Chesapeake in the Seventeenth Century: Essays on Anglo-American Society* (Chapel Hill: University of North Carolina Press, 1979), 73–95; Sharon V. Salinger, *"To Serve Well*

*and Faithfully": Labor and Indentured Servants in Pennsylvania, 1682–1800* (Cambridge: Cambridge University Press, 1987), 115–36.

5. Peter Mathias, ed., *The Transformation of England: Essays in the Economic and Social History of England in the Eighteenth Century* (New York: Columbia University Press, 1979), 134, 143–45, 158; L. A. Clarkson, *The Pre-Industrial Economy in England, 1500–1750* (New York: Schocken Books, 1972), 234–36.

6. Quote from *Pennsylvania Gazette* (Philadelphia), June 1, 1774. A comprehensive comparison of poverty in America and Europe does not exist, so it is necessary to be tentative in comparing the two areas. Unfortunately, measuring the extent of poverty among nations is extremely difficult even with the rich data available in the early twenty-first century, and evidence from previous centuries is much less reliable.

7. The most authoritative analysis of the early American economy is McCusker and Menard, *Economy of British America*. Philadelphia's economy and migration are discussed in Billy G. Smith, *The "Lower Sort": Philadelphia's Laboring People, 1750–1800* (Ithaca: Cornell University Press, 1990), esp. chaps. 2 and 6.

8. On Moraley, see Klepp and Smith, *Infortunate*. Recognizing how crucial capital was, Franklin left funds in his will to help poor artisans. See *Encouragement for Apprentices to be Sober . . . ,* broadside, 1800, Historical Society of Pennsylvania; Accounts and Ledger, Franklin Legacy, 1791–1868, Philadelphia City Archives; and L. Jesse Lemisch, ed., *Benjamin Franklin: The Autobiography and Other Writings* (New York: New American Library, 1961), 63–68, 80.

9. Almshouse quote from "General State of the Accounts of the Contributors," *Pennsylvania Gazette*, May 29, 1776. Landrum is recorded in the Daily Occurrences Docket, December 30, 1800, and January 2 and 11, 1801, Guardians of the Poor, Philadelphia City Archives. Quotes about New York, Rhode Island, and Boston are from the *Pennsylvania Gazette*, February 20, 1766; April 7, 1768; January 22, 1767. On the wandering poor and vagrants, see Douglas Jones, "The Strolling Poor: Transiency in Eighteenth-Century Massachusetts," *Journal of Social History* 8 (1975): 28–54; and Billy G. Smith, ed., *Life in Early Philadelphia: Documents from the Revolutionary and Early National Periods* (University Park: The Pennsylvania State University Press, 1995), chaps. 2–4. On the illegality of begging, see the Prisoners for Trial Docket, 1798, Philadelphia County Prison, and the Vagrancy Docket, vol. 1790–97, both in the Philadelphia City Archives.

10. Quotes from the *Pennsylvania Gazette*, November 7, 1765; November 5, 1767; February 22, 1770; May 18, 1774; September 5, 1787; and November 19, 1788. Accusations that the followers of Daniel Shays and the failure to ratify the U.S. Constitution would result in an impoverished nation are contained in numerous issues of the newspaper, including the following: September 26, 1787; October 10, 1787; November 14, 1787; April 2, 1788; and August 6, 1788.

11. The North Carolina Regulators, for example, complained about officials "grinding the face of the poor," while other early Americans used similar phrases to condemn moneylenders; *Pennsylvania Gazette*, July 11, 1771; February 13, 1772; and April 4, 1787. Accusations against monopolizers and engrossers are included in Smith, *Life in Early Philadelphia*, chap. 9. Criticism of the power of the rich is in the *Pennsylvania Gazette*, January 18, 1770.

12. *Pennsylvania Gazette*, May 29, 1760.

13. *A Complete Dictionary of the English Language, . . . By Thomas Sheridan, a.m.,* 4th ed. (Philadelphia, 1789).

14. "Letters of John Andrew," Massachusetts Historical Society, *Proceedings*, ser. 8, 1 (1864–65), 344.

15. *Pennsylvania Packet* (Philadelphia), May 25, 1772.

16. *Pennsylvania Gazette*, July 11, 1765.

## *One*

# Poverty and Politics in Early American History

### GARY B. NASH

> The contrast of affluence and wretchedness continually
> meeting and offending the eye, is like dead and living
> bodies chained together.
>
> —Thomas Paine, *Agrarian Justice* (1797)

Every society needs its myths, and the great myth of early American history is that scarce labor in a land-rich environment eliminated poverty. Poverty has not been a popular word in this country. It is offensive to the notion of a people of plenty, an insult to the bounteous natural resources of North America, a puzzlement to those who believe in the untrammeled equality of opportunity that provided a chance for everyone to succeed, and an embarrassment to those who trumpet American classlessness and exceptionalism. In her survey of history schoolbooks used in the twentieth century, Frances FitzGerald found that silence on the topic of poverty was general until the 1960s, when textbook writers began to discuss it gingerly as a problem first occurring during post–Civil War industrialization, then reappearing in the Great Depression, and once more raising its ugly head in the 1960s. The textbooks she consulted regarded poverty in the post–World War II era as "a disease, something like cancer. Its cause is unknown, its cure is hotly debated, and yet somewhere—somewhere in the regions yet unprobed by science—there is a vaccine against it." Thoroughly depoliticized in these treatments, poverty has little to do with the interests of the rich and nothing to do with capitalism, coerced labor, industrialization, or urbanization. Nor does it have much to do with gender, war, or social stratification.[1] Considering the rise of poverty rates in the United States over the last three decades (accompanied by a huge increase in income inequality that makes the United States now the leader in income inequality among advanced nations), a deeper understanding of poverty in early America may be useful in thinking about a problem that has always challenged our cherished notion of a shared citizenship.[2]

## Defining and Measuring Poverty

Historians of early American life have known for a long time that poverty pre-dated the advent of smokestack America, although the research on this topic was very sketchy before the late 1960s.[3] As early as the 1920s, social welfare historians disclosed colonial poverty as a social problem by studying statute books and local officials who managed the poor in the first almshouses and workhouses. Somewhat later, in his three studies of colonial urban life published between 1938 and 1955, Carl Bridenbaugh pointed to the emergence of poverty in the colonial cities as a major concern, though he characterized elite responses to impoverishment as the work of kindhearted urbanites creating an "age of benevolence."[4] Working almost entirely with nonquantifiable sources, these historians established that poverty was a growing problem in the eighteenth century, but they were unable to make more than general statements about the extent, nature, or causes of impoverishment or about its connection to economic development and its effects on politics. None of these studies had the slightest effect on colonial American textbooks.[5] Often beguiled by colonial promotional literature and personal reflections such as Benjamin Franklin's—"I thought often of the happiness of New England where every man is a freeholder, has a vote in public affairs, lives in a tidy, warm house, has plenty of good food and fewel with whole cloaths from head to foot, the manufacture perhaps of his own family."—historians in the main portrayed a rising people in an abundant land where "the colonies had no beggars, no poor, not even a genuine lower class."[6]

Contributing to the rise of social history in the 1960s, and influenced by the war on poverty conducted by Presidents Kennedy and Johnson, historians began to search intensively for evidence about how early American society was structured and how "the other half lived."[7] Jackson Turner Main's *The Social Structure of Revolutionary America* (1965), a pioneering study of social stratification and social mobility, reached the shocking conclusion that, even discounting slaves, as much as one-third of the population in the northern colonies and states in the revolutionary era was impoverished.[8]

Other historians excavated hitherto unused, or slightly used, sources that provided quantifiable data demonstrating that large pockets of poverty developed in most eighteenth-century communities: tax lists provided social profiles of large and small communities from top to bottom and sometimes detailed the stripping of householders from the tax collectors' lists because of poverty; probate inventories particularized the spareness of life at the bottom, in effect peering through a narrow door into the shabby dwellings of the poor; court documents cast narrow shafts of light on vagrants, criminals, and the strolling poor; registers of churches and benevolent societies gave partial views of private charity; and administrative records of overseers of the poor and almshouse managers indicated what managers of the poor thought and intended and occasionally what the poor themselves had to say. From all these data, the extent of poverty began to take shape.[9] By the late 1980s, poverty studies established eight major points indicating that if colonial America was "the best poor man's country" it was still a poor man's country for many of its citizens.[10]

First, the rate of indigence, as measured by increases in the poor tax and by the number of poor receiving public assistance, either in the form of out-relief payments or admission to workhouses and almshouses, rose in the eighteenth century as communities grew in size and some of the social and economic fluidity of the seventeenth century dried up. For example, in New York City, where members of the colony's assembly could state firmly in 1699 that "there is no such thing as a beggar in this town or country," the city teemed with paupers and vagrants by the eve of the American Revolution.[11] Other communities, small as well as large, experienced growing poverty rates by the mid-eighteenth century. Boston confronted poverty earlier, more continuously, and with the most severity of any eighteenth-century seaport.[12]

Second, the age-old victims of impoverishment—widows, foundlings and orphans, the sick, aged, and disabled—were joined increasingly by able-bodied men and women. This became evident in small and large communities, North and South, by the mid-eighteenth century. Although the poor were concentrated in the largest cities, which were points of entry for often destitute immigrants and were magnets attracting the transient, able-bodied rural poor in search of jobs, the destitute were also becoming increasingly common in inland towns. Some historians have argued that the able-bodied poor suffered only age inequality—a condition where young adults began poor but escaped poverty as they grew older.[13] It is possible that this was true in rural areas, but the only careful study of the relation between age and wealth in a seaport city—Philadelphia—demonstrates that social age accounted for little of the variation in tax assessments on the eve of the American Revolution and that those born into the bottom of society were highly unlikely to make Horatio Alger ascents to gentrified lives.[14]

Third, informal poor relief by family members, friends, and church-centered private charity also grew in the eighteenth century. Most of the "respectable poor" favored private rather than public relief. Historians have not been able to examine this group systematically since records for many churches are not extant and aid from family and friends is nearly impossible to trace. Fragmentary records indicate, however, that private aid and church charity could no longer sustain all of the "deserving poor" in the major cities during cyclical downturns in the 1720s and 1730s and were all the more incapable by the 1750s and 1760s of coping with the large influxes of immigrants and the growing number of unemployed. One historian concludes that "the level of poverty in all urban centers greatly exceeded the estimates derived from the records of public assistance" because they do not take account of the impoverished who relied on churches and charitable organizations, on family and friends.[15]

Fourth, the "strolling poor," hitherto nearly invisible to historians, multiplied rapidly in the eighteenth century, both in eastern and frontier towns.[16] For example, in Boston the number of transients warned out increased tenfold between the 1720s and 1750s.[17] This influx of poor people created pressure on town magistrates to strengthen and enforce more rigorously the residency laws that cut poor relief off from transients who took to the road in search of a job, a meal, or blind luck. By the eve of the American Revolution, warning out the transient poor became as important in the work of poor relief officials as administering to the resident poor in such towns as Boston, Providence, New York, and Philadelphia.

Fifth, responding to the increase in poor relief expenditures, which necessitated heavier tax rates, all major cities built large new workhouses and almshouses in the third quarter of the eighteenth century and constructed still larger ones in the first several decades of the new nation. Utilizing the more complete records of public assistance that have survived for the revolutionary and postrevolutionary cities, historians have shown that the ranks of the institutionalized poor were filled mostly with the sick, disabled, intemperate, and desperate urban dwellers, who, unlike the "worthy" poor, had no other options than to enter the almshouses where strict regimens were imposed.[18] In a transitional period where management of the poor was moving from outrelief to institutionalizing the poor (which was the norm by the 1820s), poor relief in most towns and cities involved a patchwork system of charity involving intermittent withdrawal of outrelief amid a growing reliance on committing the poor to highly disciplined institutions.

Sixth, more than hitherto realized, many children of the poor in most cities and smaller towns were apprenticed out or indentured by impoverished parents or were taken by magistrates from parents for indenturing, either by private arrangement or public auction. In New England, the children of the poor may have been the main source of labor from outside the family. And, as John Murray's essay in this volume argues, offspring of the poor also served an important labor function in Charleston. Everywhere in the North and upper South, the gradual emancipation of slaves during and after the Revolution put the children of free blacks at risk of growing up as servants in white middle- and upper-class families rather than in their families of nativity.[19]

Seventh, throughout the eighteenth century, poverty was particularly a feminine phenomenon, not only because women's role as childbearers and nurturers placed differential responsibilities on them but also because law and custom hindered the economic advancement of single, abandoned, or widowed women. Moreover, in the light of this, poor relief practices had a gendered dimension.[20] Recent studies, including the essays in this volume by Karin Wulf, Monique Bourque, and Ruth Herndon, have pointed to the disproportionate number of women (and their children) who were the recipients of outdoor relief or were institutionalized in urban almshouses. Particularly in New England, but also in Charleston, South Carolina, war widowhood strained poor relief resources from the late seventeenth century to the American Revolution. The "economic viability of women—shaky enough to begin with—declined" over the eighteenth century, leaving women in particular phases of their life cycle (abandoned or widowed with small children) vulnerable to destitution because their "half-wages" in low paying work were usually insufficient to sustain even a small family.[21] The early American widow, it turns out, was not necessarily an old woman; in fact, she was typically a young woman—most often an immigrant in her thirties whose ability to scrape out a living had been compromised by sickness at some point after her husband's death. Recent studies also show that the economic development of the new nation widened the inequalities between men and women. At the same time, the move in the major cities to end outrelief was particularly devastating to women because it drove them from the shelter among friends or family that outrelief payments permitted.[22]

Eighth, far more than once believed, impoverished tenancy existed throughout the colonies and early states, and lifelong landlessness expanded markedly in the eighteenth century. To point to these deep pockets of poverty—as does the essay in this book by Thomas Humphrey—is not to deny the success of a majority of free white male farmers to acquire land and achieve a decent standard of living, one that for many increased in the eighteenth century. It is only to indicate that sizable numbers were not included in gains that were widely made and that the proportion who could not acquire land was increasing.

It is possible that rural tenancy was more pervasive in the South, where slavery was deeply rooted by the 1720s, than in the Middle Colonies where coerced bondage was more an urban than rural institution. This seeming paradox cannot be resolved until comparative studies between, for example, Maryland and New Jersey or South Carolina and New York are made. But lacking such comparisons, it is clear that tenancy held large numbers of farmers in poverty's grip. For example, the most thorough study of tenancy, in Maryland, describes tenants' dwellings as "little better than hovels" and points to Chastellux's postrevolutionary description of "the miserable huts inhabited by whites whose wane looks and ragged garments bespeak poverty."[23] Representing nearly half of the white householders in the older counties of Maryland on the eve of the Revolution, very few of these tenants were able to acquire land of their own, even after proprietary manors were put up for sale in the revolutionary era because they were unable to accumulate enough capital from small-scale agricultural tenantry to purchase a freehold.

Similar conditions prevailed in North Carolina, Virginia, Pennsylvania, New York, and New Jersey.[24] Even in New England, where the usual picture portrayed is of nearly universal freehold land tenure that minimized inequality and dampened social tensions, social historians have found land tenancy prevalent in some towns where it divided communities "between rich and poor, creditors and debtors, landlords and tenants."[25] Especially on the Maine frontier (but also on the frontiers of New York and Pennsylvania), as Alan Taylor has shown, impoverishment, the fear of falling into poverty, and the feeling that the chance to acquire land was disappearing fueled tension that often burst into rampage and riot for several decades after the American Revolution.[26]

In studying the eight aspects of poverty and poor relief outlined above, historians have relied mostly on the public records relating to poor relief and taxation and the private records of churches and philanthropic societies. But recently, as many of the essays in this book demonstrate, only by expanding the definition of poverty from a condition requiring public relief and private charity to a condition of living impoverished without such relief can an appreciation be gained of how life was experienced in early America. This broader consideration of *living poor* as against *requiring poor relief* compels attention to how unfree labor was integral to the functioning of the early American economy and how the emerging market economy was not a neutral mechanism for sorting out work lives and life experiences but rather a force that introduced new levels of insecurity, as well as new opportunities, for working people.

For most of the seventeenth and eighteenth centuries about two-thirds of all white immigrants arrived as indentured servants, and a large fraction of them died before gaining their freedom. Adding enslaved Africans (nearly three of every four persons crossing the Atlantic), we can estimate that more than at least 90 percent of all people disembarking in North America arrived impoverished, and a large majority of them continued in penury for most of their lives. Nobody has argued that indentured servants and slaves were anything but poor and ruthlessly exploited, as Philip Morgan rehearses in his essay in this book, but most depictions of early America as a garden of opportunity airbrush indentured servants and slaves out of the picture while focusing on the minority of those who arrived free.[27] At all times constituting about one-quarter to one-third of the eighteenth- and early nineteenth-century population, bound laborers occupied a capacious cellar in the social system and cannot sensibly be left out of any cross-national comparisons of poverty. In fact, escaping England's dismal poverty of the early seventeenth century depended largely on keeping large fractions of colonial laboring people deprived of the fruits of their own labor. "The free sector of society could never have achieved its way of life without the support of the unfree," writes an English historian of the colonial American experience. "To appreciate the force of this point it should only be necessary to consider the possibilities that would have been open to white ambitions if black labour had been unavailable. In all probability a much more massive unfree or limited service labour force would have been drafted into the plantation colonies from the ranks of white convicts and other social outcasts—in which case the planters' privileges would unmistakably have rested on the labour of landless workers with small hope of advancement for themselves or their children."[28] In short, if most free immigrants escaped grinding poverty, and if most of them achieved a "decent competency," one of the reasons was that they were able to benefit from the oppression of the unfree. The avid appetite for escaping poverty in England, Ireland, Scotland, and Germany had its corollary in "a voracious demand for bonded laborers throughout the colonial period."[29]

Since the 1920s, historians have studied indentured servants and argued vigorously about where they came from, their social characteristics in their homelands, how much choice they had in choosing a colony in which to serve on the western side of the Atlantic, how many survived servitude, and how well the survivors fared.[30] This is a pregnant topic because the fate of the indentured servant, beginning on the bottom rung on the ladder, can be seen as the perfect test of early America's capacity for rescuing people from poverty and launching them into at least a secure material life. Some early studies, based on impressionistic evidence rather than careful studies of ex-servants, gave a picture of general success among the indentured once they gained their freedom. But Abbot Smith's first quantitative measurements of this topic yielded the conclusion that out of every ten indentured servants, only one attained a position as a farmer in comfortable circumstances and one more achieved the status of artisan. The other eight died before they obtained their freedom or became propertyless day laborers, vagrants, or denizens of the local almshouse after completing their indentures.[31]

Careful studies in recent years confirm Smith's findings about the life chances of freed servants. Although they enjoyed a better chance in the early decades of a colony's development—in Maryland until the 1660s and in Pennsylvania until the 1740s, for example—their chances for acquiring property, or avoiding poverty, worsened as the early fluidity of society disappeared.[32] A study of indentured servitude in Pennsylvania, one of the largest importers of servants in the eighteenth century, argues that "the most salient feature of the post-servitude lives of eighteenth-century indentured laborers was their obscurity." This mirrors the data on Maryland that servants arriving in the late colonial period had more difficulty finding an economic foothold after serving their terms than had earlier servants. Almost three-quarters of late arriving servants in Pennsylvania ended up on the public dole at some point in their life, and only a handful ever became property holders.[33]

One reason why the plight of the indentured servant worsened in the eighteenth century is that a sizable portion of them arrived as convicts. Nearly 45,000 felons were sentenced to transportation to the American colonies between 1718 and 1775, most of them reaching Maryland and Virginia. This represented more than 20 percent of all British immigrants arriving in North America in this era. Desperately poor on arrival, purchased to serve longer terms than ordinary indentured servants, half of them arriving without skills, and most of them ruthlessly exploited as owners thought appropriate in dealing with England's "offensive rubbish," only a few who survived their term of service escaped poverty.[34]

Although textbooks still feature the rare servant who published an account of success after servitude or the handful of servants who prospered and achieved fame—for example, revolutionary leaders such as Daniel Dulany in Maryland, Charles Thomson in Pennsylvania, and John Lamb in New York—the statistical probability for rising even to the middle class was very slight.[35] Among the mass of those who sought opportunity in the British American colonies, it is the story of relentless labor and ultimate failure that stands out. The chief beneficiaries of the system of bound white labor were not the laborers themselves but those for whom they toiled.

In thinking more broadly about the definition of poverty, historians have focused in recent decades on how closely the poor who accepted aid were connected to the laboring people in general. Mesmerized by the concept of upward mobility in the United States, historians have only lately contemplated the extent of downward mobility in particular eras and places. But in early America, most laboring people were poor at some time in their life, and large numbers fell from "a decent competency" to destitution. It took no more—in an age with no Medicare, Social Security, unemployment benefits, or workmen's disability compensation—than a fire, hurricane, severe winter, serious work accident, disease, or drought to emphasize the reality that a hard-earned climb from poverty was no guarantee of escaping its clutches for more than a short time. That they were once poor and that they were haunted by the ghost of poverty makes laboring people in many ways indistinguishable from the officially poor who accepted either private or public aid.

## Explaining Poverty's Causes

Specifying the causes of poverty in a land presumed to be filled with opportunity is not difficult so long as historians are scrutinizing the lives of the helpless and hapless. Every society has its halt and lame, its genetically and emotionally impaired, its aged, widowed, and orphaned. But historians have had more difficulty in deciphering how large numbers of able-bodied men and women fell into poverty or were unable to climb out of it. Obstructing clear thinking on this is the hoary notion that labor was North America's greatest scarcity and therefore that every able-bodied person could find available work—anywhere, anytime of the year, and unchangingly so at least through the first two centuries of European settlement. No doubt, there was a general scarcity of labor in the land- and resource-rich colonies, and this is one of the reasons why a vigorous demand for slave and indentured labor endured. But the steady availability of work at life-sustaining levels of pay over two centuries, during which the nature of work and the organization of labor underwent important transformations, is a myth.

Five main reasons, all of them inconvenient for a picture of an opportunity-filled environment, explain the poverty of the able-bodied: recurrent wars; economic fluctuations beyond the ability of colonists to control; personal crises related to sickness, death, and environmental disasters; the difficulty of many, even in good times, to move beyond a hardscrabble living in both undeveloped frontier regions and developed urban centers; and, after the American Revolution, the transition to commercialized agriculture and early industrialization.

The connection between war and poverty has not been sufficiently studied. The extent to which Indian wars impoverished communities is still unclear, but male casualty rates far greater than in modern wars, as in the case of the Pequot and King Philip's wars in New England in 1637 and

1675–76 and the 1622 and 1715 Indian wars in Virginia and South Carolina, respectively, unquestionably produced large numbers of widows, orphans, and incapacitated men, many of whom became public burdens. The eighteenth-century wars against the French and Spanish also left large numbers of widows and orphans while at the same time pumping considerable money into the colonial economies, though with differential effects and sometimes with deranging repercussions. Boston stands as a prime example of a war-ravaged economy that inflated the ranks of the poor. Massachusetts's successive assaults on French Canada left the economy of Boston crippled, its churches filled with impoverished widows and orphans, and its currency shattered by inflation. By mid-eighteenth century, Boston suffered population stagnation, a sharp decline in the number of rateable polls (householders worth ten shillings sterling), an alarming rise in almshouse admissions, and a sizable appetite for what might be called "economic cleansing"—the warning out of a flood of uprooted men, women, and children from outlying towns seeking employment in the region's major city.[36] Town officials in 1755, citing public aid for about one thousand residents, cried out that poor relief in Boston was double that of any town of similar size "upon the face of the whole Earth."[37] By the eve of the Revolution, as much as a third of Boston's householders were in the grip of indigence, much of it created by a series of wars in North America against the French.

If war disfigured Boston's society, a fluctuating economy, even in a period of generally lusty growth, produced frightening levels of poverty in Philadelphia, the capital city of pacifism. Although a house-building binge in the third quarter of the eighteenth century testified to the success of the city's upper echelon in accumulating wealth, thousands of other Philadelphians ate bitter bread. For example, in the severe winter of 1760–61, it took the invention of a wood stamp system (where the desperate received stamps entitling them to free wood from local wood sellers) to keep a sizable fraction of the city's population from freezing to death. This showed how close to the line the bottom quarter of urban populations lived. Even in kinder weather, a sharp downturn in the economy in 1761, when British troops and naval flotillas withdrew after defeating the French in the Seven Years' War, drove hundreds of families beneath the subsistence line. If this was not permanent poverty, it was a gnawing economic marginality among those who had little cushion against even brief unemployment. For them, wood was often beyond their meager earnings, especially when unemployment afflicted them for many weeks of the year and their diets and health suffered for lack of proper sustenance. "For want of Employment, many of the laboring poor, especially in Winter, are reduced to great Straits and rendered burthensome to their

Neighbours," argued promoters of a Philadelphia linen manufactory in 1764. Two years later, the city's grand jury argued on behalf of a large work-house because many "labouring People & others in low Circumstances," who were "willing to work," could not find employment. In the difficult winter of 1770–71, lack of employment again led to the laboring poor "begging bread."[38] Other proponents of manufacturing after the American Revolution took up the same refrain, arguing that hundreds of the "starving poor" who were willing to work should be provided with "suitable objects about which they can be engaged."[39] In another difficult winter, in 1790–91, a newspaper correspondent reported that he found "many willing to work, but destitute and starving for want of employ."[40] The legions of merchant seamen and laborers, shoemakers, and tailors—the lesser skilled artisans and workers—who "often eked out a precarious existence during the second half of the [eighteenth] century" in Philadelphia were matched in nearly every other urban center.[41]

Still another cause of poverty, even in good times, were fires, severe win-ters, hurricanes, and epidemic diseases that especially smote densely popu-lated seaport cities. Nine fires between 1653 and 1759 wiped out scores of families in Boston. The most terrible fire that Bostonians had ever experi-enced occurred in March 1760, tearing through the North End and burning to the ground the homes of about two hundred families, "three quarters of whom," reported a town official, "are by this misfortune rendered incapable of subsisting themselves, and a great number of them are reduced to extreme poverty and require immediate relief."[42] Such conflagrations did not, of course, single out the poor, but they did tend to spread in the most densely settled parts of town and they wreaked the greatest havoc among those with no cushion of safety who in the best of times struggled to eke out a living. For middle-class urbanites, fire could wipe out assets carefully built over many years and plunge them suddenly into near-poverty. Hurricanes could be even more devastating, such as the one that brought terrible misery to laboring people in Charleston, South Carolina, in 1728.

Along with fire came raging diseases that increased medical expenses and burial fees while reducing employment. Nine "general" smallpox epidemics alone ravaged Boston between 1649 and 1730, and another wave of smallpox swept through North America during the American Revolution. Philadelphia and New York were repeatedly assaulted by yellow fever in the 1790s. As much as a staggering 20 percent of the population that remained at risk by not fleeing the city succumbed in a single year, putting today's urban AIDS epidemics in perspective. In addition, thousands of others in the feverish cities lost wages for many weeks when the mosquito-borne fever shut down all employment.[43] Such urban catastrophes, producing "universal terror" and "a total dissolution of the bonds of society in the nearest and dearest connexions," as a contemporary account of Philadelphia in 1793 expressed it, left economic as well as emotional scars from which family members of the dead could not easily recover.[44] Bitter winters also produced mass misery—and the misery increased as the deforestation of adjacent areas drove up the price of the firewood that was essential to survive a prolonged freeze.[45]

Personal crises likewise sent large numbers of people reeling into destitution. As Simon Newman's analysis in this volume notes, in an age before OSHA, work-related accidents were common and frequently maimed mariners, construction workers, and others. The parade of laboring people through Philadelphia's Hospital for the Sick Poor testifies to the frequency of on-the-job accidents that halted wage earners in their tracks. Without workmen's compensation, the family of a permanently injured breadwinner could rarely recover its economic security. For women, abandonment was particularly a personal crisis—both emotional and economic. Deprived of her husband's wages, the woman of an absconding husband was faced with living on what her own labor commanded—typically about half the male rate of pay for waged work. In addition, the abandoned woman did not control the property of her departed husband because desertion did not legally end a marriage.[46]

War, economic downturns, and personal crises account for much of the poverty in specific locales in certain years. But often they were only contributing factors to a problem whose roots lay more fundamentally in an economy that kept large numbers of rural freemen and even more urban workers teetering on the knife edge of poverty. As early as the 1740s, the Swedish visitor Peter Kalm observed a class of people in New York City (when the economy was healthy) "who lived all year long upon nothing but oysters and a little bread."[47] In Philadelphia in the early 1770s, when a building boom was in progress, tax assessors excused nearly five hundred able-bodied residents from even the smallest tax and extracted nothing from nearly one thousand mariners.[48] Examples can be multiplied. But wherever historians have studied individual cities carefully, they have found that those who lived in or on the edge of poverty probably "comprised at least one third and probably closer to one half of the residents of America's metropolitan centers."[49] Likewise, whenever historians have examined groups known to be on the bottom of the occupational hierarchy—female domestic laborers and field hands, lumbermen, fort and road builders, shoemakers, tailors, dockworkers, laborers, fishermen, and mariners—they tell us of how typical rather than unusual was the experience of living poor.[50] If additional studies of smaller cities and rural areas confirm these estimates, then historians of early America will be obliged to speak of how "the other half lives" just as surely as historians use this term from Jacob Riis to describe industrial America in the late nineteenth and early twentieth centuries.[51]

A large majority of settlers lived in the countryside, not in the cities. But life on the frontier, where people had little capital, limited access to markets, often marginal land, and frequently poor health, was no Turnerian paradise. Charles Woodmason's portrayal of the Carolina backcountry beggars description. While scandalized by "revelling, drinking, singing, dancing, and whoring," he was shocked at the poverty that has plagued the region to the present day.[52] Half a century later on the Maine frontier, one well-situated landowner described the settlers "as destitute of food and raiment as the Vagabonds of Africa" and believed that "a few families excepted, were all their goods thrown out into the streets many men would not think it worth their while to gather them up." The very sober Reverend William Bentley of Salem, Massachusetts, described the Maine backcountry in 1787 as "inhabited by poor people, whose cottages could not be exceeded in miserable appearance by any of the most miserable in Europe."[53] To be sure, these were frontier areas, always scenes of painfully pinched existence at least in early years; but even in the most fertile and commercially connected regions, such as Philadelphia's hinterland, the trend in the late eighteenth century was toward increasing landlessness, accelerating transiency, and growing rates of poverty.[54]

In the revolutionary era, processes of economic change, partly shaped by technological developments, ratcheted up the incidence of impoverishment while at the same time generating wealth that benefited merchants, speculators, rentiers, manufacturers, and many master craftsmen. The "consumer revolution," which has claimed the attention of many historians, was real, as was the rise in the standard of living for broad swaths of the American population.[55] Inventories of wealth reveal that the ability to purchase many consumer goods beyond the wherewithal of earlier colonists was enjoyed by at least the top half of free white society. And nutritional advantages for colonists over their English cousins translated into several inches of superior height.[56] But aggregate analysis of consumerism and nutrition mask what happened in the bottom third to half of colonial society because the household goods of people in these ranks were rarely inventoried. Moreover, for some parts of North America increase in stature was mostly a seventeenth-century phenomenon, flagging thereafter, and in some rural areas, middling and poorer farmers invested less in consumer durables in the late colonial period than earlier.[57] Whatever further research may reveal on these questions, it seems clear that the American Revolution at least temporarily devastated the

American economy and that commercialization and industrialization, especially in the fast-growing eastern cities, were engines for creating wealth and poverty simultaneously.[58] In her essay in this book, Susan Klepp has analyzed infant mortality in Philadelphia to show that the increasing maldistribution of wealth and worsening health conditions in a burgeoning city undergoing commercial expansion and the early stages of industrialization produced infant mortality rates as high as in England. Her data on increasing infant mortality in the lower tiers of urban society stand as a kind of surrogate for "an economic crisis for the poor that begins in the 1780s."[59] Other studies indicate that by the 1820s and 1830s, average heights were falling in the United States at large—the result of "the maldistribution of wealth and dietary constraints in the early stages of industrialization."[60]

Although much work still needs to be done, it is apparent that the intensity of economic cycles that caused periodic impoverishment for hefty fractions of urban populations escalated in the late eighteenth and early nineteenth centuries. Mass misery in urban populations, with as much as one-quarter to one-third of able-bodied workers lacking employment, would not arrive until the depression of 1816 to 1822. But even before that, the gradual spread of wage labor placed a growing proportion of artisans and workers at the mercy of economic fluctuations. "Periodic destitution," as one historian put it, "was one structural result of the great social and economic transformations in American life" that began by the mid-eighteenth century and heightened greatly in the early nineteenth century.[61] A close examination of late eighteenth-century Philadelphia concludes that the "widespread use of wage labor ushered in a period of intense job insecurity that widened the distance between masters and workers," led to high job turnover and mounting artisan transiency, and consigned the lower tier of workers to intermittent and often incessant poverty.[62] Without owning one's labor, one courted poverty and chronic insecurity. In sum, research in recent decades indicates that what Henry George described in 1879—that whenever the highest degree of "material progress" has been realized "we find the deepest poverty"—existed before the industrial revolution.[63]

## Relieving Poverty and Controlling the Poor

If indigence was increasing and its causes growing more complex, how did legislators, town and county officials, and public leaders address what was becoming one of the eighteenth century's thorniest social issues? David Rothman provided an incomplete answer more than thirty years ago in his influential *The Discovery of the Asylum,* where he posited a change from a familial to an impersonal institutional system of poor relief that he believed occurred with the rise of industrializing cities in the early nineteenth century.[64] Since then, historians have shown that the eighteenth century was a long period of experimentation, shifting attitudes, and sharp divisions among poor relief officials—anything but a smooth transition to institutionalizing the poor and a transition that began long before the advent of swollen cities and mechanized factories.

Inherited attitudes toward the poor, greatly fortified in Puritan New England, stressed the biblical notion that poverty was the unalterable lot of the many. "'Tis the Lord," counseled Cotton Mather to his parishioners in Boston in 1712, "who has Taken away from you what He has Given to others."[65] In his essay in this book, Richard Olivas has traced ministerial pronouncements on Boston's impacted poverty in the eighteenth century. Still, there is little evidence that the poor themselves listened to advice that their poverty was divinely commissioned or that they should blame themselves.

Elsewhere, magistrates and poor relief officials did not blame God but began blaming the poor themselves. Such a view appears to have surfaced first in 1707 in New York City, when local officials required patches of cloth with the letters *N:Y* sewn on their shirts or blouses. Badging the destitute in this way attached a social stigma to poverty, forcing the poor to advertise their penniless condition as a kind of self-inflicted wound. Other cities followed this practice—Philadelphia in 1718 and Charleston somewhat later—initiating a long, slow trend toward isolating the indigent socially and treating them more as outcast than as neighbor.

In every seaport, the poor had to be relieved and managed in one way or another, regardless of who was to blame for their condition. In Boston, the city with the most severe mid-eighteenth-century poverty problem, town leaders launched the first "workfare" experiment by erecting a large linen manufactory where they urged the city's poor women, frequently war widows with small children, to work in order to drive down the cost of poor relief.[66] The failure of this venture did not deter city leaders, intent on cutting the costs of what was thought to be unacceptably expensive outrelief, from erecting large workhouses and almshouses in the third quarter of the eighteenth century.[67] Along with imposing structures, which physically and socially isolated the poor, came stricter supervision of the incarcerated—a set of shifting strategies devised by employers, magistrates, poor relief officials, and legislators to "manage" the poor or "render them submissive." Backing up the attempt to cope with spiraling poor relief costs, town officials in many places imposed harsher legal penalties against the poor (such as raising the amount of property necessary to establish town residence and thus limiting the obligation to provide for the poor); increased the registration period for establishing residence; and criminalized the taking of fish from streams, ponds, and bays by any "stranger" not resident in a town—a restriction that cut off one of the few free nutritional sources available to the poor.[68]

Wherever poor relief officials innovated, they faced formidable obstacles, the greatest of which was inadequate resources. Almost everywhere they resorted to the equivalent of modern medical triage. For the "respectable" poor, family, friends, and churches were the first line of defense. For those not so fortunately situated, small outrelief payments—in wood allotments, food, stockings, blankets, and cash—allowed both able-bodied and incapacitated people to take shelter with a friend, family member, or neighbor. Finally, for the hopelessly indigent, sick, deranged, criminal, intemperate, or disabled, the workhouse and almshouse were the prescribed remedy.

In the most fully studied case, in Philadelphia, the attempt to drive down the cost of poor relief through ending outdoor relief and forcing people into workhouses has been shown to have tested the resolve—and the capital resources—of the most dedicated urban leaders. Spurred by spiraling numbers of the indigent, a small almshouse bursting at the seams, and escalating poor taxes, a private corporation in Philadelphia, led mostly by Quaker merchants, convinced the legislature to turn poor relief over to them in 1766 and to facilitate the erection of the largest building yet constructed in the American colonies.[69]

Soon after the managers of the new Bettering House opened its doors, they vowed to end outrelief, compelling any pauper seeking public aid to take up residence in the workhouse where they were expected to labor picking oakum, weaving, and spinning. Understanding that rescinding outrelief struck hard at poor women with family responsibilities, Philadelphia's Overseers of the Poor strongly resisted the policy as cruel and misguided. Whereas fifteen years before Philadelphia's leaders had created the Hospital for Sick Poor to get laboring men back on their feet (while also ministering to the needs of women in medical need), the Bettering House managers demanded that the poor abandon familial settings. After seven years of trying to reform the poor by driving them to the Bettering House, the institution's managers confessed that the system had failed.

The building of the Bettering House in Philadelphia provides a clear picture of the changing ideological edifice of the wealthy. Although generally regarded by historians as a monument to the philanthropic impulse—a concern for relieving the needs of the rapidly growing number of the destitute—the institution was also a towering symbol of the spreading notion that the ranks of the poor were swelling because more and more people owed their poverty to intemperance or were becoming content to live the life of the idler, the profligate, or the street beggar rather than pursue an honest trade.

Philadelphia's leather-aproned hero, Benjamin Franklin, was a good barometer of this attitudinal sea change. No stranger to hunger growing up in a large family of Boston artisans, Franklin had sympathy for the poor he found in Philadelphia after arriving there in 1723 in the middle of a recession. But his spectacular success as a printer changed his mind by the time he reached his forties. As early as 1753, he expressed the view that nothing was more responsible for creating poverty than poor relief itself. He was probably fortified in this point of view by what he saw and heard in London, where he lived from 1759 to 1765 and 1768 to 1775. There municipal leaders, abandoning the earlier view that economic recession and depressed wages were the main causes of indigence, began to blame the poor themselves for their plight. In 1765, soon after returning to London, Franklin wrote in anger after the London poor mobbed grain wagons in order to prevent wheat exports at a time when bread was scarce. "The more public provisions were made for the poor," he sputtered, "the less they provided for themselves and of course became poorer. And, on the contrary, the less was done for them, the more they did for themselves, and became richer."[70] Because England led the world in caring for the poor, scoffed Franklin, that country also led the world in the creation of poverty. Repeal the poor laws, Franklin advised, and the poor would go back to work, abandoning the new national holidays they had proclaimed—St. Monday and St. Tuesday.

The emerging view of the poor that animated these comments—that the "best way of doing good to the poor, is not making them easy in poverty, but leading or driving them out of it"—became the main rationale behind the Bettering House, its name itself betokening the blurring of the line between the "deserving" and "undeserving" poor and the growing tendency to regard the needy as flawed members of society who needed to be reformed rather than relieved.[71] Although the Quaker managers of the Bettering House were intimately familiar with unprecedented economic dislocation in the mid-1760s that created widespread unemployment and a subsistence crisis for laboring people, they focused on the burden the poor were creating for taxpaying citizens rather than on the burden of being destitute. The almshouse wing of the Bettering House would care for those who could not work, but the workhouse wing would rehabilitate the able-bodied poor who would not work.

Such a view of self-created poverty triggered an argument over the causes of indigence that continued through the American Revolution, into the nineteenth century, and down to the present day. In Philadelphia, while Franklin and others ignored the blighting effects of recession, others pointed to exactly this cause of the spiraling poor lists. "It is said that our poor are indolent, and will not work," one newspaper correspondent wrote. "[But] give the poor a sufficient compensation for their work; let the demand for their exertions be constant and steady, . . . and it will soon be found that the charge of indolence, is a calumny on the most destitute part of our fellow-citizens."[72] Historians have shown in recent years that this struggle over institutionalizing the poor and subjecting them to strict discipline waxed and waned for more than half a century before the major cities moved in the 1820s from a mixed system of poor relief to a decisive end to small payments in cash, food, and fuel to outreliefers.

It is clear that the champions of almshouses had greater success in the commercial urban centers than in the less commercialized countryside, giving little support to the notion of Thomas Haskell that the spread of a capitalist ethos, centered in the cities, created more humane sensibilities toward the unfortunate.[73] To the contrary, the values of the unfettered marketplace "infiltrated the basic structure of public charity, while it often relegated poor people to items in a ledger."[74]

## Strategies of the Poor

One of the most valuable contributions of recent historians, paralleling the efforts of historians of women and African Americans, is in putting a human face on poverty by illuminating the experiences and strategies of the poor. This is part of the larger effort to recapture the plebeian lives and popular culture of the underclass while giving subordinate groups some measure of agency. American historians are behind their English counterparts in this regard, yet they have explored the networks of authority that surrounded the poor and rescued dozens of individual stories from tax lists, city directories, vagrancy dockets, almshouse admission interviews, trial records, pension applications, and other frustratingly incomplete but often revealing records.[75] In "Up From the Bottom in Franklin's Philadelphia," I charted the course of the poor silversmith Caesar Ghisilin to contrast the downward mobility of his family with that of another silversmith who made his way up the ladder of Philadelphia society. Billy Smith has constructed many vignettes of working men and women and followed two late eighteenth-century Philadelphians on a graphic tour of the city that shatters the myth that labor scarcity in early America almost always translated into high wages for anyone with an appetite for work and shows how the poor tried to stay afloat.[76] Timothy Breen has reconstructed the precarious life of a Taunton, Massachusetts, slave from his "dying speech" in 1767.[77] In the most ingeniously constructed portrait of a down-and-out American of the revolutionary generation, Alfred F. Young has unearthed the life of the picaresque Boston shoemaker, George Robert Twelves Hewes, who lived for almost a century but never escaped poverty.[78]

A distinguishing mark of all these studies is their effort to set these vignettes of impoverished individuals within economic, social, and legal contexts that show how precarious were the lives of a great portion of early American society. Hampered by elusive sources, they are less successful in the difficult process of understanding how the poor experienced the authority of those attempting to control them and devised strategies for gaining some semblance of control over their lives while, simultaneously, they were often obliged to depend on institutional relief in times of great distress.

Yet a picture, though still murky, has begun to emerge of how the officially powerless poor contended with officially powerful town officials in several important ways. One was to resist the pressure to surrender their children to the magistrates, who often bound them out for years of uncompensated labor. This was not only an emotional assault on the poor, but it also deprived them of the labor value of their children. Only the strongest impoverished parents could refuse to hand over their sons and daughters; more typically, they implored magistrates to intervene when their children were physically misused or denied at least minimal training in a useful occupation.[79]

Taking to the road was a second way of avoiding institutionalization. Ruth Herndon's essay in this book shows that while casting aside all that was familiar and familial, women tramped from place to place in late eighteenth-century New England, all the while knowing that they would be "warned out" of any town they approached and thus would be ineligible for poor relief. In an earlier study, she shows how transient Rhode Island women, representing about half of all itinerants in that colony, "tried to manipulate the system of warning out to their own advantage." Mostly young, mostly shorn of husbands, mostly with dependent children, these women frustrated town officials by hiding, darting from town when the municipal sergeant approached to interview them, or telling town fathers such heartrending stories that they permitted a newcomer to gain residence—and thus access to poor relief.[80]

The poor also made the life of almshouse and poorhouse managers miserable by defying codes of conduct and in some cases instituting rules of their own. Doubtless, much of the chaos and defiance of discipline in the urban almshouses of the revolutionary era and beyond can be charged to intemperance, insanity, and personality dysfunction. But not all of it. Sometimes the poor had their own rules and used them to frustrate their keepers thoroughly. For example, in the workhouse wing of the Philadelphia Bettering House, women rarely met the spinning quotas imposed, and if they could earn a bit of money by exceeding them, they promptly fled the house.[81] In another case, Jane Bickerdite, nurse in the Philadelphia almshouse in 1789, was on the losing end of the venereal women she attempted to govern and treat. "They quarreled with and abused her very much—and now when she was going away they mobbed her severely and raised a bawling clamorous noise and—with beating and rattling, frying pans, shovels tongs, etc., [went] after her, all of which together they called the whores march, and of which they are competent judges, as every step they have taken for several years hath been altogether in that line and true to the beat—Thus those hardened insolent husseys go on despising all rule and order here."[82]

This example of rough music—*charivari*—tells us of the attempts to administer primitive justice by largely Irish and English women who held up to scorn and abuse a German woman who, it seems, offended their sense of what had brought them to their impoverished and diseased condition.

Other women, and sometimes men, simply refused to enter institutions built to serve the poor, even if they starved or died of hypothermia. In Boston, the resistance of women with small children to leave their homes to weave and spin in the heatless linen manufactory scotched this experiment, though it would be revived many years later with an emphasis on single rather than married women. In Philadelphia, leaving their pitiful digs to enter the newly completed Bettering House was so anathema to the able-bodied poor whose sin was unemployment that "when urged to go in for relief, [they] declared in solemn manner that they would rather perish through want than go in."[83] What for poorhouse officials was often an asylum was for the poor a penitentiary.

More broadly, the poor resisted the change in attitude from those above them that turned "deserving objects of charity" into undeserving drains on the community. Such statements as "a man may be suspected of being deficient in industry, temperance, or honesty . . . who is not possessed after a certain number of years, of a moderate share of property" were taken for what they were: contempt of the laboring poor and callousness toward how, during economic downturns, those who lived closest to the line were the first to go beneath it.[84] The laboring poor insisted they were part of the community, not a drain on it. In the transition decades when outrelief was phased out and institutionalizing the poor became the economical way of servicing them, they refused to accept responsibility for their poverty; denied they created their own plight by shunning the economic opportunity theoretically available to everyone; rejected the argument that poverty was the fate of those who drank their wages away; argued instead that unemployment and poverty drove people to intemperance (a reverse causation finally adopted by the Women's Christian Temperance Union in 1886); and maintained they were entitled to relief, not as a charitable dole but as a social right in disordered societies, and had customary rights to medical care, fuel, bread, and shelter.[85]

Insisting that they had no wish to be parasites, the poor drifted in and out of American cities in search of work, avoided the workhouse whenever they could, disobeyed rules, did as little labor as possible when they were committed to these institutions, and in general resisted poor relief measures that offended their sense of what was just. Abhorring almshouses and workhouses as prisons, they took refuge there usually only as a last resort—a lying-in hospital for a woman in the final stages of pregnancy, a hospital for someone in a medical crisis, and a soup kitchen for those in a state of near starvation. Like poor relief officials, the most abjectly poor practiced their own form of triage. For many, the first remedy was moving in or out of the city in search of work; many pursued a second strategy of begging alms or appropriating food, clothes, and cash through theft; the final resort was entering the almshouse in winter when jobs were difficult to find, then fleeing in the spring when work was more readily available.[86]

In rural almshouses, which by the early nineteenth century were becoming the dominant vehicle of pastoral poor relief, inmates probably had greater leverage in shaping the terms of institutionalized existence than in the large, less personal cities. Monique Bourque's essay in this book describes how mid-Atlantic poor relief administrators in small towns were always involved in a shifting negotiation with inmates, hammering out informal contracts "which included the understanding that both aid and authority had its limits." In ways that made the lives of almshouse inmates something different than the policies intended by the county magistrates, paupers had considerable latitude to "manipulate their admission, their tasks within the institution, and their discharge." If further studies confirm these findings, the struggles of the working poor to cope with the shift from a commercial to a manufacturing economy bear some resemblance to the efforts of slaves to negotiate the terms of their labor with slave masters in the South.

## Poverty and Politics

Having discovered poverty in the land of milk and honey, historians have asked what role the poor may have played on the public scene, either by direct action themselves, as in labor organizing and crowd activity, or indirectly by convincing others that poverty was something more than self-failure at the bottom of society, thereby requiring the rethinking of fundamental social, economic, and political arrangements. Historians have provided tentative answers in recent years, but much more needs to be known. Complicating the matter is the difficulty, if not the impossibility, of treating the poor as a discrete and unchanging group with separate motives and separate agendas. Clearly this is not a fruitful way to proceed. But if it can be assumed that the poor were something more than part of "the mindless mobs," so roundly dismissed at the time for their inability to act except out of passion, then it behooves us to inquire into how the impoverished responded in political ways to the conditions of their lives. At the same time, it is reasonable to presume that the most desperately poor—the impaired, aged, and chronically sick—played virtually no role in the coming of the American Revolution and its prosecution.[87]

From early in the eighteenth century, the working poor had mingled with those a step or two above them to secure protection against privation. From city to city, county to county, and decade to decade, they loomed large in the food riots (as in Boston in the 1710s and 1720s), in public market sabotage in Boston in the 1730s, in land riots (as in New Jersey and New York in the 1730s and 1740s and in North Carolina and South Carolina in the 1760s), in election riots in Philadelphia in 1742, and impressment riots in Boston in 1747. Rarely were they leaders of the crowd actions before the 1760s, but always they were present, as the essay in this book by Thomas Humphrey makes plain. They can never be sorted out from ordinary working men and women (who themselves were usually only a work accident, a crippling disease, or brief unemployment away from poverty), but the upper-class leaders who deplored crowd actions knew the poor bulked large when they labeled the gathered crowds the "canaille," "sinister army," "tagrags," "rabble," "swinish multitude," "villainous rubbish," or "low-bred illiterates." The term most commonly applied was "the lower sort," which certainly included the poor along with those who had known destitution, had scratched their way into "the middling sort," and, in many instances, would revisit poverty.

In addition to specific grievances, nearly all of which involved basic issues of sustaining life, what has been called the "bread-nexus," the poor responded (in consort with many of those who were a rung or two above them) to the growing separation between want and wealth. The notion that poverty marred a society and rebuked its success was not an idea homegrown in America. At mid-century, a titled Englishman, whose advice was republished in Boston, pronounced that "Every Nation has the Reputation of being rich or poor from the Condition of the lowest Class of its Inhabitants."[88] Consonant with this notion, many colonial newspapers and pamphlets bristled with anger about growing social distance, almost always in times of recession and widespread unemployment. Can we doubt that the poor thickly populated the crowd that gathered outside Thomas Hutchinson's sumptuous house in 1749 when it mysteriously caught fire and the people shouted, "Let it burn! Let it burn!"[89] One year later a Boston pamphleteer stormed that "Poverty and discontent appear in every Face (except the Countenances of the Rich)" and explicitly connected the enrichment of merchants who had fattened themselves on war contracts and their manipulation of the unstable money market with the plight of job-starved fellow citizens.[90]

A decade later, the rise of radical leaders in Boston, such as James Otis and Samuel Adams, cannot be separated from the years of economic difficulty, spreading poverty, and the limited chances for advancement that so many Bostonians experienced. When a conservative writer attacked Otis and his colleagues in 1763 as "the darling idols of a dirty, very dirty, witless rabble commonly called the little vulgar," he was animated by Otis's prior attacks on Bostonians who "grind the faces of the poor without remorse, eat the bread of oppression without fear, and wax fat upon the spoils of the people."[91] When the Stamp Act riots erupted, it was entirely appropriate from the perspective of the poor and the artisans scrambling for subsistence that their initial targets should be the luxuriously appointed homes of Andrew Oliver, Benjamin Hallowell, and Thomas Hutchinson, the latter detested by the lower class since the late 1740s as the architect of a merciless deflationary policy that was seen as primarily beneficial to the rich. Governor Francis Bernard thus understood the Stamp Act riots in Boston not only as a political response to new imperial regulations but also as "a war of plunder, of general levelling, and taking away the distinction of rich and poor."[92]

In other cities, voices from below challenged the notion that the destitute bore the primary responsibility for their plight. Was it equitable, asked a New York writer in 1765, "that 99, rather 999, should suffer for the Extravagance or Grandeur of one? Especially when it is considered that Men frequently owe their Wealth to the impoverishment of their Neighbours?" Writing four years later, a New Yorker reminded his audience that "it is [to] the meaner Class of Mankind, the industrious Poor, that so many of us are indebted for those goodly Dwellings we inhabit, for that comfortable Substance we enjoy, while others are languishing under the disagreeable Sensations of Penury and Want."[93] In these statements we have evidence that the accumulation of capital that fueled consumer culture also heightened political consciousness among poorly paid workers, such as mariners and dockworkers, who made consumption of overseas products possible but shared in this consumption hardly at all.

With the advent of the American Revolution, the poor appeared on the public stage as never before. In the tumultuous decade leading up to open rebellion and in the long war that followed, the poor were omnipresent—not part of a plebeian revolution but of a revolution with "a powerful plebeian current within it."[94] Often leagued with artisans, shopkeepers, teachers, and even doctors, who usually became their spokesmen, they insisted that the public recognize their impoverishment as a disfigurement of colonial society, not their own moral deformities. Not everywhere, but in many places, they also insisted that if a cleansed new republican society was to be formed, they must be included as part of the social contract.

Within this plebeian current swam those who before the Revolution had fallen in and out of work and in and out of poverty—such men as George Robert Twelves Hewes, whose modern biographer portrays a case study of the man who was born poor, lived poor, and died poor while playing his role on the public stage.[95] Indeed, the Revolutionary War, like many American wars that followed it, turned into a poor man's fight after the *rage militaire* wore off and the better sorts looked to indentured servants, freed slaves, and the poor to shoulder the guns and don the boots for a prolonged battle of attrition. As every general knew, it was not possible to fight the war of independence successfully without the poor. "Long Bill" Scott, vividly portrayed by John Shy, was probably the typical revolutionary soldier—a man who joined the fray as an opportunity to escape poverty (in his case on the New Hampshire frontier), who returned to poverty after the war was won, and who farmed out his youngest children to his oldest son in order to set off begging a pension or job from the government. Nine times wounded during the war, he spent another decade surveying in the West before dying of "lake fever." He died a poor man, never finding the economic security that he quested for in joining the revolutionary movement.[96] His black counterpart, aptly named Salem Poor, left his hardscrabble farm in Andover, Massachusetts, to fight at Bunker Hill, White Plains, and Valley Forge.

On the home front, the Revolution was profoundly dislocating. Disruptions of supply; unpatriotic mercantile behavior in the form of forestalling and monopolizing; the creation of an army of widows, mostly needy; and rampant inflation imposed burdens differentially—and rarely to the advantage of the poor.[97] It is unsurprising, given these dislocations and the revolutionary rhetoric about equality, that the poor were involved in the more than thirty food and price riots that occurred between 1776 and 1779.[98] To be sure, these plebeian actions to seize food or force hoarding and speculating merchants to lower prices probably were as much middle as lower class in character, although no historian has found a way to dissect the exact social composition of the crowds. It is evident that women figured importantly in the protest movements.

These demonstrations of what E. P. Thompson memorably called "the moral economy of the poor" lay so close to the primary interest of the poor— the interest in staying alive—that it is not necessary to prove that they were more than participants in the mob actions.[99] Along with those above them, who lived in a floating zone where plentitude was an aspiration but penury always cast a menacing shadow, they stood at the center of "the long-term development of capitalist social relationships in America" and represented "an immediate experience of economic distress and articulate popular ideas about economic exchange, its meaning, and the crucial issues of who might claim jurisdiction over it and through what political forms."[100]

The main student of the revolutionary food riots avers that in the later years of the war the price riots had leaders from the lower classes and "became more urban and, correspondingly, more expressive of the beliefs and grievances of the cities' lower classes."[101] This was certainly true in Philadelphia, a classic case of the poor taking to the streets during a year of hyperinflation that nearly put bread out of reach for poor families whose main breadwinner was on the battlefields. In 1779, "A Fair Dealer" (perhaps Paine) warned that price increases had torn at the meager pocketbooks of ordinary people so severely as "to make the Poor almost clamerous." "Mobility" warned forestallers that "hunger will break through stone walls and the resentment executed by it may end in your destruction."[102] The Fort Wilson riot that ensued, pitting revolutionist against revolutionist along class lines, is well known. Invoking the moral economy, the crowd threatened to use force to stop Robert Morris's ships from transporting grain out of Philadelphia to distant markets where he could make fatter profits. While the shipwrights who built the ship made no "claim in the property of the vessel," they insisted that "the service of it is the right of the community collectively with the owners," because the way the vessel was used "constituted a considerable part of the advantage they hoped to derive from their labours."[103]

The grievances of the poor and their lower-class compatriots also surfaced in the weighty matter of constructing state constitutions. Although these constitutions varied in important ways, all were inspired by a strain of classical republicanism that emphasized the organic connection between economic and political power and the certainty that concentrated economic power would find its equivalent in concentrated political power. "Where there is inequality of estates there must be inequality of power," wrote the late seventeenth-century English writers James Harrington and Algernon Sidney, much quoted in the American revolutionary era, for "there is no maxim more infallible and holding in any science, than this in politics; that empire is founded in property." John Trenchard and Thomas Gordon's *Cato's Letters,* quoted widely in colonial newspapers, punctuated the point in the 1740s: "A free people are kept so by no other means but an equal distribution of property. . . . As Liberty can never subsist without Equality, nor Equality be long preserved without an *Agrarian* law, or something like it; so when Mens Riches are become immeasurably or surprizingly great, a People, who regard their own Security, ought to make a strict Enquiry how they came by them, and oblige them to take down their own Size, for fear of terrifying the Community, or mastering it."[104]

Nobody, even the most radical revolutionist, sought a perfect equality. But men as conservative as John Adams believed that "we should preserve not an Absolute Equality—this is unnecessary, but preserve all from extreme Poverty, and all others from extravagant Riches." In Philadelphia, the convention architects of a state constitution had read Harrington, Sidney, Trenchard, and Gordon carefully. If this did not convince them that in a republican society it was necessary to "discourage the Possession [of an] enormous Proportion of Property" in the hands of a "few," they had firsthand knowledge that "great and overgrown rich Men" had become oppressive and, if left to accumulate great riches, would become "an Aristocracy, or Government of the Great."[105] In North Carolina, rural citizens advised the constitution makers to "oppose everything that leans to aristocracy or power in the hands of the rich and chief men exercised to the oppression of the poor."[106]

The egalitarian thrust of the American Revolution has been observed almost from the time of the event, though historians have assigned different weights to its importance.[107] Fiercely decried by conservative revolutionaries, the leveling tendency had its source not simply in the increasing social distance between top and bottom. Absent poverty, a growing gap would not have aroused much attention. What did attract fervent attention, as noted above, was the perceived causal connection between poverty and grandiose wealth.

In the aftermath of the Revolution, some of the problems associated with colonial status were theoretically solved to the benefit of the poor by opening up the land-rich trans-Appalachian West. Yet this escape valve, while attracting thousands of the down-and-out in search of better opportunities (as yet measured only casually), seems to have shifted the scene of poverty for many while it solved it for others. The backcountry unrest of the 1780s and 1790s involved the land-nexus—disturbances originating in people losing land as much as the difficulties of gaining land and in the frustrations of those thwarted in attempts at securing self-sufficiency. It is hard to imagine any of the agrarian unrest of this era—Ely's Rebellion, Shays's Rebellion, the Fries Rebellion, the Whiskey Rebellion, and the disturbances on the frontiers of New York, Pennsylvania, and Maine—without rural poverty and stunted ambition.[108]

The Revolution also hastened the advent of a market economy and industrial development, both of which cut several ways, pleasing many while discouraging others. The rosy view of what unfettered economic activity would do for all ranks of society—all boats rising on an incoming tide—needs to be balanced by an understanding of how waged labor, replacing artisanal labor, undermined the artisan's control of his labor value and how the politics of the 1790s, both from the top and bottom of society, involved a growing concern that commercialism and the free market were not abolishing poverty but entrenching it.[109]

Recent work on three self-educated men of very ordinary means—one in Massachusetts, one in New Jersey, and another in Delaware—offer windows into the new considerations of poverty in the emerging republican order. New Jersey's Abraham Clark, a signer of the Declaration of Independence, championed the struggling husbandmen and artisans—the laboring poor—and contrasted them to the moneyed men who lived "by the labour of the honest farmer and mechanic" and "riot[ed] in luxury by means of oppression." Holding a legislature seat in the 1780s and 1790s, he urged the lawmakers to devise policies to avoid "that inequality of property which is detrimental in a republican government" and to hobble avaricious "moneyed men not yet satisfied" who looked for new opportunities to "grind the face of the needy."[110]

William Manning of rural Massachusetts joined Clark in seeing monied men as parasites who lived off the labor of the industrious poor rather than economic innovators. Likewise, he believed that the impoverishment of those with limited access to property, or who had lost it as in the dark Shaysite days, would undermine the citizenry's independence, lead toward a passive servility, and in the end doom republicanism. Writing in 1790, this autodidact opposed Hamilton's financial plans for funding and assuming the revolutionary debt, arguing that the scheme was calculated to benefit the few at the expense of the many and thus would further concentrate property in the hands of the wealthy while submerging industrious farmers and workers whose "labor is the sole parent of all property."[111] In his later "Key to Liberty," Manning made proposals for giving the laboring majority the access to knowledge that he believed the elite so jealously guarded in order to keep in check the industrious poor.

Going much farther than Clark and Manning was Robert Coram, a Revolutionary War veteran, schoolteacher, antislavery activist, and newspaper editor in Wilmington, Delaware. Coram had little faith in laissez-faire commercial development and the purported unsurpassed advantages of "civilization." "Look around your cities," he wrote, "ye who boast of having established the civilization and happiness of man, see at every corner of your streets some wretched object with tattered garments, squalid look, and hopeless eye. . . . Civilization, thy benefits are not sufficiently solid, numerous, nor splendid; we everywhere perceive that degradation and distress which thy daughter poverty has entailed upon our race." Through his *Political Inquiries, to which is Added a Plan for the Establishment of Schools Throughout the United States* (1791),[112] Coram joined the circle of Anglo-American radicals who "became increasingly skeptical about the capacity for the unregulated workings of the free market to ensure justice for every member of society." Not classical republicans attacking commerce, but deeply skeptical about the benevolence of a self-regulating, "natural" free market system, they looked for political ways to harness commerce in the interest of a more just economic order. This brought Coram close to the emerging economic and political thought of Thomas Paine, who in *Agrarian Justice* (1795) addressed the problem of a "hereditary" poverty that was the offspring of commercial society. Paine's search for political mechanisms that would ensure a more equitable distribution of what commercial society admittedly produced in abundance became the search of many disturbed by the poverty that the American Revolution could never cure. "When it shall be said," wrote Paine in *Rights of Man* in 1791–92, "in any country in the world, 'My poor are happy; neither ignorance nor distress is to be found among them; my jails are empty of prisoners, my streets of beggars; the aged are not in want, the taxes are not oppressive' . . . —when these things can be said, then may that country boast of its constitution and its government."[113]

The Painite radicals of the 1790s would not carry the day, and the poor would not find political voice or political allies strong enough to change the commercialization of society or meliorate its tendencies to concentrate wealth and engender poverty. Looming on the horizon, though it could not be known, was a depression following the War of 1812 so severe that its unemployment rate of 25 percent or higher would shake American cities to the core. This in turn would raise new questions about the sources of poverty and its remedies; and always the arguments arising out of the severe depression of 1819 to 1822 were conditioned by the history of poverty and poor relief in the eighteenth century, the history of which we have only in recent decades rediscovered.

# Notes

1. Frances FitzGerald, *America Revised: History Schoolbooks in the Twentieth Century* (Boston: Little, Brown, 1979), 110–13. Among reasons to be placed on the Daughters of the American Revolution's 1959 list of subversive textbooks were pictures of American slums and lines of unemployed citizens during the Great Depression. See Jack Nelson and Gene Roberts Jr., *The Censors and the Schools* (Boston: Little, Brown, 1963), chap. 1.

2. For contemporary poverty and secular trends, see Sheldon H. Danziger, Gary D. Sandefur, and Daniel H. Weinberg, *Confronting Poverty: Prescriptions for Change* (Cambridge: Harvard University Press, 1994).

3. In 1956, Robert Bremner produced a major work on poverty in the United States but dates the advent of a poor relief problem to about 1830. See *From the Depths: The Discovery of Poverty in the United States* (New York: New York University Press, 1956).

4. For example, Robert W. Kelso, *A History of Public Poor Relief in Massachusetts, 1620–1920* (Boston: Houghton Mifflin, 1922); Marcus Wilson Jernegan, "The Development of Poor Relief in Colonial Virginia," *Social Service Review* 3 (1929): 1–18; Jernegan, "The Development of Poor Relief in Colonial New England," ibid. 5 (1931): 175–98; David M. Schneider, *The History of Public Welfare in New York, 1609–1866*, 2 vols. (Chicago: University of Chicago Press, 1938–41); Carl Bridenbaugh, *Cities in the Wilderness: Urban Life in America, 1625–1742* (New York: Ronald Press, 1938); *Rebels and Gentlemen: Philadelphia in the Age of Franklin* (New York: Reynal and Hitchcock, 1942); *Cities in Revolt: Urban Life in America, 1743–1776* (New York: Capricorn Books, 1955).

5. "Poverty" is not an entry in the indexes of any of the colonial history textbooks published from the 1930s to 1970s. The most widely used books were: Oscar T. Barck Jr. and Hugh T. Lefler, *Colonial America*, 2d ed. (New York: Macmillan, 1968); Max Savelle and Darold D. Wax, *A History of Colonial America*, 3d ed. (Hinsdale, Ill.: Dryden Press, 1973); Oliver Chitwood, *A History of Colonial America*, 3d ed. (New York: Harper and Row, 1961); and David Hawke, *The Colonial Experience* (Indianapolis: Bobbs-Merrill, 1966).

6. Franklin to Joshua Babcock, January 13, 1772, in Albert Henry Smyth, ed., *The Writings of Benjamin Franklin* (New York, 1907), 5:362–63. The quote at the end of the sentence is from Raymond A. Mohl, "Poverty in Early America, A Reappraisal: The Case of Eighteenth-Century New York City," *New York History* 50 (1969): 5.

7. Michael Harrington's *The Other America: Poverty in the United States* (New York: Macmillan, 1962) indirectly influenced studies of early American poverty by showing how the commonly used label for post–World War II United States, "the age of affluence," masked the extensive poverty and hunger that still held 40–50 million Americans in its grip. Harrington's argument that the poor had always been present but had only disappeared from view is applicable to the historiography of early America.

8. Main, *The Social Structure of Revolutionary America* (Princeton: Princeton University Press, 1965), 41. James A. Henretta, "Economic Development and Social Structure in Colonial Boston," *William and Mary Quarterly*, 3d ser., 22 (1965): 75–92; and Allan Kulikoff, "The Progress of Inequality in Revolutionary Boston," ibid., 28 (1971): 378–403, provided more precise analyses of Boston's changing social structure in the eighteenth century. I examined poverty and poor relief in colonial Philadelphia in "Poverty and Poor Relief in Pre-Revolutionary Philadelphia," *William and Mary Quarterly*, 3d ser., 33 (1976): 3–30; and "Up From the Bottom in Franklin's Philadelphia," *Past and Present* 77 (1977): 57–83.

9. Raymond A. Mohl, "Poverty in Early America, A Reappraisal: The Case of Eighteenth-Century New York City," *New York History* 50 (1969): 5–27.

10. The much-quoted phrase "best poor man's country" was first used by William Moraley, an indentured servant in Pennsylvania and New Jersey in the 1730s. One of the rare indentured servants who published an account of his experiences, Moraley hedged his comments by noting that conditions were good for many of the poor but certainly not all of them. See Susan E. Klepp

and Billy G. Smith, *The Infortunate: The Voyage and Adventures of William Moraley, an Indentured Servant* (University Park: The Pennsylvania State University Press, 1992), 20, 89, 93, 96.

11. The New York assembly's view is quoted in Robert E. Cray, *Paupers and Poor Relief in New York City and Its Rural Environs, 1700–1830* (Philadelphia: Temple University Press, 1988), 34. Such official views should always be read with caution. A year later, New York City's church wardens, in charge of poor relief, charged that "the Crys of the poor & Impotent for want of Reliefe are Extreamly Grevious." Church Wardens Minutes, September 20, 1700, quoted in Mohl, "Poverty in Early America," 9–10.

12. For early poverty and poor relief in Massachusetts, see Charles R. Lee, "Public Poor Relief and the Massachusetts Community, 1620–1715," *New England Quarterly* 55 (1982): 564–85; and Gary B. Nash, *The Urban Crucible: Social Change, Political Consciousness, and the Origins of the American Revolution* (Cambridge: Harvard University Press, 1979), passim. For the Charleston, South Carolina, case, where poor relief expenditures grew fivefold between 1755 and 1775, see Walter J. Fraser Jr., "The City Elite, 'Disorder,' and the Poor Children of Pre-Revolutionary Charleston," *South Carolina Historical Magazine* 84 (1983): 167–79.

13. Arguments to this effect, especially by Jeffrey G. Williamson, Peter H. Lindert, and Jackson Turner Main, are reviewed in Billy G. Smith, "Inequality in Late Colonial Philadelphia: A Note on Its Nature and Growth," *William and Mary Quarterly,* 3d ser., 41 (1984): 629–31. For Main's argument, see "The Distribution of Property in Colonial Connecticut," in James Kirby Martin, ed., *The Human Dimensions of Nation Making: Essays on Colonial and Revolutionary America* (Madison: University of Wisconsin Press, 1976), 54–104.

14. Smith, "Inequality in Late Colonial Philadelphia," 629–45.

15. Billy G. Smith, "Poverty and Economic Marginality in Eighteenth-Century America," *Proceedings of the American Philosophical Society* 132 (1988): 98. See also John K. Alexander, *Render Them Submissive: Responses to Poverty in Philadelphia, 1760–1800* (Amherst: University of Massachusetts Press, 1980), 7–10.

16. Douglas Jones, "The Strolling Poor: Transiency in Eighteenth-Century Massachusetts," *Journal of Social History* 8 (1975): 28–54; Ruth Herndon, "Women of 'No Particular Home': Town Leaders and Female Transients in Rhode Island, 1750–1800," in Larry D. Eldridge, *Women and Freedom in Early America* (New York: New York University Press, 1997), 269–89.

17. Nash, *Urban Crucible,* 185; Ruth Herndon's essay in this book examines warning out trends in Rhode Island towns from 1750 to 1800.

18. Important studies include Alexander, *Render Them Submissive;* Lynne Withey, *Urban Growth in Colonial Rhode Island: Newport and Providence in the Eighteenth Century* (Albany: State University of New York Press, 1984); Cray, *Paupers and Poor Relief;* Steven J. Ross, "Objects of Charity: Poor Relief, Poverty, and the Rise of the Almshouse in Early Eighteenth-Century New York City," in Conrad Wright and William Pencak, eds., *New Approaches to Colonial and Revolutionary New York* (Charlottesville: University Press of Virginia,, 1988); Priscilla Ferguson Clement, *Welfare and the Poor in the Nineteenth-Century City: Philadelphia, 1800–1854* (Washington, D.C.: Associated Universities Press, 1985); and Barbara L. Bellows, *Benevolence Among Slaveholders: Assisting the Poor in Charleston, 1670–1860* (Baton Rouge: Louisiana State University Press, 1993).

19. Benjamin J. Klebaner, "Pauper Auctions: The 'New England Method' of Public Poor Relief," *Essex Institute Historical Collections* 91 (1958): 195–204; Barry Levy, "Girls and Boys: Poor Children and the Labor Market in Colonial Massachusetts," in Nicholas Canny, Joseph E. Illick, Gary B. Nash, and William Pencak, eds., *Empire, Society and Labor: Essays in Honor of Richard S. Dunn,* special issue of *Pennsylvania History* 64 (summer 1997): 287–307; Holly Brewer, "Constructing Consent: How Children's Status in Political Theory Shaped Public Policy in Virginia, Pennsylvania, and Massachusetts before and after the American Revolution" (Ph.D. diss., University of California, Los Angeles, 1996), chap. 6.

20. For conceptualization and context, see Linda Gordon, "The New Feminist Scholarship on the Welfare State," in Gordon, ed., *Women, the State, and Welfare* (Madison: University of Wisconsin Press, 1990).

21. Elaine Forman Crane, *Ebb Tide in New England: Women, Seaports, and Social Change, 1630–1800* (Boston: Northeastern University Press, 1998), 114; Fraser, "City Elite"; Smith, "Poverty and Economic Marginality," 106–7.

22. Lisa Wilson, *Life After Death: Widows in Pennsylvania, 1750–1850* (Philadelphia: Temple University Press, 1992), 90–100; Ruth Herndon, *Unwelcome Americans: Living on the Margins in Early New England* (Philadelphia: University of Pennsylvania Press, 2001); Karin Wulf, *Not All Wives: Women of Colonial Philadelphia* (Ithaca: Cornell University Press, 2000).

23. Gregory A. Stiverson, *Poverty in a Land of Plenty: Tenancy in Eighteenth-Century Maryland* (Baltimore: Johns Hopkins University Press, 1977), 83–84.

24. An overview of tenancy, landlessness, and rural poverty is presented in the essays by Ronald Hoffman, Edward Countryman, and Marvin L. Michael Kay in Alfred Young, ed., *The American Revolution: Explorations in the History of American Radicalism* (DeKalb: Northern Illinois University Press, 1976); for the growing reliance of eastern Pennsylvania landowners on landless wage laborers and artisans, see Lucy Simler, "Tenancy in Colonial Pennsylvania: The Case of Chester County," *William and Mary Quarterly*, 3d ser., 43 (1986): 542–69; and Paul G. E. Clemens and Lucy Simler, "Rural Labor and the Farm Household in Chester County, Pennsylvania, 1750–1820," in Stephen Innes, ed., *Work and Labor in Early America* (Chapel Hill: University of North Carolina Press, 1988), 106–43.

25. Stephen Innes, "Land Tenancy and Social Order in Springfield, Massachusetts, 1652–1702," *William and Mary Quarterly*, 3d ser., 35 (1978), 33–56. The quoted phrase is on p. 35. See also Kenneth A. Lockridge, "Land, Population and the Evolution of New England Society, 1630–1790," *Past and Present* 39 (1968): 62–80; and John J. Waters, "The Traditional World of the New England Peasants: A View from Seventeenth-Century Barnstable," *New England Historical and Genealogical Register* 129 (1976): 3–21.

26. Alan Taylor, *Liberty Men and Great Proprietors: The Revolutionary Settlement on the Maine Frontier, 1760–1820* (Chapel Hill: University of North Carolina Press, 1990); Taylor, "Agrarian Independence: Northern Land Rioters after the Revolution," in Alfred F. Young, ed., *Beyond the Revolution: Explorations in American Radicalism* (DeKalb: Northern Illinois University Press, 1993), 221–45.

27. Contemporary descriptions of servitude, such as that of William Eddis, give shocked portrayals of the wretched condition of indentured servants and note that their situation was as bad as in Britain. Eddis, *Letters from America*, ed. Aubrey C. Land (Cambridge: Harvard University Press, 1969), 40.

28. J. R. Pole, *The Pursuit of Equality in American History* (Berkeley and Los Angeles: University of California Press, 1978), 33.

29. Stephen Innes, "Fulfilling John Smith's Vision: Work and Labor in Early America," in Innes, *Work and Labor in Early America*, 10.

30. Marcus W. Jernegan's *Laboring and Dependent Classes in Colonial America, 1607–1783* (Chicago: University of Chicago Press, 1931) is the first broad work on the subject. The long subtitle of Jernegan's book—*The Economic, Educational, and Social Significance of Slaves, Servants, Apprentices, and Poor Folk*—is the first acknowledgment that the poor were significant in any book title that I have found. Jernegan produced the book for the University of Chicago's Social Service Monographs Series, a series dominated by social worker scholars in the Hull House tradition. Sharon V. Salinger provides a comprehensive discussion of recent work on servant characteristics and their choice in selecting destinations in the Americas in "Labor, Markets, and Opportunity: Indentured Servitude in Early America," *Labor History* 38 (1997): 311–38.

31. Abbot E. Smith, *Colonists in Bondage: White Servitude and Convict Labor in America, 1607–1776* (Chapel Hill: University of North Carolina Press, 1946), 297–300. A quarter century later, Richard Hofstadter reminded us that "it will not do simply to assume that freed servants, especially those from the tobacco fields, were in any mental or physical condition to start vigorous new lives, or that long and ripe years of productivity lay ahead of them." Hofstadter, *America at 1750: A Social Portrait* (New York: Alfred A. Knopf, 1972), 61.

32. Russell Menard, "From Servant to Freeholder: Status Mobility and Property Accumulation in Seventeenth-Century Maryland," *William and Mary Quarterly*, 3d ser., 30 (1973): 37–64; Lorena Walsh, "Servitude and Opportunity in Charles County, Maryland, 1658–1705," in Aubrey Land, Lois Green Carr, and Edward C. Papenfuse, eds., *Law, Society, and Politics in Early Maryland* (Baltimore: Johns Hopkins University Press, 1977); Lois Green Carr and Russell R. Menard, "Immigration and Opportunity: The Freedman in Early Colonial Maryland," in Thad W. Tate and David L. Ammerman, eds., *The Chesapeake in the Seventeenth Century: Essays on Anglo-American Society* (Chapel Hill: University of North Carolina Press, 1979), 73–95; Gloria L. Main, *Tobacco Colony: Life in Early Maryland, 1650–1720* (Princeton: Princeton University Press, 1982).

33. Sharon V. Salinger, *"To Serve Well and Faithfully": Labor and Indentured Servants in Pennsylvania, 1682–1800* (Cambridge: Cambridge University Press, 1987), 115–36; the quote is on p. 115.

34. A. Roger Ekirch, *Bound for America: The Transportation of British Convicts to the Colonies, 1718–1775* (Oxford: Clarendon Press, 1987). Parliament's Transportation Act of 1718 was described by an English pamphleteer in 1731 as "Draining the Nation of its offensive Rubbish without taking away their Lives." Quoted in ibid., 20.

35. The two most widely circulated memoirs of indentured servants give opposite views of the indentured servant's chance for success. For one servant who arrived in Philadelphia in the 1720s and who "reeled from one misfortune to another," see *The Infortunate: The Voyage and Adventure of William Moraley, an Indentured Servant*, ed. Klepp and Smith. For a success story, see John Harrower, *The Journal of John Harrower, an Indentured Servant in the Colony of Virginia, 1773–1776*, ed. Edward Miles Riley (New York: Holt, Rinehart, and Winston, 1963).

36. I have analyzed this in "Urban Wealth and Poverty," 562–64, and at greater length in *Urban Crucible*. For a parallel study of this in Rhode Island, see Withey, *Urban Growth in Colonial Rhode Island;* and Herndon, "Women of 'No Particular Home.'"

37. William H. Whitmore et al., eds., *Reports of the Record Commissioners of Boston*, 39 vols. (Boston, 1876–1908), 14:302.

38. Quoted in Alexander, *Render Them Submissive*, 14. For a broad view of the laboring poor in Philadelphia in the second half of the eighteenth century, see Billy G. Smith, "The Material Lives of Laboring Philadelphians, 1750–1800," *William and Mary Quarterly*, 3d ser., 38 (1981): 163–202; Smith, *The "Lower Sort": Philadelphia's Laboring People, 1750–1800* (Ithaca: Cornell University Press, 1990).

39. Smith, *"Lower Sort,"* 14.

40. Ibid.

41. Smith, "Poverty and Economic Marginality," 98–99.

42. Hamilton Andrews Hill, *History of the Old South Church (Third Church) Boston, 1669–1884*, 2 vols. (Boston: Houghton Mifflin, 1890), 2:51–52.

43. For smallpox epidemics, Elizabeth A. Fenn's *Pox Americana: The Great Smallpox Epidemic of 1775–82* (New York: Hill and Wang, 2001) is a starting point. For recent investigations of the impact of the 1793 yellow fever epidemic in Philadelphia, see J. Worth Estes and Billy G. Smith, eds., *A Melancholy Scene of Devastation: The Public Response to the 1793 Philadelphia Yellow Fever Epidemic* (Philadelphia: Science History Publications, 1997). Yellow fever struck Philadelphia six times between 1793 and 1805.

44. The quotations are from Mathew Carey's *A Short Account of the Malignant Fever Lately Prevalent in Philadelphia* (Philadelphia, 1793), 17, 23.

45. For desperate conditions in Philadelphia in 1740–41 and 1761–62, see Nash, "Poverty and Poor Relief," 6, 12–13.

46. The fullest study of desertion is Merril D. Smith, "'Where She's Gone to She Knows Not': Desertion and Widowhood in Early Pennsylvania," in Larry D. Eldridge, ed., *Women and Freedom in Early America* (New York: New York University Press, 1997), 211–28.

47. Quoted in Cray, *Paupers and Poor Relief*, 69.

48. Smith, "Material Lives of Laboring Philadelphians."

49. Smith, "Poverty and Economic Marginality," 99–100. In her study of Providence and Newport, Rhode Island, Lynne Withey finds that 30 to 45 percent of the householders in the late eighteenth century were "poor by any current definition." *Urban Growth in Colonial Rhode Island*, 56.

50. The literature is growing rapidly. Among the most important studies are: Smith, *"Lower Sort";* Marcus Rediker, *Between the Devil and the Deep Blue Sea: Merchant Seamen Pirates, and the Anglo-American Maritime World, 1700–1750* (New York: Cambridge University Press, 1987); Daniel Vickers, *Farmers and Fishermen: Two Centuries of Work in Essex County, Massachusetts, 1630–1850* (Chapel Hill: University of North Carolina Press, 1994); Jeffrey Bolster, *Black Jacks: African American Seamen in the Age of Sail* (Cambridge: Harvard University Press, 1997); Taylor, *Liberty Men and Great Proprietors;* Ronald Schultz, *The Republic of Labor: Philadelphia Artisans and the Politics of Class, 1720–1830* (New York: Oxford University Press, 1993); Woody Holton, *Forced Founders: Indians, Debtors, Slaves and the Making of the American Revolution in Virginia* (Chapel Hill: University of North Carolina Press, 1999); Young, *The Shoemaker and the Tea Party: Memory and the American Revolution* (Boston: Beacon Press, 1999); and the essays in Stephen Innes, *Work and Labor in Early America* (Chapel Hill: University of North Carolina Press, 1988).

51. Jacob Riis, *How the Other Half Lives: Studies Among the Tenements of New York* (New York: Charles Scribner's Sons, 1890).

52. Charles Woodmason, *The Carolina Backcountry on the Eve of the Revolution,* ed. Richard J. Hooker (Chapel Hill: University of North Carolina Press, 1953), 15 or 33.

53. Taylor, *Liberty Men and Great Proprietors,* 71–73.

54. For a review of the literature on rural poverty, see Smith, "Poverty and Economic Marginality," 108–15. For the New England case, see Kenneth Lockridge, "Land, Population, and the Evolution of New England Society, 1630–1790, and an Afterthought," in Stanley N. Katz, ed., *Colonial America: Essays in Politics and Social Development* (Boston: Little, Brown, 1971), 466–91.

55. The scholarly literature on growing consumerism is large and growing apace; it can be glimpsed in Neil McKendrick et al., *The Birth of a Consumer Society: The Commercialization of Eighteenth-Century England* (Bloomington: Indiana University Press, 1985); T. H. Breen, "An Empire of Goods: The Anglicization of Colonial America, 1690–1776," *Journal of British Studies* 25 (1986): 467–99; Breen, "'Baubles of Britain': The American and Consumer Revolutions of the Eighteenth Century," *Past and Present* 119 (1988): 73–104; Breen, "Narrative of Commercial Life: Consumption, Ideology, and Community on the Eve of the American Revolution," *William and Mary Quarterly,* 3d ser., 50 (1993): 471–501; and Richard Bushman, *The Refinement of America: Persons, Houses, Cities* (New York: Alfred A. Knopf, 1992).

56. For convenient summaries of the literature, see Lorena S. Walsh et al., "Toward a History of the Standard of Living in British North America," *William and Mary Quarterly,* 3d ser., 45 (1988): 116–70.

57. Lois Green Carr and Lorena S. Walsh, "The Standard of Living in the Colonial Chesapeake," ibid., 135; and Billy G. Smith, "Comment," in ibid., 165.

58. Even one of the most enthusiastic proponents of the wealth-generating economy of the late eighteenth century agrees that the Revolution "worked its havoc more upon the poor than the rich" and that the condition of the poor worsened in the last quarter of the eighteenth century. John McCusker, "Comment," in "Toward a History of the Standard of Living," ibid., 169. See also, Susan Grigg, "Toward a Theory of Remarriage: A Case Study of Newburyport at the Beginning of the Nineteenth Century," *Journal of Interdisciplinary History* 8 (1977): 183–220; Susan Grigg, *The Dependent Poor of Newburyport: Studies in Social History, 1800–1830* (Ann Arbor: UMI Research Press, 1984); and Clement, *Welfare and the Poor in . . . Philadelphia.*

59. For the most exacting study of changing rates of mortality, see Klepp, "Seasoning and Society: Racial Differences in Mortality in Eighteenth-Century Philadelphia," *William and Mary Quarterly,* 3d ser., 51 (1994): 473–506.

60. Susan E. Klepp's essay in this volume. For data on declining average heights (which must have been caused primarily by sharp drops in height in the lower social ranks), see Dora L. Costa

and Richard H. Steckel, "Long-Term Trends in Health, Welfare, and Economic Growth in the United States," in *Health and Welfare during Industrialization*, ed. Richard H. Steckel and Roderick Floud (Chicago: University of Chicago Press, 1997), 47–90; and John Komlos, "Shrinking in a Growing Economy: The Mystery of Physical Stature during the Industrial Revolution," *Journal of Economic History* 58 (1998): 779–802.

61. Michael B. Katz, *In the Shadow of the Poorhouse: A Social History of Welfare in America* (New York: Basic Books, 1986), 4. For an examination of the Philadelphia case, see Sharon Salinger, "Artisans, Journeymen, and the Transformation of Labor in Late Eighteenth-Century Philadelphia," *William and Mary Quarterly*, 3d ser., 40 (1983), 62–84.

62. Salinger, "Artisans, Journeymen, and the Transformation of Labor."

63. Henry George, *Progress and Poverty: An Inquiry into the Cause of Industrial Depressions, and of the Increase of Want with Increase of Wealth* (San Francisco: W. M. Hinton, 1879).

64. David Rothman, *The Discovery of the Asylum: Social Order and Disorder in the New Republic* (Boston: Little, Brown, 1971).

65. Cotton Mather, *Some Seasonable Advise unto the Poor* (Boston, 1712).

66. Gary B. Nash, "The Failure of Female Factory Labor in Colonial Boston," *Labor History* 20 (1979), 165–88; and Laurel Thatcher Ulrich, "Sheep in the Parlor, Wheels on the Common: Pastoralism and Poverty in Eighteenth-Century Boston," in Carla Gardina Pestana and Sharon V. Salinger, eds., *Inequality in Early America* (Hanover, N.H.: University Press of New England, 1999), 182–200.

67. In addition to the studies cited earlier, see Stephen E. Wiberly Jr., "Four Cities: Public Poor Relief in Urban America, 1700–1775" (Ph.D. diss., Yale University, 1975); Nash, "Poverty and Poor Relief in Pre-Revolutionary Philadelphia"; Nash, "Urban Wealth and Poverty in Pre-Revolutionary America," *Journal of Interdisciplinary History* 6 (1976): 545–84; and Nash, "Up From the Bottom in Franklin's Philadelphia."

68. The fullest studies of changing poor relief strategies in the eighteenth century, in addition to the essays in this book, are Alexander, *Render Them Submissive;* Cray, *Paupers and Poor Relief;* Bellows, *Benevolence Among Slaveholders . . . in Charleston;* and Clement, *Welfare and the Poor . . . in Philadelphia.*

69. This has been studied by Nash, "Poverty and Poor Relief," 13–30, and most fully in Alexander, *Render Them Submissive,* chaps. 5–6.

70. Quoted in Nash, "Poverty and Poor Relief," 18.

71. The quoted phrase is from Leonard Labaree et al., eds., *The Papers of Benjamin Franklin,* 35 vols. (New Haven: Yale University Press, 1959–), 13:515.

72. *(Philadelphia) Independent Gazetteer,* May 21, 1791, quoted in Alexander, *Render Them Submissive,* 14.

73. The "Haskell thesis," which originated in his response to David Brion Davis's characterization of abolitionist motives and values, has not been applied to changing attitudes about poverty. For the Haskell-Davis-Ashworth debate, see Thomas Bender, ed., *The Antislavery Debate: Capitalism and Abolitionism as a Problem in History* (Berkeley and Los Angeles: University of California Press, 1992).

74. Cray, *Paupers and Poor Relief,* 102. Cray shows that in towns outside New York City, municipal officials began switching from institutionalized relief to "pauper auctions and other kinds of public charity" in the early nineteenth century while the metropolis was moving toward a complete reliance on workhouses. Rural communities would later fall into line. For Philadelphia, see Clement, *Welfare and the Poor.*

75. For an illuminating set of essays, see Tim Hitchcock, Peter King, and Pamela Sharpe, eds., *Chronicling Poverty: The Voices and Strategies of the English Poor, 1640–1840* (London: Macmillan, 1997).

76. Smith, *"Lower Sort,"* 92–93; Smith, "The Vicissitudes of Fortune: The Careers of Laboring Men in Philadelphia, 1750–1800," in Innes, ed., *Work and Labor in Early America,* 221–22; Smith's "Walking the Streets," the first chapter of his *"Lower Sort,"* is a unique view of the "intensely insecure environment" in which most urban working people lived.

77. Timothy Breen, "Making History: The Force of Public Opinion and the Last Years of Slavery in Revolutionary Massachusetts," in *Through a Glass Darkly: Reflections on Personal Identity in Early America,* ed. Ronald Hoffman, Mechal Sobel, and Fredrika J. Teute (Chapel Hill: University of North Carolina Press, 1996), 77–92.

78. Young, *Shoemaker and the Tea Party.* This book is an extension and revision of Young's earlier "George Robert Twelves Hewes, 1742–1840," *William and Mary Quarterly,* 3d ser., 38 (1981): 561–623.

79. For the New York City case, see Cray, *Paupers and Poor Relief,* and "White Welfare and Black Strategies: The Dynamics of Race and Poor Relief in Early New York, 1700–1825," *Slavery and Abolition* 7 (1986): 273–89]; for the situation in Pennsylvania and Virginia, see Brewer, "Constructing Consent," chap. 6.

80. The best study of transient women and their strategies is Herndon, "Women of 'No Particular Home,'" 269–89. See also Herndon, *Unwelcome Americans.* A forthcoming book by Cornelia Dayton and Sharon Salinger traces the struggles of warned-out women in Boston.

81. Alexander, *Render Them Submissive,* 98.

82. Daily Occurrence Docket, December 22, 1789, Philadelphia Almshouse Records, Philadelphia City Archives.

83. Minutes of the [Philadelphia] Overseers of the Poor, 1768–74, June 15, 1769, quoted in Nash, "Poverty and Poor Relief," 26.

84. "Elector" in *Pennsylvania Journal,* October 3, 1781, quoted in Alexander, *Render Them Submissive,* 51.

85. For those who read Thomas Paine, or heard him read, they must have taken comfort in his *Agrarian Justice,* published in 1795–96, where he pled the case of the dispossessed, for whom "it is a right, and not a charity" to receive the assistance of those who paid too little for the labor of the poor and monopolized the society's resources. Philip Foner, ed., *The Complete Writings of Thomas Paine* (New York: Citadel Press, 1945), 1:612, 618–20.

86. For vivid examples of the various strategies employed by the poor in Philadelphia, see Cynthia J. Shelton and Billy G. Smith, "The Daily Occurrence Docket of the Philadelphia Almshouse, 1800," *Pennsylvania History* 52 (1985): 86–116.

87. The beginning of historical consideration of the agency of the poor and lowly begins with Staughton Lynd, "Who Should Rule at Home? Dutchess County, New York, in the American Revolution," *William and Mary Quarterly,* 3d ser., 18 (1961): 330–59; and Jesse Lemisch, "Jack Tar in the Streets: Merchant Seamen in the Politics of Revolutionary America," *William and Mary Quarterly,* 3d ser., 19 (1962), 201–19.

88. *A Letter from Sir Richard Cox, Bart. To Thomas Prior, Esq.: Shewing from Experience a sure Method to establish the Linnen Manufacture* (Boston, 1750), 10.

89. Nash, *Urban Crucible,* 226.

90. Vincent Centinel (pseud.), *Massachusetts in Agony; or, Important Hints to the Inhabitants of the Province: Calling aloud for Justice to be done to the Oppressed* (Boston, 1750), 3–5, 8, 12–13.

91. The attack on Otis is in *Boston Evening Post,* March 14, 1763; Otis's prior attack on the wealthy is in *Boston Gazette,* January 11, 1762, Supplement.

92. Bernard to Board of Trade, Aug. 31, 1765, in William Cobbett, ed., *The Parliamentary History of England* (London, 1813), 16:129–31. For the role of the humble in the street politics in Boston, see Dirk Hoerder, *Crowd Action in Revolutionary Massachusetts, 1765–1780* (New York: Academic Press, 1977).

93. *New-York Gazette,* July 11, 1765; November 13, 1769. For a fuller analysis of distrust of the wealthy in the cities, going back to the early eighteenth century, and the crescendo of attacks on the wealthy in the years leading up to the American Revolution, see Gary B. Nash, "Social Change and the Growth of Pre-Revolutionary Urban Radicalism," in Young, ed., *The American Revolution,* 4–36. The New York case is examined by Paul Gilje, *The Road to Mobocracy: Popular Disorder in New York City, 1763–1834* (Chapel Hill: University of North Carolina Press, 1987), chaps. 1–3.

94. Young, *Shoemaker and the Tea Party*, 205.

95. Ibid. For a recent treatment of underclass involvement in the revolutionary movement in Virginia see Woody Holton, *Forced Founders: Indians, Debtors, Slaves, and the Making of the American Revolution in Virginia* (Chapel Hill: University of North Carolina Press, 1999).

96. John Shy, "Hearts and Minds in the American Revolution: The Case of 'Long Bill' Scott and Peterborough, New Hampshire," in Shy, *A People Numerous and Armed: Reflections on the Military Struggle for American Independence* (New York: Oxford University Press, 1976), 163–80. In the large literature on the composition of the militia and Continental army and navy, agreement is general that as the war proceeded, the manpower was drawn from the lowest echelons of colonial society. See, e.g., Charles Royster, *A Revolutionary People at War: The Continental Army and American Character, 1775–1783* (Chapel Hill: University of North Carolina Press, 1979); and Lawrence Delbert Cress, *Citizens in Arms: The Army and Militia in American Society to the War of 1812* (Chapel Hill: University of North Carolina Press, 1982).

97. The most deeply researched case study of this is Steven Rosswurm, *Arms, Country, and Class: The Philadelphia Militia and the "Lower Sort" during the American Revolution* (New Brunswick: Rutgers University Press, 1987). For a broader look at attempts from below to cope with the revolutionary and postrevolutionary dislocations, see Ruth Bogin, "Petitioning and the New Moral Economy of Post-Revolutionary America," *William and Mary Quarterly*, 3d ser., 45 (1988): 391–425.

98. Barbara Clark Smith, "Food Rioters and the American Revolution," *William and Mary Quarterly*, 3d ser., 51 (1994): 3–38.

99. E. P. Thompson, "The Moral Economy of the English Crowd in the Eighteenth Century," *Past and Present* 50 (1971): 76–131. The ballooning literature on the "moral economy" is cited in Smith, "Food Rioters," 4–5, notes 3–5.

100. Smith, "Food Rioters," 3–4. For earlier food riots and controversies in Boston that disrupted the city for several decades, see Smith, "Markets, Streets, and Stores: Contested Terrain in Pre-Industrial Boston," in Elise Marienstras and Barbara Karsky, eds., *Autre Temps, Autre Espace— An Other Time, An Other Space: Etudes sur l'Amerique pre-industrielle* (Nancy, Fr., 1986), 181–97. For petitions on behalf of "the Poorer sort of People" in Portsmouth, New Hampshire, from 1772 to 1778, see Bogin, "Petitioning and the New Moral Economy," 399–400.

101. Smith, "Food Rioters," 17.

102. For a close examination of the Philadelphia food and price riots, see Steven Rosswurm, "'As a Lyen out of His Den': Philadelphia's Popular Movement, 1776–80," in Margaret Jacob and James Jacob, eds., *The Origins of Anglo-American Radicalism* (London: George Allen and Unwin, 1984), 300–323. The quoted passages are on p. 308.

103. Quoted in ibid., 311.

104. Charles Blitzer, ed., *The Political Writings of James Harrington* (New York: Liberal Arts Press, 1955), 98; [John Trenchard and Thomas Gordon], *Cato's Letters; or, Essays on Liberty, Civil and Religious*, 6th ed. (London, 1755), 2:16; 3:207–8. When the antiadministration group organized by Samuel Adams launched the *Independent Advertiser* in Boston in 1748, this passage from *Cato's Letters* ornamented the first issue. Adams added another sentence that asked: "But some will say, is it a Crime to be rich? Yes, certainly, At the Publick Expense."

105. The statement by John Adams was written in the draft of his *Dissertation on Canon and Feudal Law*, published in 1765, but it was extinguished in the final version. See Robert J. Taylor, ed., *The Papers of John Adams*, vol. 1 (Cambridge: Harvard University Press, 1977), 106–7n. The clause in the draft of the Pennsylvania constitution of 1776, also deleted in the final version, is quoted in Rosswurm, "Philadelphia's Popular Movement," 306–7.

106. Quoted in Michael Merrill and Sean Wilentz, ed., *The Key of Liberty: The Life and Democratic Writings of William Manning, "A Laborer," 1747–1814* (Cambridge: Harvard University Press, 1993), 5.

107. For a searching discussion of this, from J. Franklin Jameson's initial formulation to the present, see Alfred F. Young, "American Historians Confront 'The Transforming Hand of

Revolution,'" in Ronald Hoffman and Peter J. Albert, eds. *The Transforming Hand of Revolution: Reconsidering the American Revolution as a Social Movement* (Charlottesville: University Press of Virginia, 1995), 346–494; and the essays in that volume by Marcus Rediker, "A Motley Crew of Rebels: Sailors, Slaves, and the Coming of the American Revolution," 155–98; Billy G. Smith, "Runaway Slaves in the Mid-Atlantic Region during the Revolutionary Era," 199–230; and Alan Taylor, "'To Man Their Rights': The Frontier Revolution," 231–57. For other key post-Progressive statements of the egalitarian thrust, see Jesse Lemisch, "The American Revolution Seen from the Bottom Up," in Barton J. Bernstein, ed., *Towards a New Past: Dissenting Essays in American History* (New York: Random House, 1967), 5–45; Merrill Jensen, *The American Revolution within America* (New York: New York University Press, 1974); Richard B. Morris, "A Cautiously Transforming Egalitarianism," chap. 7 in Morris, *Forging of the Union, 1781–1789* (New York, Harper and Row, 1987); Morris, "'We the People of the United States': The Bicentennial of a People's Revolution," *American Historical Review* 82 (1977): 1–19; and Allan Kulikoff, *The Rise and Destruction of the American Yeoman Classes* (Chapel Hill: University of North Carolina Press, 1992). For all its celebration of the idea of equality in revolutionary America, Gordon Wood's *Radicalism of the American Revolution* (New York: Alfred A. Knopf, 1992) says little about inequality and the agency of the laboring poor in challenging the growing gap in wealth and the conservative resurgence in the 1790s. For critiques of the book and Wood's response, see essays by Joyce Appleby, Barbara Clark Smith, Michael Zuckerman, and Gordon Wood in *William and Mary Quarterly*, 3d ser., 51 (1994): 679–716. Equality is "the single most powerful and radical ideological force in all of American history" (p. 200), Wood writes, but his book barely notices those at the bottom of society—seamen, laborers, indentured servants, slaves, landless farmers, and lower-end artisans.

108. Peter Levine, "The Fries Rebellion: Social Violence and the Politics of the New Nation," *Pennsylvania Magazine of History and Biography* 60 (1973): 241–58; Richard Maxwell Brown, "Back Country Rebellions and the Homestead Ethic in America, 1740–1799," in Brown and Don E. Fehrenbacher, eds., *Tradition, Conflict, and Modernization: Perspectives on the American Revolution* (New York: Academic Press, 1977), 73–99; David P. Szatmary, *Shays's Rebellion: The Making of an Agrarian Insurrection* (Amherst: University of Massachusetts Press, 1980); Robert A. Gross, *In Debt to Shays: The Bicentennial of an Agrarian Rebellion* (Charlottesville: University Press of Virginia, 1993); Thomas P. Slaughter, *The Whiskey Rebellion: Frontier Epilogue to the American Revolution* (New York: Oxford University Press, 1986).

109. The literature on the transition to capitalism and the difficulties of the lower classes trying to negotiate the transition from agricultural to industrial labor is immense. For a discussion of the literature on this, which cites most of the relevant work, see Michael Merrill, "Putting 'Capitalism' in Its Place: A Review of Recent Literature," *William and Mary Quarterly*, 3d ser., 52 (1995): 315–26. For a case study with documents, see Paul A. Gilje and Howard B. Rock, eds., *Keepers of the Revolution: New Yorkers at Work in the Early Republic* (Ithaca: Cornell University Press, 1992).

110. The quoted passages are from Clark's 1786 pamphlet "The True Policy of New-Jersey, Defined," quoted in Ruth Bogin, "New Jersey's True Policy: The Radical Republican Vision of Abraham Clark," *William and Mary Quarterly*, 3d ser., 35 (1978), 100–109.

111. Manning's "Some Proposals for Making Restitution to the Original Creditors of Government," in Merrill and Wilentz, *Key to Liberty*, 60.

112. Seth Cotlar, "Radical Conceptions of Property Rights and Economic Equality in the Early American Republic: The Trans-Atlantic Dimension," *Explorations in Early American Culture* 4 (2000): 191–219, quoting Coram, *Political Inquiries*.

113. Foner, *Writings of Paine*, 1:446.

# PART ONE  *Lives of the Poor*

# Dead Bodies

*Poverty and Death in Early National Philadelphia*

SIMON NEWMAN

Poverty is physical.[1] It encompasses hunger and cold, joblessness and home-lessness, inferior education and health care. It is also experiential, defined by the ways in which it is perceived both by those who are and by those who are not impoverished. How a society regards and reacts to poverty is in no small part determined by the downward glances of the affluent, whose attitudes toward the poor may constitute the "major barrier" against attacks on the causes and results of impoverishment.[2] At times American society has united behind political leaders in wars against poverty, but more often leaders artic-ulate a peculiarly American desire to debate the very existence of poverty in a mythical land of plenty, arguing that it may be escaped with ease or even that it does not exist.[3] When President Ronald Reagan attacked Cadillac-driving "welfare mothers" whose freezers were full of steaks, he drew applause from those who wanted to believe that poverty did not, indeed, that poverty could not endure in the wealthiest nation the world has ever known. Indigents and the homeless, according to Reagan, simply chose to be poor. At the turn of the new millennium, during the nation's longest ever period of prosperity, the gap between rich and poor continues to expand, yet the myth of univer-sal prosperity endures. A "reality bus tour" of North Philadelphia shocked delegates to the 2000 Republican National Convention, who found the poverty they saw away from their beautified hotels "eye-opening."[4]

American historians are not immune to such myths. "Poverty and economic deprivation," contends Gordon Wood in his magisterial study of the American Revolution, "were not present" in the colonies that became the United States.[5] The historians whose research Wood ignored pointed out the absurdity of his remark,[6] but one can only wonder what the poor of revolutionary and early national America would have made of a historian who claimed that they did not exist and that their experience of insufficient food, fuel, clothing, and shelter was impossible.[7]

For the parents of eight-month-old Henry Jennings, or for the widow Margaret Clayton, or for Edward and Jane Ridley, poverty was all too real. In July 1801, Henry's father, an unemployed ship carpenter, brought his family from Boston to Philadelphia in a desperate search for work. Having spent all their money on the voyage and a small quantity of "coarse bread and salt provisions," all of which they consumed during an unexpectedly long journey, the Jennings family had no funds for further supplies, and their child expired soon after they arrived in Philadelphia.[8] The cost of poverty was just as high for Margaret Clayton, whose husband died in 1799 after a long consumptive illness during which the family lost their home and property. During an epidemic of measles in October 1801, all four of her young children fell ill, and her two-year-old son succumbed and was buried next to the father he had never known. Edward Ridley, too, may have never seen his son, Alexander, since Edward was a mariner and abroad when the eight-month-old child died. Seafaring was a poorly paid profession, yet it was the largest single occupation for adult men in the towns and cities of the young American republic. The wives and dependents of men absent on long, ocean-going voyages were forced to fend for themselves; as a nursing mother, Jane Ridley made money in one of the only ways she could, by hiring herself out as a wet nurse, while entrusting her son Alexander to another, cheaper wet nurse. Within weeks, an infection killed the child.[9]

If we fail to see and hear the poor, the fault is ours, and for a historian to ignore their presence in so many historical records and in so much scholarly work beggars belief. In the records of almshouses and workhouses, of courts and civic authorities, of prisons and charities, the poor surround the historian of early America. As names on lists, their existence may be established and quantified, but subtler investigation is required to bring their lived experiences of poverty into focus. The challenge is not to find them, but rather to give color to their lives and to make real their hunger, illnesses, underemployment, cold, poor shelter and the ways in which they dealt with such hardships. The purpose of this essay is to learn more about the lives of the poor by examining the deaths and burials of poor Philadelphians in the late eighteenth and early nineteenth centuries.

The nature and the experience of early American death appear extremely remote to the modern historian, despite the fact that death and dying were commonplace events, they often occurred within the home, and they were witnessed by almost every man, woman, and child.[10] The nature and causes of death, the manner of dying, the ways in which the living experienced the demise of others, and the rites surrounding death all provide fertile grounds for historians interested in everyday existence, culture, and belief.[11] The Grim Reaper regularly visited the households of early national America, wherein accident, sickness, and mortality were commonplace. Yet despite the ultimate leveling of the reaper's scythe, the letters and diaries of the more affluent suggest that they enjoyed better health and greater longevity than did poorer Americans. Wealthier men and women possessed the means to make projects of their bodies, feeding them a nutritional and balanced diet, exercising and molding them to Enlightenment standards of beauty, and when necessary removing them from the fetid atmosphere of city and plantation alike.[12]

The early national poor have left us far fewer of their words, rendering their experiences and manner of illness, disease, and death terra incognito, common and public events whose tenor nevertheless eludes us. We may assume that those with little or no means developed a rather more instrumental relationship with their bodies; the luxury of the body as project was unavailable to those whose physical being was a means to an end.[13] With some confidence we can speculate that insufficient quantities of food, fuel, and clothing; demanding work regimens; and exposure to myriad infections and diseases must surely have made ill health and death far more likely in poor than in wealthy households.[14] The romanticization of both life and death that was beginning to spread among the prosperous was as yet far removed from the everyday lives of "lower sort" Philadelphians, for whom death was too real, too constant, and even too mundane to allow such fanciful notions.

Poverty was far more than a condition of life requiring public action and private charity. Rather, it consisted of the day-to-day existence of living in poverty, less a condition than a way of life for the thousands of inhabitants in such communities as Southwark, a southern suburb of the Quaker City. Death came often to such people, and by knowing more about how the reaper appeared as well as by imagining how they responded to it, we may learn more about living poor in early national America. Indeed, their experiences of death will enhance our understanding of the lives and society of folk whose only appearances in written records may be no more than a brief record of their expiration.

This essay is based upon one thousand burial records inscribed by the Reverend Nicholas Collin between February 1791 and October 1809.[15] Collin served as the rector of Gloria Dei (see figure 1), the Swedish Lutheran Church and Philadelphia's oldest house of worship, which stands to this day in Southwark, a ten-minute walk south of Independence Hall. The area was home to the families of a great many sailors, laborers, journeymen, and

*Fig. 1*    William Russell Birch, *Preparation for War to defend Commerce,* engraving, 1799. The Gloria Dei Swedish Lutheran Church is in the background. The construction of the frigate *Philadelphia* at Joshua Humphreys's shipyard is indicative of the type of work engaged in by some of the laboring people who resided in this neighborhood. Courtesy of the Library Company of Philadelphia.

waterfront workers, and the pastor consequently found himself burying a good many of the city's poor.[16] These records provide valuable insight into medicine, illness, and dying during this era.

Collin's tenure at Gloria Dei was an unusually long one, stretching from 1786 to 1831. A friend of Dr. Benjamin Rush, Collin was a member of the American Philosophical Society, where he presented papers on a variety of medical and scientific subjects.[17] Medicine fascinated him, and he kept remarkably detailed records of the Philadelphians that he buried: no doctor appears to have been present in cases such as those of Elizabeth Ervin, yet Collin felt it necessary to record the length of her illness, her symptoms, and the regularity of her excretions. He saw himself as part of an Enlightenment progress that would eradicate common ailments and diseases, not least being the yellow fever that took his beloved wife in 1797. The usurpation of midwives and folk medicine by professional doctors, for example, is hinted at by Collin's brief yet moving account of the stillbirth of the young male child of Rebecca Hubbert. Living in great poverty in Mead Alley and with her seafaring husband away on a voyage, Rebecca was "in great danger" and her life was saved by taking the child "from her by instruments," most likely the forceps that in the hands of qualified yet inexperienced men were to cause such great damage to women and children alike.[18]

Although professional medicine was growing and changing rapidly, Collin drew also on a relatively static medical system, with interpretations of illness, disease, and dying that had evolved over centuries and were slow to fade away.[19] Relatively few of the records indicate that a doctor had participated in the treatment of the patient, in part because of the prohibitive expense to lower-class people. Moreover, medicine and the care of the sick were part and parcel of everyday life, family and communal endeavors built upon popular folk wisdom of long standing. Thus, sickness, dying, and even death itself remained negotiated public events, with rites of treatment and interaction between the dying and those around them that had evolved over many centuries. Doctors were often no more than occasional participants in a process that involved care and treatment of the afflicted by their family and friends. Ten-month-old John Potts, for example, who was suffering from the common infant ailment of worms, was unlikely to have been treated by a doctor; his parents administered powders in an attempt to rid his body of worms, which they may have obtained from a druggist, the Philadelphia Dispensary, or various other sources. In this case the treatment was unsuccessful, and the child died. Collin had no doubt that the worms had "been too long neglected, otherwise he would probably have overcome the vermine." Still, centuries of accrued knowledge and practice meant that folk medicine was often as successful as the remedies proposed by professional physicians in early national America.[20]

It is surprising that so few of the Southwark residents Collin buried appear to have died in a hospital. Early national Americans were well aware that hospitals were dangerous and even deadly places, wherein it was more likely that patients would compound existing problems with infections and further illness than recover. The more affluent were able to summon doctors, buy drugs, and enlist family or even paid nursing care, all within the confines of their own homes, but the poor sometimes had little option but to seek refuge in the Pennsylvania Hospital for the Sick Poor. Yet even those with insufficient means resisted the surrender of loved ones to such institutions. Although often "out of his head" as a result of a childhood head injury, Samuel Condor was institutionalized by his wife only during the four or five

months preceding his death. Collin implies that Condor had not been working for some time, and he was a drain on the meager resources of the household, but his family struggled to keep him among them. Similarly, his teenage
sister and his widowed older sister, despite their indigence, cared for the bro-
ken-backed orphan Edward Kirby for years. The Reverend Collin was never
slow to make note of such acts of familial love, for he clearly recognized the
enormous sacrifices involved.[21]

Collin's records are examples of what might be termed an amateur "medical gaze."[22] They rarely allow us to see and feel the experiences of the dying
themselves, but instead represent the thoughts and interpretations of an outsider who may not have witnessed some of the deaths that he describes. With
his layman's interest in medical science, a firm religious faith, and a conde-
scending yet compassionate attitude toward the poor among whom he lived,
Collin framed his records with precision. Like the doctors of his time, Collin
possessed no diagnostic tools beyond his own senses, which he employed
both with precision and with empathy. Integral to Collin's burial records was
his drive to understand and document how and why a person died, the ways
in which they were treated, and his own reactions to both person and process.

In the case of the unfortunate Daniel Conover, who died during the first
summer of Jefferson's presidency at the tender age of twenty-one, both popular and professional medicine concurred on the course of treatment. Collin
recorded that a horse had trodden upon and wounded Conover's foot, but
since this had healed with no apparent ill effects, Collin blamed Conover's
overexuberance on Independence Day for costing him his life. Having
"joined with other young people in the frolics of the days, and being heated
by dancing in the evening," he lay down upon the ground and consequently
contracted "a very great cold." Collin echoed the agreement of professionals
and lay people alike that the lockjaw that killed Conover was a result of the
cold rather than infection within the foot wound because an expensive
course of treatment "of mercury taken inwardly, and rubbed externally" did
little to help the young man and quite likely even speeded his departure.[23]

Interpreting Collin's records requires us to position ourselves in the middle ground between the early modern world and the scientific enlightenment. Collin, more than many of his contemporaries, comprehended
contemporary advances in understanding and treating the human body. Yet
he retained a sense of bodily health as a series of dynamic interactions with its
environment, believing that either good health or disease resulted from an
interplay between the body and its surroundings. Health depended on
achieving a balance in this interplay, hence the continued reliance on diet
and excretion to rectify disparities. Almost all medicine intended to correct

such imbalances, employing such remedies as bloodletting, emetics, and blistering to purge the body of dangerous impurities.[24] Collin shared with contemporary doctors a conviction that what one ingested and the quantities one took in were vital to one's health.

Collin's account of the weeklong illness of Mary Norbury and the treatment administered to her reflects these beliefs. Because her father was dead and her stepfather had abandoned the family, Mary had been bound out to John Grover, a justice of the peace who resided on Second Street. Sixteen-year-old Mary was sick for just over a week, and her symptoms—"first a chill, moderate headache, pain in the back, bowels & some in the stomach"— suggested what Charles Rosenberg has described as an imbalance "between constitutional endowment and environmental circumstance."[25] In accord with accepted medical practice, equilibrium between the constituent parts of Mary's body and her surroundings was sought by regulating the secretions by the application of blisters. In other instances, physicians, folk practitioners and even friends and family members may have employed tools or drugs in order to supply or diminish the body. Thus, treatment was designed to attack symptoms, and drugs were categorized by their effects—diuretics, cathartics, narcotics, emetics, and diaphoretics—rather than by disease or ailment.[26]

Collin's burial records contain the names of either Gloria Dei church members or of local residents who sought a final resting place in consecrated ground. Most Philadelphians were not church members, and as the congregation of the Swedish Lutheran Church dwindled, the numbers of nonmembers buried by Collin grew, accounting for 76 percent of the burials between 1791 and 1809, the years employed in this study.[27] Although members of Collin's congregation could expect burial free of charge, nonmembers—or "Strangers" as Collin labeled them—were required to pay ten dollars for an adult and five dollars for a child, a considerable sum. Few of the impoverished residents of Southwark could afford such fees, but in most cases Collin remitted part of the cost. Sometimes he justified this by allowing families to inter young children in the graves of their siblings, as in the case of Mary Ann Hobart, whose father was at sea when she died. Mary's mother, Rebecca, was poor, and Collin allowed Mary to be interred in the same grave as two of her siblings, enabling him to allow "a considerable abatement."[28]

On occasion, the families of Strangers were extremely vocal in their pleas for a Christian burial, as in the case of the infant son of Manuel Peterson, an "indigent" fish seller who "pleaded with tears, his desire to enter the babe in consecrated ground." Although Manuel and Abigail Peterson were unable to pay the full cost of the funeral for their five-day-old son, they paid what they could and added a string of perch, recorded by Collin with a mixture of wry amusement and respect for the pride of the bereaved couple.[29]

There were other reasons why impoverished residents of Southwark might wish to inter loved ones in the cemetery of a church to which they did not belong. Lack of funds made burial in the unconsecrated ground of Potter's Field the most viable option, but the large number of Southwark's poor who knocked upon Collin's door indicate that this was, if at all possible, to be avoided. The Petersons' gift of fish symbolizes the pride of many impoverished families, who sought to avoid the ignominy of a pauper's grave for their loved ones. Moreover, nonmembership did not mean, of course, that these people did not share elements of a basic Christian belief system or did not think it important to bury family members in consecrated ground. Perhaps most important, like the generations of European peasants from whom they were descended, the poor of Southwark were likely to gain comfort from the burial of family members close to one another, in a church cemetery in the center of their community, a fixed point that they might pass several times each day, allowing as much of a sense of connection with the dead as with the living. Collin recorded hundreds of cases where families begged him to allow burial of parents, siblings, and children beside or even in the same grave of departed relatives. Elizabeth Low's mother "was anxious to bury her . . . along with her children," and on April 24, 1801, the single mother was laid to rest alongside four of her children. Elizabeth's mother, her surviving children, and the friends who paid a token amount for the grave and burial, were unlikely to be able to afford a permanent marker for the graves of Elizabeth and her offspring. Nonetheless, all would have known the locations of the graves and may well have felt a tangible connection to those they had buried.[30]

On occasion, it was the dying themselves who pleaded for a plot in Gloria Dei's cemetery. Jane Willard "earnestly wished to be buried here," whereas twenty-nine-year-old Mary Ryan "requested on her deathbed to be buried in our cemetery, where her 2 children had been interred." Jane and George Willard were "poor people"; Mary "had for 5 years been palsical & for the last 5 mos. had a flux," and thus she was unable to work. Moreover, her husband Edward was "very indigent, owing to her long sickness & want of imployment as a ship joiner" because of the collapse of the maritime economy during President Jefferson's embargo.[31]

Collin noted full or partial addresses for almost one-quarter of the thousand decedents, and the large majority—both church members and nonmembers—lived within a few blocks of the church. Fully 85 percent of the smallpox and yellow fever victims whose addresses were recorded lived no farther away than Third Street to the west and Lombard Street to the north.

*Fig. 2*    Charles Willson Peale, *The Accident in Lombard Street*, etching, 1787. This neighborhood is more affluent than the one served by Gloria Dei a few blocks south of Lombard Street. Children, however, would have been present on all of the streets of Philadelphia. In the foreground are black chimney sweeps laughing at a young girl anguishing over her dropped pie. Courtesy of the Henry Francis du Pont Winterthur Museum.

Similarly, all of the women who died in childbirth and 93 percent of the children who were stillborn or who succumbed during infancy resided within the few blocks bounded by Fifth and Pine streets. The urban poor were Collin's neighbors, and whether or not they were members of his congregation, the minister did what he could for them, fashioning his own informal poor relief by drastically reducing the price of burials. Although striving for a dispassionate and, indeed, almost scientific objectivity in his records of death and dying, Collin, in his burial records, reveals his respect and compassion for the poor who surrounded him. While avoiding superlatives and emotional adjectives, Collin was unable to maintain his distance, and he wrote often of "affecting" cases, recording details of the condition of families that had little to do with his scientific record of the causes and nature of deaths. He was clearly moved when approached by Mary Moore, who sought burial for her infant son Dougal; Collin described her as the "wife [of] an absent seaman, struggling hard to support two children and an old sickly mother, [who] pleaded pathetically her poverty." Similarly, Collin concluded his record of

GRAPH 1. Age at Death

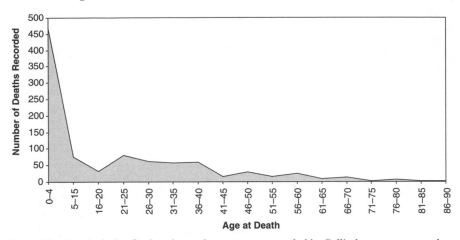

*Source:* The data include 963 decedents whose age was recorded by Collin between 1791 and 1809. Burial Records, Old Swedes Church, Pennsylvania Genealogical Society, Historical Society of Pennsylvania.

Edward Ryan's plea for the burial of his wife Mary by noting it as "a very affecting case & his grief told by a tearful sensibility."[32]

Perhaps what most affected Collin was the unremitting cycle of child mortality. As Susan Klepp's essay in this volume indicates, the majority of those buried in Southwark were children, and the fearsome infant mortality rate reveals a great deal about the straitened circumstances of their families (see graph 1). The pastor recorded both the age and the cause of death of 938 of the decedents in this sample. The mean age of death was eighteen years, although this statistic disguises how strikingly commonplace was premature death among the infants and children of poor Philadelphians. Almost one-third of those listed in Collin's records were younger than one year when they were buried, and almost one-half never reached their fifth birthdays. Once past these hurdles, life became somewhat less hazardous; only one-tenth died between their fifth and sixteenth years, and another 28 percent expired between the ages of sixteen and thirty-nine. Within Southwark's cramped and crowded confines, fewer than 16 percent of those buried by Collin lived beyond the age of forty, and just 5 percent reached the age of sixty.

That Southwark was a relatively new and rapidly growing community helps explain why so many of those who died were children and why so few were elderly. Unlike longer established sections of Philadelphia, the young people who came to live and work in the quickly expanding maritime community dominated the city's suburbs. Thousands of young people from Europe, from

GRAPH 2.  Occupations of Deceased (or Husbands or Fathers of Deceased)

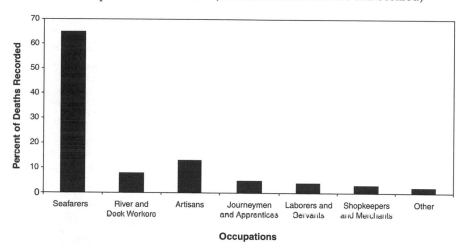

**Occupations**

*Source:* The data include 150 decedents whose occupation was recorded by Collin between 1791 and 1809. Burial Records, Old Swedes Church, Pennsylvania Genealogical Society, Historical Society of Pennsylvania.

rural America, and from other urban centers flocked to Southwark and the Northern Liberties as well as to similar areas in and around other American cities, finding what work they could and building lives and families. Collin's records demonstrate that the young, urban, migratory poor paid a high price to sustain the massive growth of cities during the early national era.

Collin's records furnish valuable information about the occupations of those living around his church, reinforcing the image of an impoverished community of the lower sort. In 157 cases, of the one thousand burial records Collin recorded the occupation of the deceased, or of the husband or father of the deceased, confirming the lowly socioeconomic status of those who lived and died within his Southwark parish (see graph 2). Of these, nearly half (46 percent) were sailors, perhaps the poorest of all free urban white men, and when those in related occupations, such as ships' carpenters, boatswain, riggers, and rivermen, are included, the figure reaches 69 percent. Most of the remainder worked at various jobs: 4 percent were bound laborers, 5 percent were apprentices or journeymen, 12 percent were artisans producing barrels, clothes, shoes, and the like. Shopkeepers accounted for a scant 1 percent and merchants for an equal number. Thus, while Collin did bury several ships' captains, mates, and masters, the great majority of the decedents hailed from the ranks of the lower sort; it is the lives and deaths of sailors, carters, apprentices, and their families that speak to us through these burial records.

Collin's interpretative frameworks require surprisingly little deciphering. On occasion, his listing of symptoms cannot satisfactorily explain the cause of death, but in many cases his lucid accounts are persuasive. In such incidents as accident, infectious disease, and childbirth, the cause of death is clear. Similarly, the infant deaths caused by teething or worms refer to the hazards of weaning and the introduction of all manner of germs to young children taking their first solid foods. Less obvious and yet very revealing are the children for whom prescribed vomiting and purging heralded an end to their existence.

Children were peculiarly vulnerable to the reaper's scythe in all of early America but especially in Southwark. A total of 543, almost 59 percent of those whose age and cause of death Collin recorded, died before reaching their sixteenth birthday (see graph 3). Seventeen percent of these young decedents had no childhood, for they were premature, stillborn, or died within a day or so of birth. Only 4 percent died in accidents, the nature of which changed as the children grew. The majority of young children in this category, such as three-year-old James Conden, died from burns or scalding, hardly uncommon in houses with fires for cooking and heating. His mother was a widow, and the greater burden of work that this condition placed on her perhaps explains how James met his death, "standing alone by the fire his cloathing catch the flames and much burnt him."[33] As the children of Southwark aged, however, they stood a far greater chance of death while playing or working outdoors. Thus, eleven-year-old apprentice Elisha Talman drowned in the Delaware Bay near the Chestnut Street Wharf.[34]

Disease and infectious illness, broadly defined, were by far the greatest dangers children faced, accounting for the demise of 70 percent of burials of people younger than sixteen. Cholera morbus, the intestinal disease commonly recorded as "vomiting and purging," killed 23 percent of all the children listed in Collin's record, including one-year-old John Bailey in August of 1804.[35] John's two-week illness and death must have been hard for his widowed mother Hester, who previously had buried three children.

Although not as pervasive as cholera, smallpox and yellow fever took a high toll, destroying the lives of 16 percent of the buried children. Yellow fever struck in occasional epidemics, but smallpox was endemic and primarily a children's ailment; both maladies reappeared with life-threatening regularity in a community visited by hundreds of ships and thousands of sailors every year. Returning about twice every decade, when a sizable population of nonimmune youngsters encouraged an epidemic, smallpox struck hardest at the youngest. For those listed in Collin's record, the disease claimed thirty children before they reached their second birthday, twenty aged two to five,

GRAPH 3.  Causes of Childhood Death

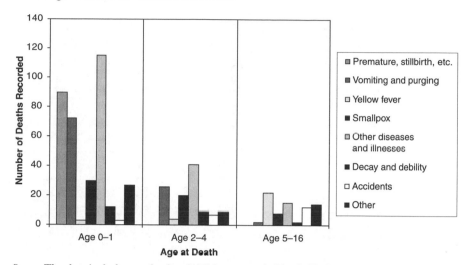

*Source:* The data include 543 deaths of children recorded by Collin between 1791 and 1809. Burial Records, Old Swedes Church, Pennsylvania Genealogical Society, Historical Society of Pennsylvania.

eight between the ages of five and sixteen, yet only eight adults. Those who survived established some immunity, at first by contracting and surviving the disease itself, and then often displaying immunity with a pockmarked visage. Others were variolated with the disease itself, which could be fatal and was resisted by many of the poor. Only after 1803 did the shift to using cowpox inoculation provide the means to eliminate the disease, although it would be decades before it completely disappeared from impoverished communities like Southwark.

In contrast, the yellow fever epidemics struck with greater venom as children grew older, claiming only seven children under the age of five yet twenty-two between the ages of five and sixteen. In adulthood, yellow fever was a potent killer, taking the lives of almost one-third of those who died between the ages of sixteen and forty; indeed, yellow fever accounted for one-quarter of all deaths of people older than sixteen. Unsanitary conditions, including standing pools of water where many of the disease-carrying mosquitoes bred, encouraged the disease to spread rapidly within families and the closely knit communities of Southwark, especially during epidemics such as that of 1793, which claimed the lives of twenty-three-year-old Thomas Parram and his mother Esther within the same week.[36] Cholera morbus was far less of a threat to adults, taking the lives of less than 2 percent of those older than sixteen.

GRAPH 4. Causes of Adult Death

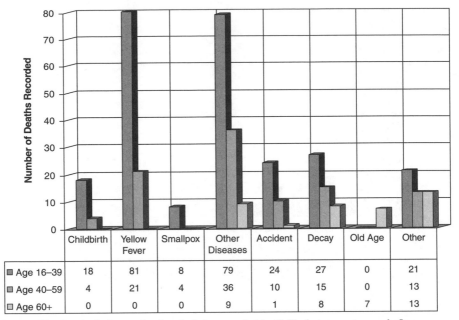

| | Childbirth | Yellow Fever | Smallpox | Other Diseases | Accident | Decay | Old Age | Other |
|---|---|---|---|---|---|---|---|---|
| ■ Age 16–39 | 18 | 81 | 8 | 79 | 24 | 27 | 0 | 21 |
| ■ Age 40–59 | 4 | 21 | 4 | 36 | 10 | 15 | 0 | 13 |
| □ Age 60+ | 0 | 0 | 0 | 9 | 1 | 8 | 7 | 13 |

*Source:* The data include 395 deaths of adults recorded by Collin between 1791 and 1809. Burial Records, Old Swedes Church, Pennsylvania Genealogical Society, Historical Society of Pennsylvania.

Disease was also a leading cause of adult mortality, but women faced additional dangers (see graph 4). Childbirth remained perilous, claiming the lives of more than 15 percent of women who died between the ages of sixteen and forty. Repeated births must have worn out many more women, like Eleanor Grey, the forty-year-old wife of a man regarded by Collin as a "worthless" mariner, who after a period of general illness "was more debilitated by childbirth" and died as a result. Collin tells us more about the role of the female community in the birthing process than about her indigent husband when he recorded that Eleanor's "female friends [who] made charitable exertions for a decent funeral."[37]

Accidents, too, claimed a far higher proportion of adults than children, and the large majority of these were men who died while at work. Twenty percent of deceased adult males between sixteen and forty years old expired as the result of accidents in their work. When sections of the Delaware froze early in 1791, twenty-six-year-old John Hastings was trapped aboard his shallup for three days; he died of cold and exposure within a day of his return. Indeed, since the river and the sea gave work to so many of those within Collin's parish, it is hardly surprising that it was responsible for the premature deaths of such men as Joseph Taylor, who died two days after falling between his ship and the wharf.[38]

Insufficient diet, infectious illness, and grueling work weakened the bodies of these Philadelphians, and with aging, they more frequently succumbed to "decay" and "mortification," general categories that signaled an erosion of good health and the withering away of bodily strength. Such conditions affected people of all ages and had a variety of causes, from juvenile tuberculosis or other wasting diseases to severe protein or vitamin deficiencies, low birth weight, and general malnutrition. Less than 1 percent of the 938 decedents whose ages and causes of death were recorded by Collin lived long enough to die of old age. Remarkable indeed were people like Heckless Fugerie, whose husband died in the American army that invaded Canada during the war for independence but who lived to see Madison elected president.[39]

The sheer normality of death is the most striking aspect of these burial records, a phenomenon that on occasion numbed Collin and never stopped distressing him. He understood firsthand how the urban poor struggled to achieve the necessaries of food, shelter, heat, and clothing and to cope with the constancy of illness and death. They saw carried home the broken bodies of those who died unexpectedly from falls, burns, shooting accidents, and drowning. So too did they see mothers, sisters, and daughters die in childbed, and they knew better than to expect that most of the neighborhood's children would survive to adulthood. Illness and disease, both familiar and unknown, surrounded them, and living as they did in a port community, they knew better than to expect a lull in its regular cull. From cholera to dropsy, from dysentery to measles, and from yellow fever to whooping cough, potentially fatal illnesses were ever present. Moreover, malnutrition and general ill health made the residents of Southwark vulnerable to conditions that would not normally have proved fatal. Thus Collin listed teething as the cause of death for 4 percent of children who died in their first two years, and worms as one of the causes of death for 12 percent who died between their second and fifth birthdays.

Living amid the poor and burying them week-in and week-out over a period of almost fifty years gave Collin a unique insight into the causes and nature of poverty. As Gary Nash noted earlier in this volume, attacks on poverty in early national America were grounded in the belief that the poor were themselves to blame for their condition, and the Bettering House stood as a monument to attempts to eliminate the "undeserving poor." Collin never adopted such attitudes, for he knew well that the poor he lived among and buried had precious little control over their circumstances. When Isaac

Richards, for example, sought to bury his four-year-old son William, Collin described Isaac as "an indigent journey-man taylor, working at very low wages, like many others." Similarly, after burying two-week-old Ann Mary Johnson, Collin lamented the pitiable state of her mother, who was "poor as the generality of seaman's wives."[40]

It was readily apparent to Collin that even those who labored hard and lived respectable lives were never far removed from poverty. When Barney Clayton died of consumption in December 1799, Collin discounted the price of burial because Clayton and his family had lost everything "in the fire in Moravian Alley some weeks ago." Economic downturns, harsh winters, and Jefferson's maritime embargo all dragged more people into destitution; when Collin made notes such as "indigent, like many others this cruel winter," he attached no blame to those who suffered through no fault of their own. Moreover, the minister recognized that even men like Andrew Dam, "an industrious" man who had enjoyed "employment sufficient for a pretty comfortable living" might slide all too easily into indigence. Dam lived far longer than most, and having bestowed much of his property upon his two daughters, "the infirmities of old age obliged him to seek a retreat in the Bettering house for the last." Rather than defining the old man by the poverty that darkened his final years, Collin preferred to remember a gentle soul who "had considerable skill in gardening and aided many in that capacity" and who "prepared for death with great devotion."[41]

Collin was never slow to condemn the moral failings of the men and women who lived around him and the "licentious manners" and an "extreme want of order" in early national society that he found quite distressing.[42] Runaway servants or young people who sought marriage without proper permission, potential bigamists, and all who treated his religious responsibilities with less than proper respect shocked and scandalized Collin. At times the minister's harsh Calvinist moralizing was quite striking, as when he condemned a young couple who sought marriage without proper permission, prompting Collin to rage against "Liberty! Liberty, in a shape often seen by me! Wretched manners!"[43] Unlike so many of his learned contemporaries, it was extremely rare for Collin to criticize the poor or to hold them responsible for their conditions. But he had little sympathy for intemperance and the suffering that it caused. The minister recorded, for example, the death of Andrew Armstrong, a fifty-year-old rigger who "had for 3 years occasional twitchings in his nerves, with low spirits and a degree of delerium after imprudent use of strong liquors." Still, Collin's experiences with the dying and their families meant that he well understood how the circumstances of their poverty were frequently beyond their control. Thus, even Armstrong's drunkenness did not lead to outright condemnation, and Collin admitted that apart from "this fault [he] was a person of good character."[44]

Collin demonstrated a good understanding of how the desperation of the poor might lead to intemperance and other evils. Although the pastor often made note of intemperance, "disorderly conduct," and "dissolute life," he did not embrace the notion that these moral failings were the primary cause of the poverty suffered by so many of the men, women, and children he buried. Only rarely did he condemn them. He took note, for example, of the conditions surrounding the death of Catherine Smith, whose demise resulted from "the unhappy life that she led with her husband, & the habit of intoxication, probably occasioned by it." Adam Smith had beaten his wife, and their neighbors "often heard her screams." Collin's compassion for her condition was matched by his disgust at the behavior of her husband; his record concludes with the prayer "God have mercy on the not few savages in this city."[45] Moral failings were always condemned by Collin, but he seldom blamed the poor for their condition, and he had considerable understanding of their quiet desperation.

While the community was unable to save Catherine Smith, in many cases family members and friends stretched meager resources to care for loved ones. Catherine Peterson had almost reached her fifth birthday when she died, but she had been so incapacitated by fits during her life as to need almost constant care and attention since she was unable to do anything for herself; she died, however, in her parents' home and not in an institution. Such care commanded Collin's respect, as in the case of Aaron and Elizabeth Bryan, who for two years had maintained Aaron's ailing father and were subsequently burdened by the death of their nine-day-old son; the minister concluded that a much reduced fee was "reasonable."[46]

While Collin's records emphasize the fragility of life among the poor in early national Southwark, they tell also of remarkable human resilience. There is both helplessness and agency here, both abject misery and defiant pride. To civic authorities, many of those Collin buried would have appeared as the undeserving poor, a segment of society to be controlled, in part, through the administration of institutional relief. At times, Southwark's indigents enjoyed little choice but to accept such assistance and the accompanying restrictions. But the tone of Collin's record communicates his respect for a community that refused to accept responsibility for their deprived condition, that lived life as fully as possible, and that demanded respect, even in death. While their deaths tell us much of the hardships of life and work, so too do they reveal a great deal about their spirit and resilience and the courage they found to confront life head on.

Even in Collin's accounts of the deaths of children, for example, we see something of how lower-class youngsters lived and played. Eight-year-old Eliza Preston "was killed in playing with other children by a pile of scantling [small timber beams] falling on her," and Thomas Turner and two friends were "playing on a bateau" which overturned, drowning all three. For the impoverished children of Southwark, there were no sheltered gardens; instead, the streets, building sites, ropewalks, and riverfront served as playgrounds. Most moving was Collin's record of the strange bruises found upon the side of thirteen-year-old orphan Anthony Nealy, an apprentice shoemaker who died of apoplexy. By noting that the marbles in the boy's pocket most likely caused the bruises, Collin acknowledged that although already working, Anthony Nealy was still a child who played.[47]

There is passion for life in these records, both in the joyous playing of children and in the raucous activities of adults. How else are we to make sense of the death of John Call, a young militiaman who was accidentally shot during an Independence Day celebration outside a tavern just south of Gloria Dei? And what of the "intemperate" Francis Cooper, who overindulged and "was taken ill on the evening of the 4th of July," or John Smith, who died after falling from a tree while trying to catch a parrot?[48] Even as death approached them, many of the poor commanded Collin's respect, for their hard work, their Christian devotion, and their irrepressible joi de vie. The pastor's admiration for fifty-nine-year-old Sarah Garrigues was obvious in his account of how, despite having been "lame with rheumatism eighteen years," she employed a chair in order to move around the house and perform her domestic tasks. So, too, did he cherish the sixteen-year-old servant Maria Sprole who sang hymns on her deathbed and seventy-one-year-old Samuel Davis who kept up his spirits during a year of confinement to his bed by imbibing "weak mixtures of wine with water" and by smoking.[49]

Collin's records suggest that the increasing popularity of evangelical religion, the culture of festive celebration, and the passion for riotous behavior and alcoholic excess were in part a struggle to comprehend or merely just to cope with the arbitrariness of death and the apparent futility of life. Such activities assumed many forms, including heaving drinking, carousing, and even violence, as in the case of rope maker Robert Jarvis, who was killed "in a tumult between the rope makers, below the church . . . and the crew of a French Privateer." Admitting that the trouble had begun "some days ago in a house of ill-fame," Collin inadvertently revealed something of the culture of the lower sort who inhabited the taverns of the Southwark riverfront and who were not slow to defend their neighborhood against those they identified as threatening or undesirable.[50] Whether struggling against illness to keep working within or without their households, or finding solace in religion as death approached, or playing children's games on the streets and waterfront, or enjoying tumultuous celebrations of Independence Day, or fighting against French sailors, Southwark's poorer inhabitants fashioned a social life and popular culture that allowed them to live short and fragile lives intensely.

Collin's records of the passing of generations of Philadelphia's poor tell us not just about the ubiquity of death, but also about their passion and enthusiasm for life. During the early nineteenth century, affluent Americans began to embrace what Philippe Ariès has referred to as the era of *la mort de toi,* a romanticization of death expressed in fiction, poetry, art, religious practice, and even the rites and conventions of burial.[51] For the poor of Nicholas Collin's Southwark, however, it was all but impossible to view, for example, a consumptive death as beautiful. There were subtle hints that perceptions of death were changing: it was new for the poor to devote scarce resources to the burial of a stillborn child, for example, as it was for parents to record in detail the lives of children who had died at a very young age. But for the "afflicted and suffering poor" of Gloria Dei parish, life was too hard and too precious for excessive romanticization, and it took all that laboring people had merely to live life and then to accept death with grace and dignity.[52]

## Notes

1. An earlier version of this essay was presented at the annual conference of the Omohundro Institute of Early American History and Culture, Austin, Texas, June 1999. The author is grateful for the comments he received at that time and for the extremely helpful suggestions of Elaine Forman Crane, Susan E. Klepp, and Billy G. Smith.

2. Robert Haveman, "The Nature, Causes, and Cures of Poverty: Accomplishments from Three Decades of Poverty Research and Policy," in *Confronting Poverty: Prescriptions for Change,* ed. Sheldon H. Danziger, Gary D. Sandefur, and Daniel H. Weinberg (Cambridge: Harvard University Press, 1994), 441.

3. See the essay by Gary B. Nash in this volume.

4. Julie Stoiber, "Poverty Activists Sponsor an Alternative Tour of Philadelphia," *Philadelphia Inquirer,* July 29, 2000.

5. Gordon S. Wood, *The Radicalism of the American Revolution: How a Revolution Transformed a Monarchical Society into a Democratic One Unlike Any That Has Ever Existed* (New York: Alfred A. Knopf, 1992), 4.

6. See, e.g., Edward Countryman, "Revolution, Radicalism, and the American Way," *Reviews in American History* 20 (1992), 480–85.

7. Definitions of poverty vary, although the lack of a means of subsistence must surely define the condition of being poor. The most basic needs of residents of early national Philadelphia were food, fuel, clothing, and shelter; those whose individual or family incomes were unable to provide sufficiently for these basic wants were, by my crude working definition, poor.

8. Nicholas Collin's record for Henry Jennings, July 30, 1801, Burial Records, Old Swedes Church, 180–81. These records are held by the Pennsylvania Genealogical Society, Historical Society of Pennsylvania (hereafter cited as Burial Records).

9. Thomas Clayton, October 23, 1801, Burial Records, 183–84; Alexander Ridley, July 6, 1802, Burial Records, 195.

10. On daily life, see Billy G. Smith, *The "Lower Sort": Philadelphia's Laboring People, 1750–1800* (Ithaca: Cornell University Press, 1990); Gary B. Nash, *The Urban Crucible: Social Change, Political Consciousness, and the Origins of the American Revolution* (Cambridge: Harvard University Press, 1979); Raymond A. Mohl, *Poverty in New York, 1783–1825* (New York: Oxford University Press, 1971); John K. Alexander, *Render Them Submissive: Responses to Poverty in Philadelphia, 1760–1800* (Amherst: University of Massachusetts Press, 1980); Robert E. Cray, Jr., *Paupers and Poor Relief in New York City and Its Rural Environs, 1700–1830* (Philadelphia: Temple University Press, 1988). Susan E. Klepp has produced the most significant work on death in early national Philadelphia. See Klepp, ed., *"The Swift Progress of Population": A Documentary and Bibliographic Study of Philadelphia's Growth, 1642–1859* (Philadelphia: American Philosophical Society, 1991); "Zachariah Poulson's Bills of Mortality, 1788–1801," in *Life in Early Philadelphia: Documents from the Revolutionary and Early National Periods,* ed. Billy G. Smith (University Park: The Pennsylvania State University Press, 1995), 219–42; and "Demography in Early Philadelphia, 1690–1860," *Proceedings of the American Philosophical Society* 133 (1989), 85–111. See also Billy G. Smith, "Death and Life in a Colonial Immigrant City: A Demographic Analysis of Philadelphia," *Journal of Economic History* 37 (1977): 863–89; Roger Lane, *Violent Death in the City: Suicide, Accident, and Murder in Nineteenth-Century Philadelphia* (Cambridge: Harvard University Press, 1979); and Tom W. Smith, "The Dawn of the Urban-Industrial Age: The Social Structure of Philadelphia, 1790–1830" (Ph.D. diss., University of Chicago, 1980).

11. This point has been made to superb effect in an exhibit at the Museum of London and the accompanying text, Alex Werner, *London Bodies: The Changing Shape of Londoners From Prehistoric Times to the Present Day* (London: Museum of London, 1988), with an introduction by Roy Porter. See also Philippe Ariès, *Western Attitudes Toward Death: From the Middle Ages to the Present,* trans. Patricia M. Ranum (London: Marion Boyars, 1994); and John McManners, *Death and the Enlightenment: Changing Attitudes to Death Among Christians and Unbelievers in Eighteenth-Century France* (Oxford: Clarendon Press, 1981).   .

12. For further discussion of the disparities in health and longevity between the wealthy and poor, see Susan E. Klepp's essay in this volume as well as her "Philadelphia in Transition: A Demographic History of the City and Its Occupational Groups" (Ph.D. diss., University of Pennsylvania, 1980), 190, 292.

13. Chris Schilling, *The Body and Social Theory* (London: Sage, 1993), 131–32. For further discussion of the body, see Bryan S. Turner, *The Body and Society: Explorations in Social Theory* (Oxford: Basil Blackwell, 1984); Anthony Synnott, *The Body Social: Symbolism, Self and Society* (London: Routledge, 1993); Gary Kielhofner and Trudy Mallinson, "Bodies Telling Stories and Stories Telling Bodies," *Human Studies* 20 (1997), 365–69; Nicole Sault, ed., *Many Mirrors: Body Image and Social Relations* (New Brunswick: Rutgers University Press, 1994).

14. Smith, *"Lower Sort,"* 92–125.

15. For further information about Collin, see Amandus Johnson, *The Journal and Biography of Nicholas Collin* (Philadelphia: New Jersey Society of Pennsylvania, 1936). Susan E. Klepp and Billy G. Smith have excerpted and commented upon some of Collin's records; see "The Records of Gloria Dei Church: Burials, 1800–1804," *Pennsylvania History* 53 (1986): 56–79, and "Marriage and Death: The Records of Gloria Dei Church," in Smith, ed., *Life in Early Philadelphia,* 177–218.

16. On the lives of early national sailors, see Simon P. Newman, "Reading the Bodies of Early American Seafarers," *William and Mary Quarterly,* 3d ser., 55 (1998): 59–82.

17. Collin was elected to membership of the American Philosophical Society on January 16, 1789. See *Pennsylvania Gazette,* February 4, 1789: Folio Four, Accessible Archives CD-ROM, item no. 5950.

18. Elizabeth Ervin, September 6, 1798, Burial Records, 124–25; Hannah Collin, September 29, 1797, Burial Records, 104–5; stillborn child of William and Rebecca Hubbert, December 18, 1805, Burial Records, 392. On the revolutionary transformations in medical practice, see Roy Porter, ed., *Medicine in the Enlightenment* (Amsterdam: Rodopi, 1995); and Morris J. Vogel and

Charles E. Rosenberg, eds., *The Therapeutic Revolution: Essays in the Social History of Medicine* (Philadelphia: University of Pennsylvania Press, 1979).

19. See, e.g., Roy Porter, ed., *Patients and Practitioners: Lay Perceptions of Medicine in Pre-Industrial Society* (Cambridge: Cambridge University Press, 1985); Dorothy Porter and Roy Porter, *Patient's Progress: Doctors and Doctoring in Eighteenth-Century England* (Oxford: Polity Press, 1989); and Guy Williams, *The Age of Agony: The Art of Healing, c. 1700–1800* (London: Constable, 1975).

20. John Potts, July 23, 1805, Burial Records, 374.

21. Samuel Condor, October 22, 1795, Burial Records, 83; Edward Kirby, November 21, 1801, Burial Records, 180.

22. Michel Foucault, *The Birth of the Clinic: An Archaeology of Medical Perception*, trans. A. M. Sheridan (London: Tavistock Publications, 1973).

23. Daniel Conover, July 10, 1801, Burial Records, 176–77.

24. Throughout this period people held to their belief that one might best counteract illness by correcting imbalances in the body; these were either in the four liquid humors (blood, phlegm, yellow bile, and black bile) or in the solid organs. Treatment was designed to top-up weakened humors or to flush them of impurities. See Charles E. Rosenberg, "The Therapeutic Revolution: Medicine, Meaning, and Social Change in Nineteenth-Century America," in *Therapeutic Revolution*, ed. Vogel and Rosenberg, 5–6.

25. Mary Speer, September 17, 1805, Burial Records, 372; Rosenberg, "Therapeutic Revolution," 5.

26. Rosenberg, "Therapeutic Revolution," 7.

27. A few of Collin's records contain little more than a brief listing of name, age, cause of death, and burial date. The majority are far more detailed, often featuring explicit descriptions of the symptoms and medical treatment, the apparent cause and nature of death, the age, address, and family of the deceased, their social and economic circumstances, and even accounts of their character. All members of the Swedish Lutheran Church were entitled to burial within its cemetery, including anyone who had moved away from Southwark.

28. Mary Ann Hobart, April 7, 1807, Burial Records, 408.

29. Male child of Abigail and Manuel Peterson, December 22, 1801, Burial Records, 185.

30. Elizabeth Low, April 24, 1801, Burial Records, 172–73.

31. Jane Willard, November 1794, Burial Records, 73–74; Mary Ryan, March 2, 1809, Burial Records, 447.

32. Dougal Moore, July 29, 1802, Burial Records, 197–98; Mary Ryan, March 2, 1809, Burial Records, 447.

33. James Conden, December 1, 1796, Burial Records, 98.

34. Elisha Talman, June 15, 1806, Burial Records, 400.

35. John Bailey, August 21, 1804, Burial Records, 354.

36. Thomas Parram, October 7, 1793, Burial Records, 65; Esther Parram, October 13, 1793, Burial Records, 68. On the yellow fever epidemic, see J. Worth Estes and Billy G. Smith, eds., *A Melancholy Scene of Devastation: The Public Response to the 1793 Philadelphia Yellow Fever Epidemic* (Canton, Mass.: Science History Publications, 1997).

37. Eleanor Grey, February 18, 1803, Burial Records, 205.

38. John Hastings, February 22, 1791, Burial Records, 54; Joseph Taylor, December 21, 1804, Burial Records, 353.

39. Heckless Fugerie, January 7, 1808, Burial Records, 425–26.

40. William Richards, December 24, 1801, Burial Records, 185–86; Ann Mary Johnson, November 2, 1807, Burial Records, 422.

41. Barney Clayton, December 8, 1799, Burial Records, 140; Andrew Dam, October 1806, Burial Records, 241–43.

42. Nicholas Collin, December 1794, May 11, 1801, as quoted in Klepp and Smith, "Marriage and Death," 188, 198.

43. Nicholas Collin, May 29, 1797, ibid., 194.

44. Andrew Armstrong, August 1799, Burial Records, 141.

45. Catherine Smith, November 11, 1803, Burial Records, 339.

46. Catherine Peterson, December 16, 1800, Burial Records, 231; William Bryan, January 13, 1805, Burial Records, 360.

47. Eliza Preston, June 29, 1805, Burial Records, 227; Thomas Turner, September 23, 1805, Burial Records, 232; John Smith, October 25, 1806, Burial Records, 397.

48. John Call, July 5, 1804, Burial Records, 349–50; Francis Cooper, July 8, 1805, Burial Records, 362; Anthony Nealy, May 19, 1807, Burial Records, 413.

49. Sarah Garrigues, January 1795, Burial Records, 75; Maria Sprole, February 2, 1808, Burial Records, 249–50; Samuel Davis, June 1800, Burial Records, 151–52.

50. Robert Jarvis, May 1795, Burial Records, 77–78.

51. Ariès, *Western Attitudes Toward Death,* 55–82.

52. Collin et al., "Address and Exhortation of the Clergy of the City of Philadelphia, November 27, 1793, *Pennsylvania Gazette,* November 27, 1793: Folio Four, Accessible Archives CD-ROM, item no. 9658. This address related to the sufferings of poor Philadelphians during the yellow fever epidemic of 1793.

*Three*

# Malthusian Miseries and the Working Poor in Philadelphia, 1780–1830

*Gender and Infant Mortality*

SUSAN E. KLEPP

> Nature, in the attainment of her great purpose [of reducing population to the level of subsistence], seems always to seize upon the weakest part.
>
> —T. R. Malthus, *Essay on Population* (1803)

Misery, Malthus argued, was the normal fate of the poor. It was the poor who lived closest to the level of subsistence, where they were prey to early death through disease, vice, war, and catastrophe. These dismal fates, blamed on a feminized "Nature" and not on the male-dominated economy or state, were the consequence of limited resources, and especially of limited food supplies. Any attempt to ameliorate the lot of the poor only caused more misery by encouraging marriage, raising the number of births, and further impoverishing the masses by increasing population pressures on finite resources. As Malthus suggested, it was the weakest, that is, the infants, who suffered most. Yet starvation was not a major cause of infant death, nor did infants absorb substantial amounts of food. Disease, unsanitary living conditions, and poor obstetric care are important causes of infant death, but other constraints on parenting afflicted the children of the poor, particularly in the early decades of American independence. These included the increasing maldistribution of wealth, shifts in the sexual division of labor, and limited economic opportunity, particularly for women. The infant mortality rates tell more about the social and economic circumstances faced by mothers and fathers than about aggregate levels of subsistence.

Despite the theoretical universality of his laws of population, Malthus made an exception for the United States. There, he argued, the relative abundance of land would allow for rapid population growth without risking the scarcities that led to miseries, at least, that is, until such time as the land was fully settled by agriculturalists. Only then would the poor of the United States experience the miseries of Old World nations. At the turn of the nineteenth century, therefore, infant mortality should have been lower in the United States than in England, especially in the mid-Atlantic where the climate was temperate and the price of wheat relatively low. This was not, however, the case.

Scattered research on infant mortality rates in Philadelphia and the mid-Atlantic region shows that infant mortality rates (IMRs, deaths under one year per thousand live births) were not lower than in old England. American urban rates of infant mortality, in the mid-200s early in the eighteenth century, certainly did not match the rates of London, which were in the very high 300s. However, American cities had populations in the tens of thousands, London in the hundreds of thousands. The gap between the English metropolis and the American metropolis began to close by the second half of the eighteenth century when IMRs in London averaged in the mid-200s and Philadelphia suffered rates in the low 200s.[1] Philadelphia's rates were equal to the rates in English commercial urban centers of similar size.[2] Average Mid-Atlantic rural rates of 192 were at the high end of the range of English rates that fell between 157 and 191 in the eighteenth century.[3] This is not what Malthus would have expected, nor is it what most historians would have predicted until recently.[4]

In the city of Philadelphia, according to one study of church records, infant mortality rates were quite high in the early eighteenth century, at 253 deaths in the first year of life. These rates fell to 187 per thousand around the turn of the nineteenth century. Louise Kantrow studied genealogies of the very wealthy in Philadelphia and found that in the eighteenth century rates averaged 163 per thousand and fell slightly, to 158, in the first half of the nineteenth century. Both studies were based on small databases. Billy Smith calculated that at Christ Church, which was changing from an inclusive Anglican parochial congregation to an exclusive, elite Episcopalian congregation over the course of the eighteenth century, infant mortality rates averaged 258 between 1751 and 1761 and 120 between 1761 and 1775.[5] In the 1820s, the first decade of Philadelphia's vital registration system, the infant mortality rate averaged 182 per thousand births.[6] The unhealthiness of the city for infants was recognized at the time, but our knowledge of urban infant mortality is confined to the population of European descent. Contemporaries noted only that African-American "children frequently die in their Infancy," and that "the death rate of Negro children is higher [due to] poverty, neglect, and particularly to lack of medical care," but observers also asserted that "deaths among the poorest whites fall little short of the proportion in the colored inhabitants."[7] Urban poverty, rather than race, kept infant mortality rates high.

We know less about the infant mortality rates in the countryside, but these rates appear to have been similar to urban rates, despite a general assumption by contemporaries and by historians that the countryside was healthier than the city. Rodger C. Henderson found IMRs of 275 per thousand births among eighteenth-century Pennsylvania Schwenkfelders, Protestants who migrated from German-speaking Silesia in 1734 and who settled primarily in Lancaster County. This rate was considerably higher than the city's average of 217 for the same period. For all of Lancaster County, rates were generally lower than Philadelphia, but rose from 148 to 178 per thousand between 1700 and 1830, so that the substantial differences between the colonial city and this hinterland county vanished by the early national period.[8] Robert Wells estimated IMRs of 210 per thousand for the small town and rural Quakers of New York, New Jersey, and Pennsylvania that he studied, again for the period between 1700 and 1830.[9] The rise in Lancaster rates seems to have been typical of rural areas and was probably a result of increasing population density and improved transportation, changes that helped to spread disease. But among the Moravians living at Bethlehem, Pennsylvania, as Beverly Smaby has shown, IMRs fell from 188 in the mid-eighteenth century, when communal child rearing was practiced, to 145 in the early decades of the nineteenth century, when nuclear families became the norm.[10] The decrease in rates at Bethlehem probably resulted from the greater individualized attention for children that was possible once centralized child rearing was abandoned. The reasons for the large differences in rates between the Schwenkfelders, Quakers, Moravians, and the residents of Lancaster are not clear, but may have to do with residence, mean wealth, relative isolation, or child-rearing practices.

In the aggregate, rural rates in New York, New Jersey, and Pennsylvania were virtually identical to urban rates. A simple summing of available studies of infant mortality in the eighteenth and early nineteenth centuries shows a mean urban rate of 189 and a rural rate of 192. There are no studies that attempt to explain these unexpectedly high rural rates, but they may have been a consequence of the relative unavailability of midwives, of the heavy physical labor required of farm wives, or of poor sanitation. The celebrated longevity of country folk appeared in later childhood and adulthood, not in infancy.

The usual gloss on the various editions of Malthus's *Essay on Population* is that positive checks (high death rates) on population growth were disappearing during Malthus's lifetime. As D. E. C. Eversley noted, "there is no sign that even at the end of his life [Malthus] knew anything in detail about industrialization. His thesis was based on the life of an island agricultural nation."[11] Economic growth associated with industrialization would change population dynamics. Higher per capita incomes presumably allowed standards of living to rise above the subsistence level, better transportation eliminated local food crises, mass production reduced the price of textiles and other necessities, and productivity was not limited by land-based wealth. These and other benefits of industrialization should have reduced mortality, even in the face of inequitable distributions of jobs, wages, and resources. Therefore it should have been increasingly prudential checks—moral restraint through delayed marriage, celibacy, and, as neo-Malthusians later advocated, birth control—that retarded population growth in the economic prosperity of the emerging industrial age, not high death rates.

The upbeat evaluation of economic change is challenged by recent work on the history of height and body mass. This research, based largely on anthropometric records of soldiers, servants, and prisoners, has found worsening health conditions accompanying the commercial expansion of the eighteenth century and the early stages of industrialization. Average heights fell for all adult inhabitants from the mid-eighteenth century in England, from the 1790s on the Continent, and from the birth cohorts of the 1830s and 1840s in the United States (where nonelite men's height fell by six centimeters). In England, where the very poor were failing to achieve the median heights of previous generations from the middle of the eighteenth century, poor London boys were so short that no modern population approximates their experience. American heights would not recover their eighteenth-century levels until the 1920s. The research on heights has uncovered the costs in health and welfare of the maldistribution of wealth and dietary constraints in the early stages of industrialization. Data on height and weight are rare, however, particularly before the middle of the nineteenth century.[12]

Differential infant mortality rates have long been used as one of the most sensitive indicators of standard of living.[13] Philadelphia provides among the best surviving data for a large population in America. It has fuller bills of mortality than other American cities, although these contain little or no information on the seasonality of death, cause of death, or the exact age or sex of the deceased. There is no data on infant deaths during the severe economic depression called the Panic of 1819. Philadelphia does have detailed burial accounts in some churches thanks to the painstaking record keeping of a few conscientious and scientifically minded ministers. None of these sources are perfect, but they are suggestive of an economic crisis for the urban poor that begins in the 1780s. The infant mortality rates for the decades around the turn of the nineteenth century allow a look at what may be an initial period of declining health by tracing a rise in infant mortality rates among the very poor. This cohort of Americans was the parent generation of the stunted soldiers born in the 1830s and after.

Family reconstitution forms—where church records of baptisms, burials, marriage, and other information are sorted by family units in order to recover family size, marriage patterns, and life expectancy—allow the most detailed look at infant mortality rates in the city. The 744 reconstituted families in the reconstitution project were divided chronologically into a colonial cohort, 1720–79, and a national cohort, 1780–1829.[14] In order to approximate differentials in economic standing, the occupation of the father (or, rarely, of the mother) was used to place children into one of three categories. The "upper sort" consists of merchants, professionals, and those identifying themselves as gentlemen. It is assumed that this was the wealthiest group. The "middling sort" contains a mix of shopkeepers, ship captains, clerks, and skilled craftsmen, while the "lower sort" includes unskilled workers, those identified as poor, and those who paid no taxes. Family reconstitution from church records does not pick up many illegitimate children, female-headed households, or transient households, and as such does not fully capture the urban experience. Still, socioeconomic standing was a crucial factor in infant mortality and its effects became exaggerated by the early national period. The upper sorts achieved a 30 percent reduction in IMRs after 1780 and the middling sorts an 8 percent decline, but the lower sort experienced a rise of 3 percent in rates despite a sharp drop in neonatal deaths (see table 1).

The differences between neonatal and postneonatal deaths and between endogenous and exogenous causes of death are commonly used to judge standard of living. Neonatal deaths are those occurring in the first month of life. Cause of death in the first month is predominantly endogenous and includes birth trauma, birth defects, or low birth weight. These are not easily preventable and largely beyond individual control, although differences in maternal nutrition, obstetric care, and breast-feeding practices can also affect these rates, particularly by influencing birth weight, birth trauma, and nutrition.[15] Postneonatal deaths occur after the first month and before the first birthday. These later deaths are caused primarily by exogenous factors, that is, the social, disease, and nutritional environment in which the child is placed, including childcare, the quality of the water supply, exposure to germs, and diet. Generally speaking, the lower the percentage of exogenous

TABLE 1. Recorded Stillbirths and Infant Mortality by Social Rank

| Category | 1720–1779 | 1780–1830 | % Change |
|---|---|---|---|
| **Upper sorts of people** | | | |
| Stillbirths per 1,000 known pregnancies | 0 | 11 | +1,100 |
| IMR[a] per 1,000 live births | 220 | 154 | −30 |
| Neonatal | 45 | 35 | −23 |
| Postneonatal | 175 | 119 | −32 |
| Survived, liveborn | 780 | 846 | +8 |
| Base number[b] | 314 | 550 | |
| **Middling sorts of people** | | | |
| Stillbirths per 1,000 known pregnancies | 5 | 13 | +260 |
| IMR per 1,000 live births | 220 | 204 | −8 |
| Neonatal | 49 | 41 | −17 |
| Postneonatal | 171 | 162 | −6 |
| Survived, liveborn | 780 | 797 | +2 |
| Base number | 906 | 1,031 | |
| **Lower sorts of people** | | | |
| Stillbirths per 1,000 known pregnancies | 4 | 15 | +375 |
| IMR per 1,000 live births | 244 | 252 | +3 |
| Neonatal | 63 | 40 | −36 |
| Postneonatal | 181 | 212 | +17 |
| Survived, liveborn | 756 | 748 | −2 |
| Base number | 510 | 403 | |

*Source:* Family reconstitution forms in the author's possession.

*Note:* The church records on which family reconstitutions are largely based do not directly measure deaths but rather the rite of Christian burial. The jump in stillbirths is an artifact of changing interpretations of the sacraments. Stillbirths were never recorded in the early eighteenth century because they were not baptized. After the middle of the century some burial rites were performed. These became common in the nineteenth century in most churches. Most stillbirths identified by gestational age were two months premature. Only a few were recorded at six months gestation and none at earlier stages of development. Obviously the incidence of stillbirths was higher than the surviving records indicate.

Approximately 5 percent of infant deaths for all groups were not baptized and had no age recorded at burial. These might have been stillbirths, neonatal deaths, or deaths of older infants or older children. While the unknown category is probably dominated by the very young, it is possible, given the sometimes lax attitudes toward baptism, that a few were older children, not infants.

[a]The infant mortality rate (IMR) is calculated excluding stillbirths and distributing those of unknown age according to known ages at death.

[b]The base number is liveborn infants.

deaths, the higher the standard of living. From 1780 to 1830, exogenous deaths accounted for 77.2 percent of IMRs among the upper sorts of Philadelphians, 79.4 percent among the middling sorts, and 84.1 percent among the lower sorts.

Except for the rates found among the lower sort in the colonial period, the proportion of neonatal deaths clustered at 45–49 per thousand births in early Philadelphia. The exception, the 63 per thousand neonatal figure for the working poor in the colonial period, may be due to the shortage of skilled midwives in early Philadelphia, with the few available midwives being beyond the financial means of the poor. Another possibility is that the mothers among the working poor were undernourished immigrants from the Old World. Malnourished mothers frequently give birth to low-weight baby girls, who in turn give birth to low-weight children, even if nutrition levels have improved for the second and third generations who were born in the New World.[16] With this one anomaly, the relative inelasticity of endogenous births is apparent for these populations. There is certainly some improvement over time and slight differences by occupational group, but compared to the volatility of postneonatal death rates, the neonatal deaths rates showed limited response to changing conditions. By the early national period, neonatal deaths for all segments of the population were in the range of 35–41 per thousand births—rates that were close to half of those found in England. In England from 1700 to 1837, 77.2 infants per thousand died before their first month of life.[17] Childbearing women in Philadelphia, no matter what their rank in society, apparently had broadly similar levels of nutrition and maternal care in the early national period.

It is in the later ages of infant death that social and economic differences appear most strongly. The wealthy substantially reduced the probabilities of deaths at ages one to eleven months between the early and late eighteenth century—a decline of 36 percent. Among the middling sorts the decline was a more modest 6 percent. Among the poor, however, mortality at these ages increased by 17 percent. This increased mortality after one month is not just an artifact of declining neonatal deaths. Put another way, lower sort postneonatal children had an excess mortality of 10 percent in the colonial period when compared to the wealthy, and an excess mortality of 78 percent in the early national period. The gap between rich and poor expanded dramatically by the end of the eighteenth century. While the affluent were increasing their ability to preserve their children's lives, poorer parents were suffering the loss of more of their children.

On the face of it, there seems to have been insufficient change in Philadelphia's environment to produce these large differences. Dirty streets, nonexistent or ineffective garbage collection, and cramped houses plagued the city from its early days to the 1830s and beyond. Water pollution was a persistent problem and the only sewers carried away street runoff, not human waste. Commerce and immigration spread disease through the port and into town.

The heat of the summer produced dysentery and other intestinal complaints through microbial infestations in the water supply and through spoiled milk and food. Tropical diseases like amoebic dysentery, yellow fever, and dengue fever could and did flourish in the heat of the summer months. In the winter, fireplaces heated rooms unevenly, and rooms were both smoky and drafty. Respiratory problems flourished as a result. Fresh fruits and vegetables were unavailable after February or March, leading to vitamin deficient diets until May or June when the first fresh food supplies appeared. Cows often stopped giving milk during the winter, so that fresh milk was either expensive or unavailable—hand-fed babies were given gruel as a filling but nonnutritious substitute. Misguided medical advice advocated excessive bleedings, harsh medicines, and the avoidance of fruit for sick children. The many deaths attributed to intestinal parasites were probably as much the result of the poisonous vermicides ingested as the worms themselves. Crowding, water pollution, dietary deficiencies, and ineffective medical advice were among the factors that persisted over the course of the eighteenth and early nineteenth centuries.[18] These continued into the second half of the nineteenth century and kept mortality rates high through the 1880s.[19]

Yet there were signs of improvement in infant care, many of which crossed socioeconomic barriers even as disparities widened. Church records indicate that newly sentimental attitudes toward children were beginning to be adopted by both the rich and the poor at the turn of the nineteenth century. An "affecting" and "tearful sensibility" could appear among the indigent as well as among the fashionable.[20] Even poorer parents paid scarce cash (between one and five dollars) to provide formal burials to memorialize stillborn children, something no one had done in the early eighteenth century. They, like the rich, sometimes named their sons for prominent men, especially George Washington, a practice that seems to reflect new ambitions for their children. They as frequently named their daughters Harriot and Clarissa after the heroines of popular novels. Both rich and poor were beginning to give their offspring middle names that recognized the child's individuality by differentiating her or him from kin with the same given name. Child-centered families and a recognition of the child's individuality probably meant that more parental resources were being regularly lavished on infants and not just at their funerals. Young children may have had more attention, been fed more regularly, and kept warmer and cleaner than had been the case earlier. Young children were deeply mourned by their parents and the details of their short lives were often recounted to the minister. Margret Lowremore, for example, was proudly remembered by her father as a prodigy because she had walked at eight months and had ten teeth at ten months.[21] Destitute parents begged for a decent burial and attempted to hold the family together even after death by burying family members in the same ground, even in the same graves.

The medical and physical environment changed by the end of the eighteenth century and affected both rich and poor. More mothers were native born after 1780 and could provide their offspring with limited immunities to the common diseases of the mid-Atlantic. Poorer parents, like the more comfortable, inoculated their children with live smallpox virus before 1803 and then switched to the safer cowpox vaccine after its introduction in America. Smallpox disappeared as a major cause of death for both rich and poor infants in the early nineteenth century. After 1797, poorer families fled yellow fever by relocating to the tent cities established to the west of the city.[22] Sentimental, affectionate parents attempted to provide the best care possible for their children, but they faced an unhealthy, germ-ridden environment.

Two parishes allow a closer look at the causes of infant death (see table 2). Gloria Dei Church, a Swedish Lutheran denomination, served a mixed group of middling and poorer Swedes, along with craftsmen, artisans, and laborers of varied ethnic backgrounds and recent migrants into the city. It was located in a southern suburb of Philadelphia near the port. From 1793 to 1831, the minister kept remarkably detailed records of final illnesses, cause of death, and economic circumstances. The less detailed records of Christ Church, a wealthier parish in the center of the city, are broadly comparable. This comparison shows that communicable diseases, respiratory complaints, and convulsions affected both groups, but these three broad categories accounted for 84 percent of infant deaths at Christ Church and 64 percent of deaths at Gloria Dei. The majority of the very wealthy and a minority of the middling parents did avoid some infectious diseases, since the proportions of exogenous deaths among the upper and middling sorts were substantially below the rate of the lower sorts. They moved to the countryside during the summer months and were replacing fireplaces with stoves for heat. They could afford to throw out curdled milk and buy vegetables in March so that their better-nourished and housed children had a greater chance of surviving many communicable diseases. Still, their larger families and household staff may have provided many opportunities for infection. Once infected, there was little wealthier parents could do to assist their children in surviving whooping cough and measles, the two most common named diseases of infancy, or the unspecified fevers and birth trauma that brought on convulsions. There was also little parents could do to prevent respiratory and throat complaints: croup, thrush, tuberculosis, colds, or pneumonia. The babies of the wealthy as well as the poor suffered in drafty houses and were surrounded by people with coughs.

TABLE 2. Causes of Infant Death, Christ Church and Gloria Dei Church, Percent Distributions

| Cause of Death | Christ Church 1770–1800 | Gloria Dei 1793–1831 |
|---|---|---|
| Communicable disease | 43.0 | 22.5 |
| Intestinal complaints | 25.0 | 36.1 |
| Fits, convulsions | 16.4 | 5.6 |
| Croup, lung, throat | 8.6 | 5.6 |
| Decay, debility, weakness | 3.9 | 12.4 |
| Worms | 0.7 | 4.5 |
| Accidents | 0.0 | 5.6 |
| Other | 2.4 | 5.6 |
| TOTAL | 100.0 | 100.0 |
| Base number | 128 | 89 |

*Source:* Family reconstitution forms.

Poorer infants succumbed in larger proportions to intestinal disease and parasites, probably caused by spoiled food, polluted water, or poor hygiene. It was clear by the end of the eighteenth century that both the public and private wells in the city and suburbs were polluted. By the end of the eighteenth century, the wealthy retreated to their country homes and even some of the middling sorts boarded in the nearby countryside in the summer, avoiding the rotting food and stinking, cloudy water of the more densely populated city. In the wake of the yellow fever epidemics of the 1790s, the city turned to the Schuylkill River for its water supply. Water was pumped into the central urban area where Christ Church was located by 1801, but the construction contracts for bringing water to suburban Southwark, where Gloria Dei Church was situated, were not issued until 1826. It was not until 1837 that the water system was complete.[23] The wealthiest families pumped water directly into their houses, and although authorities complained about illegal hookups to the water supply, most of the poor continued to rely on public pumps. This reliance on street pumps adversely affected cleanliness because water had to be lugged into the house from a distance.

There were far more cases of intestinal worms in Southwark, a consequence of poor sanitation. Diapering practices, the position and cleanliness of privies, and the frequency of hand and face washing were no doubt among the factors that contributed to the spread of these parasites. Significantly, the peak period of roundworm infestation among infants occurred from 1807 to 1809, coinciding exactly with the embargo. It was a time when unemployment rates were high and many husbands were trapped overseas by the hiatus in trade or by imprisonment. Female-headed householders peaked at 24 percent of those nonchurch members burying at Gloria Dei (compared to 14 percent for the city as a whole),[24] and 41 percent of all families appearing at the church to bury infants were impoverished (while approximately 3 percent citywide were receiving public relief).[25] Sanitation suffered. As the proportion of female-headed households seeking burial at the church declined and employment rose after 1809, the incidence of intestinal worms fell.

Poorer infants also experienced substantially higher rates of what was called "decay" and "debility." The underlying causes of these vague disease categories are unknown. These deaths may have been the consequence of neglect, juvenile tuberculosis or another wasting disease, or severe vitamin or protein deficiency from an inadequate maternal diet or an attempt to wean by substituting sweetened gruel for breast milk. In addition, it is possible that low birth weight affected these children, as Claudia Goldin found for the poorest Philadelphians in the middle of the nineteenth century.[26] Birth trauma or maternal death could be factors in these cases. Poor women could resort to the Philadelphia Dispensary for free medical assistance during childbirth after 1786, although not many did, perhaps because of the bureaucratic requirements associated with admission to the charity, perhaps because many of the doctors attached to the dispensary were young and inexperienced.[27] Poorer women were three times as likely to die in childbirth than wealthier women, and babies rarely survived the deaths of their mothers.[28] Many infants were described as sickly, weak, or decayed from birth, perhaps due to incompetent birth attendants or genetic disease. These deaths were, however, unevenly distributed through the year. Two-thirds of the debilitated died in the heat of summer or the cold of winter, only a third died in the spring or fall, suggesting that the weak could not survive temperature extremes or the shortage of milk in the winter or spoilage in the summer. Fuel scarcities and inadequate water supplies may have been contributing factors in the deaths of the already weak. A failure to thrive because of birth trauma, parental neglect, inadequate diet or shelter, or undiagnosed illness is a possible explanation for these deaths from decay and debility.

Accidents were specific to the poorer parish in Southwark, and infants were burned, scalded, dropped, or run over by carriages, usually because they were left with slightly older children or were left unattended while their parents were otherwise occupied. Two deceased infants at Gloria Dei were described as being heavily bruised in addition to having common diseases, and in one case the bruises were noted to be the size of a hand. These might now be suspected as evidence of physical abuse, but they were then apparently accepted as the by-products of excessive coughing or retching. The inability of the poorer one-third of Philadelphians to afford hired help meant little or no assistance with childcare.[29] Many inhabitants of Southwark were migrants lacking supportive kin networks. Still, among those burying at Gloria Dei, accidental deaths were highest at the turn of the century and virtually disappeared as a cause of death by 1830. Even poor children were apparently more carefully supervised by the 1820s and 1830s. But despite improvements in childcare, poor infants faced a larger number of disease and environmental risk factors during their first year of life than did their wealthier contemporaries.

The very sensibilities that brought greater concern for the individuality and uniqueness of infants also brought ideals of female domesticity that further restricted women's already limited economic opportunities.[30] These new sensibilities were accompanied by the physical separation of home and work. The deputy husband role that allowed women to carry on their husband's occupation in his absence or after his death became less possible in the early republic, both because of new ideologies of domesticity and because of the capitalization requirements of production in the early republic.[31] Poorer women left their babies with wet nurses while they sought employment as servants in the city or in the countryside, working at inns or tending tollgates. They sewed, boarded single workers, wet-nursed, kept small grocery or grog shops, or sold oysters or fish or thread or soup. Often they tried several employments. Some turned to prostitution. Work conflicted with breastfeeding and other childcare routines. For all these desperate women, fresh milk and other foods may have been extravagant luxuries. The work requirements of women with infants were additional factors that affected infant mortality rates. Public and personal sanitation, attention, and length of breast-feeding caused differences in viability for wealthier and poorer children and were linked to the economic status of women.

The proportion of women heads of household consistently increased in Philadelphia in the early republic. In 1770, 14 percent of all taxpayers were women, a figure that rose to 21 percent in 1776, a year into the Revolutionary War. Not all taxpayers were heads of household. According to the first federal census in 1790, women headed 13 percent of Philadelphia's households. By 1800, it was 14 percent. In 1810, after the embargo, women headed 16 percent of households in the census, while during the Panic of 1819 women headed 18 percent of households. The return of an expanding economy did not stop the trend, and women headed 19 percent of households in 1830.[32]

The figures for female-headed households at Gloria Dei Church do not show the same pattern as the federal census figures. In part this is because many of these women would not have appeared as heads of household in the census. Some women heads of household in Southwark were married with absent or absconding husbands and so would have appeared under their husbands' names in the census. Some lived with kin. Some were single women with illegitimate children living as servants or boarders. Some were, or claimed to be, widows. The exact marital status of these women is not always clear from the record and the minister occasionally discovered that some women had invented nonexistent husbands when applying for their child's burial. These female heads of families increased from 10 percent of all those burying at Gloria Dei between 1793 and 1805, to a high of 24 percent during the embargo. The percentage was slightly lower during the War of 1812. After that the percentage of women fell sharply to 9 percent of households during the Panic of 1819 and 5 percent thereafter. Some husbands did return after the embargo and war. Yet many husbands are known to have left in search of work during the postwar depression.

Since this dramatic reduction in female-headed households after 1816 runs counter to census trends, it probably indicates that the majority of women trying to cope without a man's earning capacity could not even afford a church burial for their offspring after 1816. This shift corresponds with the severe restriction of outdoor (at home) relief for women by the overseers of the poor, justified on the grounds that these women were "insolent, demanded relief 'as a right' and were not properly thankful." In the city as a whole, more women than men received the shrinking amounts of public outdoor aid before the mid-1820s; afterward, the sex ratios were reversed, when "women received less of the most substantial types of aid than men."[33] These women, with so few economic options, were being forced by deepening poverty to inter their children in the public burying ground, the local potter's field. It was just one of the indignities afforded the poor that no records were kept of those buried there.

About one-quarter of all men and women appearing at the church were impecunious and did not possess sufficient cash to pay for a burial. Since not all burial entries noted the mode of payment, the actual percentage of the destitute was undoubtedly higher. There were substantial gender differences in access to cash (see table 3). Men had greater institutional resources for claiming cash and these resources promised sustained assistance. Women more often had to beg for sympathy and charity on an occasional basis as an immediate crisis forced them into a semipublic role. These women appear to have been pitiable rather than insolent, humble objects of charity rather than entitled, and appropriately thankful for the pittances allotted them. Widow Rebecca Mariner "lament[ed] her poverty, having 2 small children to support by a paltry shop." The minister reduced the required fee, but "ordered

TABLE 3. Sources of Burial Fees by Gender of Payer, Gloria Dei, 1800–1825, Percent Distribution

| Source of Burial Fee | Female | Male |
|---|---|---|
| Minister's discretion | 36.3 | 22.9 |
| Church charitable funds | 20.3 | 24.1 |
| Friends, neighbors | 21.7 | 9.7 |
| Kin | 13.0 | 7.2 |
| Employers, masters, coworkers | 2.9 | 8.4 |
| Almshouse, hospital, institutions | 5.8 | 27.7 |
| TOTAL | 100.0 | 100.0 |
| Base number lacking cash | 69 | 83 |
| Number of burials | 304 | 357 |
| Percentage lacking cash | 22.7 | 23.2 |

Source: Gloria Dei Burial Records, Historical Society of Pennsylvania.
Note: These figures are based on adult burials because mode of payment was less regularly recorded for infant burials. They provide a rare insight into the economic resources of poor women and men.

the body [of her eleven-month-old son] placed out of the row," an indignity that she did not object to.[34]

More than half of all impecunious women received charity from the church and nearly one-half of all men did, but women were far more likely to appeal directly to the minister to reduce or waive fees, while men more often applied for relief from the established charitable funds. Men in Southwark were also more likely to get cash assistance from government or private welfare programs, such as the Almshouse or the Pennsylvania Hospital. Men could borrow from employers or coworkers. Women more often drew on private sources of aid. More than a third of all women depended on friends, neighbors, and kin to collect money in times of need. The church records show that men also depended on friends and neighbors for cash, but they were more likely to borrow the necessary funds from a single person. The voluntary door-to-door canvassing of neighbors to raise the burial fee seems to have been an almost entirely female activity designed to afford the family of a local woman a decent burial. These female groups often formed when the details were particularly tragic, as when women were abused, abandoned, or faced multiple problems. It is doubtful that female neighbors and kin had enough money to give more than crisis aid, whereas institutions, as parsimonious as they were, might provide continuing assistance. Men and women were both poor, but women's sources of aid were more evanescent and precarious.

For reasons that are not clear, it was poor boy babies who bore the brunt of poverty, whereas girls died more frequently among those with greater financial resources (see table 4). Because infants were too frequently recorded only as, for example, "the child of John and Mary Jones" at baptism or burial, without name or sex being recorded, it is not possible to measure sex ratios before 1780 or for many congregations after 1780. But the evidence from the nineteenth-century gentry, and from Christ Church and Gloria Dei between 1780 and 1830 is consistent. Middle and upper sort girls died in infancy more often than boys did, while among the lower sorts the sex differentials were reversed. This was not the effect of differing sex ratios at birth. At Gloria Dei there were 95 male stillbirths and 91 female stillbirths, and 94 male and 91 female deaths in the first four weeks following birth—both close to the nor-

TABLE 4. Sex Differentials in Infant Mortality Rates, 1720–1830

| Study Population | Male | Female | Sex Ratio[a] |
|---|---|---|---|
| **Philadelphia Gentry** | | | |
| 1700–1800 | 154 | 172 | 112 |
| 1800–1850 | 163 | 154 | 94 |
| **Christ Church, 1780–1830** | | | |
| upper sorts | 132 | 113 | 86 |
| middling sorts | 126 | 116 | 92 |
| lower sorts | 139 | 280 | 209 |
| **Gloria Dei** | | | |
| middling sorts | 200 | 131 | 66 |
| lower sorts | 143 | 174 | 122 |
| **Nonurban** | | | |
| Schwenkfelders to 1800 | 263 | 287 | 109 |
| Lancaster County | | | |
| to 1741 | 155 | 140 | 90 |
| 1741–1770 | 171 | 181 | 106 |
| 1771–1800 | 175 | 182 | 104 |

*Source:* Louise Kantrow, "Life Expectancy of the Gentry in Eighteenth- and Nineteenth-Century Philadelphia," in *The Demographic History of the Philadelphia Region, 1600–1860*, ed. Susan E. Klepp (Philadelphia: American Philosophical Society, 1989), 324–27. Family reconstitution forms. Rodger Craige Henderson, "Comparative Mortality Rates and Trends: Eighteenth-Century Lancaster County, Pennsylvania, British North America, and the Caribbean," Paper presented to the Philadelphia Center for Early American Studies, April 15, 1983, 22, 38, 51. None of the studies of rural mortality rates comments on time trends or sex differentials in infant deaths.
[a]Sex ratio: proportion of male infant deaths for every 100 female infant deaths.

mal birth ratio of 105.5 males for every 100 females. But after the first month of life there were 132 male deaths for every 100 female deaths. Members of the church—those who could afford to keep up with their pew rents—were buried for free. There were no savings to the family in burying girls in the potter's field, yet the sex ratio was 117 for postneonatal burials among church members. The conclusion has to be that life became more precarious for poor infant boys, just as it was for well-to-do girls. These large sex-based mortality differentials were urban phenomena. In rural areas these differences were muted or nonexistent.

There are a few theories that attempt to explain differences in infant death rates by sex—it is not a subject that has received much attention. The simplest theory is that the causes are biological and environmental, not the result of parental preference for one or another sex. Parents valued children regardless of their sex. Males have weaker immune systems than females, so that if infants were exposed to disease, more males were apt to die. Poorer children were more likely to experience disease; therefore more males would die among the poor, particularly from tuberculosis, a disease that can thrive in crowded households.[35] There is considerable merit to this argument. Tuberculosis was more than twice as common among poorer adult workers as among the middling and upper sorts of people.[36] Most parents did value children, and they did what they could to protect them against smallpox through inoculation and then vaccination. During the yellow fever epidemics whole families fled. But this theory does not explain why upper and middling sort girls would die at a higher rate than boys. If wealthier infants were sheltered from communicable diseases, then one would expect equity in death rates, not an excess of female deaths. However, the children of the wealthy experienced a higher proportion of infectious disease mortality than did the children of the poor at the turn of the nineteenth century (see table 2). It would seem that there should have been an even greater surplus of male deaths among the "better" sort than among the lower sort if male susceptibility to infectious disease were the cause.

Biologist Ingrid Waldron finds both gender preference and genetics at work in differential rates. "Where girls have higher mortality than boys, one important cause appears to be sex discrimination resulting in less adequate nutrition and health care for females. In contrast, higher infant mortality among males appears to be due primarily to inherent biological disadvantages."[37] But the national-level statistics on which this argument is based, like the rural rates that would have dominated eighteenth-century Pennsylvania and New Jersey, do not exhibit the large excess male deaths of the postrevolutionary, industrializing city's poor.[38]

A third argument posits parental preferences for sons or daughters that vary according to circumstance, particularly according to the economic experiences of the parents. These may be conscious choices expressed through infanticide or unconscious choices played out through differential treatment by sex. While most preindustrial and early industrial societies preferred males for inheritance purposes, prestige, and labor, unfavorable economic conditions might cause too many sons to become a liability.[39] A preference for males is not universal in developing economies. Where populations were expanding because of economic growth, according to a study of eighteenth- and nineteenth-century Germany, males were preferred because they could take advantage of new opportunities. This was especially the case among those wealthy parents who had the resources to place their sons in advantageous positions. In stagnant economic situations competition for local resources was intense and females were preferred because they would not require land but could possibly marry into landed families. Poorer families generally had higher female preferences than wealthier families, and this was exaggerated during periods of economic stagnation.[40] This theory fits many of the known characteristics of Philadelphia around the turn of the nineteenth century.

Impoverished Penrith, a parish in northern England, was, according to a study by Susan Scott and C. J. Duncan, "a saturated community," that is, economically stagnant and creating few new jobs for future generations. Only the eldest sons could hope to find employment; the others were "supernumerary": they were forced to leave in order to find work. In this environment, which lasted from the eighteenth into the nineteenth century, the less valued male infants died at much higher rates than did their sisters, probably because girls were nursed longer than boys and thus avoided intestinal complaints while still young. The statistics suggest that boys were normally weaned between two and four months, girls not until eight months. How this apparent distinction was justified was not explored.[41]

These findings concerning parental gender preferences fit many of the known circumstances in early national America. The American population was generally expanding rapidly between 1780 and 1830, creating opportunities for young men, especially those in a position to take advantage of speculative activities. Wealthy young women required dowries that did not directly benefit their birth families. Girls, as is well known, did get fewer of the resources of wealthy families: boys were substantially better educated, they were allowed to travel more widely, they inherited more valuable assets, and they were obviously the pride and joy of their families.

Among poorer families, as the work of Billy Smith shows for an earlier period and the registers of Gloria Dei Church show for the turn of the century, unemployment and, more frequently, underemployment were common, even during nominally prosperous times like the mid-1820s. Men turned to oystering, hauling, and other unskilled labor because they could not find work in their craft. They left their families behind as they traveled south and west looking for work. They sailed overseas and left their wives and children in immediate poverty while awaiting a small windfall at the end of the voyage. They faced a loss of wages because of illness, injury, adverse weather, or war. The survival of the family often depended on the labor of women whose sewing, wet-nursing, washing, huckstering, or daywork supplemented their husband's income or entirely supported their families. It was a rare occasion, and cause for comment, when a wife, "occupied by the sick children a long time, could earn nothing."[42]

Girls and young women also provided the brewing, baking, spinning, sewing, nursing, childcare, and washing that more comfortable households paid cash for. Girls might well be preferred in such a situation where opportunities for boys were so limited and the small amounts earned by women so essential to the family economy. For example, when the Baker family fell on hard times in the first decade of the nineteenth century due to the alcoholism and illness of the male head, the women put up boarders, established a small day school, took in sewing, and opened a shop. The eldest son was sent to sea. The labor of three women partially compensated for the loss of an adult male's income.[43] In addition to providing goods, services, and income, married daughters usually provided homes for elderly parents, so parents preparing for possible invalidism in old age would want daughters rather than sons. Interestingly, the infant sex ratio reversed among the poor only during the War of 1812 when military service and military contracts temporarily opened up employment opportunities for white men. Under more normal circumstances, however, having several daughters may have been more advantageous and desirable than having sons in an industrializing economy. Other explanations of parental preferences have pointed to the rewards or drawbacks of having sons, or to the increased hardships of too many daughters under certain circumstances. None have considered that there might have been very positive economic and social reasons for privileging daughters.

The problem with parental preference theory is that the mechanism for inducing or allowing higher mortality among the less desirable sex is not usually discussed. Even the suggestion by Scott and Duncan that differential weaning may have been the means for producing the desired sex ratios among surviving children is not explained.[44] In the eighteenth century infanticide seems to have been uncommon—even illegitimate children were apparently more likely to be abandoned than killed. G. S. Rowe found only ninety-two cases of child murder in all of Pennsylvania between 1682 and 1800, including seventy-eight cases of neonatal death. Of course not all cases came to the attention of the authorities, but the number of unknown cases would have to have been quite large to have even reached the level of an instance a year in each of the counties.[45] Deliberate neglect seems unlikely. In both wealthier and poorer families sentimental attitudes would probably work against neglect or abuse of boys or girls. These suppositions cannot be tested based on the information in table 1. The limited numbers of cases culled from family reconstitutions that give any information beyond date of death prevents a closer analysis of the circumstances of infant mortality.

The next best source for studying infant mortality is the burial register at Gloria Dei Church in the suburb of Southwark during the period that Reverend Nicholas Collin kept the records, 1793–1831. This source gives names, ages, cause of death, economic circumstances of the parents and, in many cases, information on occupation (see table 5). There are chance, unsystematic comments on place of origin, kin networks, sources of money borrowed for the burial, sobriety, illiteracy, and other circumstances. In addition, the register is divided between "Members," parishioners who inherited, bought, or paid rent on a pew, and "Strangers," those who were not formally attached to the church. The Members were generally artisans and laborers like most in Southwark but tended to be better established with wider kinship networks for economic and social support. None were counted as impoverished and fewer than 4 percent of member households were female-headed. Members accounted for 14 percent of the stillbirths and infant deaths at the church. Strangers were more likely to be transients, immigrants, and the impoverished. Ten percent of the Strangers are known to have been poor; 9 percent were from female-headed households. Among Strangers, an average of 20 infants were buried each year during the peak of yellow fever epidemics, 1783–1805. This rose to 25 during the embargo, fell to 16 during the War of 1812, shot up to 36 during the Panic of 1819, and reverted to 25 from 1824 to 1831. The 1,066 cases permit a more detailed examination of the environments of infant deaths. The weakness in this data set is that the population at risk and survival rates cannot be computed because most of these infants were not baptized—all we can recover is their deaths. In addition, only a handful of wealthy individuals attended the church, none of whom experienced the loss of an infant. This source will not permit an investigation of the circumstances of the upper sorts.

Stillbirths are nominally those who died before birth, but the term was used loosely and probably encompassed at least a few children who died soon after

TABLE 5. Gloria Dei Records, 1793–1831

| | Stillbirths (%) | Postneonatal Deaths (%) | Sex Ratio postneonatal deaths | Base Number |
|---|---|---|---|---|
| Total | 17 | 77 | 132 | 841 |
| Total Members | 25 | 79 | 117 | 115 |
| Total Strangers | 20 | 77 | 140 | 726 |
| Male deaths | 17 | 79 | — | 457 |
| Female deaths | 20 | 74 | — | 365 |
| Unknown sex | 64 | 63 | — | 19 |
| Female-headed households | 16 | 83 | 126 | 92 |
| Poor households | 14 | 73 | 139 | 74 |
| Illegitimate children | 12 | 57 | 300 | 14 |
| Nurse children | 0 | 100 | 600 | 16 |
| Members, 1793–1805 | 19 | 81 | 133 | 42 |
| Members, 1806–23 | 27 | 82 | 94 | 38 |
| (War years, 1812–17) | 30 | 78 | 137 | 14 |
| Members, 1824–31 | 31 | 74 | 127 | 34 |
| Strangers, 1793–1805 | 18 | 79 | 109 | 211 |
| Strangers, 1806–23 | 20 | 76 | 141 | 367 |
| (War Years, 1812–17) | 20 | 66 | 92 | 50 |
| Strangers, 1824–31 | 24 | 75 | 192 | 149 |
| January–March | 15 | 74 | 113 | 174 |
| April–June | 26 | 77 | 143 | 168 |
| July–September | 13 | 78 | 132 | 352 |
| October–December | 22 | 69 | 180 | 155 |

Note: Stillbirths represent a percentage of all infant deaths and stillbirths. Postneonatal deaths are a proportion of neonatal and postneonatal deaths. Sex ratios of deaths are based on those dying at ages one to eleven months. The base numbers are postneonatal infant deaths by category.

birth. The time series in table 5 show that members, whose membership privileges included free burial plots, more commonly buried stillbirths than did Strangers, who had to pay for both cemetery space and the sexton's services. But both groups increasingly into the nineteenth century provided "decent" burials for the very young, reflecting the rise of sentimental attitudes toward children. The fact that women heads of household, who tended to be the poorest of the poor, had a slightly higher rate of stillbirth burial than the poor generally might indicate that even impoverished women were committed to the emerging domestic and child-centered ideals of the early republic. Not surprisingly, the lowest stillbirth burial rates were found in the least wanted pregnancies. Illegitimacy dampened, but did not entirely extinguish sentiment.

A recent article by Nicky Hart cautions that stillbirth rates are not constant but have been historically as volatile as other measures of mortality. She argues that "a high stillbirth rate implicates maternal health and physique as a primary factor in mortality."[46] That the peak of this Philadelphia suburb's stillbirth mortality came in April, May, and June, when the nutritional deprivations of the winter months were greatest, is one sign that the stillbirth rate's rise may also signal the growing nutritional problems that anthropometric research has recovered for a slightly later period in American history. This seasonal concentration of stillbirths appears only during and after the Panic of 1819. From 1793 to 1806 only 15 percent of stillbirths occurred in the spring. By 1823–31, 39 percent were in the spring. An increasingly vitamin-deficient diet through a shortage of fresh fruits and vegetables might explain this shift in the seasonality of stillbirths. The dietary shortfall could be the result of rising prices for vitamin-rich foods in the spring or of long-term shifts in dietary preferences toward coffee, tobacco, sugar, and alcohol: the drugs that allowed workers to work longer.

The calculations of the proportion of postneonatal deaths in table 5 often run counter to expectations. The proportions were higher among church members than among Strangers. The percentage of postneonatal deaths rose, as expected, among church members during the difficult years of the embargo, War of 1812, and Panic of 1819, but fell for Strangers. There may be several factors at work. One is that this was not a closed population. The very poorest families may have shifted to a pauper's burial for their children during hard times, as seems to have happened for female-headed households after 1816, changing the social and economic composition of the Strangers seeking out church services. Members, who received free burial plots, would not have been forced to accept a less dignified burial even in cases of unemployment or poverty. The other possibility is that higher and rising endogenous mortality may have caused a lower percentage of postneonatal deaths among Strangers. Less nutritious diets for pregnant women or a declining quality of obstetric care during childbirth could have increased the percentage of deaths at less than one month and decreased the percentage over one month. Without knowing the populations at risk of burying at Gloria Dei these suppositions cannot be tested. It may be useful to remember that these explanations are not mutually exclusive: both could be operating.

The seasonality of postneonatal deaths shows not only the healthier conditions in the fall, when the harvest was in and colder weather killed germs and preserved food longer, but also the rise in deaths as winter gave way to spring. During these late winter and early spring months diets became more monotonous and less nutritious. The peak period of postneonatal death was in the heat of summer when intestinal disease flourished as a result of spoiled food, polluted water, and sour milk.

Female-headed households had the highest proportion of postneonatal deaths. Poverty undoubtedly was a primary cause of the high percentage of deaths at older ages of infancy, as insufficient food, clothing, and distracted (and often sick) mothers adversely affected the health of their children. It is also possible that pregnant women actually fared better when on their own because the old custom of wives waiting on their husbands during meals and then eating the leftovers may have meant that women ate better in their husbands' absence. Improved nutrition and heavier birth weights might have reduced the proportion of neonatal deaths and elevated postneonatal deaths. The lowest proportion of postneonatal deaths occurred among illegitimate children. Inadequate care during pregnancy, birth, and the first month was certainly a major cause. Attempts to hide the pregnancy by reducing weight gain or by binding the abdomen might have injured the fetus, causing its early demise. Drugs taken to abort could have caused injury as well. Giving birth without attendants was also risky.

Calculations of the proportion of exogenous deaths are suggestive but not conclusive. Still, the sex ratios at ages one to eleven months show the predominance of male deaths in virtually all categories. Only during the War of 1812 did the sex ratio briefly reverse for Strangers. For Strangers the discrepancy between boys and girls grew over time. The disease environment may explain part of this increase since the incidence of respiratory disease steadily increased from 13 percent of deaths to 24 percent of all deaths during the same period, and young males are particularly susceptible to pulmonary disease. The sex ratios by major disease category in table 6 indicate substantially elevated male susceptibility to a number of major complaints: respiratory disease, intestinal problems, and that vague category of decay and debility. The intestinal problems and decay could be the result of early weaning as well as of local health conditions.

Males also died at especially high rates in the fall and in the early spring. The spring months were when nutritional shortfalls occurred and the absence of fresh foods might particularly affect newly weaned boys. The evidence on the seasonality of death also shows that in the healthiest season, October to December, when the number of deaths were lowest, the preponderance of male deaths was the greatest, at 180, followed by the spring months when fresh food and milk were expensive (143) and the intestinal diseases of the summer (132). Yet in the depths of winter when respiratory diseases prevailed—diseases that should have produced the most sizable difference—the ratio was most equitable (113). Girls, despite their stronger immune systems, had higher death rates from the most common communicable diseases, smallpox (prevalent only until the introduction of vaccination in 1803), whooping

TABLE 6.  Sex Ratios by Cause of Death, Gloria Dei, 1793–1831

| Cause of Death | Sex Ratio[a] |
| --- | --- |
| Weanling diseases[b] | 475 |
| Decay, debility | 200 |
| Lung and throat | 185 |
| Intestinal | 150 |
| Convulsions, fits | 105 |
| Miscellaneous | 73 |
| Communicable disease | 67 |

[a]Sex ratio: the number of male deaths for every 100 female deaths.
[b]Weanling diseases, which include vomiting, diarrhea, worms, and "teething," are those associated with weaning and the introduction of solid foods.

cough, and measles. There was no difference between boys and girls in the incidence of convulsions or fits.[47] This suggests that it was not disease but early weaning or neglect that resulted in higher death rates for poor boys. The very high imbalance in infant deaths from weanling diseases (vomiting, diarrhea, worms, and "teething") confirms these speculations. Boys were almost five times as likely to die of these diseases than girls. In addition, boys who died of these diseases before their first birthday were, on average, 9 months old, whereas girls were 10.75 months. A larger portion of male babies was weaned early, and they died from the germs in food, milk, and water, or they failed to thrive on solid foods and died of decay and other wasting illnesses.

Precisely why this behavior existed and how parents justified these risky practices awaits study. Were boys more exposed to colds and pleurisy, were they weaned earlier or fed foods of dubious quality so that they more commonly experienced diarrhea, did they fail to thrive because of neglect or because of tuberculosis? Did poor parents expect boys to be heartier and more responsive to rougher treatment while girls were thought to be more delicate and in need of shelter, or did they favor girls over boys for economic reasons? In this regard, it is noteworthy that female-headed households had the lowest differential sex ratios, which may indicate that women, even though they tended to be poorer, were less influenced by a cost analysis approach than men. When women appeared as the sole parent, the sex ratio in infancy was 123; when men were listed as the sole parent, the ratio was 132. Two-parent households fell in the middle, with a ratio of 127. This may indicate that fathers were somewhat more likely than mothers to make calculated decisions about a particular child's care.

Despite these many uncertainties, the sex ratios in table 5 indicate that the deliberate neglect of boys was operating in two small subgroups of the population. Among illegitimate infants three boys died for every girl and among children placed out at nurse six boys died for every girl, probably because more boys than girls were placed out. Neither illegitimacy nor the presence of a wet nurse was recorded regularly, so other infants would certainly have fallen into these categories. Illegitimate children were reared by their mothers, by the putative fathers, by masters or mistresses, or by the Almshouse. Most caretakers seemed burdened by the task. James Reeves, a married laborer from New Jersey, brought the body of his six-month-old son for burial, explaining that Elizabeth Penton had "sworn it to him, wrongly as he says, by which he was obliged to foster it. He pleaded poverty also."[48] Reeves not only resented raising the boy but also paying to bury "it." Wet-nursed children were placed out by working mothers, by widowers who lost their wives in childbirth, by parents who had left the city to work in the countryside, or by the overseers of the poor. The women who worked as wet nurses ranged from the wives of skilled craftsmen, who were well known in the community, to impoverished seamen's wives, who were forced to put out their own babies to accept another's for pay. Small numbers and missing details prevent a fuller analysis of the wet-nursing business, but the risk of sending a child out was known at the time. In England, mercenary wet nurses were known as "angelmakers." Nurse children in Philadelphia, mostly boys, were secondary to the work schedules of their parents or guardians. Excess male mortality seems to have been partly the result of disease. Weaning practices appear to have played a major role, but parental intentions remain obscure. In a small minority of cases, particularly among those born illegitimately and those selected for fostering, these infant deaths were, if not actively encouraged, then not entirely unwelcome.

The inability of many men to find work in their craft, the worsening economic position of working women, the maldistribution of city services, particularly of water, were some of the important causes of the growing disparities in infant mortality between the upper and middling sorts and the lower sorts. Infant mortality rates reflected social and economic disparities that had developed over the course of the eighteenth century. As Billy G. Smith has noted, in the most prosperous American city, the "material circumstances of the lower sort were considerably worse, their position at the bottom more permanent, and their chances to achieve . . . more limited than scholars sometimes have assumed." Tom W. Smith found that "American economic development in general and industrialization in particular tended to increase the concentration of wealth. In Philadelphia's case the increased concentration seems to be related to the declining membership in the middle class as early industrialization thinned out the small proprietor ranks."[49]

Recent studies have found that infant mortality among the poor rises with the increase in the wealth share of the upper 5 percent of the population, even when the absolute income of the poor is unaffected. One suggested causal factor might be "the government's relative concern with the rich and poor."[50] Certainly the state and local governments were more concerned with provisioning the wealthier neighborhoods with clean water in the early nineteenth century. Street cleaning, garbage collection, and other services were also unequally distributed. Another study of current disparities finds that the social cohesion and optimism that can be found in economically egalitarian societies brings health whereas income inequality fosters hostility both on the part of the wealthy toward the poor and on the part of the poor toward the wealthy. With anger comes violence, homicide, accidents, and alcohol and drug abuse. Poorer nations have better health than wealthier nations when they are more socially cohesive.[51] There is scattered information on alcohol abuse, spousal abuse, and despair among the poor at Gloria Dei, none full enough to plot change over time. But the impression is that the poor before the War of 1812 faced underemployment because their skills were undervalued, while the poor of the postwar period had no skills. There are more mentions of drunken women, of illegitimacy, of wet-nursing, and of the physical abuse of husbands, wives, and children after the war. Indeed, 1816 seems a major turning point for the working poor. Infant mortality rates went up, stillbirths increased, sex ratios became increasingly skewed, respiratory complaints rose, as did signs of malnutrition and other environmental causes of infant death, women heads of household disappeared from the church as relief payments were cut off and sources of employment restricted. Fathers left their families to find work; parents left their children to find work. Despite some improvements in preventing smallpox and the accidental deaths of small children, the difficulties faced by families in Southwark multiplied and infant boys died in large numbers and infant girls in smaller but still significant numbers.

The records on infant mortality are imperfect, but they suggest that the inability of many men to find employment in their craft, the worsening economic position of working women, and the maldistribution of city services (particularly of water) were among the most important causes of the growing disparities in infant mortality between the upper and middling sorts and the lower sorts. There is a now hackneyed saying that "it takes a village to raise a child," but in the early republic it seems that it took two parents, a servant or two, and summers in the country to keep infants healthy. Boys, rather than girls, were the primary beneficiaries of this exceptional care. Poorer two-parent households struggled, with wives torn between the demands of childcare and the need to earn money to supplement their husbands' earnings. Mothers embraced ideals of loving childcare at the same time that they were severely restricted in their opportunities to earn money or to acquire charitable support. Ironically, the reduced earning power of women seems to have made girls more valuable: more girls were needed to maintain the income, services, and productivity of the female economy that substituted for the income of often absent men. Most fathers and mothers did what they could for all their children. For a small number of parents, enough to affect the sex ratio in infant deaths, selective neglect, especially through early weaning and the out-placement of boys were the consequences of economic dislocations in the late eighteenth and early nineteenth centuries. The weakest part of mankind was a social construction as well as a biological reality and might describe infant boys as well as girls.

# Notes

1. John Landers, "Mortality and Metropolis: The Case of London, 1675–1825," *Population Studies* 41 (1987): 64.

2. E. A. Wrigley and R. S. Schofield, *English Population History from Family Reconstitution, 1580–1837* (New York: Cambridge University Press, 1997), table 6.17, 274.

3. Wrigley and Schofield, *English Population History*, 215.

4. These eighteenth-century rates compare to total U.S. IMRs of 99 per thousand at the beginning of the twentieth century and 7 per thousand in 1998. Only the most impoverished and war-torn countries in the twentieth century begin to approximate the death rates of eighteenth-century England and America. Sierra Leone had an IMR of 195 in 1998, but the less developed world as a whole had a rate of 64.

5. Billy G. Smith, *The "Lower Sort": Philadelphia's Laboring People, 1750–1800* (Ithaca: Cornell University Press, 1990), 209.

6. Susan E. Klepp, *"The Swift Progress of Population:" A Documentary and Bibliographic Study of Philadelphia's Growth, 1642–1859* (Philadelphia: American Philosophical Society, 1991), 244–65.

7. Anthony Benezet to Granville Sharp, May 20, 1773, Granville Sharp Letterbook, Library Company of Philadelphia; J. P. Brissot, *New Travels in the United States of America, 1788,* trans. M. S. Vamos and D. Echeverria (Cambridge: Harvard University Press, 1964), 232n; Gouveneur Emerson, "On Mortality," in Pennsylvania Society for the Abolition of Slavery, *The Present State of the Free People of Color of the City of Philadelphia and Adjoining Districts* (Philadelphia, 1838), 35.

8. Rodger C. Henderson, "Eighteenth-Century Schwenkfelders: A Demographic Interpretation," in *Schwenkfelders in America: Papers Presented at the Colloquium on Schwenkfeld and the Schwenkfelders,* ed. Peter C. Erb (Pennsburg, Pa.: Schwenkfelder Library, 1987), 39–40; and Henderson, "Comparative Mortality Rates and Trends: Eighteenth-Century Lancaster County, Pennsylvania, British North America and the Caribbean," Philadelphia Center for Early American Studies, April 15, 1983, 22, 51.

9. Robert V. Wells, "A Demographic Analysis of Some Middle Colony Quaker Families of the Eighteenth Century" (Ph.D. diss.: Princeton University, 1969), 136–38. Philadelphia Quakers accounted for between 5 and 20 percent of his samples.

10. Beverly Prior Smaby, *The Transformation of Moravian Bethlehem: From Communal Mission to Family Economy* (Philadelphia: University of Pennsylvania Press, 1988), 83.

11. Quoted in John R. Weeks, *Population: An Introduction to Concepts and Issues* (Belmont, Calif.: Wadsworth, 1992), 65.

12. For summaries of this work, see Dora L. Costa and Richard H. Steckel, "Long-Term Trends in Health, Welfare, and Economic Growth in the United States," in *Health and Welfare during Industrialization,* ed. Richard H. Steckel and Roderick Floud (Chicago: University of Chicago Press, 1997), 47–90; and John Komlos, "Shrinking in a Growing Economy: The Mystery of Physical Stature during the Industrial Revolution," *Journal of Economic History* 58, no. 3 (1998): 779–802. Also, Stephen Nicholas and Deborah Oxley, "The Living Standards of Women during the Industrial Revolution, 1795–1820," *Economic History Review* 46 (1993): 723–49; and Komlos, "A Malthusian Episode Revisited: The Height of British and Irish Servants in Colonial America," *Economic History Review* 46, no. 4 (1993), 768–82; Timothy Cuff, "Variation and Trends in Stature of Pennsylvanians, 1820–1860," in *The Biological Standard of Living in Comparative Perspective,* ed. John Komlos and Jorg Baten, vol. 1 (Stuttgart: Franz Steiner, 1998).

13. W. Parker Frisbie, Douglas Forbes, and Richard G. Rogers, "Neonatal and Postneonatal Mortality as Proxies for Cause of Death: Evidence from Ethnic and Longitudinal Comparisons," *Social Science Quarterly* 73 (1992): 535–49; Paul Huck, "Infant Mortality and Living Standards of English Workers during the Industrial Revolution," *Journal of Economic History* 55 (1995): 528–50; Claudia D. Goldin and Robert A. Margo, "The Poor at Birth: Infant Auxology and Mortality at Philadelphia's Almshouse Hospital, 1848–1873," National Bureau of Economic Research, Working Paper #2525, 1988; Steven L. Gortmaker, "Poverty and Infant Mortality in the United States," *American Sociological Review* 44 (1979): 280–97; Smith, *"Lower Sort,"* 209–12; Richard M. Titmuss, *Birth, Poverty and Wealth: A Study of Infant Mortality* (London: Hamish Hamilton, 1943).

14. In my 1989 study, infant mortality was not studied separately from childhood mortality. The requirement that a family be under observation for fifteen years from the birth of a child through adolescence restricted the number of cases among the highly mobile Philadelphians to 2,819 cases. By re-examining the same family reconstitutions under the requirement of a single year's observation from birth to first birthday, the number of cases increased to 3,714. Klepp, *Philadelphia in Transition: A Demographic History of the City and Its Occupational Groups, 1720–1830* (New York: Garland, 1990), 244–65.

15. Frisbie et al., "Neonatal and Postneonatal Mortality"; Kathryn Sowards, "Premature Birth and the Changing Composition of Newborn Infectious Disease Mortality: Reconsidering 'Exogenous' Mortality," *Demography* 34 (1997): 399–409. That these assumptions about cause of death by age apply to the period under consideration can be seen in the following table, based on the causes of death from the detailed observations of the Reverend Nicholas Collin of Gloria Dei Church, 1793–1831, and organized by major categories.

Primary Cause of Infant Death by Age at Death, Gloria Dei Church, 1793–1831, percent distribution (continued on p. 90)

| Cause of Death | Neonatal (died before 1 month) | Postneonatal (died 1–11 months) |
| --- | --- | --- |
| **Endogenous** | | |
| Premature/birth defect | 48.6 | 1.1 |
| Difficult birth/twin | 23.6 | 2.0 |
| Jaundice | 2.8 | 0.0 |
| **Mixed** | | |
| Fits/convulsions | 13.9 | 11.0 |

*Source:* Gloria Dei Burial Records, Historical Society of Pennsylvania. Comparatively few infants dying under one month of age had a cause of death recorded. Although many infants had multiple symptoms recorded at death, only the primary cause is included here. The exclusion of secondary and tertiary causes particularly undercounts the incidence of intestinal worms in older infants.

Primary Cause of Infant Death by Age at Death, Gloria Dei Church, 1793–1831, percent distribution *(cont'd)*

| Cause of Death | Neonatal (died before 1 month) | Postneonatal (died 1–11 months) |
|---|---|---|
| **Exogenous** | | |
| Intestinal complaints | 8.3 | 33.8 |
| Decay/debility/weakness | 1.4 | 9.1 |
| Worms | 1.4 | 1.1 |
| Infectious disease | 0.0 | 22.1 |
| Croup, lung, and throat | 0.0 | 15.6 |
| Accident | 0.0 | 1.4 |
| Inoculation, live smallpox virus | 0.0 | 1.4 |
| **Other** | 0.0 | 1.4 |
| TOTAL | 100.0 | 100.0 |
| Base numbers | 72 | 438 |

Prematurity, small size (low birth weight), and various physical defects were the most frequent causes listed for stillbirths and neonatal deaths around the turn of the nineteenth century. Complicated deliveries, including twin births and instrument births, were the next most common cause for babies younger than one month. Fits and convulsions might have any number of causes, from disease or injury of the nervous system to vitamin D deficiency to high, spiking fever. In neonates, brain injury during birth is a likely cause, whereas high spiking fever would be an expected cause in older infants. Environmental causes dominate postneonatal deaths. After one month of age, intestinal complaints, the plague of the summer months when water was contaminated and food spoiled, was the largest category. The frequency of vomiting, purging, colic, and other complaints tired the Reverend Nicholas Collin, who sometimes merely jotted down "the usual disease" as the cause of death or failed to record any cause. Communicable diseases, particularly whooping cough and measles, were the second most frequent causes of death among postneonatal infants. Croup and other lung and throat diseases were important causes, particularly in the winter, as were various wasting diseases, which might also be reflective of a more generalized failure to thrive. Childcare practices are reflected in accidental deaths, in the incidence of intestinal worms, and in deaths from smallpox inoculation as well as in other categories.

16. Susan Scott and C. J. Duncan, "Interacting Effects of Nutrition and Social Class Differentials on Fertility and Infant Mortality in a Pre-Industrial Population," *Population Studies* 54, no. 1 (2000): 71–87.

17. Wrigley, *English Population History from Family Reconstitution*, table 6.4, 226.

18. Carole Shammas, "The Space Problem in Early United States Cities," *William and Mary Quarterly*, 3d ser., 62, no. 3 (2000): 505–42; Charles S. Olton, "Philadelphia's First Environmental Crisis," *Pennsylvania Magazine of History and Biography* 98, no. 1 (1974): 90–100. Even infants were bled and dosed with opiates and other dangerous substances, see Samuel X. Radbill, "The Pediatrics of Benjamin Rush," *Transactions and Studies of the College of Physicians of Philadelphia*, 4th ser., 40, no. 3 (1973): esp. 157–70.

19. Gretchen A. Condran and Rose Cheney, "Mortality Trends in Philadelphia: Age- and Cause-Specific Death Rates, 1870–1930," *Demography* 19 (1982): 97–123; Rose A. Cheney, "Seasonal Aspects of Infant and Childhood Mortality: Philadelphia, 1865–1920," *Journal of Interdisciplinary History* 14 (1984): 561–85.

20. Gloria Dei Burial Records, Mary Ryan, March 2, 1809.

21. Gloria Dei Burial Records, December 12, 1796.

22. John K. Alexander, *Render Them Submissive: Responses to Poverty in Philadelphia, 1760–1800* (Amherst: University of Massachusetts Press, 1980), 130–31.

23. [Philadelphia] Bureau of Water, *Description of the Filtration Works and Pumping Stations, Also a Brief History of the Water Supply, 1789–1909* (Philadelphia, 1909), 56–71.

24. Tom W. Smith, "The Dawn of the Urban-Industrial Age: The Social Structure of Philadelphia, 1790–1830" (Ph.D. diss.: University of Chicago, 1980), 178.

25. Priscilla Ferguson Clement, *Welfare and the Poor in the Nineteenth-Century City: Philadelphia, 1800–1854* (Rutherford, N.J.: Fairleigh Dickinson, 1985), 49.

26. Goldin and Margo, "Poor at Birth."

27. Samuel P. Griffitts et al., "A Return of the Diseases of the Patients of the Philadelphia Dispensary from December, 1786, to November, 1791," *Transactions of the College of Physicians, of Philadelphia*, vol. 1, pt. 1 (1793), 3–42.

28. Klepp, *Philadelphia in Transition*, 184.

29. Smith, "Dawn," 64–66.

30. Claudia Goldin, "The Economic Status of Women in the Early Republic: Quantitative Evidence," *Journal of Interdisciplinary History* 16 (1986): 375–404; Elaine F. Crane, *Ebb Tide in New England: Women, Seaports and Social Change, 1630–1800* (Boston: Northeastern University Press, 1998), esp. 132–38; Jeanne Boydston, *Home and Work: Housework, Wages, and the Ideology of Labor in the Early Republic* (New York: Oxford University Press, 1990).

31. Laurel Thatcher Ulrich, *Good Wives: Image and Reality in the Lives of Women in Northern New England, 1650–1750* (New York: Alfred A. Knopf, 1982); Goldin, "Economic Status."

32. Smith, "Dawn," 178; Karin Wulf, "Assessing Gender: Taxation and the Evaluation of Economic Viability in Late Colonial Philadelphia," *Pennsylvania Magazine of History and Biography* 121 (1997): 219.

33. Clement, *Welfare and the Poor*, 74–76.

34. Gloria Dei Burial Records, July 29, 1807.

35. D. T. Courtwright, "The Neglect of Female Children and Childhood Sex Ratios in Nineteenth-Century America: A Review of the Evidence," *Journal of Family History* (1990): 318–19. Also Saeko Kikuzawa, "Family Composition and Sex-Differential Mortality among Children in Early Modern Japan: Evidence from Yokouchi, 1671–1871," *Social Science History* 23 (1999): 99–127; Maggie Jones, "The Weaker Sex: From Nursery to Nursing Home, Men Face Daunting Odds," *New York Times Magazine*, March 16, 2003, p. 56.

36. Klepp, *Philadelphia in Transition*, 285.

37. Ingrid Waldron, "Sex Differences in Infant and Early Childhood Mortality: Major Causes of Death and Possible Biological Causes," in Population Division, Department of Economic and Social Affairs, United Nations, *Too Young to Die: Genes or Gender* (New York: United Nations, 1998), 64.

38. For national figures, see Dominique Tabutin and Michel Willems, "Differential Mortality by Sex from Birth to Adolescence: The Historical Experience of the West (1750–1930)," in Population Division, *Too Young to Die*, 17–52.

39. S. Ryan Johansson, "Welfare, Mortality, and Gender: Continuity and Change in Explanations for Male/Female Mortality Differences over Three Centuries," *Continuity and Change* 6 (1991): 135–77.

40. Eckart Voland, Robin I. M. Dunbar, Claudia Engel, and Peter Stephan, "Population Increase and Sex-Biased Parental Investment in Humans: Evidence from Eighteenth- and Nineteenth-Century Germany," *Current Anthropology* 38 (1997): 129–35. The authors posit a generational lag in sex preferences that does not appear in Philadelphia.

41. Scott and Duncan, "Interacting Effects," 84; fig. 1, 75.

42. Gloria Dei Burial Records, William Smith, July 29, 1820.

43. Susan E. Klepp and Susan Branson, "A Working Woman: The Autobiography of Ann Baker Carson," in *Life in Early Philadelphia: Documents from the Revolutionary and Early National Periods*, ed. Billy G. Smith (University Park: The Pennsylvania State University Press, 1995), 155–74.

44. Scott and Duncan, "Interacting Effects."

45. G. S. Rowe, "Infanticide, Its Judicial Resolution and Criminal Code Revision in Early Pennsylvania," *Proceedings of the American Philosophical Society* 135 (1991): 207; Sharon Ann Burnston, "Babies in the Well: An Underground Insight into Deviant Behavior in Eighteenth-Century Philadelphia," *Pennsylvania Magazine of History and Biography* 106 (1982): 151–86.

46. Nicky Hart, "Beyond Infant Mortality: Gender and Stillbirth in Reproductive Mortality before the Twentieth Century," *Population Studies* 52 (1998): 215–29.

47. In the twentieth century these same patterns prevail. Infant boys are more vulnerable to infectious disease and respiratory complaints; girls have higher mortality from measles. Waldron, "Sex Differences," 72–73.

48. Gloria Dei Burial Records, Jonathan Reeves, June 23, 1811.

49. Gary B. Nash, "Urban Wealth and Poverty in Pre-Revolutionary America," *Journal of Interdisciplinary History* 6 (1976): 545–84; Richard G. Miller, "Gentry and Entrepreneurs: A Socioeconomic Analysis of Philadelphia in the 1790s," *Rocky Mountain Social Science Journal* 12 (1975): 71–84; Billy G. Smith, *"Lower Sort,"* 149; Tom W. Smith, "Dawn," 167.

50. Robert J. Walman, "Income Distribution and Infant Mortality," *Quarterly Journal of Economics* (November 1992): 1283–1302, quote on 1299.

51. Richard G. Wilkinson, "Comment: Income, Inequality, and Social Cohesion," *American Journal of Public Health* 87, no. 9 (1997): 1504–6. Three other articles in this issue address aspects of the income-health connection.

# Four

# Slaves and Poverty

PHILIP D. MORGAN

In most early American societies slaves were the poor. This claim would not be true if the poor are defined as only those meriting charity, those unable to sustain themselves, "the impotent poor," to use early modern terminology. If living from hand to mouth, toiling manually for survival, and leading a precarious and tenuous existence define the able-bodied—the "labouring poor" (a term apparently coined by Daniel Defoe in 1701)—then slaves preeminently qualify. They worked without remuneration, legally owned no property, suffered often arbitrary and excessive punishment, and lived at minimal subsistence levels. They experienced, in Orlando Patterson's eloquent phrase, a form of "social death." As Edmund Morgan noted of Virginia, but by implication of much of early America, "Slavery, more effectively than the Elizabethan Statute of Artificers, made the master responsible for the workman and relieved society at large of most of its restive poor." Slaves composed the majority of the able-bodied poor in a colony such as Virginia. Virginia's metamorphosis into a slave society also transferred the responsibility for the aged, the disabled, and the young—the dependent poor—from the parish to the individual plantation owner. In a sense, then, slavery "solved" the problem of the poor, whether dependent or able-bodied, by privatizing it, at least in the colonies that were full-fledged slave societies.[1]

Distinguishing between dependent (deserving) and able-bodied (undeserving) is one useful historical way to think about the poor, but conceptions of poverty are not straightforward. Poverty, it might be thought, is a state of near or actual starvation, a denial of the basic requirements of survival, but malnutrition is not always easily gauged, nor are all the poor necessarily malnourished. Poverty is low income or relative deprivation, it also might be thought, but again specifying precisely the relation, distinguishing, for example, between feelings of inadequacy and conditions of deprivation or drawing the line between absolute dispossession and some minimum standard of necessities, is not easily achieved. For the most capacious definition of poverty, Amartya Sen simply describes the condition as "the lack of freedom to have or to do basic things that you value." These "basic things" involve, as he puts it, "the deprivation of elementary capabilities." For Sen, poverty is not just low income but undernourishment, ill health, illiteracy, insufficient clothing, inadequate shelter, and the like—the lack of basic capabilities. By this broad definition, slaves supremely qualify as the poorest of the poor, denied the most basic of freedoms.[2]

Thus exploring the white poor in early America seems a somewhat misplaced activity if the far more sizable group of black poor is ignored. All discussions of poverty in early America should begin with slaves, not free whites. That such discussions have rarely occurred is surely because, as Hannah Arendt perceptively noted, "the institution of slavery carries an obscurity even blacker than the obscurity of poverty." The numbers of white poor in British America were certainly not negligible, and in many places they increased over time. But in relation to the Old World where poverty was far more extensive, white poverty in early America was small scale. Peter Lindert and Jeffrey Williamson, for example, argue that "in the aggregate colonial inequality [by which is meant among free householders] was stable at low levels." It is all very well to say, as Gary Nash does, that "poverty [by which is meant largely white poverty] was a growing problem in the eighteenth century," but by how much had it grown by the end of the period? Was it growing everywhere? How extensive was it? How did it compare to Europe? Colonial America was undoubtedly "the best poor man's country," as Nash concedes, but it emphatically was not "a poor man's country nonetheless," as he also claims—unless slaves are encompassed. Alice Hanson Jones's conclusion that the standard of living in British America on the eve of the American Revolution was "probably the highest achieved for the great bulk of the population in any country up to that time" seems accurate. Or, as John McCusker and Russell Menard put it, "The colonies experienced little if any of the abject [white] poverty found in contemporary Europe or in the United States in the early nineteenth century." They continue, "Among the white colonists it seems that while the rich got richer the poor prospered as well, but at a slower rate." For white folk, colonial America was a middling person's country, where the majority enjoyed a modest competency, far more so than for their European counterparts.[3] What the New World had in abundance that the Old World lacked was not just land, which of course provided the basis for the modest competency of many whites, but rather a large group of people— slaves—who were exploited in unprecedented ways. Even Europe, with all the barbarities suffered by its poor, had no group as immiserated as slaves. It is thus misguided to exaggerate the dimensions of white poverty in early America, real though the distress suffered by a minority of whites undoubtedly was, when a much larger group of truly impoverished people should garner most attention.

Although slaves were the true poor in colonial America, they were far from being a homogeneous group and, in some respects, were materially better off than some white people. Without question, then, some whites in early America were devoid of basic necessities, and some of them were even poorer in a material sense than at least some slaves. The life expectancy of slaves, for example, was quite high for an early modern population, as was their stature. Some slaves had greater access to property, better levels of subsistence, and even opportunities to earn cash than other slaves—and some poor whites. In some places and at certain times, many slaves experienced a material status superior to that enjoyed by poor folk.

This essay seeks to accomplish two goals. First, it compares the lot of slaves to that of other poor people. It identifies various groups—from urban dwellers to Indians—that constituted many of the impoverished and then contrasts their living conditions and quality of life with that of slaves. Second, it disaggregates the monolith, slaves, and considers some key variations, particularly over time, across space, and by occupation among them. As J. H. Plumb noted many years ago in a comment still true today, "Yet in all this wonderful range of work on slavery, as exciting, as deeply original, as any going forward on any aspect of American social history, there is one singular omission. There is no comparative study of slavery and poverty."[4]

This exercise in comparison should not mask a major contrast between the conventional poor and slaves. Poverty generally is a relative condition, and it varies according to the prevailing standards of time and space. Furthermore it was rarely a static state: a core of permanently poor usually existed and the condition of poverty often passed from generation to generation, but also a person typically moved in and out of poverty over a lifetime—when times were bad, for instance, or as they grew old—or through a family life cycle, because the poor were often children; the typical French beggar, as Olwen Hufton notes, was the child. The poor in England were, in Paul Slack's words, "a jumble of social groups and individuals with little in common besides their poverty." Or, as Stuart Woolf describes the European poor, "The very fluidity and relativity of the condition of being poor denies the fixity of all categorizations." Although slavery was not uniform, an undeniable permanence or fixity attached to its status. An individual slave's status certainly varied along a broad spectrum of rights, powers, and protections, but a New

World slave did not generally move in and out of the condition. True, some slaves—a tiny fraction in British America—moved from slavery to freedom through manumission, but most New World slaves remained slaves all their lives, as did their children and children's children. Slavery is a legal institution; poverty a material state. While slavery was an absolute, poverty among whites was more frequently a relative condition.[5]

The nonslave poor can be organized into two main groups. One comprised the free poor, those who were tenuously integrated into the economy. They included some urban dwellers, tenants, rural laborers, Native Americans, and the traditional dependents. The other were bound laborers—primarily servants, convicts, and redemptioners—who were temporarily poor due to their status and because their owners regulated and restricted their consumption.

Much focus on the white poor is targeted at urban centers. Without a doubt, poverty increased markedly over the course of the eighteenth century in the major cities and towns of British America. But by the Revolution no more than about 10 percent of any city's residents received some form of public assistance, although the proportion of urban dwellers who lived at or below subsistence was perhaps three or even four times the size of those receiving charity. Urban poverty in America was on a much smaller scale than in Europe, where in some cities perhaps two-thirds or more of the population lived below or close to the poverty line, often in stinking slums, half-starving to death. Furthermore, urban life itself was far more exceptional in America than in Europe; indeed, relative to the total population, fewer Americans lived in cities at the end of the eighteenth century than at the beginning. On the eve of the American Revolution only 5 percent of the British North American population were urban residents. The urban poor in America was therefore a tiny fraction of the overall poor population.[6]

Tenancy, often associated with grinding poverty and oppressive landlords, increased markedly in eighteenth-century British America. In some older settled areas, particularly in Maryland, Virginia, Pennsylvania, Massachusetts, and New York, as much as a half or more of the free population were tenants by the time of the American Revolution. In one Maryland county—Prince George's—the proportion of landless householders reached 69 percent by 1800. Not only was tenancy widespread, for many it was a permanent condition. Yet although a significant number of tenants were near the bottom rung of the social ladder, many were far from impoverished. Indeed, most tenants in America were in a far better position than their European counterparts; the most important privilege that American tenants generally enjoyed was the ownership of their improvements. In colonial Virginia, some tenants were frequently behind in their rents and owned few possessions, yet others were "bold" enough to sell their lots and do "as they please[d] with the land." Poverty was endemic, Gregory Stiverson argues, among tenants on proprietary manors in Maryland, and yet most had secure long-term leases, were able to develop tracts with almost no interference from landlords, and paid rents that were only slightly higher than quitrents. In most respects, Stiverson concedes, proprietary tenants were "barely distinguishable from small freeholders." Stiverson assumed that proprietary tenants were better off than private tenants because the former paid a lower rent and held long-term leases, but two subsequent studies of tenants on private estates have found surprising levels of prosperity. Life leases on a Jesuit-owned estate in Charles County, Maryland, gave tenants long-term security, a saleable asset, an inheritance for at least one child, the same political privileges as freeholders, and the same living standards as small freeholders in the area. Similarly, many tenants on Carrollton manor in the Monocacy Valley, Maryland, were, by contemporary standards, well off. Many owned slaves and either owned or could afford to purchase land off the manor; they achieved wealth levels equal to or in excess of many landowners. Finally, most tenants in both New York and Pennsylvania were fairly independent and prosperous. Two conclusions about tenants seem warranted: they were not a homogenous group, and many, perhaps a majority, were far from being poor.[7]

Other landless workers existed in early America. The number of workers who called themselves "labourers" grew over the course of the eighteenth century. By the mid-eighteenth century in parts of New England as many as a third of men were landless laborers. Transients began tramping the roads in search of work, and communities began expelling or "warning out" an increasing number of newcomers who had no visible property. Even in a slave society such as the Chesapeake, free white laborers rapidly increased in number. By the end of the eighteenth century, many of the landless, perhaps a majority, were laborers, either overseers or those who worked for wages. Young single men and women in particular often worked for pay. The growth of slavery particularly expanded the work available to hired white women. Laborers were not always destitute; some employed capital equipment, most obtained a basic education, and a few even employed other workers. Typically, too, laborers were young men who were either waiting to inherit land from fathers or preparing to enter a craft. According to Christine Daniels, "they often achieved at least a meager competency" even if they also "lived close to disaster."[8]

Native Americans too can be included among the poor, although with wants scarce and means fairly plentiful, they might be said to be remarkably

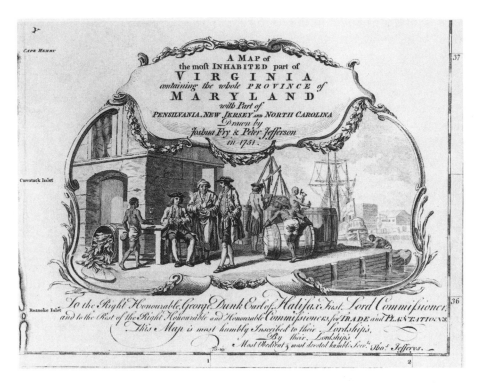

*Fig. 3*    A wharf scene in the Chesapeake region, with scantily dressed slaves doing the work. Cartouche from Joshua Fry's and Peter Jefferson's *A Map of the Most Inhabited Part of Virginia . . . ca. 1755*. Courtesy of the John Carter Brown Library at Brown University.

free of material pressures, even if they experienced a low standard of living. Able to satisfy most of their people's needs quite readily, Indian communities can merit Marshall Sahlins's term "the original affluent society." Many Indians remained apart from the conventional colonial economy before 1800; they relied on a mixed economy of hunting, gathering, and farming, and, as Claudio Saunt notes, they "measured worth in battle feats and spiritual power" rather than in material possessions. Chiefs gained renown for what they gave away, not what they owned. Indians often valued European goods primarily for their aesthetic properties and ceremonial uses. When fur traders described Hudson Bay Indians (who were subject to more constraints than most other Indian groups) as "starving," they might indeed be referring to their literal lack of food—walking skeletons "scarcely possessed of a necessary article to enable them to procure a living," as one trader put it—but equally they might be speaking of their priorities, their actual avoidance of starvation, by hunting for food rather than obtaining furs. So when an Indian said, "I am starving," he could be excusing his failure to supply furs or even engaging in a form of self-deprecatory etiquette.[9]

Increasingly, however, Native Americans were drawn into the colonial economy—whether by farming the land intensively, engaging in animal husbandry, peddling baskets and pots, going to sea, working for wages, toiling as bound laborers and as domestics, or consuming English goods. Over the course of the seventeenth and eighteenth centuries, Indians experienced a sharpened social stratification, not only in comparison to white colonists but also among themselves. A few quite wealthy and a large number of poor Native Americans became the norm. Indeed, so integrated were Indians into the colonial economy that two scholars have recently argued that the transfer of resources from Indians to colonists and the resulting lower incomes Indians experienced may well account for the real output per capita gains, estimated at about 0.6 percent per year as a maximum, generated by the eighteenth-century British North American economy. Perhaps the best glimpse into the marked inequality among native groups are the claims for property lost by the Mohawks during the American Revolution and for property damaged or destroyed that belonged to Creeks during the Redstick War of 1813 and 1814. Among the 58 Mohawk claimants, the top 4 owned about a third of all lost property; among the Creeks, the top decile of 589 claimants owned two-thirds of all destroyed property. That the vast majority of both Mohawks and Creeks seemingly owned little property (80 percent of Creeks, for example, held just a fifth of the claimed property) indicates the pervasiveness of the near-propertyless and the deep split between rich and poor in Indian society.[10]

Some of the poorest segments among free Americans were no doubt the so-called traditional or deserving poor—the infirm, disabled, widowed, and orphaned—but their overall numbers were smaller in North America than Europe. Women certainly endured poverty more often than men in early America. Widowed, separated, or abandoned women, many with children, comprised a large part of the transients warned out of New England towns. The young and the elderly, especially those lacking a support network, were most at risk. Yet far more women were married in America than Europe. "Families in early modern England," Daniel Scott Smith notes, "were more than twice as likely to be headed by a woman as were white households in late eighteenth-century America"; and these women-headed households were "disproportionately prone to be impoverished." In the Chesapeake and Caribbean, the incidence of orphanhood may well have been higher than in Europe, but the proportion of elderly was smaller. Many young people were poor for only part of their lives and escaped poverty as they matured. In fact, the proportion of younger adults (aged twenty-five to forty-four) among the poor declined quite markedly in New England—from 39 percent in the mid-seventeenth century to 24 percent in the third quarter of the eighteenth century—as their proportion among the general population also declined. Apparently, the rural New England economy benefited poorer people.[11]

Those whites who were temporarily poor because of bound labor probably outnumbered the free white poor, particularly at certain periods of time. Throughout the seventeenth century, for example, servants were far more numerous than the urban poor. Between 1580 and 1775, colonial British America imported about 500,000 white bound laborers, approximately two-thirds of all white immigrants to the colonies. A majority of these bound laborers were indentured servants, who faced a harsher lot in the New World than did servants in England. A typical servant spent from three to five years paying off the costs of his or her transportation. Since they were under contract (or indenture) for a number of years, a master might buy and sell the remainder of that contract—in effect, the servant—"like a damnd slave," as one Virginia servant put it. By contrast, servants in husbandry in England generally worked for a master for only one year and their contracts were not negotiable currency. Corporal punishment was probably more common in the colonies than in England because masters had fewer institutional checks on their behavior in the New World than the Old. In seventeenth-century Virginia, John and Alice Proctor beat two servants to death, on one occasion administering 500 lashes to one of them. Yet New World masters probably did not engage in widespread physical abuse because harming their servants reduced profits, although the tendency for a master to extract as much work as possible from a servant whose term would expire was undoubtedly real.[12]

The experiences of indentured servants varied greatly. Many, particularly in the seventeenth-century Chesapeake and West Indies, never survived their terms—largely because they succumbed to a new disease environment. On the other hand, some servants had their terms extended because they ran away or, in the case of women, had a child. By contrast, other masters provided their servants with more than the legally required minimum levels of food and clothing, and some even paid wages to their servants or made bargains with them to release them early from their terms. Servants could choose their destinations, and thus the least favored destinations had to offer incentives to attract them. Most important perhaps, servants had basic legal rights: they could petition courts for redress of grievances. In one study of 260 complaints submitted to Maryland courts between 1652 and 1797, indentured servants won 83 percent of the time. Servants, unlike slaves, had precious legal protections. Furthermore, through at least the first half of the seventeenth century, those servants who managed to survive their terms in the Chesapeake generally did well, often getting access to land and even modest political offices, although toward the end of the seventeenth and into the eighteenth centuries, ex-servants' opportunities for upward mobility declined markedly. Thus, in the eighteenth century immigrants and pamphleteers usually advised against coming to America as an indentured servant, although one recent immigrant in 1772 still thought the prospects were good, especially for the "younger Class" whose "Servitude for a few years, is in my opinion of service to them & may be looked on only as an apprenticeship." For those of "advanced years," however, "the change of Climate, hardships they often undergo, during their Servitude, under tyrannical masters, with the pressure upon their minds on being rank'd & deemed as Slaves, are such, that they seldom surmount."[13]

Not all servants were indentured. Perhaps about a half of all the seventeenth-century white immigrants came without a contract and thus served according to "the custom of the country," which usually meant longer terms than experienced by indentured servants. Customary servants generally were younger and probably possessed fewer skills than indentured servants. They also were less likely to win in the courts than indentured servants, although in Maryland even they prevailed 70 percent of the time. Yet another group of servants arrived without an indenture, but they typically fared better than the customary servants. They were redemptioners, allowed a specific length of time upon their arrival in America to raise the unpaid portion of the costs of their transportation. Only if they failed did they or members of their family become indentees whose length of service was determined in part by the amount owed. Because redemptioners negotiated their own labor agreements or those of their children, their contracts could not be sold without their assent. One final form of servitude was debt peonage. A person who had been imprisoned for debt, for example, might bind himself, without time restriction, to a master until the obligation had been repaid. Although debt servants generally served shorter terms than indentured servants, their situation was susceptible to exploitation because masters could extend the terms through exorbitant subsistence charges and interest on the debt. Indian whalemen on Nantucket often served two- or three-year stints to pay off their debts to an individual merchant, but the cycle of dependence might often be nigh continuous.[14]

Convicts were far less numerous than indentured and other types of servants, and their lot was probably the harshest of all bound white laborers. Between 1718 and 1775, Britain banished about 50,000 convicts—about a quarter of all British immigrants—to its American colonies. They served longer terms than servants: about three-quarters were sentenced to seven years, most of the remainder as long as fourteen, with a few servitude for life. Confined in prisons for about two months before boarding, shackled in chains, crowded onto ships, sold almost naked and half-starved at wharfside or driven in coffles from town to town by "soul drivers"—"Going to Hell in a Cradle" was how one prisoner described the process—convicts experienced conditions close to slavery. Indeed, convicts sometimes compared their condition to slavery and one female felon believed "many Negroes are better used." Yet technically convicts chose their fate; some in fact elected not to be transported and suffered death as did one convict who "had rather die than live under Bondage for so many Years" or another who "had rather bear strangling for a minute than to make sugar all his life-time" alongside slaves. Convicts apparently knew the rigors that awaited them: Benjamin Franklin said convicts "must be ruled with a Rod of Iron," and in general masters were said to be "cruel, barbarous, and unmerciful" toward convicts. Convicts were probably the one white group to receive floggings about as frequently as slaves. But the convicts' recourse, as with other servants, was their ability to petition courts for relief—an option limited in practice and in its chances of success. And over time colonial legislatures stripped away the rights of convicts, so that by the last third of the eighteenth century in both Virginia and Maryland convicts could not testify in court, and in Virginia they were also denied freedom dues. Once freed, convicts probably enjoyed better opportunities in America than they would have experienced at home; nevertheless, Roger Ekirch concludes, "very few felons enjoyed even modest success."[15]

In conclusion, then, despite pockets of serious poverty, particularly among the temporarily unfree, a general sense of well-being was pervasive for most free colonists in early America. As Jackson Turner Main says of one New England colony, "the great majority of Connecticut's people fared as well in 1774 as in 1700 or 1670, and . . . this majority included virtually all of the married men and their families. Indeed, by contrast with most other preindustrial societies, these men did not simply escape poverty but enjoyed real plenty." If this was true of most white families in Connecticut, how much more must it have been true of most white families in the mid-Atlantic and Southern colonies where prosperity was even more evident than in New England? In fact, Crevecoeur, an astute observer of early America, thought a "pleasing uniformity of decent competence appears throughout our habitations." Even Allan Kulikoff, who has a keen nose for inequality, observes that an "astonishingly high percentage—two-thirds of colonial families—owned land."[16]

If most white Americans shared a "decent competence," more precise measurements of well-being need to be analyzed. This section explores six main

indicators of the elementary capabilities outlined by Sen: demographic performance; diet; stature and general state of health; clothing; shelter; and
work demands. These are not the only measures of the gap between competence and poverty of course. Educational levels and basic literacy constitute
another useful yardstick. Unfortunately, little concrete information is available on education, although the contrast was surely extreme—the vast majority of slaves were illiterate, and although many white poor shared the
condition, they were not deprived of an elementary education to anything
like the same degree. Nevertheless, these six measurements are some of the
most basic, and a fair amount of information is available, allowing some comparisons between the experiences of black and white populations.[17]

Perhaps the best guide to general well-being is the remarkable demographic performance of the early North American population. By the late
eighteenth century, Robert Fogel notes, white Americans had "a twenty-year
advantage in life expectancy at birth over the English" and had "reached levels of life expectancy that the general population of England and even the
British peerage did not attain until the first quarter of the twentieth century."
Overall, the mainland white population grew by an average of about 3 percent per annum in the eighteenth century—with the Mid-Atlantic and Lower
South regions registering the fastest growth rates. During the same period,
the black population increased in size at an even faster rate. The black population grew just over 3 percent per year in the northern colonies, about 4.5
percent in the South. The Caribbean was a much less rosy story; there, the
white population was largely static, and the black population grew only about
1.5 percent a year, despite heavy forced migration.[18]

As the Caribbean experience especially indicates, immigration accounts
for much of the population growth, and how immigrants arrived in the New
World reveals a major difference in the experiences of the enslaved and the
free. Mortality was always three or four times higher for slaves and crews of
slavers than for white migrants and their crews. The slave trade on average
recorded about 60 deaths per month per thousand people shipped. This rate
was four times greater than that among German emigrants to Philadelphia in
the eighteenth century and about five times higher than that among British
convicts to Australia in the late eighteenth and early nineteenth centuries.
The only group to approximate mortality rates on slavers were British convicts to North America in the early eighteenth century (56 deaths per month
per thousand between 1719 and 1736), and their mortality levels soon
improved significantly (dropping to 12 per month per thousand between
1768 and 1775). No recorded voyage in the North Atlantic appears to have
generated the appalling conditions typical for a slave vessel and almost no

ship carrying servants or convicts crowded its passengers on anything like the scale of slave ships, which generally included far more individuals per unit of space than did other vessels.[19]

Important as immigration was, by the eighteenth century at least, the North American population grew primarily from natural increase. A starving population, generally speaking, cannot reproduce itself; to that extent, natural increase is a minimal indicator of well-being. What is impressive about the North American population, both white and black, is the speed at which it increased naturally. From 1730 down to 1800, the natural rate of increase of Virginia's black population was about 2 or more percent a year. Even South Carolina's slave population grew through reproduction by more than 1 percent a year from 1760 onward, except for the Revolutionary War years and their immediate aftermath. The one exception to this remarkable success story—unprecedented for slave populations in the New World to this point—concerned cities (where, of course, proportionately few North American slaves lived) such as Philadelphia, where fertility among slave women was sufficiently low and mortality in general so high that births failed to exceed deaths. Overall, from the early eighteenth century onward the mainland slave population grew faster from natural increase than contemporary European populations. Apart from the dislocations of the very first years of settlement, almost no North American, white or black, starved. Virtually all North Americans benefited from living in an environment where a few days' labor could produce a maize crop that would feed a person for a year and where two sources of protein—fish from the ocean and meat (either game or livestock)—were widely available. In addition, extensive forests provided timber for housing and firewood, and low population density reduced the spread of communicable diseases.[20]

By contrast, throughout most of the British Caribbean, slave populations registered high rates of natural decrease. By 1750 the West Indies had imported almost 800,000 Africans, but deaths had so far exceeded births that the slave population then stood at less than 300,000. Only slave populations in marginal colonies such as the Bahamas were able to increase naturally during the eighteenth century, although the Barbadian slave population was beginning to do the same by the end of the century. Perhaps the single most important reason why the Caribbean was a graveyard for slaves and the mainland a breeding ground can be summed up in one word: sugar. Sugar cultivation was so onerous that it was literally a killing work regime. In addition, because the Caribbean islands generally had more hostile disease environments and more fragile ecologies than the mainland, seasonal and episodic cases of nutritional stress occurred. The "hungry times" in Caribbean islands,

*Fig. 4*    "Planting the Sugar Cane on Bodkins Estate," with men and women under close supervision and a windmill in the background (note the head-carrying by slaves and the use of hoes). William Clark, *Ten Views in the Island of Antigua . . .* (London, 1823). Courtesy of the John Carter Brown Library at Brown University.

which lasted from June to September, occurred after the end of the sugar harvest, when the access to cane juice declined and food crops were not yet available. Drought-induced famines occurred fairly frequently, hurricanes caused periodic devastation, and naval blockades during wartime—most notably, the American Revolutionary War—led to many thousands of slaves dying from starvation because of insufficient imported foods. The demographic performance of Caribbean slaves points to significant material deprivation and epidemiological stress.[21]

For the poor, whether white or black, how they lived was primarily how they ate. The diet for both poor whites and slaves was predominantly composed of cereals. Whites generally ate a range of grains, but for most slaves, certainly those in the Chesapeake, corn was the staff of life. The maize ration for slaves was not generous but was roughly the same as white indentured servants and convicts received—about thirteen to fifteen bushels a year. Although maize was a primary staple in the Lower South and Caribbean, it did not dominate either diet to the extent it did in the Chesapeake. In the lowcountry, rice and chickpeas were major components of the slave diet; and

*Fig. 5*    "Holeing a Cane-Piece on Weatherell's Estate," with gang of slave men and women preparing the fields for the planting of sugar cane (note children working and the black driver). William Clark, *Ten Views in the Island of Antigua* . . . (London, 1823). Courtesy of the John Carter Brown Library at Brown University.

in the Caribbean, Guinea corn (sorghum or millet), plantains, and yams were important food crops. Contemporaries praised the nutritional content of maize; perhaps, therefore, the reduced corn intake of Caribbean and low-country slaves was to their nutritional detriment. Wherever plantations were not present—as in the Bahamas, Anguilla, and Barbuda in the Caribbean—or in towns, or on farms throughout North America, slaves experienced a better than average diet.[22]

Slaves undoubtedly ate less protein than servants or poor whites in America, though probably more protein than many European poor folk. A little salt pork or salt fish was the typical allotment for slaves. The distribution of meat to slaves seems to have been more common in the Chesapeake than in the lowcountry, and more common on the mainland than in the islands. In the Chesapeake, wildlife and pork were more important in poor white and slave diets than in that of the wealthy, though in all groups domestic mammals constituted the most common meat protein. Slaves supplemented their rations by hunting, trapping, fishing, gardening, and raising fowl—but the more the slaves provided their own food, particularly through provision grounds, as was particularly common on some Caribbean islands, the more likely it was that they suffered nutritional stress. One indicator in the colonial Jamaican slave population, for instance, is the presence of rats as rare items of protein in their diet. Even when slaves did not go hungry, their intake of proteins and vitamins was often inadequate; rickets, scurvy, and allied deficiency diseases were common. Analysis of slave skeletons at some sites has revealed health levels comparable to Native American populations threatened with extinction, although at other slave sites the levels were little different from that of whites. Dietary deficiencies help account for a description of a dozen slave men and women on one low-country estate as "all misshapen or disfigured." Similarly, an inadequate diet probably explains why a traveler thought that Carolina slaves were "shrivelled and diminutive in size, compared with those in Virginia." But, in fact, few travelers described slaves in the way some observers described entire villages in parts of Europe where, in Hufton's words, "the inhabitants were crippled or physically distorted."[23]

The daily caloric intake of slaves is almost impossible to measure, in part because rations varied from region to region, even from master to master, and in part because the slaves' independent activities may well have provided roughly as many calories as the masters' allocations. Nevertheless, historians have not refrained from offering such estimates: for example, the average estate ration in the late eighteenth-century Caribbean was supposedly between 1,500 and 2,000 calories a day, whereas in eighteenth-century Philadelphia slaves apparently received about 1,800 to 2,400 calories a day at a time when the city workhouse may have provided 2,600. Such intakes, even if they are reliable estimates, do not seem to have been enough to meet the energy demands of a field hand or laborer, which have been put at about 3,000 calories per day, but then again some healthy modern West Indian populations subsist on less than 2,000 calories daily. Overall, few slaves (mostly confined to the Caribbean and during particular years or seasons) starved, even if some were malnourished.[24]

Somewhat more precise than estimates of caloric intake are measurements of height at maturity, which are fairly good indicators of net nutritional status. In the eighteenth century, the average height of white American men was about sixty-eight inches, or approximately two inches taller than their European counterparts. In fact, native-born white Americans seem to have been the tallest people in the world, and their average height was close to that attained in modern times. Heights did increase slightly over the course of the eighteenth century. Occupational differences in stature were modest; farmers were not appreciably taller than artisans, for example. The most important variation was regional: native-born white American men from the southern colonies were taller than their northern counterparts. Nutritionally, then, white men in America seem to have been exceptionally well off.[25]

By the time of the Revolution native-born North American blacks were almost the same height as whites—on average less than an inch shorter. In the late eighteenth century, the mean height of adult male slaves was about 67.2 inches. Creole slaves were thus about an inch taller than most Europeans; indeed, their physical stature was closer to that of European aristocrats than to that of peasants. By all accounts, then, most North American slaves avoided permanent undernourishment, the lot of many poor people in Europe. Slaves born in North America were taller than those born in the Caribbean, who in turn were generally taller than those born in Africa. The one exception was early nineteenth-century Berbice where adult male creoles were somewhat shorter than male Africans—presumably a sign of that colony's extreme nutritional inadequacy, unfavorable environmental conditions, and harsh work regime. Sugar colonies produced consistently shorter creole slaves than non-sugar-producing colonies. In the early nineteenth century American-born slaves were, on average 1.6 inches taller than even Africans from the Bight of Benin—the coastal region with the tallest slaves. The same regional variation was true of blacks as whites: American-born slaves were taller in the Upper South than in the Lower South. Slave children, particularly below the age of five, seem to have been staggeringly small (in the Caribbean they were considerably shorter than the factory children in the satanic mills of industrializing Britain—contrary to the arguments of proslavery advocates). However, their catch-up as teenagers was remarkably rapid and seems to have been largely attributable to the distribution of meat when they began working. During the second half of the eighteenth century, a decline in stature seems to have occurred among North American slaves, but whether due to wartime disruptions of the American Revolution or to a southward shift of the slave trade catchment areas, which brought shorter slaves from West-Central Africa in greater numbers than before, is not clear.[26]

During the eighteenth century, masters began paying greater medical attention to their slaves than in the previous century—and slaves might well have had more access to doctors than poor whites—but it is doubtful that the slaves' health improved much, if at all. Some medical measures probably did more harm than good. The natural increase of a slave population cannot be correlated, for example, with the number of available European-trained doctors. Smallpox inoculation and vaccination, probably the only medical advances to benefit slaves, were helpful, but they did not reduce mortality rates drastically. As Barry Higman notes, "The most direct intervention of the slaveowner aimed at reducing mortality levels, the provision of European medical attention, probably had a negative effect." There were probably more doctors and certainly more hospitals proportional to the population in the lowcountry than in the Chesapeake, but neither were sufficient to overcome the significant fertility and mortality differentials between the two regions. Similarly, those slaves who were most isolated from European medical practitioners, those living in the nonplantation colonies of the Caribbean (where environmental conditions were already conducive to longevity, it must be conceded) survived longest.[27]

Slaves and poor whites seem to have worn much the same kinds of clothing, although if possible masters clothed their slaves more cheaply than they did white servants. In 1691 substandard military clothing was deemed sufficient for slaves. Unbleached linens, such as crocus, rolls, and "osnaburg," and inexpensive woolens, such as Welsh plains, Yorkshire kersey, and Kendal cotton, constituted the most common materials. Homespun was rare before the American Revolution, but in 1711 Virginia's governor noted that some colonists mixed cotton with their wool "to supply the want of coarse Cloathing and Linnen, not only for their Negros, but for many of the poorer sort of house keepers"—another indication that the same type of cloth was destined for blacks and the white poor. Laboring folk of both races generally wore durable, coarse, uncomfortable, ill-fitting clothes. Textiles with trade names that touted their sturdiness—whether Foul Weather, Fearnothing, or Everlasting—were widely distributed. Men from all ranks wore leather breeches, dubbed the "blue jeans of the eighteenth century." An extant hunting shirt worn by a white soldier seems much the same as the description of a light blue hunting shirt, "plaited in the sleeves," worn by a slave. Working men, whether slave or free, usually wore a jacket or waistcoat, shirt, breeches, and hat or cap; women typically wore a jacket and a petticoat. Some occupations had distinctive garbs: some slaves were identifiable by the "Dress such as Sailors wear" or "such Clothes as Watermen generally wear"; slave blacksmiths donned the emblem of their trade, the leather apron; and male house slaves, like domestic servant men more generally, might wear livery. Convicts reported that they rarely had shoes; many slaves, particularly field hands, went barefoot. Manual workers, whether white or black, usually appeared in their own hair; few sported wigs. Poor children, both white and black but particularly slaves, seem to have had few clothes, sometimes nothing at all.[28]

Despite similarities, there were differences in the appearance of slaves and poor whites. Because of shortcomings in the provision and distribution of clothing, many adult slaves—far more than poor whites, it would seem—were scantily clad. Field hands frequently wore only a mere rag around their loins, a "Breech Clout" or "Arse-Cloth" in contemporary parlance. Breechcloths or waist ties for men and wraparound skirts for women were a distinctive feature of African-American dress; and nakedness or seminakedness was a condition associated primarily with slaves. In addition, as Linda Baumgarten notes, "the absence of stays among the clothing assigned to female field slaves is another example of discrimination through clothing." Even English women living in the poor house were expected to have stays (made of bone or leather and designed to shape the female figure into a cone from waist to bust), and only American women in the backwoods left off their stays in the hottest summer months. Moreover, slaves probably preferred to wear scanty, loose-fitting clothing as a matter of choice, although masters shortchanged them too. As another matter of choice, slaves apparently believed heads should generally be covered; certainly they wore headcloths far more widely than whites, although white women in the Caribbean followed the practice fairly extensively (the headwrap had African origins, but headgear in general signified submissiveness and subjection). In part because their sartorial resources were so limited, slave clothing was distinctive for the extent to which it was patched and edged, often with bright colors. Slaves often used natural dyes to add a welcome touch of color to their drab uniforms. Yet over time, it would seem, slaves—especially on large plantations—came to be associated with a standardized form of clothing, even if the range of imported cloths grew more varied and slaves gained greater access to variety in their leisure-time dress. Masters referred to their slaves as "clothed in the usual manner of laboring Negroes," "clothed in the common dress of field slaves," or wearing "the usual winter clothing of corn field negroes."[29]

Poor people, even slaves, could wear clothes above their supposed station. A Jamestown cow keeper wore scarlet silk on Sundays; a lowly collier's wife, also in Jamestown, flaunted a beaver hat and a silk suit; two Mohawk Indians on horseback were "dressed a la mode Francois with laced hats, full trimmed coats, and ruffled shirts"; a maroon captain in Jamaica wore "a ruffled shirt, blue broad cloth coat, scarlet cuff to his sleeves, gold buttons, & he had with [that ensemble a] white cap, and black hat, white linen breeches puffed at the rims, no stockings or shoes on." Whites regularly complained of extravagantly dressed slaves, particularly on Sundays and holidays. In 1672 the justices of the peace of Surry County, Virginia, observed that the "apparrell commonly worne by negroes" heightened their "foolish pride" and so banned white linen and ordered only "blew shirts and shifts" for slaves. One visitor to South Carolina noted that "there is scarce a new mode" of fashion "which favourite black and mulatto women slaves are not immediately enabled to adopt." A correspondent in the Chesapeake spoke of "the great Liberties" allowed slaves "particularly in their Dress." According to this observer, slaves stole "purely to raise Money to buy fine Cloaths, and when dressed in them, make them so bold and impudent that they insult every poor white Person they meet with." Wearing "Sunday or Holyday Cloaths" made slaves, he thought, as "bold as a Lion."[30]

Colonists in general experienced poorer housing than Europeans. Lavishing most of their time and resources on farm development, the earliest settlers scrimped on their accommodations. They generally huddled together in cramped, drafty, dark, impermanent structures—nothing more than ramshackle and temporary huts. Most dwellings had no foundations but were constructed on posts placed directly into the ground, with clapboard siding, earthen floors, and wooden chimneys. In material terms, the first couple of generations in America tended to lead a crude, spartan existence often associated with poverty in Europe. While middling farmers gradually invested in better housing over time, a broad cross section of the eighteenth-century American population continued to live in crude, earthfast, one- or at best two-room houses without plaster walls, a lick of paint, wood floors, or glass windows. Houses were tiny. In late eighteenth-century Maryland the most common size for a house was 16 by 20 feet; in Worcester County, Massachusetts, one-sixth of the houses were less than 500 square feet; and urban tenements were even smaller. If being poor meant living in one room, many Americans in the colonial period were poor. Frontier settlers even as late as the American Revolution were often said to be living in primitive conditions.[31]

Although slaves and poor whites suffered similar housing conditions, slaves tended to be the worst off. For one thing, many slaves lacked separate quarters, but rather lived in outbuildings, in kitchens, or, particularly in northern cities, in out-of-the-way spaces in principal dwellings—in attics, cupboards, or under the stairs. Only the poorest domestic white servant had to experience this lack of privacy. For another, many slave spaces were extremely small. cabins of between 150 and 250 square feet were commonplace (although poor tenant housing in the Chesapeake, for example, was not much bigger, and the median house size for free whites in Spotsylvania County, Virginia, in 1798 was just 280 square feet). The average living space for Caribbean slaves has been estimated at between 30 and 60 square feet each (in more than half of the dwellings of the poor in early nineteenth-century Amsterdam, less than 60 square feet were available per person). Doors were small, windows rare, making for smoke-filled, dark, and unventilated spaces. Third, whereas whites increasingly lived privately during the eighteenth century, slaves increasingly lived communally in cramped, unsanitary villages, which were breeding grounds for communicable diseases. Finally, masters generally invested little in the flimsy and dilapidated huts that dotted their plantations; often the only items they bought for the construction of these huts were nails. Wattle-and-daub dwellings, thatched with canes or grasses, were the most common form of slave housing in the Caribbean. They cost almost nothing but labor to construct. In 1800 the per capita value of shelter in the United States has been estimated at six dollars for free persons and three dollars for slaves.[32]

Poor folk, both white and black, not only inhabited squalid hovels but generally lacked basic household amenities. A few cooking utensils, bedding, and clothes often constituted the total assets of a poor person. Laborers furnished their houses with little more than a mattress or two, a cooking pot, and some chests. Slaves usually had less than this minimum: their "beds" were often collections of straw, old rags, a rush mat, or some animal skins. Tables, chairs, and bedsteads were usually out of reach of the white poor and almost certainly to the vast majority of slaves. Many of the poor ate from coarse earthenware or woodenware and rarely saw a mirror. Sleeping on a dirt floor, eating a pot-boiled stew, using fingers or a spoon, sitting on a box, or just squatting for lack of a stool were typical household experiences for the poor, not just slaves. Perhaps the only housing advantage the rural American poor had over their European counterpart was that they did not need to share their hovels with livestock for heating purposes. In tropical climes, of course, slaves generally did not need heat; in temperate regions, "a good fire," as one master put it, was "the life of a negro," and enough firewood was usually available to keep warm. But even this advantage narrowed over time. Firewood became increasingly scarce and expensive by the end of the eighteenth century. Even in rural areas landowners began restricting tenants to using only fallen wood, and some planters did the same to slaves. Firewood was a major item in outdoor poor relief budgets in northern towns and cities.[33]

Over the course of the eighteenth century, the poor's amenities benefited from a prospering economy. Dr. Alexander Hamilton once stayed in a poor family's home and observed "a looking glass with a painted frame, half a dozen pewter spoons and as many plates, old and wore out but bright and clean, a set of stone tea dishes, and a tea pot." Of the family's meager possessions, the "tea equipage," a symbol of luxury, gave the gentleman the greatest offense. Even the inmates of the public hospital of Philadelphia, the city poorhouse, insisted on having tea. By the late colonial era, tea and teaware appeared in about a quarter of poor estates in some Chesapeake counties. Some poor folk came to own chairs, bedsteads, coarse ceramics, linens, perhaps a book or two, table knives, and forks. By the late eighteenth century, some poor folk began to acquire some of the amenities previously beyond their reach.[34]

Even some slaves shared in these improvements in both household amenities and housing. Some acquired flatware, even an occasional piece of porce-
lain, as well as the odd remnants of tea services. An occasional slave cabin
exhibited a few more comforts than normal, as in one Virginia slave dwelling
that contained chairs, a bed, an iron and brass kettle, an iron pot, a pair of
pot racks, a pothook, a frying pan, and a beer barrel. On another Virginia
estate, those slaves who possessed large numbers of chickens traded them for
stools. Slave housing, too, became more substantial and orderly over time.
Single cabins and duplexes gradually supplanted dormitories; houses with
sills, brick foundations, and plank floors little by little replaced earthfast
dwellings; wooden chimneys gradually gave way to brick chimneys. In the
Caribbean stone or boarded dwellings, with shingle roofs, sometimes took
the place of wattle-and-daub structures. On the more established plantations,
slaves began constructing two- and even three- or more room structures.[35]

Diet, shelter, and clothing, all affected the ability to perform work—the
prime activity of slaves and the laboring poor. Because of the chronic labor
shortages in early America, labor participation was higher in the New World
than the Old—as was the range of servitude. This effectiveness in extracting
labor was most apparent for slaves, who began to enter the labor force as
early as age three or four but more widely at ages eight to ten and toiled until
virtually in the grave. Among the free American population (both in the
North and South), about one-third was in the labor force; among slaves, the
proportion was two-thirds. As David Eltis notes, "Europeans put African
women to work in whip-driven field gangs in the Americas but were not prepared to see European women work under like conditions." Underemployment, a common feature of early modern European labor, was also less
widespread in America. About a fifth of the early modern English population
was too malnourished for regular work. Because of unemployment due to
weather, illness, season, the interval between jobs, and simple lack of work,
the typical working man in eighteenth-century Europe worked about 200 to
210 days a year, and the poor worked even fewer days. In America, free laborers worked about 280 to 290 days, and slaves between 280 and 310 days,
depending mostly on the crop. A more precise measure of the general conditions of labor is the number of hours involved. Slaves cultivating sugar had
the most onerous schedule, with first-gang field laborers toiling on average
about 3,500 hours a year (in Barbados the average was 3,200 but in Jamaica a
staggering 4,000 hours). In North America, slaves averaged about 2,800
hours annually, although there were variations by crop.[36]

The heightened intensity of labor per hour associated with gang-driven
slave labor, as Robert Fogel has pointed out, was more important than the

actual number of hours worked. In this regard, no other crop had such an extreme pace of labor as that of sugar. Not just the extreme hours of heavy labor, but the demands of night work during crop season, which lasted at least six months of the year, and the brutality of the gang-driving system made its regime extraordinarily onerous. In sugar's earliest phases in Barbados, white servants worked at the crop, but they soon learned of its rigors and avoided it at all costs; the crop became the preserve of slaves. Rice was another arduous crop, because of its long production cycle, the heavy pounding by hand, and the harsh environment in which it was grown—even though it was subject to a task, rather than gang, system. Like sugar, rice became associated solely with slave labor in the Lower South. Tobacco was the least physically demanding southern crop to produce. It was initially grown largely by servant labor, and well into the eighteenth century many a servant and convict worked as a common field hand in the Chesapeake. "Among the Negroes to work at the Hoe" was how a Virginia convict described his fate. White servants complained about the drudgery, the sheer backbreaking toil, that such work entailed, although their lot was almost certainly better than slaves, who had no claim to the customary rights (such as a rest in the heat of the day or the many traditional holidays) that English servants brought with them from the Old World. Even in an activity, such as ironworking, that often employed slave and free labor together, the owners supervised slaves more closely and punished them more harshly than their white counterparts, whether free or indentured, and frequently relegated slaves to the dirtiest and most arduous tasks—mining, charcoal-making, and woodcutting.[37]

Although coercion was fundamental, the intense labor of slaves was not extracted solely by force; positive incentives also played a role, just as they did for free labor. The most important rewards masters offered slaves were holidays or rest days, special allowances of material goods, various tasking or piece-rate arrangements, and cash payments. Apart from the Christian holidays of Christmas, Easter, and Whitsuntide, planters generally kept Sundays free from estate labor and then gave occasional other days as indulgences, usually for good work. On eighteenth-century Caribbean islands where the provision ground system operated, slaves were usually allowed every other Saturday out of crop to tend their provisions. Such slaves typically had about fifteen free days as well as Sundays. Masters were usually willing to trade with their slaves, thereby displaying their benevolence, rendering slavery a little more humane, while also buying the products at below market price, thereby serving their own self-interest. The slaves preferred to exchange their provisions, fish, poultry, small livestock, and craft products for cash. Tasking, which gave slaves some latitude in apportioning their time, was common in many slave work settings—especially rice, coffee, timber, and naval stores production, and increasingly in some sugar and cotton operations. So-called overwork—production that exceeded a quota—was common in ironworking. Also, masters sometimes paid cash to get slaves to perform extra work, perhaps on a Sunday, or long into the night.[38]

In sum, there are two ways of assessing the material standards of early American slaves. On the one hand, they experienced a thoroughly spartan material existence. They worked extraordinarily hard and in many cases for more hours than free laborers. Harsh taskmasters drove them onward, the whip being the ubiquitous instrument. Just as Africans experienced higher mortality and more crowded conditions than any other transatlantic traveler, so once in America they lived in the flimsiest, most cramped quarters. Their everyday attire was as mean as their shelter. Masters forced slaves to wear cheap, drab, uncomfortable clothes. Many adults and most children went naked and barefoot. Slaves were as poorly fed as they were clothed. Their diet was high in starch, low in protein, and extremely monotonous in content. Richard Parkinson, a perceptive observer, noted that slaves were "both clothed and fed at less expence" than free men; the livelihood of the southern planter, he continued, was "pinched and screwed out of the negro."

At the same time, poor whites experienced material conditions not all that dissimilar to slaves. In some respects, many slaves were better off than poor whites in strictly material terms. Certainly the stature of slaves suggests that their diet was no worse, perhaps even better, than that of many poor whites. Slaves rarely starved, even if they were malnourished. As J. R. Ward notes, "by emancipation [and probably well before] an adult British West Indian slave's material state, measured by quantity of food eaten and yards of cloth worn, at least matched that of many British workers." Some slaves, particularly on the mainland, worked fewer hours than free workers in the northern colonies. And, of course, slaves were far from experiencing the same conditions; marked variations existed among them—and these need now to be explored.[39]

The slaves' bedrock material conditions were not uniform, even though social differentiation among slaves was always much less than among free people. Opportunity for individual advancement was obviously much more restricted for the unfree than for the free. Slaves rarely could change masters or move voluntarily. Their *peculiam*, the small items of movable property that they might acquire—such as produce from gardens or provision grounds, small livestock, occasionally horses and cattle, extra clothing, or their own craft products—were always by their master's leave. Possession was always tenuous for slaves; legal ownership was never possible. Collective action to remedy grievances was also difficult; slaves tended to act individually rather than in groups. Nevertheless, although slavery always allowed much less room for maneuver than freedom, the institution was not homogenous or monolithic. The slave experience varied, most significantly in five major ways: over time, across space, according to the status of masters, through a hierarchy among slaves, and finally by the differential struggles of the enslaved.[40]

The material conditions of slaves, much like those of whites, changed over the course of the colonial period. As frontier societies became more settled, planters built more secure housing, displayed their wealth through their plantation establishment, and in general regularized the material conditions of their laborers. Housing evolved from barracks or quarters to family cabins and duplexes; domestic life moved from public to private, perhaps symbolized best by the growing appearance of padlocks on slave cabin doors and the presence of personal subfloor storage pits inside many cabins; earthfast structures slowly gave way to more permanent architectural forms; and slave settlements grew more autonomous over time. Although eighteenth-century slaves never wore a uniform, their dress grew more standardized. Similarly, cereals, vegetables, and some fish or meat protein became the core of the slave diet. In some cases innovations, such as pounding machines and the use of tidal flows in rice cultivation or more plowing and ratooning to reduce hand manuring and cane holing in sugar cultivation, eased the labor of slaves at particular points of the year. As plantations grew larger and more slaves escaped field labor, the material lives of an increasing minority of slaves improved.[41]

But not all slaves, or the poor, experienced material progress. The regularization of conditions created a diminution of material standards in some cases. Some planters more precisely measured the yardage of cloth or food rations in order to cut costs; some imposed a more geometric, ordered layout to housing that slaves might not have preferred; some increased labor requirements, perhaps by undertaking elementary time and motion studies to accelerate work pace; some tried to monitor pilfering and nighttime activities. The late eighteenth-century trend by which masters increasingly regularized the material and work conditions of slaves parallels attempts by local authorities to do much the same with respect to the free poor—curtailing outdoor relief and forcing them into hospitals and workhouses. The same urge ostensibly to "improve," "standardize," and "ameliorate" material conditions by reducing autonomy seems at work.

Another way in which slavery changed over time was according to the life cycle of the individual slave. Newly enslaved Africans, typically in their teens or early adult years, were at their most destitute when they landed in America.

Literally stripped of almost everything—possessions, kin, their health, even memories—they arrived on New World soil virtually naked, physically debilitated, perhaps still smarting from a shipboard brand, soon to be separated from even shipmates, and sold most commonly as individuals. Disoriented and alienated, many would sicken and die within the first year. Often placed in the hut of another slave, perhaps even to be exploited by that host slave, it would be many years before the newcomer ever acquired anything. But, if the slave survived, job allocations depended above all on age. On sugar estates, for example, children usually worked in the third gang between the ages of five and twelve, progressed to the second gang between twelve and eighteen, and then to the third gang between eighteen and forty-five, before returning to the second gang when past their prime, usually over forty years of age. Typically, drivers had to wait for their appointment until they were in their mid-to-late thirties. Those slaves who entered trades usually did so much later than free persons. Most masters could not afford to apprentice slaves at the usual age (early teens), but rather had to single out a likely field slave, usually a mature adult, for on-the-job training. Watchmen were almost always old and weak. Life cycle changes, then, clearly determined different jobs.[42]

Native-born slaves or creoles experienced slavery very differently from Africans. Creoles had more resistance to the local disease environment and were almost always taller and better nourished than Africans. Creoles almost completely abandoned the bodily aesthetic so important to Africans—cicatrization and teeth filing—in part because those practices had lost their function in the New World and in part because masters placed their own marks on the slaves' bodies. In place of permanent forms of bodily adornment, creoles channeled their interest in fashion and their commitment to personal style in varied and changing hairstyles, inventive headgear, occasional jewelry, and brightly colored clothes. Often described as brisk, lively, sharp, and sensible, or conversely as bold, saucy, sly, and cunning, native-born slaves inspired admiration and provoked consternation from masters in almost equal amounts. Planters generally thought that creoles made better skilled workers than Africans, and almost everywhere native-born men dominated the artisan ranks. In late eighteenth-century Saint Domingue, for instance, one in four creole men, compared to only one in ten African men, held positions outside the field. Native-born slaves of mixed racial ancestry were the most likely to avoid field labor. Mulatto or light-colored women were particularly overrepresented among domestics. Considered physically weak and yet superior because of their light skin, and indeed often related to the slave-owner or his white employees, mulattoes were highly favored in occupational allocations. The light-skinned Hemings family's monopoly of household positions at Monticello was not unusual. Visitors to Jefferson's home who stayed close to the house would have encountered only Hemingses.[43]

Slavery varied not just over time but across space. Three spatial distinctions are conspicuous. First were the obvious regional differences—between island and mainland, between large island and small island, between lowcountry and Chesapeake, between tidewater and piedmont, between highlands and lowlands, between yeoman and plantation worlds. Slaves on large islands, for example, usually had access to mountain provision grounds; slaves on small islands relied mostly on imported foods. Also, slaves tended to be much healthier and fertile in interior rather than in coastal locations, in hilly or mountainous territory rather than in lowland ecosystems. Second, crops shaped slave life in fundamental ways. In Jamaica, for instance, the death rate on sugar plantations was 50 percent higher than on coffee plantations; in Trinidad it was nearly three times as high on sugar as on cotton plantations; and in South Carolina a slave child on a rice plantation was almost half as likely to survive to maturity as a child elsewhere in the South. Finally, slavery was markedly different in urban, as opposed to, rural environments. In the Caribbean, somewhat counterintuitively, living in a town generally increased the chances of survival. The superior housing and clothing of urban slaves probably helped ward off diarrhea and dysentery, the great killers in the cramped plantation quarters. In North America, on the other hand, living in a city generally reduced a slave's chance of survival. The difference is largely explained by the far more thinly dispersed rural populations of the mainland as compared to the densely settled sugar plantations of most islands. Also, urban living in North America reduced a slave's chances of survival because of a limited diet due to a lack of access to garden plots and because working for wages reduced time for self-sufficient activities. Craft opportunities were much greater in towns than in the countryside, not only in number but in range, and the ability of a slave to hire his or her own time (and thereby earn money) was also greater in towns than in the countryside.[44]

The status of the master had enormous ramifications for slave life. Just as use of the term "servant class" to describe London's domestic servants gives a misleading impression of homogeneity, so slavery and the "slave class" were similarly differentiated. Perhaps the greatest distinction was between slaves living in the household of a small farmer and that of a large planter. Small planters generally provided their slaves less clothing and flimsier accommodations, although not necessarily less food, than most large planters. In fact, the subsistence priorities of many small planters often guaranteed more food to their slaves than those owned by commercially oriented large planters. The size of the plantation, as Robert Fogel has noted, was far more important than occupation in determining slave household structure. Mother-headed slave households were common on small plantations; two-parent-headed slave households and extended slave households were common on large plantations. Slave families were more stable, less subject to disruption, on large than on small plantations. To be poor in Africa was usually to be without relatives, to have no kin connections, to be solitary; for many slaves, particularly of course the African newcomer, the same condition applied, but for creoles in particular, especially those on large plantations, kinfolk were often present and families acted as a haven in a cruel world.[45]

Just as the status of the master varied, so did that of the slave, although within a much narrower range. Skilled slaves and domestics usually enjoyed more comforts than field hands, even than many poor whites. Slave artisans might wear collars and cuffs made from lace or other expensive materials, gold-laced hats, shoes with metal buckles, beaver hats, and superfine cloth coats. One carpenter was only somewhat more ostentatious than usual in flourishing a silver watch, silver shoe buckles, and a brown wig. Personal manservants were the best dressed slaves. One such waiting man cut a fine figure in his "blue Plush Breeches," "fine Cloth Pompadour Waistcoat," white shirt, neat shoes with silver buckles, and "fine Hat cut and cocked in the Macaroni Figure." Tradesmen generally experienced better nutrition and health than domestics and, to an even greater extent, field laborers. The death rate of field hands in the Caribbean was more than double those of privileged slaves. Slave ironworkers, in part because of the "overwork" system which allowed them to acquire cash or goods for surpassing daily or weekly production quotas, were able to purchase extra linen, clothing, bedding, and food to improve their quality of life. At one Chesapeake ironworks the ration was six pounds of meat a week; when a slave foreman at a nearby plantation heard the news he said he would flee his plantation unless sent to the foundry. An investigation of sixteen adult skeletons dating to the late eighteenth century from Catoctin Furnace in Maryland found not only that the men outlived the women but that male ironworkers outlived nineteenth-century plantation workers. The opportunity to travel was another benefit that came to privileged slaves. Boatmen and sailors, manservants, and tradesmen who hired their own time were the most widely traveled slaves. Probably the most common privilege of skilled slaves—a regular supply of alcohol—owed to the customary right enjoyed by English artisans. Finally, privileged slaves could often bequeath an inheritance, something not usually associated with slaves: they regularly transmitted their skills to their children. On some plantations a few slave families came to monopolize privileged positions.[46]

Nevertheless, occupational distinctions should not be exaggerated. On one Jamaican plantation studied in great detail, privileged slaves—drivers, carpen-

ters, coopers, masons, blacksmiths, and domestics—were more likely to be
sheltered under shingled than thatched roofs, but that was the extent of the
improvement in housing that their status brought. Houses on this plantation
were no bigger or better for slaves of mixed racial ancestry or for high status
workers than they were for field hands. Furthermore, the typical domestic and
many skilled slaves (for example, sawyers) often engaged in drudge labor,
sometimes in the fields. The work of a washerwoman was no more glamorous
than that of a field hand. Indeed, for women in general occupational differentiation was seriously limited. Skilled labor was generally considered to be
men's work. Removing men from the field meant that women composed the
greater portion of those remaining. By the early nineteenth century, Richard
Dunn found that a young man's chances of remaining a prime field hand on
Mesopotamia plantation, Jamaica, was one in two; for a young woman, it was
five in six. Occupational distinctions meant little to slave women.[47]

Finally, slavery varied in large part because slaves, like the white poor,
actively strove for the means of their own survival. Individual slaves worked
on their own time, hunted and gathered, fished, tended private gardens and,
in some cases, provision grounds, raised livestock, and hawked the products
of their labors. Some slaves were gifted healers, others renowned conjurors;
some were noted preachers, others celebrated musicians; some were jockeys,
others goldsmiths. Some traded in town markets, others stole from masters.
Slaves were not defenseless, mere victims of their impoverishment. Some
slaves acquired considerable cash and property. In late eighteenth-century
Jamaica, slaves held perhaps about a fifth of the coins circulating on the
island, although the average slave probably owned little more than a shilling.
A few slaves earned large sums for selling livestock or hiring their time. In the
1790s slaves typically carried goods worth ten to twelve shillings sterling when
they went to market. A small minority of slaves earned enough to buy their
freedom. Some slaves managed to accumulate substantial estates, at times
equivalent to those of moderately successful free artisans or farmers, and
some were able to bequeath those estates to their loved ones at death.[48]

Most of all, slaves, like the poor in both Europe and Africa, learned to survive;
they engaged in strategies, "a whole series of ploys and subterfuges," akin to
Olwen Hufton's classic portrayal of an "economy of makeshifts." For slaves, just
as for the English poor, "reciprocity and neighbourlines were crucial. Although
they lacked the real capital which enabled the better-off to weather difficult
times without outside help, the poor could and did accumulate 'social capital.'
By lending tools and possessions, and by offering physical and psychological
assistance to neighbors and kin in times of need, they invested in the future,
being able to draw on the resources of others." Families and kinfolk were just as

important for slaves as for the white poor. Just as the mother in a conventionally poor household taught her children how and where to beg, so the slave mother who often brought up her children alone was the dominant figure in their lives. For slaves too, just like the African poor, "by hawking or begging or stealing, by endurance or industry or guile, by the resourcefulness of the blind or the courage of the cripple, by the ambition of the young or the patience of the old—by all these means the African poor survived in their harsh world."[49]

It is easy to dismiss these variations in the experiences of slaves as trivial. The material conditions of slaves were so impoverished, it can be argued, that it is futile to draw distinctions among them. Moreover, the material conditions of slaves rested heavily on the fortunes, decisions, and whims of individual masters; and, in that sense, distinctions between the slaves may seem merely idiosyncratic and arbitrary. But significant variations in slave life did occur, and they were patterned, not random. Some improvements occurred over time; age, birthplace, and color determined occupational allocations; territorial distinctions mattered; crops profoundly shaped slave experiences; size of plantation counted; status in the slave hierarchy was consequential; and slaves, like poor whites, always strove both individually and collectively to shape their material state.

A major, perhaps the defining, experience of the conventional poor is their risk of dependency. Vulnerability, as Olwen Hufton notes, "was the main characteristic of the *pauvre*." The poor "lived under the constant threat" of "hunger, cold, pain, or physical deprivation." Life-cycle poverty was premised on insecurity. Thus a recently married couple with two or three young children could easily experience temporary poverty. Perhaps the wife was unable to work, the children too young to earn, the father ill equipped to bring in enough money to meet the increased expenses. Another period of life— advancing years—was often a stage to fear. Earnings could dry up, and lack of familial support might be unavailable. Ordinary everyday happenings like sickness or an increase in the price of basic foodstuffs could throw people on the margins of survival into poverty.[50]

Slaves faced all sorts of insecurities—about whether they might be sold, or whipped, or have to endure some fresh humiliation. Slaves were the dependent par excellence; the whim of a master determined a slave's fate. But the one compensation for such dependence was that a slave generally could expect a minimal subsistence. The master had an obvious and real incentive to see that the slave survived. The birth of a slave child would not strain a family budget— because the slave family had no budget. The conventional poor lived, as Hufton notes, "in a perpetual state of debt," but no slave suffered this fate. If a master had too many children among his slaves he might sell some of them—thereby making it tragically clear that no slave family could ever feel secure—but he would have every inducement to keep them alive. Some masters did try to evade the expense of feeding aging slaves by freeing them, but such an action was rare; growing old was not a stage of life slaves had especially to fear. Nor did sickness or debility, say following childbirth, generally mean a reduction in rations. The insecurity of staying alive—of having no food, no clothing, no roof over one's head—was the one vulnerability the condition of slavery minimized. In some cases, then, the material conditions of slaves were not always inferior to other temporarily unfree or even free laborers. Almost all slaves were *pauvre*, struggling continuously to keep body and soul together, but few of them were *indigent*, always hungry and in chronic need of the means of survival. Such a comparison may seem to come dangerously close to the racism of George Fitzhhugh, but I prefer to see it as closer to the clear-eyed vision of say, J. H. Plumb, who wrote, "Slavery and poverty [in the early modern period] are not different in kind but different in degree, and the disadvantage was not always the slave's for, as property, he might be treated with greater consideration in sickness or in old age than the wage slave."[51]

To say that slaves had some material benefits, that few were absolutely destitute, is not to say that their lot was somehow better than the white poor. In the nineteenth century, Irish famine deaths proved to some people that wage slavery caused greater horrors than chattel slavery. Frederick Douglass would have none of it: "The Irishman is poor," he noted, "but he is not a slave. He is still the master of his own body." The Irish could at least organize, remonstrate, and emigrate. American slavery, that "grand aggregation of human horrors," rendered its victims as mute as the "silent dead," echoing Orlando Patterson's depiction of slavery as social death. The escaped slave Harriet Jacobs added, "I would ten thousand times rather that my children should be the half-starved paupers of Ireland than to be the most pampered among the slaves of America." Slaves strove to throw off the chains of slavery even if freedom brought starvation and economic deprivation. Conversely, Frederick Douglass found no takers among white workers when he advertised the job vacancy, with all its alleged material comforts, created by his having fled slavery.[52]

## Notes

1. Paul Slack, *The English Poor Law, 1531–1782* (Basingstoke, Eng.: Macmillan, 1990), 12 (terminology); Orlando Patterson, *Slavery and Social Death: A Comparative Study* (Cambridge: Harvard University Press, 1982); Edmund S. Morgan, *American Slavery, American Freedom: The Ordeal of Colonial Virginia* (New York: W. W. Norton, 1975), 340–41, 385–86. For an altogether different

context, but interesting parallels, see Dharma Kumar, *Land and Caste in South India: Agricultural Labour in the Madras Presidency During the Nineteenth Century* (Cambridge: Cambridge University Press, 1965), 48 and passim. (I owe this reference and much else to Stanley L. Engerman.) For the purposes of this chapter, "America" is British America, encompassing mainland and islands.

2. Amartya Sen, *Poverty and Famines: An Essay on Entitlement and Deprivation* (Oxford: Clarendon Press, 1981), 9–23; Sen, *Development as Freedom* (New York: Alfred A. Knopf, 1999), 20 (quote), 87–110; "How to Define Poverty? Let Us Count the Ways," *New York Times*, May 26, 2001, A15, A17 (quote).

3. Hannah Arendt, *On Revolution* (New York: Viking Press, 1963), 66; Peter Lindert and Jeffrey Williamson, *American Inequality: A Macroeconomic History* (New York: Academic Press, 1980), 10–11, and, for an update, see Peter H. Lindert, "Three Centuries of Inequality in Britain and America," in Anthony B. Atkinson and François Bourguignon, eds., *Handbook of Income Distribution* (Amsterdam: Elsevier, 2000), 167–216; Gary Nash, essay in this volume. For the best summary of wealth estimates, drawing on the work of Jones and others, as well as a good summary of the debate between those who argue increasing inequality over time, such as Nash, and those, most notably Lindert and Williamson, who see stability at low levels, see John J. McCusker and Russell R. Menard, *The Economy of British America, 1607–1789* (Chapel Hill: University of North Carolina Press, 1985), 55–61 (quote from Jones on p. 55, and their own assessment on p. 59) and 258–76. For two superb articles that show the importance of including blacks in poverty estimates, see Carole Shammas, "A New Look at Long-Term Trends in Wealth Inequality in the United States," *American Historical Review* 98 (1993): 412–31 and Daniel Scott Smith, "Female Householding in Late Eighteenth-Century America and the Problem of Poverty," *Journal of Social History* 28 (1994): 83–107.

4. For comparisons of material conditions between slaves and the poor, largely in the nineteenth century, see most importantly, Robert William Fogel and Stanley L. Engerman, *Time on the Cross: The Economics of American Negro Slavery* (Boston: Little, Brown, 1974). See also Eric Vaughn Snow, "Who Was Better Off? The Standard of Living of American Slaves and English Farmworkers Compared, 1750–1875" (M.A. thesis, Michigan State University, 1997); J. H. Plumb, "Slavery, Race and the Poor" in *In the Light of History* (1972), repr. in *The American Experience: The Collected Essays of J. H. Plumb*, vol. 2 (Athens: University of Georgia Press, 1989), 135.

5. Paul Slack, *Poverty and Policy in Tudor and Stuart England* (London: Longman, 1988), 7; Stuart Woolf, *The Poor in Western Europe in the Eighteenth and Nineteenth Centuries* (London: Methuen, 1986), 2, 4–5 (quote), 50. See also Tom Arkell, "The Incidence of Poverty in England in the Later Seventeenth Century," *Social History* 12 (1987): 23–47; Steven King, *Poverty and Welfare in England, 1700–1850: A Regional Perspective* (Manchester: Manchester University Press, 2000), 78–87; Olwen Hufton, *The Poor of Eighteenth-Century France, 1750–1789* (Oxford: Clarendon Press, 1974), 2, 7. Poverty can be considered an absolute condition—as the minimum necessary to maintain a person's survival—but how to measure that minimum varies from society to society and over time. See John Iliffe, *The African Poor: A History* (Cambridge: Cambridge University Press, 1987), 1–2.

6. Billy G. Smith, "Poverty and Economic Marginality in Eighteenth-Century America," *Proceedings of the American Philosophical Society* 132, no. 1 (1988): 85–118, esp. 91, 96, 99–100, and his "Poverty," in *Encyclopedia of the North American Colonies*, ed. Jacob E. Cooke (New York: Scribner's, 1993), 1:483–93, esp. 489–91; Woolf, *Poor in Western Europe*, 6.

7. Willard Bliss, "The Rise of Tenancy in Virginia," *Virginia Magazine of History and Biography* 58 (1950): 427–41 (quote on p. 437); Gregory A. Stiverson, *Poverty in a Land of Plenty: Tenancy in Eighteenth-Century Maryland* (Baltimore: Johns Hopkins University Press, 1977), 13, 48, 57, 137, and passim; Lorena S. Walsh, "Land, Landlord, and Leaseholder: Estate Management and Tenant Fortunes in Southern Maryland, 1642–1820," *Agricultural History* 59 (1985): 373–96; Mary C. Jeske, "Autonomy and Opportunity: Carrollton Manor Tenants, 1734–1790" (Ph.D. diss., University of Maryland, 1999), and her "Prosperous Landholders: Carrollton Manor Tenants during the Era of the American Revolution" (unpub. paper, 2000); Steven Sarson, "Landlessness and

Tenancy in Early National Prince George's County, Maryland," *William and Mary Quarterly,* 3d ser., 57 (1999): 569–98; Lucy Simler, "Tenancy in Colonial Pennsylvania: The Case of Chester County," ibid., 3d ser., 43 (1986): 542–69; Sung Bok Kim, *Landlord and Tenant in Colonial New York: Manorial Society, 1664–1775* (Chapel Hill: University of North Carolina Press, 1978). See also Bernard Bailyn, *The Peopling of British North America: An Introduction* (New York: Alfred A. Knopf, 1986), 83–85, 157–59.

8. Douglas Lamar Jones, *Village and Seaport: Migration and Society in Eighteenth-Century Massachusetts* (Hanover, N.H.: University Press of New England, 1981); Esther L. Friend, "Notifications and Warnings Out: Strangers Taken into Wrentham, Massachusetts, between 1732 and 1812," *New England Historical and Genealogical Register* 141 (1987): 179–202, 330–57, and 142 (1988), 56–84; Steven Sarson, "Landlessness and Tenancy in Early National Prince George's County, Maryland," *William and Mary Quarterly,* 3d ser., 57 (1999): 569–98; Zachary Ryan Calo, "From Poor Relief to the Poorhouse: The Response to Poverty in Prince George's County, Maryland, 1710–1770," *Maryland Historical Magazine* 93 (1998): 393–427; Paul Clemens and Lucy Simler, "Rural Labor and the Farm Household in Chester County, Pennsylvania, 1750–1820," in *Work and Labor in Early America,* ed. Stephen Innes (Chapel Hill: University of North Carolina Press, 1988), 106–43; Lucy Simler, "The Landless Worker: An Index of Economic and Social Change in Chester County, Pennsylvania, 1750–1820," *Pennsylvania Magazine of History and Biography* 114 (1990): 163–99; Christine Daniels, "Gresham's Laws: Labor Management on an Early-Eighteenth-Century Chesapeake Plantation," *Journal of Southern History* 62 (1996): 205–38; Christine Daniels, "'Getting His [or Her] Livelyhood': Free Workers in Slave Anglo-America, 1675–1810," *Agricultural History* 71 (1997): 125–61 (quotes on pp. 143–44); Laurel Thatcher Ulrich, *A Midwife's Tale: The Life of Martha Ballard, Based on Her Diary, 1785–1812* (New York: Alfred A. Knopf, 1992), 80–82, 160–62; Daniel Vickers, *Farmers and Fishermen: Two Centuries of Work in Essex County, Massachusetts, 1630–1850* (Chapel Hill: University of North Carolina Press, 1994), 52–53, 241–42, 249–50, 302–3.

9. Claudio Saunt, "Taking Account of Property: Stratification among the Creek Indians in the Early Nineteenth Century," *William and Mary Quarterly,* 3d ser., 57 (2000): 733–60; Marshall Sahlins, *Stone Age Economics* (Chicago: Aldine, 1972), 1–39; Mary Black-Rogers, "Varieties of 'Starving': Semantics and Survival in the Subarctic Fur Trade, 1750–1850," *Ethnohistory* 33 (1986): 353–83.

10. On the integration of Indians into the colonial economy, a huge literature now exists. Selective examples include Arthur J. Ray, *Indians in the Fur Trade: Their Role as Trappers, Hunters, and Middlemen in the Lands Southwest of Hudson Bay, 1660–1870* (Toronto: University of Toronto Press, 1974); John A. Sainsbury, "Indian Labor in Early Rhode Island," *New England Quarterly* 48 (1975): 378–93; Ray and Donald B. Freeman, *"Give Us Good Measure": An Economic Analysis of Relations between the Indians and the Hudson's Bay Company Before 1763* (Toronto: University of Toronto Press, 1978); Ray, "Indians as Consumers in the Eighteenth Century" in Carol M. Judd and Arthur J. Ray, eds., *Old Trails and New Directions: Papers of the Third North American Fur Trade Conference* (Toronto: University of Toronto Press, 1980), 255–71; Christopher L. Miller and George R. Hammell, "A New Perspective on Indian-White Contact: Cultural Symbols and Colonial Trade," *Journal of American History* 73 (1986): 311–28; James Merrell, *The Indians' New World: Catawbas and Their Neighbors from European Contact through the Era of Removal* (Chapel Hill: University of North Carolina Press, 1989), 49–91; Daniel Richter, *Ordeal of the Longhouse: The Peoples of the Iroquois League in the Era of European Colonization* (Chapel Hill: University of North Carolina Press, 1992), 75–104; Ann M. Carlos and Frank D. Lewis, "Indians, the Beaver, and the Bay: The Economics of Depletion in the Lands of the Hudson's Bay Company, 1700–1763," *Journal of Economic History* 53 (1993): 465–94; Donna Keith Baron, J. Edward Hood, and Holly V. Izard, "They Were Here All Along: The Native American Presence in Lower Central New England in the Eighteenth and Nineteenth Centuries," *William and Mary Quarterly,* 3d ser., 53 (1996): 561–86; Daniel R. Mandell, *Behind the Frontier: Indians in Eighteenth-Century Eastern Massachusetts* (Lincoln: University of Nebraska Press, 1996); Jean M. O'Brien, *Dispossession by Degrees: Indian Land and Identity in*

*Natick, Massachusetts, 1650–1790* (Cambridge: Cambridge University Press, 1997), 133–38, 156–57, 189–213; Ruth Wallis Herndon and Ella Wilcox Sekatura, "The Right to a Name: The Narragansett People and Rhode Island Officials in the Revolutionary Era," *Ethnohistory* 44 (1997): 433–62; Peter C. Mancall and Thomas Weiss, "Was Economic Growth Likely in Colonial British North America?" *Journal of Economic History* 59 (1999): 17–40; Peter C. Mancall, Joshua Rosenbloom, and Thomas Weiss, "Measuring Indigenous Economies: Quantitative Estimates for the Carolinas and Georgia during the Eighteenth Century" (paper presented at American Historical Association meeting, 2001); Jean R. Soderlund, essay in this volume; on property claims, see David B. Guldenzopf, "The Colonial Transformation of Mohawk Iroquois Society" (Ph.D. diss., State University of New York at Albany, 1986) and Claudio Saunt, "Taking Account of Property," *William and Mary Quarterly*, 3d ser., 57 (2000): 733–60. For stratification of another Indian nation a little later in time, see William G. McLoughlin and Walter H. Conser Jr., "The Cherokees in Transition: A Statistical Analysis of the Federal Cherokee Census of 1835," *Journal of American History* 64 (1977): 678–703.

11. Daniel Scott Smith, "Female Householding in Late Eighteenth-Century America," *Journal of Social History* 28 (1994): 83–107; Gloria L. Main and Jackson T. Main, "The Red Queen in New England?" *William and Mary Quarterly*, 3d ser., 56 (1999): 135.

12. Philip D. Morgan, "Bound Labor: The British and Dutch Colonies," in *Encyclopedia of North American Colonies*, ed. Cooke, 2:17–32; Morgan, *American Slavery, American Freedom*, 106–7, 126–29, 216–18, 281–82, 311; Darrett B. Rutman and Anita H. Rutman, *A Place in Time: Middlesex County, Virginia, 1650–1750* (New York: W. W. Norton, 1984), 51–52, 72–75, 129–38, 175–76. See also Abbot Emerson Smith, *Colonists in Bondage: White Servitude and Convict Labor in America, 1607–1776* (Chapel Hill: University of North Carolina Press, 1946); David W. Galenson, *White Servitude in Colonial America: An Economic Analysis* (Cambridge: Cambridge University Press, 1981); Margaret M. R. Kellow, "Indentured Servitude in Eighteenth-Century Maryland," *Histoire Sociale-Social History* 17 (1984): 229–55; Sharon V. Salinger, *"To Serve Well and Faithfully": Labour and Indentured Servants in Pennsylvania, 1682–1800* (New York: Cambridge University Press, 1987); Hilary McD. Beckles, *White Servitude and Black Slavery in Barbados, 1627–1715* (Knoxville: University of Tennessee Press, 1989), who exaggerates the similarities between indentured servitude and slavery; for more accurate analyses, see David Eltis, *The Rise of African Slavery in the Americas* (Cambridge: Cambridge University Press, 2000), esp. chaps. 2–3 and M. L. Bush, *Servitude in Modern Times* (Cambridge: Polity Press, 2000), 28–38, 57–68. For an impressive, downward revision of the number of indentured servants in British America (although the essay treats only the mainland), see Christopher Tomlins, "Reconsidering Indentured Servitude: European Migration and the Early American Labor Force, 1600–1775," *Labor History* 42 (2001): 5–43.

13. In addition to n12, see Christine Daniels, "'Liberty to Complaine': Servant Petitions in Maryland, 1652–1797," in Christopher L. Tomlins and Bruce H. Mann, eds., *The Many Legalities of Early America* (Chapel Hill: University of North Carolina Press, 2001), 219–49; Russell R. Menard, "From Servant to Freeholder: Status Mobility and Property Accumulation in Seventeenth-Century Maryland," *William and Mary Quarterly*, 3d ser., 30 (1973): 37–64; Lois Green Carr and Russell Menard, "Immigration and Opportunity: The Freedman in Early Colonial Maryland," in Thad Tate and David Ammerman, eds., *The Chesapeake in the Seventeenth Century: Essays on Anglo-American Society and Politics* (Chapel Hill: University of North Carolina Press, 1979), 206–42; Lorena Walsh, "Staying Put or Getting Out: Findings for Charles County, Maryland, 1650–1720," *William and Mary Quarterly*, 3d ser., 44 (1987): 89–103; Bernard Bailyn, *Voyagers to the West: A Passage in the Peopling of America on the Eve of the Revolution* (New York: Alfred A. Knopf, 1986), 172–73; Barbara DeWolfe, ed., *Discoveries of America: Personal Accounts of British Emigrants to North America during the Revolutionary Era* (Cambridge: Cambridge University Press, 1997), 149–58; and for a recent summary of the literature, see Sharon V. Salinger, "Labor, Markets, and Opportunity: Indentured Servitude in Early America," *Labor History* 38 (1997): 311–38; cf. Farley Grubb, "Labor, Markets, and Opportunity: Indentured Servitude in Early America, a Rejoinder to Salinger," *Labor History* 39 (1998): 235–41.

14. Farley Grubb, "Redemptioner Immigration to Pennsylvania: Evidence on Contract Service and Profitability," *Journal of Economic History* 46 (1986): 407–18 and his "The Auction of Redemptioner Servants, Philadelphia, 1771–1804: An Economic Analysis," ibid. 48 (1988): 583–603; Richard B. Morris, *Government and Labor in Early America* (New York: Columbia University Press, 1946), 310–23, 345–63; Christine Daniels, "'Without Any Limitation of Time': Debt Servitude in Colonial America," *Labor History* 36 (1995): 232–50; Daniel Vickers, "The First Whalemen of Nantucket," *William and Mary Quarterly*, 3d ser., 40 (1983): 560–83 and his "Nantucket Whalemen in the Deep-Sea Fishery: The Changing Anatomy of an Early American Labor Force," *Journal of American History* 62 (1985): 277–96. See also Arnold Bauer, "Rural Workers in Spanish America: Problems of Peonage and Oppression," *Hispanic American Historical Review* 59 (1979): 34–63.

15. A. Roger Ekirch, *Bound for America: The Transportation of British Convicts to the Colonies, 1718–1775* (Oxford: Clarendon Press, 1987), 27, 59–60, 63, 86, 87, 92, 99–100, 120, 122–23, 125, 129, 147–56, 177–85; Bailyn, *Voyagers to the West*, 261–64, 292–95, 314–25, 334, 346; Farley Grubb, "The Transatlantic Market for British Convict Labor," *Journal of Economic History* 60 (2000): 94–122; Eltis, *Rise of African Slavery*, 73–74.

16. Jackson Turner Main, *Society and Economy in Colonial Connecticut* (Princeton: Princeton University Press, 1985), 151; Hector St. John de Crevecoeur, *Letters from an American Farmer and Sketches of Eighteenth-Century America*, ed. Albert J. Stone (New York: Penguin, 1981), 67; Allan Kulikoff, *From British Peasants to Colonial American Farmers* (Chapel Hill: University of North Carolina Press, 2000), 3, 127–63.

17. The generally accepted proportion of slaves who were literate is about 5 percent, although this estimate is pure guesswork. For a recent estimate of literacy among one region's poor, showing marked differences along gender, wealth, and particularly racial lines, see Ruth Wallis Herndon, "Research Note: Literacy Among New England's Transient Poor, 1750–1800," *Journal of Social History* 29 (1996): 963–65.

18. Henry A. Gemery, "The White Population of the Colonial United States, 1607–1790," in Michael R. Haines and Richard H. Steckel, eds., *A Population History of North America* (Cambridge: Cambridge University Press, 2000), 143–90, esp. 149; Lorena S. Walsh, "The African American Population of the Colonial United States," in ibid., 191–240; Robert William Fogel, *The Fourth Great Awakening and the Future of Egalitarianism* (Chicago: University of Chicago Press, 2000), 141; E. A. Wrigley and R. S. Schofield, *The Population History of England 1541–1871* (Cambridge: Cambridge University Press, 1981), 208–9.

19. Raymond L. Cohn, "Maritime Mortality in the Eighteenth and Nineteenth Centuries: A Survey," *International Journal of Maritime History* 1 (1989): 159–91; Robin Haines, Ralph Shlomowitz, and Lance Brennan, "Maritime Mortality Revisited," ibid. 8 (1996): 133–72; Ralph Shlomowitz, Lance Brennan, and John McDonald, *Mortality and Migration in the Modern World* (Aldershot, Eng.: Variorum, 1996); Herbert S. Klein and Stanley L. Engerman, "Long-Term Trends in African Mortality in the Transatlantic Slave Trade," *Slavery and Abolition* 18, no. 1 (1997): 36–48; Stephen D. Behrendt, "Crew Mortality in the Transatlantic Slave Trade in the Eighteenth Century," ibid., 49–71; Stanley L. Engerman, Robin Haines, Herbert S. Klein, and Ralph Shlomowitz, "Transoceanic Mortality: The Slave Trade in Comparative Perspective," *William and Mary Quarterly*, 3d ser., 58 (2001): 93–117; Eltis, *Rise of African Slavery*, 78, 116–28, 156–58. The one exception regarding crowding is, for a brief period, in the German redemptioner trade; see Marianne S. Wokeck, *Trade in Strangers: The Beginnings of Mass Migration to North America* (University Park: The Pennsylvania State University Press, 1999), 79. Roger Ekirch found that slave ships entering Maryland were three times as crowded as convict ships (180 slaves versus 60 convicts per 100 tons): *Bound for America*, 100.

20. Philip D. Morgan, *Slave Counterpoint: Black Culture in the Eighteenth-Century Chesapeake and Lowcountry* (Chapel Hill: University of North Carolina Press, 1998), 81, 84; Susan E. Klepp, "Seasoning and Society: Racial Differences in Mortality in Eighteenth-Century Philadelphia," *William and Mary Quarterly*, 3d ser., 51 (1994): 473–506; Richard H. Steckel, "Nutritional Status in the Colonial American Economy," ibid., 3d ser., 56 (1999): 44; Lois Green Carr and Lorena

S. Walsh, "Changing Lifestyles and Consumer Behavior in the Colonial Chesapeake," in Cary Carson, Ronald Hoffman, and Peter J. Albert, eds., *Of Consuming Interests: The Style of Life in the Eighteenth Century* (Charlottesville: University Press of Virginia, 1994), 60.

21. Stanley L. Engerman and B. W. Higman, "The Demographic Structure of the Caribbean Slave Societies in the Eighteenth and Nineteenth Centuries," in *UNESCO General History of the Caribbean*, ed. Franklin W. Knight, vol. 3, *The Slave Societies of the Caribbean* (London: Macmillan, 1997), 45–104; J. R. Ward, *British West Indian Slavery, 1750–1834: The Process of Amelioration* (Oxford: Clarendon Press, 1988), 23–24, 119–89; B. W. Higman, *Slave Populations of the British Caribbean, 1807–1834* (Baltimore: Johns Hopkins University Press, 1984), 303–78; Richard B. Sheridan, "The Crisis of Slave Subsistence in the British West Indies during and after the American Revolution," *William and Mary Quarterly*, 3d ser., 33 (1976): 615–41.

22. Hufton, *Poor of Eighteenth-Century France*, 46; Morgan, *Slave Counterpoint*, 134–35; Ward, *British West Indian Slavery*, 18–29, 105–18; Higman, *Slave Populations*, 205–10. For a good summary of nutrition among the European poor, see Robert Jutte, *Poverty and Deviance in Early Modern Europe* (Cambridge: Cambridge University Press, 1994), 72–78; for the diet of the urban laborer in North America, see Billy G. Smith, *The "Lower Sort": Philadelphia's Laboring People, 1750–1800* (Ithaca: Cornell University Press, 1990), 95–103; for the late eighteenth and early nineteenth centuries, see Lorena S. Walsh, "Consumer Behavior, Diet, and the Standard of Living in Late Colonial and Early Antebellum America, 1770–1840," in *American Economic Growth and Standards of Living before the Civil War*, ed. Robert E. Gallman and John Joseph Wallis (Chicago: University of Chicago Press, 1992), 217–61. See also Carole Shammas, "The Eighteenth-Century English Diet and Economic Change," *Explorations in Economic History* 21 (1984): 254–69 and *The Pre-Industrial Consumer in England and America* (Oxford: Clarendon Press, 1990), 121–56. In eighteenth-century rural France, 95 percent or more of the poor's diet was cereal—perhaps a larger proportion than the diet of some slaves.

23. Morgan, *Slave Counterpoint*, 136–40, 143; Henry Miller, "An Archaeological Perspective on the Evolution of Diet in the Colonial Chesapeake, 1620–1745," in *Colonial Chesapeake Society*, ed. Lois Carr, Philip D. Morgan, and Jean Russo (Chapel Hill: University of North Carolina Press, 1988), 176–99; Joanne Bowen, "Foodways in the Eighteenth-Century Chesapeake," in *The Archaeology of Eighteenth-Century Virginia*, ed. Theodore R. Reinhart (Richmond: Archaeological Society of Virginia, 1996), 87–130, Higman, *Slave Populations*, 217–18; B. W. Higman, *Montpelier Jamaica: A Plantation Community in Slavery and Freedom 1739–1912* (Kingston, Jamaica: University Press of the West Indies, 1998), 208; Kenneth F. Kiple, *The Caribbean Slave: A Biological History* (Cambridge: Cambridge University Press, 1984), 89–103; Richard H. Steckel, Paul W. Sciulli, and Jerome C. Rose, "Skeletal Remains, Health, and History: A Project on Long Term Trends in the Western Hemisphere" in *The Biological Standard of Living in Comparative Perspective: Contributions to the Conference Held in Munich January 18–22, 1997, for the XIIth Congress of the International Economic History Association*, ed. John Komlos and Joerg Baten (Stuttgart: F. Steiner, 1998), 139–54, esp. 150; Hufton, *Poor of Eighteenth-Century France*, 46.

24. Robert Dirks, "Resource Fluctuations and Competitive Transformations in West Indian Slave Societies," in *Extinction and Survival in Human Populations*, ed. Charles D. Laughlin and Ivan A. Brady (New York: Columbia University Press, 1978), 122–80; Kiple, *Caribbean Slave*, 76–88; Klepp, "Seasoning and Society," 481–85. In the nineteenth century, the daily energy intake of adult slaves is said to be "probably in the neighborhood of 2,500 to 3,000 calories": Robert William Fogel, *Without Consent or Contract: The Rise and Fall of American Slavery* (New York: W. W. Norton, 1989), 132. See also Jutte, *Poverty and Deviance*, 77, and Hans-Joachim Voth, *Time and Work in England, 1750–1830* (Oxford: Clarendon Press, 2000), 162–71.

25. Steckel, "Nutritional Status in the Colonial American Economy," *William and Mary Quarterly*, 3d ser., 56 (1999): 31–52; Kenneth L. Sokoloff and Georgia C. Villaflor, "The Early Achievement of Modern Stature in America," *Social Science History* 6 (1982): 453–81; Steckel, "Stature and Living Standards in the United States," in *American Economic Growth and Standards of Living*, ed. Gallman and Wallis, 265–308; Fogel, *Fourth Great Awakening*, 140–41. See also John Komlos,

"A Malthusian Episode Revisited: The Height of British and Irish Servants in Colonial America,"
*Economic History Review* 46 (1993): 768–82; Farley Grubb, "Withering Heights: Did Indentured
Servants Shrink from an Encounter with Malthus? A Comment on Komlos," ibid. 52 (1999):
714–29; John Komlos, "On the Nature of the Malthusian Threat in the Eighteenth Century,"
ibid. 52 (1999): 730–48; and Farley Grubb, "Lilliputians and Brobdingnagians, Stature in British
Colonial America: Evidence from Servants, Convicts, and Apprentices," *Research in Economic History* 19 (1999): 139–203.

26. David Eltis, "Nutritional Standards in Africa and the Americas: Heights of Africans,
1819–1839," *Journal of Interdisciplinary History* 12 (1982): 453–75; Robert A. Margo and Richard
H. Steckel, "The Heights of American Slaves: New Evidence on Slave Nutrition and Health,"
*Social Science History* 6 (1982): 516–38, esp. 521; Gerald C. Friedman, "The Heights of Slaves in
Trinidad," ibid. 6 (1982): 482–515; Higman, *Slave Populations,* 280–93; Richard H. Steckel, "A
Peculiar Population: The Nutrition, Health, and Mortality of American Slaves from Childhood
to Maturity," *Journal of Economic History* 46 (1986): 721–42; Fogel, *Without Consent or Contract,*
138–47; Steckel, "Work, Disease, and Diet in the Health and Mortality of American Slaves," in
Robert W. Fogel and Stanley L. Engerman, eds., *Without Consent or Contract: Technical Papers*
vol. *11,* vol. 4 (New York: W. W. Norton, 1992), 489–507; David Eltis, "Welfare Trends among the
Yoruba in the Early Nineteenth Century: The Anthropometric Evidence," *Journal of Economic History* 50 (1990): 521–40; John Komlos, "The Height of Runaway Slaves in Colonial America,
1720–1770," in *Stature, Living Standards, and Economic Development: Essays in Anthropometric History,*
ed. Komlos (Chicago: University of Chicago Press, 1994), 93–116, also included in his *The Biological Standard of Living in Europe and America, 1700–1900* (Aldershot, Eng.: Variorum, 1995), in
which also see his "Toward an Anthropometric History of African-Americans: The Case of the
Free Blacks in Antebellum Maryland"; Philip R. P. Coelho and Robert A. McGuire, "Diets Versus
Diseases: The Anthropometrics of Slave Children," *Journal of Economic History* 60 (2000): 232–46,
and Richard H. Steckel, "Diets Versus Diseases in the Anthropometrics of Slave Children: A
Reply," ibid., 247–59. See also more generally, Roderick Floud, "Anthropometric Measures of
Nutritional Status in Industrialized Societies: Europe and North America since 1750," in *Nutrition and Poverty,* ed. S. R. Osmani (Oxford: Clarendon Press, 1992), 219–41, esp. 231, 237.

27. Higman, *Slave Populations,* 261–302, 376; Ward, *British West Indian Slavery,* 160–65,
184–85, 207; Richard B. Sheridan, *Doctors and Slaves: A Medical and Demographic History of Slavery
in the British West Indies, 1680–1834* (New York: Cambridge University Press, 1985); Morgan,
*Slave Counterpoint,* 321–25.

28. Beverly Lemire, *Dress, Culture and Commerce: The English Clothing Trade before the Factory,
1660–1800* (Basingstoke, Eng.: Macmillan, 1997), 34; Morgan, *Slave Counterpoint,* 125–33; Linda
Baumgarten, "Plains, Plaid and Cotton: Woolens for Slave Clothing," *Ars Textrina* 15 (1991):
203–21; Robert A. Brock, ed., *The Official Letters of Alexander Spotswood* (Richmond: Virginia Historical Society, 1882), 1:72 (I am grateful to Linda Baumgarten for this reference); Ward, *British
West Indian Slavery,* 151–53; Higman, *Montpelier,* 229–37; Linda R. Baumgarten, "Common Dress:
Clothing for Daily Life," MS (again I am most grateful to the author for allowing me to see this
important work); Linda R. Baumgarten, "Leather Stockings and Hunting Shirts," in *American
Material Culture: The Shape of the Field,* ed. Ann Smart Martin and J. Ritchie Garrison (Winterthur,
Del.: Henry Francis du Pont Winterthur Museum, 1997), 251–76, esp. 266; Ekirch, *Bound for
America,* 149. For clothing among the European poor, see Jutte, *Poverty and Deviance,* 78–82, and
John Styles, "Clothing the North: The Supply of Non-Elite Clothing in the Eighteenth-Century
North of England," *Textile History* 25 (1994): 139–66.

29. Morgan, *Slave Counterpoint,* 128–29, 130, 132–33, 598–601; Baumgarten, "Common
Dress"; Helen Bradley Griebel, "The West African Origin of the African-American Headwrap," in
*Dress and Ethnicity: Change Across Space and Time,* ed. Joanne B. Eicher (Oxford: Berg, 1995),
207–226; Ward, *British West Indian Slavery,* 152, 210; Higman, *Slave Populations,* 223–25, 257.

30. Karin Calvert, "The Function of Fashion in Eighteenth-Century America," in Carson et
al., eds., *Of Consuming Interests,* 257, and Cary Carson, "The Consumer Revolution in Colonial

British America: Why Demand?" ibid., 551; Timothy J. Shannon, "Dressing for Success on the Mohawk Frontier: Hendrick, William Johnson, and the Indian Fashion," *William and Mary Quarterly*, 3d ser., 53 (1996): 14; Douglas Hall, *In Miserable Slavery: Thomas Thistlewood in Jamaica, 1750–1786* (London: Macmillan, 1989), 17; "Management of Slaves, 1672," *Virginia Magazine of History and Biography* 7 (1899–1900): 314; Morgan, *Slave Counterpoint*, 601–2. See also Shane White and Graham White, "Slave Clothing and African-American Culture in the Eighteenth and Nineteenth Centuries," *Past and Present* 148 (August 1995): 149–86.

31. Edward A. Chappell, "Housing a Nation: The Transformation of Living Standards in Early America," in *Of Consuming Interests*, ed. Carson et al., 167–232, esp. 169, 175–76, 181, 206–7, 210; Kulikoff, *British Peasants to Colonial American Farmers*, 121–22; James Horn, *Adapting to a New World: English Society in the Seventeenth-Century Chesapeake* (Chapel Hill: University of North Carolina Press, 1994), 296–333; Lee Soltow, *Distribution of Wealth and Income in the United States in 1798* (Pittsburgh: University of Pittsburgh Press, 1989), 49–93. For the best European information, see Jutte, *Poverty and Deviance*, 62–71, and Shammas, *Pre-Industrial Consumer*, 157–93.

32. Bernard L. Herman, "Slave and Servant Housing in Charleston, 1770–1820," *Historical Archaeology* 33 (1999): 88–101; Morgan, *Slave Counterpoint*, 107–8, 110–12; Chappell, "Housing a Nation," in *Of Consuming Interests*, ed. Carson et al., 191–92; Stiverson, *Poverty in a Land of Plenty*, 56–84; Higman, *Montpelier*, 152, 176; Higman, *Slave Populations*, 218–23; Douglas V. Armstrong and Kenneth G. Kelly, "Settlement Patterns and the Origins of African Jamaican Society: Seville Plantation, St. Ann's Bay, Jamaica," *Ethnohistory* 47 (2000): 369–97; Mancall and Weiss, "Was Economic Growth Likely in Colonial British North America?" *Journal of Economic History* 59 (1999): 23. Thomas Jefferson expected that free workers would demand both more space and more independent access to it than slaves: Fraser Neiman, "Modeling Social Dynamics in Colonial and Antebellum Slave Architecture: Monticello in Historical Perspective" (unpub. paper, 1998), which also reports the Spotsylvania County data. Of the European poor, Jutte notes that "the cottages in which the day-labourers, cottagers and paupers lived were usually single-roomed, with an earth floor, mud walls, a thatched roof, a hole in the wall for a window and another for smoke to escape from the open hearth"—not all that dissimilar from the accommodation of slaves (Jutte, *Poverty and Deviance*, 68).

33. Carr and Walsh, "Changing Lifestyles and Consumer Behavior," in *Of Consuming Interests*, ed. Carson et al., 63; Carson, "The Consumer Revolution in Colonial British America," ibid., 498, 598; Morgan, *Slave Counterpoint*, 121–22; cf. Hufton, *Poor in Eighteenth-Century France*, 50.

34. Carl Bridenbaugh, ed., *Gentleman's Progress: The Itinerarium of Dr. Alexander Hamilton, 1744* (Chapel Hill: University of North Carolina Press, 1948), 54–55, as cited in Ronald Hoffman's preface in *Of Consuming Interests*, ed. Carson et al., viii; Carr and Walsh, "Changing Lifestyles and Consumer Behavior," ibid., 67, 80–81, 145; T. H. Breen, "'Baubles of Britain': The American and Consumer Revolutions of the Eighteenth Century," ibid., 457; Carson, "The Consumer Revolution in Colonial British America," ibid., 617. See also Lorna Weatherill, *Consumer Behaviour and Material Culture in Britain, 1660–1760* (London: Routledge, 1988); Shammas, *Pre-Industrial Consumer*; John Brewer and Roy Porter, eds., *Consumption and the World of Goods* (London: Routledge, 1993); Peter King, "Pauper Inventories and the Material Lives of the Poor in the Eighteenth and Early Nineteenth Centuries" in *Chronicling Poverty: The Voices and Strategies of the English Poor, 1640–1840*, ed. Tim Hitchcock, Peter King, and Pamela Sharpe (Basingstoke, Eng.: Macmillan, 1997), 155–91.

35. Morgan, *Slave Counterpoint*, 104–24; Higman, *Montpelier*, 146–90, 238–40.

36. Fogel, *Fourth Great Awakening*, 11, 42, 75–77, 185–86; Voth, *Time and Work in England*, 121–30; Edmund S. Morgan, "Slavery and Freedom: The American Paradox," *Journal of American History* 59 (1972): 26–27; Eltis, *Rise of African Slavery*, 85–113; Robert M. Schwartz, *Policing the Poor in Eighteenth-Century France* (Chapel Hill: University of North Carolina Press, 1988), 109; Higman, *Slave Populations*, 188; Fogel, *Without Consent or Contract*, 28, 52–54, 77–78; Hugh Cunningham, "The Employment and Unemployment of Children in England, c. 1680–1851," *Past and Present* 126 (1990): 115–50. For some general comparisons, free northern farmers averaged

about 3,200 hours per year, factory workers in early nineteenth-century Britain 2,900, and the modern U.S. worker about 1,700 (1,600 in Germany and 1,400 in Sweden).

37. Fogel, *Without Consent or Contract*, 78–79; Beckles, *White Servitude and Black Slavery*, 115–67; Morgan, *Slave Counterpoint*, 147–59, 164–70, 175–78; Ekirch, *Bound for America*, 152, 156; Wayne K. Durrill, "Routine of Seasons: Labour Regimes and Social Ritual in an Antebellum Plantation Community," *Slavery and Abolition* 16 (1995): 161–87; Lorena Walsh, "Slave Life, Slave Society, and Tobacco Production in the Tidewater Chesapeake, 1620–1820," in *Cultivation and Culture: Labor and the Shaping of Slave Life in the Americas,* ed. Ira Berlin and Philip D. Morgan (Charlottesville: University Press of Virginia, 1993), 176–77; John Bezi-Selfa, "Slavery and the Disciplining of Free Labor in the Colonial Mid-Atlantic Iron Industry," *Pennsylvania History* 64, special supplemental issue (summer 1997): 270–86; idem, "A Tale of Two Ironworks: Slavery, Free Labor, Work, and Resistance in the Early Republic," *William and Mary Quarterly*, 3d ser., 56 (1999): 677–700; idem, "American Crucible: Adventurers, Ironworkers, and the Struggle to Forge an Industrious Revolution, 1640–1830," chap. 3 (MS). I am grateful to Mr. Bezi-Selfa for sharing this chapter with me.

38. Higman, *Slave Populations*, 202–4; Ward, *British West Indian Slavery*, 112, 200–202; Morgan, *Slave Counterpoint*, 195, 359–66, 373–76; Betty Wood, "'Never on a Sunday?' Slavery and the Sabbath in Lowcountry Georgia 1750–1830," in *From Chattel Slaves to Wage Slaves: The Dynamics of Labour Bargaining in the Americas*, ed. Mary Turner (Bloomington: University of Indiana Press, 1995), 79–96; Fogel, *Without Consent or Contract*, 191–94, 392; Philip D. Morgan, "Task and Gang Systems: The Organization of Labor on New World Plantations," in *Work and Labor*, ed. Innes, 189–220; for ironworks, see n33 and Charles B. Dew, *Bond of Iron: Master and Slave at Buffalo Forge* (New York: W. W. Norton, 1994), 108–21, 155–56, 162–63; O. Nigel Bolland, "Proto-Proletarians? Slave Wages in the Americas: Between Slave Labour and Free Labour," in *From Chattel Slaves to Wage Slaves*, ed. Turner, 123–47.

39. Parkinson, *A Tour in America, in 1798, 1799, and 1800 . . .* , 2 vols. (London: J. Harding, 1805), 1:27; Ward, *British West Indian Slavery*, 263, 286–88.

40. On slaves' propensity to act individually, see Peter Kolchin, *Unfree Labor: American Slavery and Russian Serfdom* (Cambridge: Harvard University Press, 1987), esp. 257–301.

41. Morgan, *Slave Counterpoint*, 102–254; Barbara J. Heath, *Hidden Lives: The Archaeology of Slave Life at Thomas Jefferson's Poplar Forest* (Charlottesville: University Press of Virginia, 1999), 63–64; Fraser Neiman, "Sub-Floor Pits and Slavery in Eighteenth and Early Nineteenth Century Virginia" (unpub. paper, 1997); Ward, *British West Indian Slavery*, 72, 82, 88.

42. Morgan, *Slave Counterpoint*, 443–59; Ward, *British West Indian Slavery*, 18, 110–11; Higman, *Slave Populations*, 189–99.

43. Higman, *Montpelier*, 249–57; Morgan, *Slave Counterpoint*, 463–64, 594–609; Barbara J. Heath, "Buttons, Beads, and Buckles: Contextualizing Adornment Within the Bounds of Slavery," in Maria Franklin and Garrett Fesler, eds., *Historical Archaeology, Identity Formation, and the Interpretation of Ethnicity* (Williamsburg, Va.: Colonial Williamsburg Research Publications, 1999), 47–69; Fogel, *Without Consent or Contract*, 48; David P. Geggus, "Sugar and Coffee Cultivation in Saint Domingue and the Shaping of the Slave Labor Force," in *Cultivation and Culture*, ed. Berlin and Morgan, 73–98; Higman, *Slave Populations*, 194–97; Lucia Stanton, "'Those Who Labor for My Happiness': Thomas Jefferson and His Slaves," in *Jeffersonian Legacies*, ed. Peter S. Onuf (Charlottesville: University Press of Virginia, 1993), 151.

44. Fogel, *Without Consent or Contract*, 127; William Dusinberre, *Them Dark Days: Slavery in the American Rice Swamps* (New York: Oxford University Press, 1996), 80, 412; Higman, *Slave Populations*, 376; Klepp, "Seasoning and Society," 473–506; Morgan, *Slave Counterpoint*, 229.

45. Tim Meldrum, "London Domestic Servants from Depositional Evidence, 1660–1750: Servant-Employer Sexuality in the Patriarchal Household," in *Chronicling Poverty*, ed. Hitchcock, 49; Fogel, *Without Consent or Contract*, 178–79, 182; Iliffe, *African Poor*, 7, 33–35, 54, 57, 59, 63, 72, 76, 85–87; Morgan, *Slave Counterpoint*, 498–558.

46. Morgan, *Slave Counterpoint*, 131, 136, 246, 347, 545–46; Higman, *Slave Populations*, 245–46, 288–89, 333–35, 345–47; S. Max Edelson, "Affiliation without Affinity: Skilled Slaves in Eighteenth-Century South Carolina," in *Money, Trade, and Power: The Evolution of South Carolina's Plantation Society*, ed. Jack P. Greene, Rosemary Brana-Shute, and Randy J. Sparks (Columbia: University of South Carolina Press, 2001), 221–59.

47. Higman, *Montpelier*, 180–81; Morgan, *Slave Counterpoint*, 244–53; Richard S. Dunn, "Sugar Production and Slave Women in Jamaica," in *Cultivation and Culture*, ed. Berlin and Morgan, 49–72.

48. Higman, *Montpelier*, 243; Morgan, *Slave Counterpoint*, 358–76, 469–70, 537–38; Berlin and Morgan, eds., *Cultivation and Culture*, 31, 35, 37; Larry E. Hudson, ed., *Working Toward Freedom: Slave Society and Domestic Economy in the American South* (Rochester, N.Y.: University of Rochester Press, 1994); Betty Wood, *Women's Work, Men's Work: The Informal Slave Economies of Lowcountry Georgia* (Athens: University of Georgia Press, 1995).

49. Hufton, *Poor of Eighteenth-Century France*, 7, 69–127; Hitchcock, *Chronicling Poverty*, 12; Iliffe, *African Poor*, 8. See also Jutte, *Poverty and Deviance*, 83–99, 143–57, and Marco H. D. van Leeuwen, "Logic of Charity: Poor Relief in Preindustrial Europe," *Journal of Interdisciplinary History* 24 (1994): 589–613.

50. Hufton, *Poor of Eighteenth-Century France*, 20. See also Mary E. Fissell, *Patients, Power, and the Poor in Eighteenth-Century Bristol* (Cambridge: Cambridge University Press, 1991), 3.

51. Iliffe, *African Poor*, 2; Hufton, *Poor of Eighteenth-Century France*, 20; Plumb, "Slavery, Race and the Poor," 139.

52. David Roediger, "Race, Labor, and Gender in the Languages of Antebellum Social Protest," in *Terms of Labor: Slavery, Serfdom, and Free Labor*, ed. Stanley L. Engerman (Stanford: Stanford University Press, 1999), 175, 177.

# PART TWO    *Poor Relief*

# "Who Died an Expence to This Town"

*Poor Relief in Eighteenth-Century Rhode Island*

RUTH WALLIS HERNDON

As Gary Nash points out in his essay in this volume, scholars have studied poverty and various systems of poor relief in early America, especially in the urban centers, but the limitations of the records have frustrated their efforts to paint a portrait of the poor.[1] In this essay I will endeavor to sketch a human face on both the recipients and the administrators of poor relief in one British North American colony during the latter half of the eighteenth century. My argument is fourfold: that the enterprise of poor relief involved the entire community; that the familial and face-to-face nature of community relationships gave the poor some latitude in designing their own relief; that women, especially women of color, were less likely than men to receive direct assistance; and that the stresses of the revolutionary era produced both more occasion for relief and experimentation with new methods of providing relief.

A typical occasion for relief was recorded in May 1798, when the town leaders of Charlestown, Rhode Island, voted to reimburse Jack Paul for "nursing, bording, and necessaries furnished Margaret Clark in her last sickness, and funeral expences included." Margaret Clark had never previously been the object of official concern and she never would again. The clerk described her only as "a black woman belongin to this town who died an expence to this town."[2] This fleeting mention of the death of one poverty-stricken woman illustrates many of the salient aspects of poor relief in eighteenth-century Rhode Island. Margaret Clark did not die alone; she was tended in Jack Paul's household. Although the town treasury covered the costs of her daily maintenance and medical care, the money did not go to an institution but to an individual householder who had worked out an agreement with the leaders

of the town. It was not mere chance that Margaret Clark received such meager assistance in her "last sickness"; it was usual for women of color to be
relieved only when they were mortally ill and when a grave digger could be
foreseen as the last person to provide them care. Finally, although Margaret
Clark was supported in 1798 much as she would have been in 1748, a change
was underway. In the postwar depression of the 1780s, officials in Charlestown
(as elsewhere in Rhode Island) felt overwhelmed by the human need within
their jurisdiction and sought new ways to meet that need, first admonishing
the neighboring Narragansett Indian tribal council to "maintain their poor"
who were residing in Charlestown and then issuing a blanket order for "all
idle persons belonging to this Town and those that are supported by said
Town" to be bound out "to labor."[3] Although Charlestown did not resort temporarily to a poorhouse (as did all the surrounding communities), belea-
guered officials in this rural, sparsely populated town still had cause to find
new ways of alleviating the poverty within their borders.

The following analysis of poor relief in eighteenth-century Rhode Island
contributes to a better understanding of early American poverty and poor
relief. First, it details exactly how those in need came to the attention of town
officials, how those officials made their decisions to relieve need in a particular way, and how the poor themselves participated in shaping their own relief.
Second, it analyzes an entire region, considering the administration of poor
relief in both commercial and agrarian areas simultaneously. Third, it analyzes the factors of gender and race and their connection to poverty. While
previous studies have significantly illuminated the emerging mechanisms and
institutions of relief in cities like Boston, Philadelphia, and New York,[4] I focus
on the particular people who engaged in daily exchanges of welfare in both
agrarian and commercial Rhode Island communities, bringing the very
human faces of poor relief in early America into our historical vision.

New Englanders did not invent poor relief. They inherited it, along with the
rest of English law. Parliamentary legislation during the seventeenth and
eighteenth centuries (referred to collectively as the "Poor Law") codified and
regularized the various means of poor relief that had sprung up in the sixteenth century after the dissolution of the manors, monasteries, and guilds
that formerly had given aid to the needy. The Poor Law made local governments responsible for poor relief and implicitly assured all inhabitants that
their basic material needs would be provided in times of crisis. The Poor Law
also equipped governing officials with three principal instruments to manage
the lives of desperately poor people. *Warning out* rid the community of people who "belonged" legally to another town—a hometown—where they were

entitled to public support. *Orphan* or *pauper apprenticeship* put indigent children and adults into labor contracts with local residents, who agreed to provide the necessities of life in exchange for work. And *poor relief* placed the destitute in the care of other townspeople, who would receive payment in money or goods from the town treasury for their support of the poor. Rhode Island town leaders made liberal use of all three instruments as they shaped their own particular policies to deal with the poor of their communities.

This essay draws on the records of officials tasked with the responsibility of poor relief in half of Rhode Island's towns between 1750 and 1800. These fifteen towns—Charlestown, Cumberland, East Greenwich, Exeter, Glocester, Hopkinton, Jamestown, Middletown, New Shoreham, Providence, Richmond, South Kingstown, Tiverton, Warren, and Warwick—fairly represent the wealth, age, population, economic orientation, and geographic location of Rhode Island's thirty towns in the late eighteenth century. The methods used by town officials to deal with the poor varied little throughout the New England colonies, and the information drawn from Rhode Island towns applies as well to towns in Connecticut, Massachusetts, New Hampshire, and Vermont. But the town records of these other colonies do not contain the same wealth of detail about indentures, warning out, and poor relief administration. Rhode Island towns enjoyed an unusual autonomy in relation to colony government, and town clerks took extra pains to document town business. The resulting richness of the town records allows Rhode Island to serve admirably as a window into the entire New England region.

The Rhode Island records show that the administration of poor relief involved an entire network of people, at the center of which sat five or six elected town councilmen. These familiar faces were civic-minded white men who labored for years on end to govern the affairs of their towns, men of means who lived in greater comfort than their neighbors and did not rely on the paltry financial rewards of office to maintain themselves and their households. They were "fathers of the town" who acted within a communitarian understanding of patriarchy; they saw themselves as heads of a public family, with all the town's inhabitants coming under their power and laying claim to their care. From the moment of their annual election, the fathers of the towns assumed it was their right to manage the lives of others—to claim others' wealth to support the poor or to direct the details of the lives of the poor.[5]

These town fathers functioned as both administrators of poor relief and guardians of the public purse. Mindful that relief funds originated in yearly taxes paid by their neighbors, town leaders examined the circumstances and asked questions before disbursing money. The first question was whether or not the needy person was legitimately the town's responsibility. Colonial poor law directed town officials to provide the necessities of life for those in distress. But town officials felt obliged only to those people who were legally settled inhabitants of the town. Colonial settlement laws, which undergirded the poor laws, stipulated how a person acquired a legal settlement—by birth, servitude, or purchase of real estate. Persons who moved away from their home enjoyed no claim to relief in the new towns where they were living. Town leaders and "respectable" inhabitants made vital distinctions about their indigent neighbors. Some they rejected as "transients" without a legal settlement: these people (who were disproportionately female and non-white) were warned out of town rather than assisted.[6] They embraced others as "belonging" to the town and entitled to relief. In the imagery of communitarian patriarchy, there were, in effect, legitimate children who deserved care and "bastard" children who did not.

Once it was established that the poor person was a legally settled inhabitant of the town—a legitimate member of the family—councilmen posed a second question: Might there be other sources of support? Rhode Island law required grandparents and parents, if of ability, to take care of their grandchildren and children and vice versa. "If of ability" was the key phrase, and many relatives of indigent people barely scraped by themselves. If able-bodied family members were slow to support their own, councilmen prodded them along. The town records contain many tales of adult children being summoned to the town council to explain why they neglected their ailing and aged parents.[7] If no family members could help, friends and neighbors might be counted on to ease the financial difficulties of people in distress, as was the case when the injured and indigent sailor Primus Thompson paid his room, board, and doctor bill with some money "charitably given" to him.[8] Congregations might take up a special offering for needy members, as did Newport's Trinity Church in 1772 when it collected £47 12s "for the poor of all denominations."[9] A church might give extra assistance to a longtime member, as did the Friends Meeting when it took Middletown inhabitant Elizabeth Barker under their care when she became senile.[10] Or a group of prosperous inhabitants might put on a public performance of charity, as happened on an August afternoon in Providence in 1767, when "a few gentlemen" organized "a great feast for the poor" that featured the barbecue of a 120-pound hog, half a sheep, and a whole lamb, all "dressed in the best manner."[11]

If no private sources of support could be discovered, officials might grant assistance short of actual poor relief. In most towns voters instructed their tax assessors to "consider the poor" and grant tax exemptions as needed, and in some towns voters combined the offices of tax assessor and overseer of the poor, enabling officials to both identify need and relieve it. But individuals also petitioned the town meeting directly when assessors overlooked them. Seventy-year-old Thomas Rathbun, for example, won a tax exemption when he pled inability to work because he was disabled by gout; for sixteen years he had been unable to ride on horseback or "walk one step on foot without crutches or two staves."[12] Beyond tax exemptions, town leaders sometimes granted the destitute the privilege of gathering and cutting firewood from town property, grazing their occasional cow or sheep on common land, or planting a vegetable garden in the town's burying ground. Only when all other private and public resources had been exhausted did town leaders provide direct relief.

The third question councilmen asked was whether poor relief was truly necessary. An endless variety of misfortune and catastrophe rendered people unable to support themselves. For those living on the edge of ruin, a very small push could send them into abject poverty. Illnesses and accidents stripped people of their ability to labor. Fires left families homeless. Wives with young children were impoverished by husbands and fathers who were sent to jail, who drank away their earnings, who absconded from the family, or who necessarily were absent for long periods of time while earning a living—a particular problem for the families of sailors and soldiers. The councilmen considered the circumstances and determined how much relief each person received. Three principles guided this determination: that poor relief be as brief as possible, that it be as cheap as possible, and that recipients contribute to their support with their own labor.

The first principle—limited duration of poor relief—was accomplished through a careful and constant scrutiny of the poor of the town by officials and neighbors. When the indigent were deemed capable of caring for themselves again, relief was reduced or terminated. Most people received welfare for only a few months or, at most, a few years; their condition was temporary and so was the remedy. In 1799, for example, Mary Harvey was unable to support herself during the advanced stages of her pregnancy, and the Charlestown council temporarily assumed the costs of her care. But Harvey quickly recovered, and by the time the midwife submitted her charges to the council, Harvey's period of indigence was already referred to in the past tense—"when she was one of the poor of the town."[13] Disabled people whom the town supported for decades, or even a lifetime, were a rare exception. The time limitations of poor relief are underscored poignantly by the many references to the last form of assistance granted to many a frail and aged inhabitant—watchers for the corpse, grave clothes, a coffin, and a decent burial.

The second principle—providing relief as cheaply as possible—was accomplished by careful calculations of just what each poor person needed. If partial support would solve the problem, councilmen tried it. Towns sometimes provided housing for distressed families, but more often officials removed the poor from their own households and put them under the care of others.[14] Even those towns that constructed a workhouse or a poorhouse continued to farm out most of the poor with individual inhabitants of the town. The Glocester councilmen fashioned a typical poor relief contract in 1794 when they agreed to pay Seth Hunt £8 per year to provide widow Elisabeth Smith and her children with "house rent, firewood, priviledge of sauce [garden produce] & fruit; and reasonable pay at the direction of the council for all other necessaries & trouble."[15]

Whether partial or full support, relief was frugal charity. Town leaders obtained goods and services for indigents on "as cheap terms as may be."[16] Thus Rachel Burdick received only such clothing as Hopkinton officials deemed "really necessary," and Abigail Sweet was boarded at the cost of £4 per week while East Greenwich officials looked for a place where they could "get her kept cheaper."[17] This focus on frugality resulted in an informal competition among townspeople to offer the lowest price for the business of supplying goods and services to the poor at the town's expense. An example of such negotiations occurred in 1766 when Benjamin Potter proposed to the Exeter authorities that he take over the care of Hannah Remick at a lower rate than the town was paying to her present caretaker, widow Alice Albro. The Exeter councilmen sent a representative to Albro, advising her to slash her weekly rate in half; Albro did so to avoid losing her charge to her competitor.[18] How, one wonders, did Albro make such a drastic reduction in her expenses and still furnish Remick with the necessities of life? But such dramatic cost-cutting was routine, suggesting that public support was of the most limited and spartan nature. Thus paupers undoubtedly suffered because they were supplied with only the barest of absolute essentials.

To achieve the third principle—that poor relief recipients should labor as much as possible toward their own support—town leaders spurred industry among indigents in a variety of ways. In some cases, the tools of work were provided. For instance, an Exeter man who owned a plow was paid to turn up the ground around a needy man's house so that the struggling family could grow their own food. Similarly, several of Tiverton's poor were provided with cows (on loan), so they could supply their own milk, butter, and cheese.[19] In other cases, councilmen appointed overseers who put idlers to work.[20] In still other cases, official prodding took the form of forced labor contracts, usually for six months or a year.[21]

Councilmen also did a brisk business binding out children in a particular form of indentured servitude known as "orphan apprenticeship" or "pauper apprenticeship." By this means, illegitimate and destitute youngsters—as well as orphaned ones—were taken from their parents and raised to adulthood in more "respectable" households. It was not until well into the nineteenth century that Rhode Island authorities began placing such children in orphanages akin to that pioneered by officials in Charleston, South Carolina, as John Murray discusses in his essay in this volume. The numbers of minors bound out in every Rhode Island town were, however, sufficient to fill such a group home. Under the terms of these individual indentures, the master (head of household) was obliged to provide the child servant with all the necessities of life as well as education and training in some manual skill. In return, the child was obliged to live with, obey, and labor for the master. Orphan apprenticeship thus provided cheap labor for many masters, but it did not necessarily benefit the children, who frequently were immobilized at what officials deemed to be their appropriate station in life and trained only for menial service to their betters in adulthood. Sometimes children were bound out over the objections of their parents, and at very tender ages: the average age at binding was seven, but more children were indentured at four than any other age, much younger than apprentices who did not belong to poor families. Indentures of this sort demonstrated official power to break up and reorganize indigent families and also served official goals by removing children from the ranks of those needing poor relief. Further, many of these young servants were exploited by masters striving for economic profit, and their lengthy contracts—usually lasting until eighteen for girls and twenty-one for boys—suggests that bound children, as Barry Levy and Lawrence Towner have argued, provided an important source of labor for New England communities.[22]

Identifying needs of the poor and alleviating those needs depended on a pipeline of information that flowed through the town and poured its contents into the ears of the town councilmen. It started with a "complaint." Occasionally, people in need brought their complaint directly to town leaders, some boldly "throwing themselves upon the town" and requesting or even demanding full support.[23] But more typical was a sequential relay of information from a needy person to a concerned neighbor to a town leader.[24] The everyday dramas of the poor, described in the town records, show how this pipeline of information operated. In 1767, for example, Tent Anthony, an Indian, "was taken with a numb palsey fit" at the house of Josiah Arnold (probably her employer) in Jamestown. After being stricken, she remained "bad" on one side and lay "in a helpless condition." Arnold reported Tent Anthony's situation to overseer of the poor Matthew Greenold, who relayed the information to the Jamestown councilmen, who arranged for the care of the ill woman.[25]

The pipeline reversed its flow when councilmen made their decision about relief. It carried goods, services, and money to those in need. Once again, a wide network of townspeople participated. Virtually all inhabitants could contribute to supporting the poor and thereby earn extra income in the way of payments from the town treasury. Some were paid for making clothes for the poor, others for making shoes. Some were paid for providing cornmeal, meat, milk, and cheese; others were paid to deliver those foods to the poor. Some were paid to build houses for the poor; others were paid to repair their windows and chimneys. Some were paid to nurse the poor and deliver their babies; others were paid to make their coffins and dig their graves. Those most heavily involved in poor relief, however, were those who took in the poor as lodgers, daily providing food, shelter, and heat and making the poor person a part of the household. From the wealthiest squire to the poorest laborer, nearly every inhabitant could and did participate in poor relief.

As this flow of information indicates, poverty was everybody's business in face-to-face communities where need could rarely be concealed. Given the daily human interactions of people living close together and the general lack of privacy in early America, residents of small towns inevitably had intimate knowledge of each other. The complaints brought to the town councilmen show how neighbors keenly observed each other's circumstances, down to details of clothing, bedding, diet, and health.[26] Sarah Whitman was described as "almost naked for want of shifts and a coat." Lois Marshall and her four children were reported as "destitute of firewood so as to make them comfortable." Neighbors complained that Clement Weaver was "very sick and not able to take care of himself and family."[27]

Being on relief was similarly public knowledge. Unlike modern America, the poor were not segregated in their own enclaves. Rather, indigents were tucked into other households or maintained in their own humble homes under the oversight of a town official. Receiving town charity did not remove the poor from daily interactions with their more prosperous neighbors. On the contrary, it intensified those interactions since the president of the town council was just as likely as someone of humbler means to be a caretaker for an indigent. For paupers, then, accepting relief meant a further reduction of the already minimal privacy that residents could expect in eighteenth-century New England.

To become one of the poor of the town also meant the loss of control over one's domestic life. Indigents were usually moved into other households and became dependent on and under the power of the head of that household. In some cases they might have been accepted as an integral part of the household, but in others they were treated as servants. Their daily care was arranged by town authorities and caretakers, and those arrangements might be changed frequently and abruptly by councilmen seeking the cheapest terms or by caretakers tiring of their charges. Hopkinton widow Elisabeth Odell, apparently a difficult or costly charge, was moved twelve times during the last six years of her life. Whatever trouble she caused to her caretakers, she herself must have been distressed by the frequent moves, changes in eating and sleeping arrangements, and adjustments to a new household with its routines and rules dictated by the head of the family.[28]

Equally difficult for poor mothers and fathers was the loss of parental authority when their children were placed as orphan or pauper apprentices in other homes. Surviving parents often had continued contact with their bound-out offspring and could appeal to authorities if they suspected abuse, but someone else exercised day-to-day management of their sons and daughters. It must have been a parent's nightmare when a master was demonstrated to have treated an apprentice "in a nonhuman manner," as happened on occasion.[29] Further, occupational hopes these parents had for their children were often dashed by the realities of hard labor in tender years. One concerned guardian was grieved that his young ward worked such long hours and received little schooling while bound out to a master. "I should be glad you would consider the orphan and do by him as you would have others do by yours," the guardian wrote, and added, "Don't think hard of my wanting the child to have learning, for that is the chief [thing] he will have to depend on."[30]

To become one of the poor of the town was also to lose status. The town records indicate that people who depended on the town for support were relegated to a different category in the eyes of their neighbors. Peleg Sheeps's caretaker was directed to provide room, board, and clothing "suitable for such a person." John Johnson's caretaker was ordered to supply clothing "suitable to his station & condition." When Sarah Budlong became one of the poor of the town, her gold necklace and chest of drawers were taken from her because they were of "no advantage to her under [her] present situation"; in exchange she was given "two pair of good new leather shoes."[31] Even though special badges were no longer worn by the poor of the town in the late eighteenth century, their "suitable" clothing and diet advertised their diminished status to the rest of the community.

Not surprisingly, then, needy people often left their hometowns in search of work. When Priscilla Blackmar applied to the Glocester council for the official certificate that poor people needed to reside in another town, she told them that "she could procure a better living in the town of Cranston."[32] Similarly, Salisbury Stoddard explained that he was moving his family from Little Compton to Middletown "for the better support and maintenance of themselves," and he immediately asked permission to keep a tavern in his Middletown lodgings.[33] By frequently and readily producing the necessary certificates, town officials appeared to welcome the departure of inhabitants who might otherwise need relief, and sometimes authorities even fostered such relocations. When widow Mary Brown moved herself and her child to Middletown, the Hopkinton councilmen ordered that she "be helped forward to Narragansett Ferry."[34] Providence officials encouraged "poor and destitute" Michael Field to leave town by giving him a certificate plus six shillings in travel money, and they also gave six shillings to Christopher Moore to "defray his expences" when he "left the workhouse to take a walk into the country" to look for a job.[35] Such cases emphasize how moving elsewhere seemed a good option both to the poor and to town officials.

Those who stayed and received relief in their hometowns sometimes actively tried to influence the shape of their support. In face-to-face meetings with town leaders, some individuals suggested arrangements that revealed their understanding of the town's resources and their desire to retain some control over their own lives. Mary Campbell of South Kingstown and Phebe Allen of Glocester successfully negotiated with their councils to move from one caretaker to another.[36] At one Warwick council meeting, John Bennett convinced officials to let him build a house on town land since he owned no real estate of his own, and widow Hannah Scranton persuaded them to build her a small house "in some convenient place, where wood and water was plenty" and where "with her industry she should be able to maintain herself and children."[37] Christopher Sylvester successfully petitioned the Providence council for a free tavern license to assist him in launching a small "shopkeeping business"; common labor was impossible for him, thanks to a "mserabel state of health" occasioned by "sickness" contracted five years earlier when he was a sailor aboard a ship that voyaged to the East Indies.[38]

Some impoverished parents tried to use the orphan apprenticeship system to their own and their children's benefit by directly pressuring authorities. William Booth's mother was able to persuade the East Greenwich councilmen to find another master because she was "very unwilling" to release her son to the man they first chose.[39] Betty Church consented to the Providence council's arrangements for her son only when the terms of the indenture obligated the master to educate the boy more extensively than was typical for such servants.[40] Eleanor Spencer disappeared with her three-year-old daughter at a strategic moment, effectively preventing the bound-out child from being taken to another colony when her master moved.[41]

Rather than negotiating indentures directly, black and Indian mothers sometimes actively placed their children in particular households, "leaving" them where they would receive the necessities of life and other care; this amounted to an informal selection of the masters to whom the children eventually would be bound. Marcy Scooner "left" her daughter Hannah at the household of Matthew Greenold before journeying to another town in pursuit of work.[42] Moll Pero "left her son, a mustee boy about five years of age," in the household of Joseph Underwood, who later asked the Jamestown councilmen to bind the boy to him.[43] Sometimes these strategic placements had an air of desperation about them, as in the case of two-year-old Sarah, "left" at George Babcock's house by an "Indian squaw" who was "unknown" to Babcock; Babcock quickly persuaded the South Kingstown council to bind the toddler to him until she turned twenty.[44] Other times, women of color "left" siblings together in the care of a master who eventually obtained indentures of both. Dan Weeden asked the Jamestown councilmen to bind to him two Indian children, a four-year-old boy and a fifteen-year-old girl, whose mother, Indian "squaw" Betty Jack, had "left" them with him "for a maintenance" six months earlier.[45] Other sibling pairs left together by their mothers included "mustee" children Harry and Sarah in South Kingstown, "Negro" children Simon and Patience Talbury in East Greenwich, and "black" children John and Isabel Brown in Exeter.[46] The recurring pattern of such placements, often interpreted by authorities as abandonment, suggests that watchful mothers, unable to raise their children on their own, selected where and with whom the children would live.

By such strategies as leaving town, bargaining with officials over poor relief arrangements, and influencing the choice of their children's masters, poor people helped shape their experience of poor relief. In so doing, they made it clear that poverty did not make them helpless or passive victims of official management; often enough they actively selected the best alternative open to them.

Who was aided by poor relief? Rhode Island town records show that, despite the gender-neutral and color-neutral wording of poor laws, black and Indian women were the least likely to benefit from town-administered relief. Some people of color, in an effort to maintain control over their lives, may have attempted to avoid official attention by not applying for support. Still, the remarkable absence of black and Indian women in the relief records and their pronounced presence in the warning out records suggests that officials were well aware of need among women of color but reluctant to grant assistance.

Councilmen tended to keep a close eye on women of color who lived independently within Rhode Island towns, a scrutiny prompted in part by official responsibility to relieve the poverty that always lurked outside the door of women struggling to support themselves and their children on the meager wages of a domestic servant or farm laborer. But officials were also on the alert because Indian and black women often lived in households without male heads, raising the children in one place while their mates worked elsewhere as sailors, soldiers, or laborers. To town authorities, these women were out of their proper places, disconnected from the patriarchal households on which white New England was officially built. They were wives without husbands and daughters without fathers, but also, and perhaps most important, people of color without masters. Women so completely out of place posed a threat to order, and this threat had a distinctly sexual overtone, as evidenced by the accusations of prostitution leveled at women of color and by the frequent, easy assumption of town officials that the children of these women were "bastards" whom the town fathers would eventually have to bind out with indentures.[47]

For these reasons, officials concerned with "maintaining good order" in their towns monitored women of color and took appropriate measures when they deemed it necessary. Yet this scrutiny and intervention seldom resulted in relief; instead, town leaders tended to warn out women of color. Between 1750 and 1800, women of color constituted more than 13 percent of all household heads warned out of Rhode Island towns, yet such women constituted much less than 5 percent of the general population. Town leaders, it seems, were especially assiduous in removing black and Indian women from their communities, thus shifting the responsibility for their care to other towns.[48]

Women in general dominated the ranks of those warned out and removed from Rhode Island towns: fully two-thirds were adult females. Many of these women were hidden in the official record because only their husbands were questioned by officials and named on the removal order. Men headed only half of the warned-out households (50.4 percent); women without husbands headed the other half (49.6 percent). When wives and female household heads are combined, women emerge as the people most often warned out.[49] People of color also were overrepresented among people warned out. Between 1750 and 1800, about one-fifth (22 percent) of those warned out were identified as "Indian," "mustee," "mulatto," "Negro," "black," and "of color."[50] This proportion is much higher than historical reconstructions of the African-American and Native American populations, which show people of color as a declining presence in Rhode Island's population, from around 12 percent in 1755 to about 5 percent in 1800.[51] The warn-out statistics show the opposite trend: the percentage of people of color among those warned out increased significantly in the 1780s and 1790s. When the Providence councilmen warned out "Boston Nance" (a transient "mulatto" woman) in 1800, people of color constituted half of all those warned out of Rhode Island towns. This is an astonishing statistic in light of the census data that "Negroes" comprised only 5 percent of the population that year.[52]

Analyzing the gender and race of warned out people is far easier than discovering the gender and race of relief recipients. No clerk ever conscientiously recorded every recipient, much less every disbursement; instead, clerks typically recorded a few individual accounts, but then lumped together the next few accounts as vague expenditures "for the poor of the town" without further detail. Nevertheless, some clerks in some towns during some years provided sufficient detail to make possible a sampling of recipients during three peak years of relief expenditures (1764, 1788, and 1791). The sampling reveals that women and men received money and goods in fairly equal proportions: women received 53 percent of the disbursements in 1764, 61 percent in 1788, and 46 percent in 1791. This near parity is surprising, considering how frequently women struggled to maintain households without the support of husbands and fathers. Women and men alike fell into ill health and feebleness in old age, but women alone bore the disruptions of childbirth and attendant health problems. If poor relief accurately reflected the economic vulnerability of women, then disbursements on behalf of women—both in total cost and in number of expenditures—should have exceeded those for men.

People of color, despite the need occasioned by their poorly paid labor, were likewise underrepresented in relief disbursements. Black and Indian recipients are rarely mentioned in the record. When they are included, they are usually women, and they are usually quite aged. The poor relief supplied to them was most frequently the expenses of final illness and a decent burial. Typical in this regard were Margaret Clark (whose story opened this essay) and Sarah Fitten, who never received any support when she was alive, but only after she died: a meager amount for "bords & making of a coffin" and for "one gallon of rum & half gallon molasses sugar expended at the burial."[53] No town supported a woman of color for more than a few months; only white men and women enjoyed the possibility of virtual pensions by the town, with a few (such as Elisabeth Odell) spending years on relief. Several white women who were mentally disabled spent decades on support; no woman of color ever did.

Women of color were thus in a precarious position regarding poor relief: in times of need, they were likely to be warned out and unlikely to receive significant assistance. But they were not passive victims. The record is dotted with examples of black and Indian women forging their own way in defiance of official dictates. Some women frustrated authorities by failing to appear in council meetings, by giving unintelligible answers to questions or changing their stories at each telling, by refusing to sign or mark the transcriptions of their testimonies, or by returning to a town from which they had been warned out. Sarah Gardner, an Indian woman, returned to Providence four times after being forcibly removed. Even the threat of whipping didn't deter her or the four adult daughters who accompanied her. The council considered the five women to be "of bad character and reputation" and clearly wanted them elsewhere, but the Gardners' determination to live in Providence was even stronger.[54] Sarah Mathewson, a "mulatto" woman, showed her sophisticated grasp of the system when, after returning illegally to Providence, she "concealed herself from the officer until she got into her present pregnant state when . . . it became improper to inflict the punishment prescribed by law."[55] By these and similar actions, women of color demonstrated that they had resources and alternatives invisible to town officials who tried to manage their lives.

The latter half of the eighteenth century brought two wars, periodic economic depression, and demographic change, all of which affected the condition of indigents and the administration of poor relief. The focal point of distress occurred in the 1780s, when the most severe depression, following on the heels of the Revolutionary War, disrupted the lives of countless Rhode Islanders. People dislocated by the British occupation of their towns fled inland as refugees, swelling the population—and the relief problems—of those more secure towns. Adding to their numbers were emancipated people of color who gained their freedom when they fled servitude, served in the military during the war, or successfully bargained with their masters for their liberty. The passage of gradual emancipation laws in Rhode Island and Connecticut in the early 1780s also nudged masters into freeing slaves and encouraged slaves to struggle even harder for their independence. Freed people then moved about in search of work and a congenial community. Men who had found work as soldiers and sailors during the war searched for employment afterward, adding to the flood of postwar transients. Even transient people who had lived comfortably for years in towns where they had no legal settlement found themselves unable to pay their rent and purchase food. When their need became critical, councilmen warned them out, regardless of their long employment and neighborly ties in the town.

People who stayed in place suffered from the rising costs of food and supplies during the Revolution and the postwar depression. In 1779, for

GRAPH 5. Per Capita Poor Costs, 11 Rhode Island Towns (in Constant Dollars)

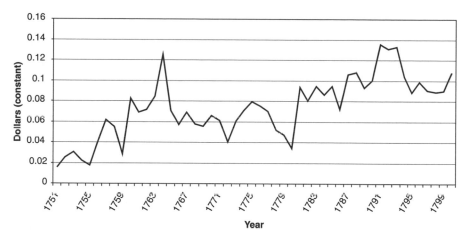

*Source:* Town meeting and town council records, 1750–1800, Cumberland, East Greenwich, Exeter, Glocester, Hopkinton, Jamestown, Richmond, South Kingstown, Tiverton, Warren, and Warwick.

example, Glocester inhabitant Stephen Aldrich found himself unable to support his large family because "provisions [were] so dear." In 1786, Providence's poor inhabitants were unable to find firewood that they normally could scavenge from town land.[56] Town governments faced the same problems. Poor costs climbed sharply upward at the beginning of the 1780s and remained high (graph 5). People on the move in search of better fortune were unlikely to find it.

Voters, flinching at their astronomically high tax bills during the war and the subsequent depression, demanded that town leaders minimize relief costs. Councilmen responded by carefully examining the accounts of caretakers and lopping off part of the charges. In 1780, for example, the Exeter councilmen denied Oliver Spink and George Pierce one-quarter of their charges for keeping John Albro, one of the town's poor. Since Pierce was himself the council president and an overseer of the poor, it seems unlikely that the adjustment implied a suspicion of fraud; rather it was a time when all involved in town government tightened their belts. In 1788, the Warwick voters demanded that Doctor William Aldrich appear at a town meeting and explain what seemed to them to be very high charges for "visits and medicins" for one of the town's poor. Aldrich drew up a detailed list of dates and costs and commented that he had attended his patient only when asked by town officials and that he had made several visits gratis. The town paid him, but its unease about the bill emphasized the economic difficulties under which many officials labored.[57]

These small economies were not enough. In the 1780s, overworked councilmen and overtaxed voters in numerous towns called for "a new method of supporting the poor."[58] The favored method: constructing workhouses or poorhouses where the poor of the town could be boarded together and kept to some kind of profitable task. Well before the Revolution, the more densely populated towns—Newport, Providence, Warwick—had opened workhouses, and a few smaller towns had discussed trying them.[59] During the Revolution and the postwar depression, however, towns that had never even considered a poorhouse suddenly found compelling reason to build or purchase one: Richmond in 1779; East Greenwich in 1781; Tiverton and Middletown in 1783; Hopkinton in 1785; Warren in 1786; South Kingstown in 1787; Glocester in 1790.[60] Hopkinton voters succinctly expressed the rationale behind this flurry of activity: they wanted a workhouse "for the use of the poor & idle inhabitants of this town as well as stragling persons who shall come into this town."[61]

The Hopkinton voters' resolve underscores the disorder sensed by inhabitants of Rhode Island towns in the 1780s. "Stragling persons" had become a problem even in rural, sparsely populated communities where paupers had always been familiar faces. Towns like Hopkinton had never seen reason to draw up "an exact list of the names of such persons as are maintained at the expence of this Town as poor thereof," as did Providence in 1753, because in Hopkinton the town councilmen could tick off by memory exactly who was receiving relief.[62] That changed in the 1780s, when the increasing presence of needy strangers helped propel voters into at least trying institutional care for the destitute among them, known and unknown. Historian Robert Cray has found this same trend toward institutionalization in the rural areas around New York City during the revolutionary era; both rural New York and rural Rhode Island were moving toward the landscape of institutions that Monique Bourque analyzes in this volume.[63]

These initial attempts to create group homes for the poor did not prove entirely satisfactory. Sometimes an overseer could not be found for the house; sometimes the house fell into decay and was no longer safe for dwellers; sometimes the house did not achieve the economic savings that voters had anticipated. As a result, most towns soon returned to more traditional methods of placing the poor in households. Now, however, there was a qualitative difference in the way caretakers were identified and paupers placed, indicating that voters had begun to think of poor people as a collective unit. In several towns, voters bargained with one prosperous householder to take in all the paupers for an agreed-upon sum, effectively creating an informal poorhouse. In 1794 the South Kingstown voters agreed that Samuel Stanton would "take, keep and maintain all and every of the poor of this town" for one year for $400. The South Kingstown voters also agreed that one physician attend to the medical needs of the poor each year for a set price, a strategy previously employed only in the most populous towns such as Providence.[64] Other towns organized "poor auctions," at which interested householders would bid for the opportunity to board certain "lots" of poor people. The lowest bidder won. Warwick councilmen, for example, conducted their first poor auction in 1788, when they disposed of "sundry poor children" to the lowest-bidding households.[65] This auction system not only turned indigents into objects, it almost certainly ensured that the winner would provide the most inexpensive care to his or her charges.

During the revolutionary era, then, even rural Rhode Island communities began thinking about collective care of the poor, causing this corner of New England to join the wider eighteenth-century shift of attitudes toward poor relief in America, which Gary Nash discusses in his essay in this volume. For Rhode Islanders in Providence as well as Charlestown and Hopkinton, the transformation of poor relief had begun, and in the early 1800s poor farms and poorhouses would spring up and stay. Those initial forays of the 1780s showed taxpayers both the convenience and the problems of group arrangements—the potential for saving money and also the potential for reducing human beings to objects in the eyes of their neighbors. Perhaps this threatened transformation in human relations helps explain why most towns drew back from the poorhouse idea after an initial burst of activity. Even in Providence, that magnet for transient and impoverished people, more indigents were placed in other private households rather than in the workhouse in the last decade of the 1700s. Although the idea had been planted and tested, it would be another generation before Rhode Island communities turned wholeheartedly to institutions for care of their poor.

Even if the methods of poor relief did not change significantly under the stress of war and postwar depression, did the amount of care increase in response to social distress? Yes, in two ways. The number of people warned out rose sharply, indicating that town leaders forced out more and more needy people who were not legal inhabitants. The money spent on poor relief likewise increased.

Warning out serves as a good measure of increase and decrease in poverty in the region, charted over the period 1750–1800 in graph 6. The number of warn-out orders fell sharply at the outbreak of the Seven Years' War (1756)

GRAPH 6. Warn-Outs Annually, 13 Rhode Island Towns

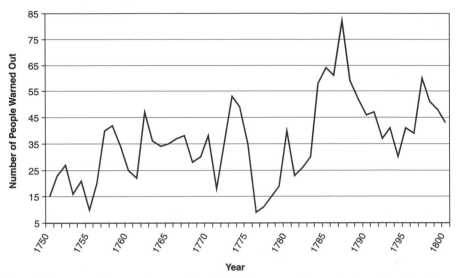

*Source:* There were 1,832 people warned out in the town council records, 1750–1800, Cumberland, East Greenwich, Exeter, Glocester, Hopkinton, Middletown, New Shoreham, Providence, Richmond, South Kingstown, Tiverton, Warren, and Warwick.

and the Revolutionary War (1776). Officials, distracted by more urgent problems, temporarily ignored the needy and troublesome transients within their borders; at the same time, employment opportunities increased and some of those needy people disappeared. Some poor men found a temporary livelihood as soldiers and sailors; others, both men and women, found work by following the army and supporting the troops; still others found work in farms and shops that needed extra hands as their owners took advantage of increased demand for food and clothing. They left the towns where they had been living on the edge of destitution to pursue wartime opportunities.

Warning out resumed rapidly after the outbreak of these wars and peaked during the early 1760s and again during the mid-1780s, evidence of the economic depression that settled on New England especially hard in the wake of the Revolutionary War. But sheer numbers do not tell the whole story. In most Rhode Island towns, the population grew rapidly after the Revolutionary War, and if transient removals are measured as a percentage of the population, a different pattern emerges. The percentage of warn-outs fell to an all-time low in 1776, jumped to a near-record high in 1784, and then rapidly diminished to its lowest peacetime levels in the 1790s (see graph 7). Thus, after 1784 a decreasing proportion of people were actually being sent out of town.

GRAPH 7. Percentage of Households Warned Out of 13 Rhode Island Towns

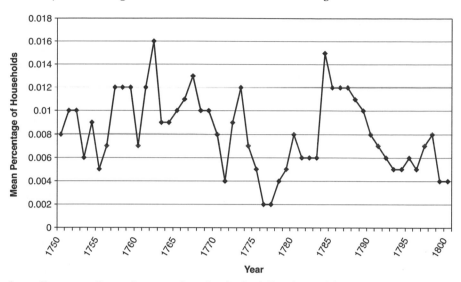

*Source:* Town council records, 1750–1800, Cumberland, East Greenwich, Exeter, Glocester, Hopkinton, Middleton, New Shoreham, Providence, Richmond, South Kingstown, Tiverton, Warren, and Warwick.

This decline in warning out in the 1780s and 1790s may have been due to a more tolerant policy on the part of town officials toward transient residents, and it may also indicate a decline in the number of people who fell into desperate need of the sort that usually prompted the intervention of authorities. Some poor people may have been able to find work more easily as the postwar economy improved, or they may have left Rhode Island in search of better jobs elsewhere. While the pattern of warning out may not prove a straightforward indicator of changing economic conditions throughout the revolutionary era, its peak in the mid-1780s underscores the negative impact of the postwar depression on poor people, who were thrown into such difficulty that authorities were prompted to order them back to their hometowns.[66]

Nowhere did transients keep officials busier in the 1780s than in Providence, where weary councilmen convened numerous meetings just to keep track of the flood of new arrivals. Between 1750 and 1800, Providence officials warned out 682 people, five times the number for any other town; thus, Providence's councilmen were five times as busy at this task as any of the other six-man councils throughout the state. With its expanding mercantile economy, rising upper class, and promising market for crafts and trades, Providence was very much Rhode Island's great attraction in the late 1700s. In the years

TABLE 7. Hopkinton Expense Categories as Percentage of Total Town
Budget, 1760–1789

| Year | Poor Relief | Military | Roads | Administrative Costs | Other Expenses |
|------|------------|----------|-------|----------------------|----------------|
| 1760 | 62.1 | 0.0 | 6.5 | 30.8 | 0.5 |
| 1766 | 52.8 | 0.0 | 17.2 | 15.3 | 14.8 |
| 1775 | 53.8 | 1.0 | 17.0 | 27.4 | 0.7 |
| 1776 | 21.9 | 36.6 | 3.6 | 37.9 | 0.0 |
| 1777 | 3.5 | 23.3 | 1.1 | 72.1 | 0.0 |
| 1781 | 5.0 | 32.3 | 7.7 | 53.7 | 1.2 |
| 1782 | 1.2 | 71.6 | 1.1 | 22.0 | 4.0 |
| 1783 | 22.6 | 0.0 | 3.5 | 73.5 | 0.4 |
| 1784 | 19.8 | 4.7 | 9.9 | 54.9 | 10.8 |
| 1785 | 62.7 | 0.0 | 5.7 | 21.7 | 10.0 |
| 1786 | 73.4 | 0.0 | 1.8 | 23.2 | 1.6 |
| 1788 | 53.9 | 0.0 | 3.8 | 29.2 | 13.1 |
| 1789 | 63.4 | 0.0 | 4.0 | 31.0 | 1.6 |

Source: Town meeting and town council records, vols. 1 and 2, Hopkinton.

following the Revolutionary War, Providence outshone Newport, formerly
Rhode Island's largest town. The bombardment and occupation of Newport
by British troops drove away many residents, interrupted trade, and damaged
farms, shops, and ships. After the war, job hunters migrated to Providence, not
Newport, and they came from a considerable distance to try their fortune.
Well over half of the people warned out of Providence in the latter part of the
eighteenth century originated in towns at least twenty miles away—from New
London, southern Rhode Island, western Massachusetts, Boston, Cape Cod,
and myriad more distant locations, including Europe. No other Rhode Island
town drew people from that kind of distance in this era of slow and deliberate
travel; in towns outside Providence, the majority of people warned out were
from neighboring towns and had come less than ten miles. The problem of
needy, transient people was concentrated in Providence.[67]

Still, not urbanized Providence, but agrarian Hopkinton serves as the most
representative case of the rise and fall of poor relief for settled inhabitants
during the revolutionary era. Hopkinton's records provide complete
accounts of the town's expenditures for sixteen years between 1760 and
1789, allowing a crude reconstruction of the town's budget and a view of the
Revolutionary War's effect on that budget (see table 7). The figures show
that, when there was no war, the costs of caring for the poor dominated the
budget, generally accounting for at least half of the town's disbursements.
This supports Bruce Daniels's findings that relief costs were the principal

cause of "local financial problems" in eighteenth-century Rhode Island.[68] The second most costly budget item, administrative costs (payments to tax assessors and collectors, auditors, the town sergeant, the town clerk, the town treasurer, and deputies to the legislature), generally amounted to half of what was spent on the poor.

It was not mere rhetoric, then, when voters complained about the costs of relief as they grudgingly levied taxes on themselves. In a typical situation, the East Greenwich town meeting agreed in 1754 to a tax of £300 to refill the "very much exhausted" treasury because of the "many persons having considerable demands upon the treasurer for the supporting of the poor."[69] In Glocester that same year, a tax of £600 was levied because "this Town is very much in debt by reason of the many poor that are constant[ly] maintained by the Town."[70] December and January saw the greatest number of poor taxes assessed to provide needy residents with housing, firewood, and clothing necessary to survive the cold. In December of 1787, for example, Warwick voters levied a tax of £400 on themselves because "a considerable sum will also be wanting to support the poor of the Town the ensuing winter."[71] And in January of 1789, the same town ordered a tax to be spent for "clothing the poor [and] procuring bedding & bunks necessary for them to lodge in."[72]

This concentration on poor relief changed dramatically during the Revolutionary War when military costs dominated the disbursements, and in one critical year, 1782, such expenses represented nearly three-quarters of the total budget. Military expenses included the cost of preparing munitions for the defense of the town, bounty money for men who agreed to enlist in the army on behalf of the town, and supplies for the town's soldiers. In 1782, the peak year of military expenditures, Hopkinton taxpayers were hit belatedly with a cluster of bills from townspeople who had provided various supplies during the previous few years; the cessation of hostilities in Rhode Island gave these suppliers time to organize their accounts and apply for reimbursement.

Administrative costs also increased significantly during wartime, reflecting the extra work that fell on officials who calculated and collected more taxes and attended extra sessions of General Assembly. Such expenses continued to be high for several years after the war as well, reflecting the ongoing barrage of state and Continental taxes in the wake of the war. While Hopkinton voters (like many other Rhode Islanders) were willing to levy taxes upon themselves, they loudly protested these taxes imposed by the state legislature and, in the 1780s, they delayed payment so repeatedly that their treasurer was jailed by the county sheriff as a way of pressuring the taxpayers into paying their bill.[73] The extra labor performed by officials as a consequence of heavy taxes drove up administrative costs significantly.

TABLE 8.  Hopkinton Per Capita Expenditures, 1760–1789 (in constant dollars)

| Year | Poor Relief | Military Costs | Administrative Costs |
|------|-------------|---------------|----------------------|
| 1760 | 0.039 | 0.000 | 0.017 |
| 1766 | 0.042 | 0.000 | 0.013 |
| 1775 | 0.054 | 0.001 | 0.027 |
| 1776 | 0.024 | 0.040 | 0.042 |
| 1777 | 0.006 | 0.041 | 0.127 |
| 1781 | 0.011 | 0.087 | 0.114 |
| 1782 | 0.006 | 0.340 | 0.104 |
| 1783 | 0.058 | 0.000 | 0.190 |
| 1784 | 0.065 | 0.016 | 0.181 |
| 1785 | 0.151 | 0.000 | 0.052 |
| 1786 | 0.197 | 0.000 | 0.062 |
| 1788 | 0.217 | 0.000 | 0.140 |
| 1789 | 0.104 | 0.000 | 0.054 |

*Source:* Town meeting and town council records, vols. 1 and 2, Hopkinton.

The Revolutionary War years were a disaster for the impoverished residents of Hopkinton. Although some poor people left town to follow the army or found local war-related jobs, those unable to labor—and those charged with their care—simply had to scrape by without much help from the town. Poor relief disbursements were cut abruptly in 1776, slashed again in 1777, and stayed at significantly reduced levels until the mid-1780s, when military expenditures had ceased and administrative costs were once again under control. This reduction in support meant not only that the poor received a smaller percentage of the total budget, but also that they collected less real money. The actual amount paid out to the poor of the town, computed as some per capita expenditure for each of the town's residents, is listed in table 8. In 1777 and 1782, per capita disbursements reached an all-time low, so that each inhabitant was spending less than a penny a year to support the town's paupers. Clearly, the care of the poor took a back seat to the expenses of running the war, and not until the guns were laid aside completely did the needs of the poor dominate the budget again. Then the per capita expenditures rebounded dramatically, reflecting the great human distress of the poor during the postwar depression. Disbursements were particularly high in 1788 when the voters scrambled to cover a bevy of past-due accounts from caretakers of the poor.[74] Whether or not Hopkinton's paupers received better care in the late 1780s, certainly more was spent on them than ever before.

In the latter part of the eighteenth century, the Rhode Island system of poor relief was both highly personalized and very public, a community endeavor both in the identification of need and in the alleviation of it. Because the three principal instruments—warning out, orphan apprenticeship, and caretaking of the needy—were administered on an individual basis, the system was subject to manipulation by town officials, by taxpayers, by caretakers for the poor, and by the poor themselves. Although the most powerful inhabitants initially determined who received relief and in what form, recipients were still able to apply pressure to the situation and retain some control over their own circumstances. And although certain members of the community, most notably women of color, were unlikely to receive support, the system's flexibility softened this prejudicial administration, enabling these most disadvantaged people to find ways around and through official dictates.

Given such individualized and personal exchanges at the local level, most Rhode Islanders were well acquainted with the dramatic increase in poverty in their communities during the Revolutionary War and its aftermath. They saw the human reality in needy strangers straggling into their towns and eventually felt it in substantially increased local taxes. In response, they tried out new forms of collective poor relief in poorhouses, workhouses, and caretaker auctions. These brief forays soon foundered and taxpayers returned to more traditional methods, but the idea of collective care had been well planted. As the costs of relief mounted in the late 1780s, weary taxpayers continued to search for more economical methods of assisting the indigents in their midst. Within a few decades, the poor would be segregated in farms, orphanages, and other institutions, no longer a daily presence in the homes of community members and no longer mentioned by name in the council minutes. Fifty years after Margaret Clark died "an expence to this town," paupers like her were far more effectively hidden from view, both on the town's landscape and in the town's records.

## Notes

1. My thanks go to Monique Bourque, Susan Klepp, Daniel Mandell, Billy G. Smith, and Karin Wulf for their helpful comments on earlier versions of this essay. Abbreviations used in notes:

TCM=town council meeting
TCR=town council records
TM=town meeting
TMR=town meeting records
PTP=Providence town papers

All records except those for Providence are housed at the town halls of the individual towns, unless otherwise noted. The Providence records are housed at the Providence City Archives (TCR and TMR) and at the Rhode Island Historical Society (PTP).

2. TCM, May 7, 1798, Charlestown TCR 5:139.

3. TCM, April 7, 1783, and April 7, 1788, Charlestown TCR 3:132, 4:2.

4. See, e.g., Gary Nash, "Urban Wealth and Poverty in Pre-Revolutionary America," *Journal of Interdisciplinary History* 6 (spring 1976): 545–84; John K. Alexander, *Render Them Submissive: Responses to Poverty in Philadelphia, 1760–1800* (Amherst: University of Massachusetts Press, 1980); Raymond A. Mohl, *Poverty in New York, 1783–1825* (New York: Oxford University Press, 1971); Billy G. Smith, *The "Lower Sort": Philadelphia's Laboring People, 1750–1800* (Ithaca: Cornell University Press, 1990). Robert E. Cray has investigated gender and racial biases in poor relief as well as the differences in relief administration in rural and urban areas; his work has helped frame new questions about the identity of the poor and the nature of the relief they received. See *Paupers and Poor Relief in New York City and Its Rural Environs, 1700–1830* (Philadelphia: Temple University Press, 1988) and "White Welfare and Black Strategies: The Dynamics of Race and Poor Relief in Early New York, 1700–1825," *Slavery and Abolition* 7:3 (December 1986): 273–89.

5. Ruth Wallis Herndon, *Unwelcome Americans: Living on the Margin in Early New England* (Philadelphia: University of Pennsylvania Press, 2001), 1–10.

6. Herndon, *Unwelcome Americans* and "Women of 'No Particular Home': Town Leaders and Female Transients in Rhode Island, 1750–1800," in *Women and Freedom in Early America*, ed. Larry D. Eldridge (New York: New York University Press, 1996), 269–89. For earlier studies of warning out, which do not address race and gender as categories of analysis, see Josiah Henry Benton, *Warning Out in New England, 1656–1817* (Boston: W. B. Clarke, 1911; repr. Freeport, N.Y.: Books for Libraries Press, 1970), and Douglas Lamar Jones, "The Strolling Poor: Transiency in Eighteenth-Century Massachusetts" *Journal of Social History* 8 (1975): 28–54.

7. *Acts and Laws of Rhode Island* (1767), 201. In 1751, for example, Glocester councilmen determined to sue David Thornton if he did not repay the town what they had spent on clothes and other necessities for his father Benjamin, who was "in real want of support." In 1760, the Exeter councilmen ordered Robert, Ebenezer, James, and Peleg Moon to come to the next council meeting and explain why they had neglected to care for their mother Elizabeth Moon, who had become "chargeable" to the town. (TCM, August 31, 1751, Glocester TCR, vol. 1.; TCM, October 14, 1760, Exeter TCR 2:97.)

8. Examination of Primus Thompson, TCM, January 20, 1775, Jamestown TCR 2:117–18.

9. *Newport Mercury,* December 28, 1772.

10. TCM, October 20, 1788, May 18, 1789, and June 21, 1790; Middletown TCR 2:183, 2:194, 2:201–202.

11. *Providence Gazette,* August 15, 1767. The originators of the plan apparently misjudged the number of poor persons who were willing to attend the feast as there was enough left over afterward to provide a full meal for the benefactors and their households. Or perhaps that was one of the reasons for the "entertainment." The following week, the recipients of this charity expressed their gratitude in a newspaper notice that echoed the florid style of the original invitation, asking that "the Fatness of Heaven drop down upon their Hearts" (*Providence Gazette,* August 22, 1767).

12. Petition of Thomas Rathbun Jr., June 1, 1779, Exeter Town Records, Rhode Island Historical Society; TM, June 1, 1779, Exeter TMR, vol. 3.

13. TCM, September 2, 1799, Charlestown TCR 5:170.

14. Councils lodged poor people with their own kin as often as possible, perhaps as an informal application of the law that required relatives to support each other. But these caretakers were too poor themselves to support their even poorer kin without assistance from the town. Numerous sons and daughters received stipends for boarding their mothers and fathers; grandparents lodged with their grandchildren. "Bastard" children (who were taken on as the poor of the town if their mothers were needy) typically grew up in the same household with their mothers and

grandparents—at least, until they were old enough to be bound out as indentured servants, and then it was often those same grandparents who signed the contract as masters and mistresses to their grandchildren.

15. TCM, January 18, 1794, Glocester TCR 2:104.

16. The Hopkinton councilmen used this phrase when they were looking for a caretaker for Susannah Hall in 1793. (TCM, April 1, 1793, Hopkinton TCR 3:31.) The Cumberland authorities used another common phrase when they took on the care of indigent Jeremiah Plimpton in 1759: they determined to provide care "in the best manner they can with the least cost." (TCM, August 29, 1758, and April 18, 1759, Cumberland TMR 1:45A and 1:47A.)

17. TCM, January 2, 1797, Hopkinton TCR 3:94; TCM October 29, 1768, East Greenwich TCR 3:116.

18. Albro had been receiving £6 (Rhode Island old tenor currency) per week; the new competitive rate was £3 10s. (TCM, May 14, 1765, August 6, 1766, and August 21, 1767, Exeter TCR 3:8, 3:25, 3:39.) In another instance of this informal competition, two Richmond townspeople proposed to supply such necessities of life to a poor family in the town "for two thirds of what it cost the town [for] the year past"—an offer the taxpayers promptly accepted. (TM, June 6, 1780, Richmond TMR 3:501.)

19. TCM, December 8, 1772, Exeter TCR 3:131; TM, January 5, 1784, May 15, 1786, August 28, 1787, and June 10, 1789, Tiverton TMR, vol. 2.

20. Informal (not contracted) coercion to labor was usually exercised with women. For example, when Martha Remington, "a person of ability of body to work and earn her own living," sought to extend her sojourn at Warwick's town workhouse, the councilmen "would not consent to support her there any longer" and turned her out so that she had to fend for herself. And when the Glocester councilmen learned that Keziah Grant was "so slack" in her industry that she had brought herself and her three children into a state of need, they ordered that she receive certain necessities but also ordered that Grant herself be kept "properly to work." (TCM, December 14, 1767, Warwick TCR 2:293; TCM, May 27, 1786, Glocester TCR 2:12.)

21. These formal contracts were usually for men. For example, the Hopkinton councilmen decided to "bind out" James Phillips if he did not "apply him self to business in supporting his family." And when Jack Marsh of Jamestown became "old & very decrepit," the councilmen bound out his "idle" and "dissolute" son Japhet for a year, with the proceeds going to support the older man, since "it is the incumbent duty of all children, to contribute as much as in them lies, toward the support of their aged parents." (TCM, June 21, 1785, Hopkinton TCR, 2:238; TCM, August 27, 1754, Jamestown TCR 1:76.)

22. Barry Levy, "Girls and Boys: Poor Children and the Labor Market in Colonial Massachusetts," *Pennsylvania History* 64 (1997): 287–307; Lawrence Towner, "A Good Master Well Served: A Social History of Servitude in Massachusetts, 1620–1750" (Ph.D. diss., Northwestern University, 1955), repr. as *A Good Master Well Served: Masters and Servants in Colonial Massachusetts, 1620–1750* (New York: Garland Press, 1998); and "The Indentures of Boston's Poor Apprentices, 1734–1805," *Colonial Society of Massachusetts Publications* 43 (1966): 417–33, repr. in *Past Imperfect: Essays on History, Libraries, and the Humanities,* ed. Robert W. Karrow Jr. and Alfred F. Young (Chicago: University of Chicago Press, 1993), 36–55; and John E. Murray and Ruth Wallis Herndon, "Markets for Children in Early America: A Political Economy of Pauper Apprenticeship," *Journal of Economic History* 62, no. 2 (June 2002): 356–82.

23. Some sufferers even approached the town voters and leaders assembled in town meeting, perhaps calculating that a public appeal would be more effective than a private petition. In 1770, for example, Samuel Bailey announced to the Richmond town meeting that "his circumstances are very poor and his wife in a weak condition" and asked for some assistance from the town. The town meeting gave Bailey 7s 6d to tide him over his difficulties. (TM, July 2, 1770, Richmond TMR 2:337.)

24. Some towns elected separate overseers of the poor, who served as the council's eyes, ears, and hands in their dealings with the poor. Overseers provided information to councilmen,

awaited their decisions, and carried out their directives. In the most populous towns, with the largest population of poor people (Providence, for example), overseers had considerable discretion and latitude in dispensing town funds to the poor, and some even maintained their own account books. In less populated towns and towns less troubled by needs of the poor, voters elected men to serve simultaneously as councilmen and overseers of the poor, underscoring how central poor relief was to the business of town leadership.

25. TCM, May 19, 1767, Jamestown TCR 2:2. Although the carriers of information are usually identified as male in the town records, there are occasional references to female involvement. In 1784, for example, Rebecah Nun and overseer of the poor Lawton Palmer jointly brought complaint to the Hopkinton council about a poor man who was "not well used" by his caretaker. The pairing of Nun (the observant neighbor) with Palmer (the town official) suggests the true provenance of much information—female neighbors who were the first to be aware of needy circumstances and who nudged their husbands, sons, and fathers to carry the information to official parties. As a result of the joint complaint, the Hopkinton town council ordered the poor man's caretaker to appear before them to answer the complaint. (TCM, March 9, 1784, Hopkinton TCR 2:128.)

26. The concerned "neighbors" who started information down the pipeline were often family, who naturally had the best chance of observing the circumstances of suffering firsthand. Families were essentially economic units in colonial America, and when a member (laborer) in that economic unit was prevented from labor by illness, handicap, or death, the town stepped in to fill the gap. In 1772, Widow Bugbee informed the Warwick councilmen that her mother "through age and infirmity of body, was rendered unable to do anything to support herself." Widow Bugbee reported "she was willing to do what was in her power to help her mother, but it was too hard to do it all" and she wanted financial help from the town so that she could hire someone to assist her in caring for her mother. The councilmen granted Bugbee a little over one shilling per week to help support her mother. (TCM, September 14, 1772, Warwick TCR 3:17–18.) Similarly, in 1795, Deborah Greene reported to the Warwick councilmen that her grandfather, James Tallman "is very much unwell, and his wife blind, & they are therefore rendered incapable of supporting themselves." Greene asked for an allowance for them from the council. The council granted the Tallmans a weekly stipend of 6s (3s for the husband; 3s for the wife). (TCM, September 14, 1785, Warwick TCR 4:377.)

27. TCM, June 19, 1757, Exeter TCR 2:15; TCM, December 29, 1785, Hopkinton TCR 2:243; TCM, June 25, 1791, East Greenwich TCR 4:143.

28. Elisabeth Odell's story is told in fragments, primarily through references to her caretakers being repaid. She is first mentioned as being cared for by Daniel Coon in 1771 (TCM, September 10, 1771, Hopkinton TCR 2:9); she is last mentioned when an inventory of her meager estate was taken after she died some six years later (TCM, March 2, 1778, Hopkinton TCR 2:97).

29. Examination of James Anderson Morgan, TCM, July 18, 1768, New Shoreham TCR 4:174. Town councilmen made this judgment after they viewed "the marks on the boy's body."

30. William Maxson Jr. to Mr. Champlin, December 4, 1791, miscellaneous clerk's papers, Hopkinton Town Clerk's Office.

31. TM, February 10, 1797, New Shoreham TMR 5:308; TCM, December 11, 1780, Warwick TCR 3:93; TCM, December 28, 1782, and June 9, 1783, Warwick TCR 3:126, 3:137.

32. TCM, April 12, 1763, Glocester TCR 1:58.

33. TCM, June 17, 1754, Middletown TCR 1:279.

34. TCM, June 2, 1788, Hopkinton TCR 2:292.

35. TCM, November 6, 1786, Providence TCR 5:402; Overseer of the Poor Account, January 29, 1794, PTP 19:108.

36. TCM, April 9, 1781, South Kingstown TCR 6:81, and TCM, September 28, 1751, Glocester TCR 1:E.

37. TCM, June 11, 1764, Warwick TCR 2:246–48.

38. Petition of Christopher A. Sylvester, November 3, 1794, PTP 20:140.

39. TCM, November 16, 1778 and January 26, 1779, East Greenwich TCR 3:191–92, 3:194.

40. Indenture of Benoni Church, November 30, 1795, PTP 23:53.

41. TCM, June 3 and September 9, 1771, Warwick TCR 3:5–7. The Warwick councilmen terminated the girl's indenture, apparently in response to the mother's action, but there was probably a question as to whether a child bound out by public officials could legally be moved outside the colony's jurisdiction.

42. TCM, September 3, 1766, Jamestown TCR 1:229.

43. TCM, March 27, 1762, Jamestown TCR 1:143–44.

44. TCM, April 9, 1770, South Kingstown TCR 5:228.

45. TCM, August 27, 1754, Jamestown TCR 1:75–76.

46. TCM, October 13, 1772, South Kingstown TCR 6:7; TCM, March 27, 1773, East Greenwich TCR 3:142–43; TCM, July 4, 1800, Exeter TCR 6:200–201.

47. Ruth Wallis Herndon, "Women as Symbols of Disorder in Early Rhode Island," in *Women and the Colonial Gaze*, ed. Tamara L. Hunt and Micheline R. Lessard (Basingstoke, Eng.: Palgrave, 2002), 79–90.

48. Herndon, *Unwelcome Americans*, 18–19, 205.

49. Herndon, "Women of 'No Particular Home,'" 269–89, and *Unwelcome Americans*, 16–18.

50. In the first part of the eighteenth century, town clerks generally used "mustee" to refer to people of mixed Indian and European ancestry and used "mulatto" to refer to people of mixed African and European ancestry. But these terms became increasingly ambiguous and slippery toward the end of the century, as clerks began to describe Indian people as "black" or "Negro" or "mulatto." (See Ruth Wallis Herndon and Ella Wilcox Sekatau, "The Right to a Name: Narragansett People and Rhode Island Officials in the Revolutionary Era," *Ethnohistory* 44, no. 3 [summer 1997]: 433–62.) Further, clerks did not consistently note the race of the person being warned out. Where no race is mentioned, I assumed the person was white; but almost certainly, some of those people were not white, and these are thus low estimates for the number of nonwhite people in the warned out population.

51. In 1755, people of color constituted 11.6 percent of the population in Rhode Island; in 1783, Indians constituted 0.9 percent and blacks 4.5 percent of the population (Evarts B. Greene and Virginia D. Harrington, *American Population Before the Federal Census of 1790* [Gloucester, Mass.: Peter Smith, 1966], 67–70). Later counts show blacks representing 6.3 percent of Rhode Island's population in 1790 and 5.3 percent in 1800 (U.S. Bureau of the Census, *Negro Population 1790–1915* [Washington, D.C.: Government Printing Office, 1918], 51).

52. Herndon, "Women of 'No Particular Home,'" 269–70.

53. TCM, July 16, 1751, Jamestown TCR 1:44.

54. TCM, March 5, 1770, February 17, 1772, March 20, and April 4, 1780, and October 1, 1787, Providence TCR 4:299, 4:322, 5:168–69, 5:172, and 6:23; PTP 10:148.

55. Letter to Rehoboth Overseers of the Poor, TCM, May 18, 1778, Providence TCR 5:113–15. The punishment referred to was a public whipping.

56. TCM, May 3, 1779, Glocester TCR 1:40; TCM, December 10, 1786, Providence TCR 5:404.

57. TCM, April 24, 1780, Exeter TCR 4:73; TM, August 26, 1788, Warwick TMR 3:316; William Aldrich Account, Warwick TMR 1:311, Rhode Island Historical Society.

58. TM, June 5, 1786, Glocester TMR 1:183.

59. TCM, December 17, 1768, Providence TCR 4:282; TM, January 4, 1763, Warwick TMR, 2:272–73; TCM, December 9, 1765, Warwick TCR, 2:267–68; TM, August 27, 1751, and August 27, 1754, Glocester TMR, vol. 1; TM, May 20 and December 16, 1754, Tiverton TMR 2:3–4.

60. TM, September 10, 1779, Richmond TMR 3:565; TM, February 17, 1781, East Greenwich TMR, vol. 2; TM, October 6 and December 13, 1783, Tiverton TMR 2:157–58; TM, May 28, 1783, Middletown TMR 1:148; TM, April 20, 1785, Hopkinton TMR, vol. 1; TM, December 4, 1786, Warren TMR 1:217; TM of March 6, June 5, and June 9, 1787, South Kingstown TMR 2:235–43; TM, August 31, 1790, Glocester TMR 2:18.

61. TM, April 20, 1785, Hopkinton TMR, vol. 1. In the 1700s, most Rhode Island towns made no distinctions between poorhouses and workhouses. Some who entered the Warwick "workhouse," for example, were totally incapable of working and contributed nothing toward their support. The terms seem genuinely interchangeable in most town records and to refer generally to a group setting in which needy people would be housed. Providence was the exception. The 1773 rules for their workhouse make clear that profitable employment was demanded of all inmates. In addition, this workhouse had a "cage" where disorderly or troublesome inmates would be put for correction. (Rules for the Providence Workhouse, October 8, 1773, PTP 2:82.) By 1775, this cage was being used to house disorderly transients and poor inhabitants who were not inmates of the workhouse; and by 1796, a "Bridewell" had been constructed next to the workhouse, a prison to hold the increasing numbers of troublesome poor and vagrant people. (TCM, November 8, 1775, Providence TCR 5:343; TM, June 23, 1796, Providence TMR 7:376–77.)

62. TM, January 22, 1753, Providence TMR 5:43.

63. Cray, *Paupers and Poor Relief*, 67–68, 83–99.

64. TM, July 7, 1794, South Kingstown TMR 2:345; TM, August 26, 1794, South Kingstown TMR 2:347. As early as 1773, Providence authorities announced to "all the doctors in this Town" that they were prepared to issue a contract to one of them "to doctor all the poor of this Town per annum"; the winning bid would be the one "who will undertake for the smallest sum for a year if the council shall judge it to be reasonable." (TM 3d Wednesday of April 1773, Providence TMR 6:np.)

65. TCM, October 4, 1788, Warwick TCR 3:235.

66. Herndon, *Unwelcome Americans*, 12.

67. Ibid., 14–15. On Providence and Newport, see Lynne Withey, *Urban Growth in Colonial Rhode Island: Newport and Providence in the Eighteenth Century* (Albany: State University of New York Press, 1984); Elaine Forman Crane, *A Dependent People: Newport, Rhode Island in the Revolutionary Era* (New York: Fordham University Press, 1985); and Florence Parker Simister, *The Fire's Center: Rhode Island in the Revolutionary Era, 1763–1790* (Providence: Rhode Island Bicentennial Foundation, 1979).

68. Bruce C. Daniels, *The Fragmentation of New England: Comparative Perspectives on Economic, Political, and Social Divisions in the Eighteenth Century* (Westport, Conn.: Greenwood Press, 1988), 40.

69. TM, November 26, 1754, East Greenwich TMR 2:np.

70. TM, November 4, 1754, Glocester TMR 1:30.

71. TM, December 17, 1787, Warwick TMR 3:287.

72. TM, January 17, 1789, Warwick TMR 3:337.

73. TM, 1st Monday of July 1782, June 3, 1783, June 1, 1784, Hopkinton TMR 1:150, 1:232.

74. TCM, January 7 through November 10, 1788, Hopkinton TCR 2:285–300.

# Six

## Gender and the Political Economy of Poor Relief in Colonial Philadelphia

KARIN WULF

In the six cases they considered at their weekly meeting on September 1, 1768, the overseers of the poor for the city of Philadelphia confronted many of the typical needs and circumstances of people in poverty. After deliberating, the overseers decided to send Catherine Porter and her son back home to Chester County, thereafter to become the responsibility of poor relief officials in that locale. They recommended that four women be sent to Philadelphia's Bettering House, opened less than a year earlier. These included three pregnant women, abandoned by husbands, who were sent to the almshouse wing of the Bettering House, the section designated for needy poor unable to work. One woman was sent to the house of employment wing, where she would be expected to contribute her labor. And Fanny McCulloch, who had been sent away from the city's jail while ill, was deemed cured; the woman who had nursed and boarded McCulloch at the overseers' expense needed to be paid.[1]

At that fall meeting the overseers of the poor confronted a constant feature of the city's poor relief system: the preponderance of women seeking and receiving relief. But the overseers also faced a very new feature: recent reforms had shifted the emphasis of poor relief from traditional "out relief"—the awarding of small sums for food, board, medical care, and even burial services directly to the needy—to institutionalization. Previously the overseers likely would have given needy women some firewood and perhaps money to pay for rent or nursing care. Under the new system, the overseers had little choice but to send pregnant and abandoned women to the Bettering House, where they would be confined and compelled to work (if capable) until able to provide for themselves and their dependents. A probable scenario involved the forced indenture of their children as apprentices.

These types of welfare practices, endemic in urban centers in the late eighteenth and early nineteenth centuries, have long been a subject of academic analysis. Scholars have examined why places like Philadelphia turned from a system of out relief rooted in the English parish-based notion of collective community responsibility for the "traditional poor"—women, children, the infirm, and the elderly—toward a scheme of institutionalization.[2] Such diverse scholars as David Rothman and Michel Foucault have interpreted these institutions as reflecting the shift from early modern to modern sensibilities and the concomitant development of new means of class surveillance. In many accounts, the significance of increased poverty among men was profound. In Gary Nash's classic formulation, for example, economic depression and increasing poverty among able-bodied men after the Seven Years' War stimulated the construction of institutions, such as Philadelphia's Bettering House. Among these newly impoverished men, however, were born the seeds of class consciousness that would flower into some of the most radical aspects of the American Revolution.[3]

Historians of the nineteenth and twentieth centuries have recently paid a great deal of attention to the place of women and the role of gender ideologies in shaping welfare policies. Feminist scholars, such as Linda Gordon, focused on the modern, expansive, interventionist state in perpetuating inequalities between men and women. These scholars developed structural critiques of welfare and its antecedents, pointing to the ways in which welfare policies reflected specific gender definitions. While this literature has grown more sophisticated in theorizing the sources and meanings of women's poverty and their interaction with state policies, its fundamental achievement remains, as Gordon contends, that "welfare as an academic topic or a social issue cannot be understood without particular attention to the situation of women and the gender system of the society."[4]

A similar analysis of gender and welfare is possible for earlier periods. In Philadelphia, the most studied among colonial British American cities, ideas about gender were central to shaping both poverty and poor relief policies. Although later, national welfare policies reflected gendered notions in ways that synchronized with the complex of modern governmental and civic forms, traditional ideas about household and dependency shaped men's and women's differential experiences of poverty and poor relief and the subsequent generations of relief policies.

By examining Philadelphia, in this essay I will argue that ideologies of gender shaped both the realities of poverty among men and women and the changing poor relief policies that were implemented in the colonial period.[5] After sketching the nature of poverty and poor relief in early Philadelphia,

I will examine the differential treatment of men and women within those systems. Finally, I will analyze how gender informed a political economy of poor relief.

The concept of political economy provides a useful way of understanding the interconnections between gender and poor relief. Students of early America will recognize Drew McCoy's formulation of "political economy" as the economy's embodiment of political goals and values and, conversely, the effort of politicians and others to shape the economy accordingly. Scholars of gender and modern welfare have extended this idea, arguing that rather than being independent of social and cultural forces, economic policies result from dominant concepts about community, including race, class, gender, and sexuality. Political economy thus inheres in the formulation of such governmental policies as poor relief. In colonial Philadelphia, notions about gender helped shape a political economy of poor relief.[6]

Four features of poverty and poor relief characterized eighteenth-century Philadelphia. First, two kinds of poor relief were provided: out relief and institutionalization. The former was the predominant form of aid throughout most of the colonial period. It allowed a needy person to collect assistance and remain within the community, and it was available in several different forms. The overseers of the poor provided onetime provisions, consisting of small sums of money or specific goods or services. They made the occasional loan for rent, paid maintenance for pregnant indigents during their lying in, and supplied specific essential items, such as firewood in the winter and apprenticeships for poor children. In 1709, for example, officials purchased a "pr shoes for Gideon Eaches child" and "a cord of wood for Mary Whitman" and paid 8 shillings to "Widd[ow] Blancy for Whitman in her lying in."[7] Overseers also paid for funereal services, including "winding sheets" to wrap the corpse, grave digging, burial fees, and even liquor to serve the mourners.[8]

Relief payments often were made in the hopes of getting people in need back on their feet and on the road to self-sufficiency. For example, after determining that Mary Bennan, who was "in great want" in October 1751, was a legal resident of Philadelphia, the overseers "pd her 15 s[hillings] to carry on her Buss[iness]."[9] Officials and relief recipients apparently preferred these short-term provisions since they both allowed the independence of recipients and comported with social values that emphasized communal interdependence and hostility to long-term dependence. Officials rarely awarded long-term pensions to the poor, and even these were quite small, perhaps several shillings in the late 1730s. Most indigents remained on the pension rolls only a few months, although a handful received support for up to a year.[10]

The other type of government assistance, "indoor" or institutional relief, began in 1732 when Philadelphians constructed an almshouse. It was small and never housed as many needy as the overseers aided through out relief.[11] Only in 1768, with the erection of the Bettering House, did institutions become an important and ultimately the sole component of the relief system in Philadelphia.

The second feature of poor relief was that it comprised a growing proportion of the city's budget during the first three-quarters of the eighteenth century. Beginning in the 1730s, lawmakers increased the poor tax to cover mounting costs. After the Seven Years' War, an economic downturn created considerable unemployment, which, combined with several harsh winters and a growing number of immigrants and ex-soldiers, produced more needy people. As costs increased, city officials searched for new and cheaper ways to deal with indigents. Constructing a Bettering House was an attempt to curtail rising costs.[12]

Third, unmarried women were particularly vulnerable to poverty and they often had to provide for children. Whether widowed, abandoned, or never married, these women suffered financial distress due to systemic and life-cycle developments, including pregnancies and other medical conditions that kept them from working, childcare responsibilities that hindered their work opportunities, and the low wages paid women in the early modern economy. Similar to today, women with children but without husbands experienced poverty often and acutely.[13]

Fourth, colonial relief officials evaluated both the character of the poor and the nature of their need, going to great lengths to ensure that public funds aided only "proper objects" of relief.[14] One issue that officials debated was whether an individual should even receive assistance from the city or the charity to which he or she had applied, or whether that person should be treated elsewhere (either in another locale or by another group). Officials also wanted to know the extent of a person's need and whether relief constituted an appropriate response; this required investigation. By virtue of Pennsylvania's poor law of 1706, the overseers of the poor could not grant relief to anyone until "that person or persons have procured an order from two justices of the peace for the same," and those orders came only after an investigation of the applicant.[15] Relief officials may have been likely to find women suitable "objects" of relief because so many of them were so needy, or because the cultural image of women as dependent was fitting, or a combination of both. Ultimately, evaluations of the poor were often based on gender—how well or how ill a man or woman conformed to the standards of gendered behavior expected of a person in economic deprivation. As those expectations changed, the forms of poor relief altered to reflect them.

The last two of these factors—unmarried women's particular economic vulnerability and the inclination of poor relief officials to find women especially suitable recipients of relief—explain why unmarried women, in contrast to single men or married couples, were the primary constituents of public poor relief in colonial Philadelphia.[16] This was especially true of out relief, which was the most flexible, appropriate, and desirable form of assistance for women, largely because it could be combined with low-waged or part-time work and familial unity.[17]

With these basic features of the colonial relief system in mind, and by comparing the treatment and experience of men and women within the system, we can better understand the ways that ideas about gender shaped both poor relief policies and practices. Extant records show who applied for poor relief. They also illustrate the kinds of decisions overseers of the poor made about the disposition of those applications and the amount they allotted to needy men and women in out relief, institutional care, and pensions. In addition, the records suggest much about how relief officials distinguished between appropriate and inappropriate aid recipients and how they then continued to evaluate the needy poor in their care. The centrality of gender to the processes of application and receipt of relief, and the practices of official evaluation, is evident.

Such relief records are extant for only select years; they are, however, fairly evenly spread over the colonial period, and they illustrate different aspects of the poor relief system. One commonality among the different kinds of records is the predominance of women among both applicants and recipients of out relief. Thirty-one of forty-five surviving directives to the overseers from Robert Strettel and William Plumstead, mayors of Philadelphia between March 1751 and March 1752, for example, concerned poor women in need.[18] The public poor relief process was set in motion when individual Philadelphians notified officials that a person was in need. These referrals might come in the form of a complaint, as when Jane Collins informed Mayor Robert Strettel in October 1751 that "a poor man who lodges at her house is very destitute of every thing necessary to support life and must perish if not speedily relieved."[19] With winter approaching, Collins probably could ill afford to keep the man herself. After a referral, the mayor directed the overseers to investigate these applications.

Just as women comprised the majority of out relief applicants, they also constituted the majority of out relief recipients. Cash payments went to women twice as often as to men in 1709, and in 1739 thirteen of eighteen payments of cash or provisions of wood or clothing were provided to women. In 1758–59, the overseers of the poor paid rent for seven women and six men and gave cash to seven women and no men. The overseers spent considerable money aiding pregnant women, providing them with cash, nursing and midwifery services, and food. They also helped pay traveling expenses for twenty-four women, but only ten men, perhaps presuming that women were more likely to add to the city's population of needy and that removing them from the city would be cost beneficial. These strategies did not always work, as in the case of Margaret Neal, who received 3 shillings in December of 1758 to move out of the city. But the next week, the overseers paid "Grany Pauling for laying [in of] Peg Neal," and again in March they paid Neal another shilling.[20]

Women also collected the majority of poor relief pensions. In 1709, ten of fourteen pensions were provided to women, and in 1739, twenty-three of thirty-one pensioners were women.[21] Thirty-three women and nine men collected regular pensions in 1751.[22] Most received pensions for short periods, suggesting that women experienced intermittent poverty and made use of multiple sources of aid.[23] Pensions represented a kind of middle ground in poor relief strategies, reflecting the authorities' recognition of long-term need, but they stopped short of institutionalization. That middle ground disappeared in the late colonial period.

The overseers of the poor continued to provide reduced amounts of out relief through July 1769, even after they had been directed to begin sending all appropriate persons to the new Bettering House. Most of those who appeared on a list of "Necessitous Persons to whom small sums were Advanced for their immediate Relief" were female. The expenditures for the overseers of the poor for one month during this period demonstrate that women collected more than twice the amount provided men. In April 1767, women were awarded about £9 in out relief, while men garnered about £4; 13 shillings were allotted to children's care.[24]

In short, during the era when out relief was the principal form of poor relief, whether distributed as money, goods, or services, and even when it was minimally available during the late 1760s, it was most often formally sought by and allocated primarily to women.[25] Whether the disproportionate number of women in the relief system was shaped by the reality of poverty's differential impact on women and men or the predisposition of poor relief officials to find women more worthy of relief than men is hard to say with certitude. Most likely both factors played a role.

During the eighteenth century, the rise of exclusively institutional forms of aid and increasing attention to male poverty substantially changed both men's and women's experiences with poor relief in Philadelphia. Well before the Bettering House was built in 1767, Philadelphians were familiar with smaller, more discreet institutions designed to house the poor in conjunction with out relief. The city almshouse was constructed in 1713, and the Pennsylvania Hospital for the Sick Poor began accepting patients in a private home in 1752. The hospital moved into its own building on Spruce Street (where it still stands) in 1756.[26] These institutions worked alongside the overseers of the poor in their administration of out relief. Rather than having an entirely separate set of officials, the overseers of the poor made referrals to the almshouse, and poor Philadelphians accepted simultaneous or consecutive ministrations from the overseers and the hospital.[27]

Although out relief was predominantly awarded to women, institutions accommodated men and women in more equal numbers. For the early eighteenth century, only the account books of the overseers of the poor can tell us who was sent to the city almshouse. In 1739, for example, five of seven people the overseers transported to the almshouse were women, and all three whose almshouse board was paid by a third party (as in the case of a maid of Charles Cox who was presumably either ill or pregnant or both) were women.[28] The best surviving figures are for 1751, when the warden of the almshouse made a report about the inmates and their respective situations. In that year, women comprised 76 percent of the applications for temporary relief and 79 percent of the pensioners paid regularly by the overseers. But while women commanded such a substantial majority of the out relief resources, almost equal numbers of women and men (twenty-six and twenty-four, respectively) resided at the Almshouse.[29]

Part of the reason for the parity in institutional care might be the willingness of poor relief officials to provide out relief to women even when their condition suggested that institutionalization was more appropriate. For example, the overseers paid to keep disabled or sick women out of institutions by granting them small pensions.[30] "Crazy" Mary Charton lived in Elizabeth Heany's house at the corner of Chestnut and Second Streets, and received 2 shillings, 6 pence a week from the overseers of the poor. Other pensioners were considered incapable of handling their own funds, like "Crasy" Bridgit Sullivan, whose unusually large pension of 7 shillings, 6 pence the overseers paid directly to Catherine Smith, presumably Sullivan's landlord. Mary Mills was bedridden, and "an Old Woman" received a pension of 5 shillings on her behalf. The overseers' case notes indicate that they supported other aged or ill female pensioners in their own lodgings (albeit usually in someone else's house) rather than send them to the Almshouse. As we will see, this pattern did not extend to men in need.

The overseers' seeming preference for granting women out relief as opposed to institutionalizing them at the almshouse is one of a number of important differences in the evaluation and disposition of poor men's and women's situations. A sheaf of applications for relief written in 1751 and a unique report of the almshouse warden on the conditions of his inmates in the same year illustrate both how men and women became impoverished differently as well as how the overseers represented and responded to their poverty. The overseers assessed two factors: the causes associated with poverty, and whether the condition of the destitute necessitated relief.

According to relief applications and the almshouse warden's report, the causes of men's and women's poverty diverged. Men were much more likely than women to be severely disabled or very aged, making them permanently unable to work. In 1751, twelve of the twenty-four men lodged in the almshouse had a permanent disability, such as blindness or paralysis, while only two women were described as severely disabled.[31] Similarly, most of the men who applied for relief were described by themselves or by others as sick or disabled, and their illness or disability was described relative to their ability to work. A petition for Robert Maxfield, for example, stated that he "labours under a disorder in his Legg by which he is rendered unable to gett a subsistence—and . . . he belongs to this city."[32]

Women who petitioned for aid or were lodged at the almshouse in 1751, in contrast, were usually not sick, disabled, or permanently prevented by physical incapacity from working. Most simply cited poverty as the reason for their application for relief. Ann Campbell was a "very Poor and Distressed Object"; Elizabeth Smith was "unable to maintain herself and destitute."[33] Most of these women were unmarried. A few were wives of jailed debtors or of men who had abandoned them, but all lacked the financial advantage of a working husband.[34] The presence of children in seven of thirty-one women's petitions, and the absence of children in all of the men's, suggest at least one other marked difference in the situations of destitute men and women. Martha Adams, for example, was simply "incapable to maintain her Self & Child being very Poor."[35]

While the causes of men's and women's poverty were represented to be quite different, poor relief officials' decisions about how to treat their respective cases was also distinct. In most cases the mayor's directives to the overseers of the poor to investigate poor relief applicants were not accompanied by information about the disposition of their application. But a handful of cases in which the overseers reported their findings to the mayor make plain the onus on poor men to demonstrate their needs in ways that reflected the cultural valuation of masculine independence. Thomas Dason, for example, suffered from an "indisposition of body" and was "rendered unable to support himself & family." The overseers found that Dason was not a resident of

Philadelphia; "he has not gaind any Settlement here." The overseers were thus not obligated to assist him, although they also found him "not in other respects a proper Object."[36] In other words, they might as they did in other cases, particularly with needy women, have helped Dason anyway. But they found him not a suitable candidate for relief. Was it his failure to provide for his family that made him such an unappealing case for charity? Samuel Blamey lay ill "in a consumption" and was similarly unable to provide for his family. Instead of rejecting his case outright, the overseers sent Dr. Shippen, one of the doctors at the hospital, to examine Blamey.[37] The cases in which men were most easily able to compel the overseers sympathies and resources were more straightforward: these were men who were elderly, clearly incapable of labor, and no longer expected to head households or care for others. They had served their families and their communities and now, in the absence of younger kin to care for them, deserved a small share of the poor relief monies. James Armstrong, for example, was "a Poor Man an Ancient Inhabitant past his Labour." The overseers determined he had been a "Ditcher & Sawer of Wood" and gave him a shilling to help with his maintenance.[38]

The ways that poor relief authorities evaluated men and women already lodged in the almshouse likewise demonstrates the different sets of expectations and assumptions about men's and women's capacities for labor and deservedness for relief. In the report on the condition of almshouse inmates in 1751, the almshouse warden was much more likely to find men "fit" for release from the almshouse, while even women who were described as healthy or were cited as unruly were not turned out. Although Elizabeth Boon, for example, seemed "fit to do something for her own Maintenance," the warden did not recommend that she be expelled.[39]

In contrast, almost every man the warden described as "fit" was slated for release. The descriptions of their conditions demonstrate how liberally the warden used that term when referring to men. Tellingly, he identified most men by their occupation. He judged sixty-year-old James Sidbotham, a barber, able to "do for himself," and butcher Jonathan Richards "well enough to go out" even though he was "very ragged." The warden assessed "old Taylor" Hugh Ross and Gabriel Green, another "old Barber," as fit to "go out during the summer." Thomas Tanten had been in the almshouse since 1748 and was "an old infirm lame Butcher." Nevertheless, the warden thought Tanten "yet might p[er]haps do something" for his own keep and recommended him for release. The warden simply called Thomas Savory "no proper person for the Alms House."[40] The definition of "fitness" was clearly much more expansive for men than it was for women, and the warden expected that, though quite aged and perhaps somewhat disabled, men would or should be able to provide for themselves. Women, no matter what their health, were understood to be less capable of sustaining themselves and their families economically.[41]

The striking difference, then, in men's and women's applications for poor relief in 1751 and in the descriptions of the male and female almshouse inmates' conditions was that men were represented as unable to work because of their physical state, while women were described as simply unable to support themselves. Both petitioners and petitioned believed that men could and should labor, while women were less able to do so for a complex of reasons. These determinations suggest that the authorities found women more needy and more deserving of relief and that men were held to a much stricter standard.

With the rise of larger institutions engineered to address the problems of poverty in the mid-eighteenth century, elites and some officials began to calculate gender, need, and poor relief somewhat differently. Beginning with the reformers who built the Pennsylvania Hospital for the Sick Poor in 1753, some authorities began to focus increasingly on male poverty, although the sex ratio of the poor—and ultimately even the sex ratios of the relieved poor—changed only a little. These reformers, because they addressed primarily male rather than female destitution, concluded that new kinds of relief efforts were necessary not only to provide aid to the poor in times of extreme need, but to get to the root causes of poverty. In reformers' eyes, male poverty, unlike female destitution, was not systemic but instead was caused by illness or injury to male householders or by the men's moral failings. Institutional care would set men on the road back to physical, moral, and ultimately financial health. It was good for the individual male, good for his impoverished family, and good for the community that no longer wanted to pay for their aid; institutional reforms thus promised much. As we will see, this new calculus failed to account fully for the realities of women's, but also men's, poverty. It was a significant departure from the traditional commitment to out relief as the best way to address those realities.

At the same time the almshouse warden was harshly rating the condition of his male inmates, a group of Philadelphians hatched a plan to get more poor men back to work. Opened in 1752, the Pennsylvania Hospital for the Sick Poor was a semipublic institution whose funding came from private contributors and a matching grant from the colonial assembly. The brainchild of Thomas Bond and Benjamin Franklin, the hospital was based in large measure on the voluntary hospitals springing up in England. The drive for such hospitals combined interests in reducing public poor relief expenditures and in making the poor both more grateful for assistance and more contented with their lot.[42] In urban areas, poverty was on the rise, and the evidence of the poor population was ever more visible. The old system of relief based on the notion that communities were responsible for the care of those born in and residing within their geographic boundaries now seemed ill suited to urban destitution. Reformers began to see out relief as a kind of "handout" that encouraged neediness, rather than a temporary measure that helped ameliorate the harshest effects of poverty and economic dependency, particularly among women with children. They thus envisioned new forms of relief that would better reflect their new understanding of poverty.

The hospital's founding also reflected the ideological connection between the character of the poor, specific family forms, and political economy. English writers had more energetically derided the "idle" poor since the early eighteenth century and now began to valorize their counterpart, the "industrious poor."[43] Whereas the discourse of evaluation in the earlier period contrasted the "worthy" poor or "proper objects of charity" with the unworthy and the improper, by the 1750s a new language had emerged to describe the problems of poverty. Increasingly, authorities and philanthropists contrasted a shocking inclination to "live in Sloth and Idleness" with "industrious" poverty, finding the poor exhibiting more of the former and less of the latter as the eighteenth century advanced.[44]

Ultimately, the "industrious" and the "idle" began to replace the worthy and the unworthy as the principal categories of the poor.[45] Significantly, these new categories largely described types of poor men, whereas previous categories had often simply contrasted women ("proper objects") with men (not proper objects).[46] The industrious poor were usually described as men whose poverty should abate with recovery from illness or injury, and whose wives and children would be simultaneously aided by affording them medical attention. The Pennsylvania Hospital, Franklin noted, would allow the sick poor to be "useful to themselves, their families, and the public."[47] The hospital organizer's original petition to the Pennsylvania assembly stressed that the sick poor would, "by the judicious Assistance of Physic and Surgery, be enabled to taste the blessings of health, and be made in a few weeks Useful Members of the Community, able to provide for themselves and families."[48]

Thus, despite the fact that most women relieved by these organizations were not married, either because they were widowed or never married, and that the majority of the needy poor were women, officials increasingly focused on the rehabilitation of poor men as a solution to women's poverty. Questioning the benefits of direct or out relief and advocating institutional reforms, the author of an essay appended to the hospital's annual report for 1764 opined that although "of some Kinds of Charity the Consequences are dubious; some Evils which Beneficence has been busy to remedy, are not certainly known to be very grievous to the sufferer, or detrimental to the Community." "No man can question," he continued, "whether it not be worthy . . . to restore those [men] to Ease and usefulness, from whose Labours Infants and Women expect their bread."[49] The author elided the realities of poverty among women that the overseers had long struggled with. Not mentioning the higher rates of poverty among women without husbands—or at least the large numbers of such women who had sought and received poor relief—the author suggested that men at labor were the obvious solution to all poverty.

To ensure that the hospital met its goal of assisting only what Franklin called the "useful and laborious" poor, the hospital's managing board adopted a set of guidelines and procedures. These "Rules Agreed to by the Managers of the Pennsylvania Hospital for the Admission & Discharge of Patients" clearly privileged men over women by mandating that "women having young Children . . . not be received unless their Children are taken care of elsewhere that the Hospital may not be burthened with the maintenance of such Children nor the Patients disturbed with their noise."[50] Thus, in practice the hospital refused to admit pregnant women for the delivery of their child. Midwives, at the expense of the overseers of the poor, continued to care for pregnant indigent women, or as a last resort the expectant mothers were sent to the almshouse.[51]

The prohibition on children, together with the hospital's stated goal of rehabilitating poor men to laboring condition and its program of admission recommendations, meant that the hospital admitted fewer poor women than men. The number of men and women resident in the hospital during the month of May (a month of careful accounting after the annual surveys conducted in April) for the years 1757 (when the new hospital building opened) through 1768 (when the Bettering House opened) is shown in table 9. On average, 68 percent of the hospital's residents during those months were men, and 32 percent were women.

Comparing records of the overseers of the poor, the almshouse, and the Pennsylvania Hospital suggests two important aspects about gender, poverty, and poor relief in Philadelphia before the erection of the largest poor relief institution, the Bettering House, in 1768. First, poor relief officials were much more likely to award relief to women than to men. Second, when relief was designed for men, as in the case of the hospital, it was of a variety meant literally to heal the very temporary causes of their poverty rather than to address any daily, ongoing needs. While women received (albeit in small amounts) money, food, blankets, wood, or other material assistance, men received short almshouse stays in extreme cases or medical care for the duration of their

TABLE 9. Pennsylvania Hospital Residents, May 1757–1768

| Year | Women (%) | Men (%) | Total Number |
|------|-----------|---------|--------------|
| 1757 | 42 | 58 | 19 |
| 1758 | 32 | 68 | 28 |
| 1759 | 28 | 72 | 36 |
| 1760 | 37 | 63 | 46 |
| 1761 | 42 | 58 | 50 |
| 1762 | 34 | 66 | 56 |
| 1763 | 29 | 71 | 84 |
| 1764 | 30 | 70 | 101 |
| 1765 | 28 | 72 | 107 |
| 1766 | 28 | 72 | 106 |
| 1767 | 34 | 66 | 115 |
| 1768 | 35 | 65 | 101 |

*Source:* Admission and Residence Records, Archives of the Pennsylvania Hospital, American Philosophical Society, Philadelphia.

infirmity. The assumption was that only illness or injury could or should make men unable to care for themselves and their families, whereas many other factors contributed to women's poverty. The increasing emphasis on men's poverty could not eradicate the corollary to the cultural presumptions of the common law of coverture: women were dependent, perhaps by nature, certainly by social design.

Although the Pennsylvania Hospital reflected shifting sentiments about poverty (and its relation to the enactment of appropriate gender roles), it was not until another group of reformers began to agitate for the Bettering House that the elision of the systemic sources of female poverty was complete. What caused a few Philadelphians to propose the Bettering House scheme, and what probably caused other Philadelphians to give the idea credence, was the economic crisis precipitated by the end of the Seven Years' War. The end of wartime requisitioning combined with taxation to pay off war debts helped bring on a depression.[52] The increasing costs of consumer basics, such as food and housing, and an unemployment problem that owed much to the economic crisis as well as high immigration meant that the city's poor became poorer, and more people joined their ranks.[53] The poor relief system was severely strained, and taxes to pay for the increasing demand for relief increased at a rapid clip.

In 1765, the overseers of the poor raised the ordinarily quite modest poor tax an extraordinary 66 percent.[54] The almshouse was overflowing, they reported, and the number of poor they aided had doubled between 1755 and 1764.[55] The overseers even briefly advocated the construction of a work-house to deal with the teeming population of unemployed. But when the assembly did adopt a scheme for a new institution, it shifted poor relief responsibility and tax authorization almost entirely to a new body: a group of twelve managers of the new Bettering House to be elected from among its private contributors.[56] In essence, the managers of the Bettering House would now control the money that had previously funded the activities of the overseers of the poor, and out relief would be phased out.[57]

The overseers of the poor strongly opposed the adoption of this plan, especially the elimination of out relief. They cited prominently all the reasons why poor women preferred out relief to almshouse admissions.[58] Moreover, they argued that many poor simply could not work for their keep at the Bettering House because of "age, Infirmity, or sickness," but if left to cobble together available resources as they had in the past, they could scrape by. Many poor people, the overseers contended, "found means at present to support themselves upon a small pension." Additionally, the overseers understood that moving to the almshouse meant forfeiting home, neighbors, and perhaps possessions, which would be "cruel" to those who needed only short-term help—a category that obviously included pregnant women. The overseers also believed the physical accommodations of the almshouse were inadequate. "In the case of man and wife especially," they reported, the lack of "apartments" suitable for joint lodging was "a great discouragement to many" to avail themselves of the almshouse facility. No overseer, and by implication no almshouse manager, could "in discretion" advocate that married couples, no matter what their financial position, live "in a separate state." Lastly, the overseers warned that the poor simply did not like the almshouse. Rather than be coerced into the place, the "wicked & profligate" among them "would rob & steal rather than go in or wd be begging." The almshouse managers were dissatisfied with this report of conditions among the poor and demanded that the overseers visit each of their pensioners and encourage them to go to the almshouse.

As is evident from that exchange, the overseers of the poor and the new Bettering House managers operated on the basis of quite distinct ideas about the poor and about how best to help them and society at large.[59] The overseers viewed poor relief as a means of temporarily or even seasonally, albeit possibly cyclically, assisting those whom the economic system made least able to help themselves. The Bettering House managers viewed poor relief as a means of educating the poor about the improprieties of their conduct, which had made them poor, and of making the poor at least minimally productive by requiring many of them to labor for their upkeep in the publicly funded

TABLE 10. Bettering House Adult Admissions, 1770–1775

| Year | Women | | Men | | Total Number |
|------|-----|-----|-----|-----|--------------|
|      | *N* | (%) | *N* | (%) |              |
| 1770 | 199 | 65  | 107 | 35  | 306 |
| 1771 | 175 | 61  | 113 | 39  | 288 |
| 1772 | 141 | 56  | 110 | 44  | 251 |
| 1773 | 130 | 54  | 111 | 46  | 241 |
| 1774 | 140 | 49  | 143 | 51  | 283 |
| 1775 | 203 | 55  | 165 | 45  | 368 |

*Source:* Almshouse Managers Minutes, 1766–80, Philadelphia City Archives.

institution. While the overseers' frame of reference was the women whom they had long seen as their primary constituents, the Bettering House managers viewed poor relief in terms of the men whose reform would create self-sustaining patriarchal households.

Ultimately the overseers of the poor lost this debate about the nature and future of poor relief, and henceforth the assembly devoted all poor relief monies to the operations of the Bettering House.[60] Despite their deep misgivings, the overseers resolved on June 23, 1769, not to pay any more pensions or to provide any more short-term aid but only to recommend "proper objects" to the almshouse. Poor women and men who had depended on the overseers to provide aid during times of crisis now faced an unpleasant choice: the Bettering House or nothing.

The transformation in poor relief was striking in some respects but remained the same in others. Whereas the old almshouse had played only a small role in public poor relief, between the Pennsylvania Hospital and the Bettering House institutionalization had become the principal form of relief. The demise of out relief marked a sharp change in the way that public relief was distributed, but also in the ways that poor relief was experienced. The proportions of men and women receiving poor relief, however, changed only a little. Women had been the majority of out relief recipients and at least half of all the residents of the old city almshouse, and they immediately comprised a clear majority of the Bettering House admissions (see table 10). Between 1770 and 1775, an average of 57 percent of admissions to the Bettering House were women.

Significantly, women were much more often confined to the almshouse wing of the new Bettering House, and men to the workhouse, suggesting that ideas about who was fit and unfit to work continued to be structured along gendered lines. Between 1769 and 1775, 59 percent of women at the Bettering House lodged at the almshouse, while 59 percent of men lived at the workhouse. This division also suggests that women still comprised the majority of the occasionally poor who needed help intermittently, and in situations such as advanced pregnancy when they could not be of much use in the workhouse.[61]

Women may also have been sent to the almshouse rather than the workhouse side of the Bettering House because they needed to care for the children they brought with them. From 1770 to 1775, children comprised between 16 percent and 30 percent of all persons admitted to the almshouse. Records show that those children were usually sent to the Bettering House not as orphans awaiting indenture, but with their mothers. Of twenty children sent to the almshouse between March and July of 1768, for example, ten accompanied their mothers. Three went with both a mother and a father, and seven children went alone. Of the seven children who went to the almshouse without a parent, presumably so that the overseers of the poor could bind them out, four were identified as having fathers (which did not exclude their having mothers as well), whereas three children had only mothers. In sum, thirteen of twenty poor children in the almshouse had poor mothers with them, while four had poor fathers, and three had both.[62]

Thus, women were confined to the Bettering House much more frequently than men, and they brought children with them much more frequently than did men. During that same period in 1768, the overseers recommended to the Bettering House thirty women and fourteen men; among these were three married couples. Forty-three percent of the women brought children with them; 33 percent of the women were unmarried and brought children. Only 21 percent of the men had children with them, and all of these men were married.[63] Whether poor mothers chose to indenture their children or to attempt a difficult course of patchwork economic strategies, children were the most substantial factor in the economics of their household.[64] Looking at the indentures arranged for poor families by another group, the guardians of the poor, for example, suggests the very young age at which children were apprenticed, and that the poorer they were, the younger they left home for apprenticeship.[65]

Somewhat surprisingly given the number of pregnant women aided by the overseers of the poor, the fact that the Bettering House did provide some medical care for its inmates, and that the Pennsylvania Hospital did not accept women expecting children, between 1770 and 1775 an average of only twenty-four babies per year were born in the Bettering House.[66] It may be that women simply preferred to try to make it on their own rather than accept institutionalization even when close to delivering a child.

Women may have also actively resisted being lodged at the Bettering House. The proud announcement in July 1770 that fourteen inmates had been discharged, "several of whom behaved during their residence very orderly and have obtained places of service," was followed by less auspicious developments. The managers began reporting runaways in December of that same year. The overseers' original predictions about the unappealing nature of the Bettering House proved to be particularly true for women. The managers of the Bettering House rarely acknowledged runaways among the discharges, but on the occasions when their monthly reports specified the sex of runaways, they noted that twice as many women as men had "absconded without leave of the steward."[67] Certainly conditions in the Bettering House were bleak: few if any poor Philadelphians could be extraordinarily grateful for the guarantee of shelter and food provided once they were committed. The punitive aspects of the Bettering House were dramatically different from the "small sums" and pensions that had kept poor Philadelphians, and particularly women, somewhat independent. British doctor Robert Honyman reported that women begged him "to try to get them out" of the Bettering House.[68] He expressed surprise at their desire to escape; he may not have known how many were committed against their will. For the couple of years that the managers of the Bettering House distinguished between those admitted and those committed to their care, fully 70 percent of those committed to the Bettering House were women.[69] In 1770, the first full year of operation, sixty-one women and only twenty-four men were committed to the workhouse for the mandatory term of one month.[70]

Although poor women may have resisted commitment to the Bettering House when they were able, they had little alternative when they were sick. Even after the Bettering House opened and out relief was curtailed, the Pennsylvania Hospital continued to admit a large majority of men (see table 11). Some women were attended by doctors while at the almshouse; the minutes of the Bettering House managers recorded annual salaries to several doctors, referred to the almshouse as having a "Laying in Ward" and when pressed for funds in 1775 pleaded that, rather than a Bettering House, they had been running "really and fully an Hospital . . . a Laying in Hospital, where upwards of 30 poor destitute women in a year, are carefully delivered and comfortably provided for in that extremity."[71]

Comparing the numbers of men and women resident in each institution supports the notion that the focus of poor relief resources, as well as the discourse about poor relief, was now aimed more often at men than in the past. Although women had always predominated among out relief recipients, and when the old city almshouse and out relief had functioned together women

TABLE 11. Pennsylvania Hospital Admissions, 1769–1775

| Year | Women (%) | Men (%) | Total Number |
|---|---|---|---|
| 1769 (May–December) | 29 | 71 | 252 |
| 1770 | 27 | 73 | 415 |
| 1771 | 33 | 67 | 382 |
| 1772 | 34 | 66 | 358 |
| 1773 | 29 | 71 | 413 |
| 1774 | 28 | 72 | 429 |
| 1775 | 23 | 77 | 465 |
| TOTAL | 29 | 71 | 2,714 |

Source: Board of Managers Minutes, American Philosophical Society, Philadelphia.

still commanded a majority of poor relief resources, now those resources seemed to be more evenly divided. From mid-1769 to mid-1770, the average number of men and women aided by either the hospital or the Bettering House was almost even (see table 12). Perhaps this parity reflected the new reality of poverty: men now comprised a larger proportion of the needy than they ever had before.

No dramatic shift in the character, as opposed to the numbers, of the poor accounts for the seeming parity of men and women as treated by both the major institutions of poor relief. Rather, these figures highlight the nature of the admissions policies in each place and show how poor relief still targeted men and women very differently. It is unlikely that the Bettering House managers privileged poor women over poor men in admissions given their interest in capturing and rehabilitating men to industry and the expressed interest of women in refusing entry to, or in escaping from, the Bettering House.[72] It is also clear that the hospital did admit men rather than women; it is unlikely that men contracted diseases or suffered injuries more than women given women's higher rates of mortality from childbearing.[73] In other words, the larger proportion of men in the hospital, which evens out the numbers of Philadelphians receiving some form of poor relief, does not reflect a proportional picture of the needy population. Rather, it reflects the interest of elites and poor relief officials in addressing poverty generally through getting men back to work, either on their own after recuperation or in the workhouse.

Evidence continued to point to women's (especially unmarried women's) vulnerability to poverty, even while poor relief forms less frequently reflected this reality. Although out relief did not aid more than a significant fraction of poor women, it was designed to meet the predictable, expected, albeit

TABLE 12. Bettering House and Hospital Residents by Sex,
June 1769–May 1770

|  | Bettering House | | Hospital | | |
|  | Almshouse | Workhouse | Poor | Paying | Total |
|---|---|---|---|---|---|
| Women | 83 | 60 | 24 | 5 | 172 |
| Men | 36 | 58 | 60 | 14 | 168 |

*Source:* Board of Managers Minutes and Almshouse Managers Minutes, Philadelphia City
Archives.

intermittent events in a woman's life given her precarious economic condition. The designers of institutional relief, however, did not recognize cultural or structural causes of poverty, such as women's dependent status under the law and by cultural tradition; rather, institutional officials of the Pennsylvania Hospital and the Bettering House acknowledged only the temporary calamities of illness or injury, or moral failures such as idleness, to be the cause of poverty. In sum, although it looks that by the 1760s poor men and women in Philadelphia simply received aid from different sources, they received relief that accorded with the evolving connections between gender and a political economy of poor relief. Poor relief had always reflected the important role of gender in political economy. What was new was the changed emphasis from the issue of expected feminine dependence to the promotion of masculine independence.

Ultimately the Bettering House failed to deliver on its promises to reduce both poverty and the costs of poor relief, and in fact after 1775 its managers began to offer some out relief again. Institutionalization alone had proved ineffective in aiding the kind of intermittent poverty that women in particular endured, and perhaps their continuing plight became impossible to ignore. Certainly the numbers of poor Philadelphians continued to increase, and the Bettering House was no more economical than out relief. The failures of Philadelphia's Bettering House, however, could not stop the tide of institutionalization. In the years after the American Revolution, groups promising similar innovations and efficiencies created institutions to treat any number of social ills, including penitentiaries and asylums.[74]

Historians have long pointed to the important role of emerging class consciousness and tensions as an impetus for these institutions in the eighteenth and nineteenth centuries. They have noted that reformers advocating the institutional solution to poverty complained about the idleness of the poor and that debates about whether or not employment was available for the poor reflected rising tensions in a nascent capitalist economy.

What has been less directly addressed is the importance of ideas about gender and the consequently different experiences of men and women within the poor relief system in toto. Colonists understood poor relief as having an organic relation to the economy and to household, the central social structure. Those two conceptual categories, economy and household, were deeply embedded in a patriarchal context. Thus the original notion of poor relief was to interact with and accommodate what were understood to be the natural by-products of that household and economic structure, namely, the dependency of women, the very elderly or infirm, and children. Reformers substituted a radical new idea, institutionalization as the exclusive form of relief, for the out relief that was meant for those traditionally needy folks. Yet those reformers, both those who built the Pennsylvania Hospital and those who supported the Bettering House, remained tethered to the same Anglo-American concepts of patriarchal household in which men headed households and women and children lived within them. They simply changed their primary focus from those who were made dependent under that system to those who ought to have been independent within it. Thus despite an extraordinary shift in the enactment and experience of poor relief, colonial welfare policies remained beholden to a traditional conception of gender and political economy.

## Notes

1. Minutes of the Overseers of the Poor, 1768–74, Philadelphia City Archives (hereafter PCA).

2. David J. Rothman, *Discovery of the Asylum: Social Order and Disorder in the New Republic* (Boston: Little, Brown, 1971); Michel Foucault, *Discipline and Punish: The Birth of the Prison*, trans. Alan Sheridan (New York: Pantheon, 1977).

3. See Gary B. Nash's essay in this volume, along with his *The Urban Crucible: The Northern Seaports and the Origins of the American Revolution* (Cambridge: Harvard University Press, 1986); John K. Alexander, *Render Them Submissive: Responses to Poverty in Philadelphia, 1760–1800* (Amherst: University of Massachusetts Press, 1980); Billy G. Smith, *The "Lower Sort": Philadelphia's Laboring People, 1750–1800* (Ithaca: Cornell University Press, 1990).

4. Linda Gordon, "The New Feminist Scholarship on the Welfare State," in Gordon, ed. *Women, the State, and Welfare* (Madison: University of Wisconsin Press, 1990), 30. Other important essays in this volume (for the purposes of my study) include Virginia Sapiro, "The Gender Basis of American Social Policy"; Barbara J. Nelson, "The Origins of the Two-Channel Welfare State: Workmen's Compensation and Mother's Aid"; and Frances Fox Piven, "Ideology and the State: Women, Power and the Welfare State." An important early contribution to this literature is Mimi Abramovitz, *Regulating the Lives of Women: Social Welfare Policy from Colonial Times to the Present* (Boston: South End Press, 1988), and a recent contribution to the subject of the feminization of

poverty in early America is Elaine Crane, *Ebbtide in New England: Women, Seaports, and Social Change, 1630–1800* (Boston: Northeastern University Press, 1998). On the disciplining of impoverished men through a discourse of gender in the modern era, see Michael Willrich, "Home Slackers: Men, the State, and Welfare in Modern America," *Journal of American History* 87 (September 2000): 460–89.

5. I use "gender" here, as Joan Scott defined the term, as constitutive of social relationships based on ideas about the differences between the sexes, and as a way of signifying relationships of power. Scott, *Gender and the Politics of History* (New York: Columbia University Press, 1988), 42–43.

6. Drew McCoy, *The Elusive Republic: Political Economy in Jeffersonian America* (Chapel Hill: University of North Carolina Press, 1980), see esp. 5–7. For the modern era see esp. Gordon, "New Feminist Scholarship."

7. Peter J. Parker, "Rich and Poor in Philadelphia, 1709," *Pennsylvania Magazine of History and Biography* 88 (1975): 6–7.

8. For example, in 1739 the overseers gave Katherine Davis 4 shillings for the seven weeks before she died, and then paid another 2 shillings to have her buried. Poors Day Book, March 1739–March 1740, Gratz Collection, case 17, box 4, Historical Society of Pennsylvania (hereafter HSP).

9. "To the Overseers of the Poor from Mayor Robert Strettel," October 9, 1751. Stauffer Collection, HSP.

10. In 1739, twenty-three women and nine men received pensions for between one and eight weeks; three women and four men received pensions for between twelve and twenty-five weeks; and five women and two men received pensions for between forty-four and fifty-two weeks. Poors Day Book, Gratz Collection, case 17, box 4, HSP.

11. Quakers built an almshouse for needy Friends in 1717, but it only held perhaps a half dozen people; the city also built a punitive workhouse in 1719. For more on the building of these facilities, see Gary Nash, "Poverty and Poor Relief in Pre-Revolutionary Philadelphia" *William and Mary Quarterly*, 3d ser., 33 (January 1976): 3–30; and Carl Bridenbaugh, *Cities in the Wilderness: Urban Life in America, 1625–1742* (New York: Capricorn Books, 1964). The only extant accounts of the early city almshouse are for 1751. See discussion of those records below.

12. A summary of these developments can be found in Nash, "Poverty and Poor Relief."

13. Gary Nash has argued that crucial changes in the composition of the poor population followed the economic downturn after the Seven Years' War, when many more able-bodied men joined the traditionally needy—women, children, the disabled, and the elderly. But however many men joined the ranks of the poor in the mid-eighteenth-century city, it is not at all clear that the ratios of men to women among the poor changed at all. The best evidence of a sharper increase in poverty among men, a larger number of men formally excused from taxation for inability to pay, conceals the informal process by which women were similarly excused. Karin Wulf, "Assessing Gender: Taxation and the Evaluation of Economic Viability in Late Colonial Philadelphia," *Pennsylvania Magazine of History and Biography* 121 (July 1997): 201–35.

In addition, women were likely as affected by unemployment as men, either as potential independent wage earners themselves or as the dependents of men. Thus, while there is a logical argument to be made that women were more vulnerable to poverty, there is no clear evidence that poverty among men increased disproportionately compared to women. On the characteristics and evidence of the poverty of women, particularly women without husbands, see Ruth Wallis Herndon, "Women of 'No Particular Home': Town Leaders and Female Transients in Rhode Island, 1750–1800," in *Women and Freedom in Early America*, ed. Larry D. Eldridge (New York: New York University Press, 1996), 269–89; N. E. H. Hull, *Female Felons: Women and Serious Crime in Colonial Massachusetts* (Urbana: University of Illinois Press, 1987), 54–55; Gary B. Nash, "The Failure of Female Factory Labor in Colonial Boston," *Labor History* 20 (1979): 165–88; Alexander Keyssar, "Widowhood in Eighteenth-Century Massachusetts: A Problem in the History of the Family," *Perspectives in American History* 8 (1974): 111–16; Sharon V. Salinger, "Spaces, Inside and

Outside, in Eighteenth-Century Philadelphia," *Journal of Interdisciplinary History* 26 (summer 1995): 28; Sharon Salinger and Charles Wetherell, "Wealth and Renting in Pre-Revolutionary Philadelphia," 835; Carole Shammas, "The Female Social Structure of Philadelphia in 1775," *Pennsylvania Magazine of History and Biography* 107 (January 1983): 69–83; Daniel Scott Smith, "Female Householding in Late Eighteenth-Century America and the Problem of Poverty," *Journal of Social History* 27 (fall 1994): 83–107.

14. The Committee to Alleviate the Poor, for example, was interested in helping only "real objects of charity" as opposed to "ill designing persons."

15. Quoted in Parker, "Rich and Poor," 4–5. In 1751, for example, Mayor Robert Strettel pointed the overseers to the problems of Martha Adams, who was "represented . . . incapable to maintain her Self & Child being very Poor." Strettel instructed the overseers to "inquire into her Circumstances and do for her as you shall find right." Robert Strettel to the Overseers of the Poor, December 12, 1751, Society Miscellaneous Collection, box 7A, HSP. Strettel regularly instructed the overseers to provide such relief "as you shall judge right." Many of his directions, as well as those of William Plumstead, can be found in the Dreer (Mayors of Philadelphia), Society, and Balch-Shippen Collections at the HSP. For another example of Strettel's use of this same language and the direction of the overseers to make evaluations, see the petition of Comfort Boyd, discussed below.

16. See Karin Wulf, *Not All Wives: Women of Colonial Philadelphia* (Ithaca: Cornell University Press, 2000), 153–79. Usually a woman's marital status was quite explicitly noted in the records as widowed, abandoned, or the mother of children by a man not her husband. Women who appear by name, and without mention of a husband, in the public poor relief records, such as those of the overseers of the poor, the city almshouse, or the Bettering House, are assumed to be unmarried—that is, widowed, never married, abandoned, or otherwise separated. Married women rarely appear in these records and usually with their husbands in the rare cases when the entire family was taken into the almshouse. In only a very few cases, women whose sick husbands needed care at home petitioned for financial help. Men mentioned alone cannot be considered unmarried, of course, especially when they collected any form of out relief.

17. Studies of poor relief in other colonial urban places confirm that women outnumbered men among relief recipients. In colonial New York, where an almshouse was built in 1735, out relief and institutionalization continued to function together until much later in the eighteenth century. Steven Ross has found that 62 percent of poor in the almshouse and 57 percent of poor on out relief in New York between 1691 and 1748 were women. Ross, "Objects of Charity: Poor Relief, Poverty, and the Rise of the Almshouse in Early Eighteenth-Century New York," as quoted in Robert E. Cray Jr., *Paupers and Poor Relief in New York City and Its Rural Environs, 1700–1830* (Philadelphia: Temple University Press, 1988), 47. Women outnumbered men by similar margins among those on out relief and the institutionalized poor in colonial Boston. Crane, *Ebb Tide in New England*, 8, 112–13. In the early nineteenth century women continued to predominate among recipients of out relief. See Priscilla Ferguson Clement, *Welfare and the Poor in the Nineteenth-Century City: Philadelphia, 1800–1854* (Rutherford, N.J.: Fairleigh Dickinson University Press, 1985), 70; Susan Grigg, *The Dependent Poor of Newburyport: Studies in Social History, 1800–1830* (Ann Arbor: UMI Research Press, 1984), 19–30. For an analysis of widows on outdoor relief in Philadelphia between 1828 and 1832, see Lisa Wilson, *Life After Death: Widows in Pennsylvania, 1750–1850* (Philadelphia: Temple University Press, 1992), 79–85.

18. Some of these directives are found in the Society Miscellaneous Collection, box 7A, while others are in the Balch-Shippen, Gratz, Society, and Stauffer Collections, HSP.

19. Robert Strettel to the Overseers of the Poor, Philadelphia, October 9, 1751, Stauffer Collection, #2146, HSP.

20. "City of Philada. for Disbursements for the Poor," bound at the back of Christopher Marshall's diary "B" (1774–81), HSP.

21. For 1709, Parker, "Rich and Poor"; for 1739, Poors Day Book, Gratz Collection, case 17, box 4, HSP.

22. "Pensions as pd by the Last overseers of the Poor," Society Miscellaneous Collection, box 7A, folio 1.

23. In 1739, 65 percent of women received pensions for fewer than eight weeks, while only 33 percent of men did. Ibid.

24. Women collected most of their out relief in cash. For example, in April 1767, the categories and amounts of expenditures for out relief included: Cash, £4 18s 3p; Goods, 3.7.2; Services, 0.8.6; Travel, 0.10.3 (total expenditures on out relief for women: 9.4.2). Expressed in pounds, shillings, and pence, from the city almshouse ledger, 1767–68, HSP. Undoubtedly kept by the overseers of the poor, the ledger debited out relief and almshouse supplies from the city almshouse account and credited fines, etc., due to the overseers (by tradition) to the same account. In another example, from March through July 1768, months for which the records are quite clear, the overseers gave "small sums" of out relief to almost three times as many women as men. Twenty women and seven men received such sums. Minutes of the Overseers of the Poor, 1768–74, PCA.

25. Records of private charities reflect the same phenomenon. The Committee to Alleviate the Poor of 1761–62 gave wood, blankets, and stockings to 129 women and 75 men. Presumably some of those men had wives, so the actual number of women aided by the society, as when the overseers of the poor gave out relief to men, would be even larger. "Accounts of Wood, blankets, & stockings given to the poor, 1762," Wharton-Willing Papers, oversize #26, HSP.

26. J. Thomas Scharf and Thompson Westcott, *History of Philadelphia, 1609–1884,* 3 vols. (Philadelphia: L. H. Everts, 1884) 1:191, 205–6; William H. Williams, *America's First Hospital: The Pennsylvania Hospital, 1751–1841* (Wayne, Pa.: Haverford House, 1976), 15, 24.

27. Use of the hospital's records is predicated on not revealing any individual names or case histories. I have found multiple cases through a comparison of the hospital admissions and residence accounts of names that correspond to those found among the extant overseers' records.

28. Poors Day Book, 1739, Gratz Collection, case 17, box 4, HSP. On resistance to institutionalization among poor women in Boston, see Nash, *Urban Crucible,* 117–20.

29. List of almshouse inmates, Society Miscellaneous Collection, box 7A, folio 1, HSP.

30. The system of keeping the poor in the homes of other citizens was more common in rural areas or in small towns. See Cray, *Paupers and Poor Relief.*

31. Ibid.

32. Stauffer Collection, p. 336, HSP.

33. Society Miscellaneous Collection, HSP.

34. Comfort Boyd and Susanna Condon, for example, were both married to jailed debtors. The husbands of Ann Pillets Singer, Mary Driver, and Mary Howell had simply abandoned them. Ann Pillets was indentured to Joseph Graver before she married Morris Singer. There is no record of the reason for Singer's abandonment of his wife and young sickly child. He could practice his trade while traveling; he was apprenticed as a shoemaker. Mayor Strettel to Overseers, November 25, 1751 (concerning Ann Pillets Singer), box 7A, Society Miscellaneous Collection, HSP. Hugh Driver and Mr. Howell left sick wives and small infants, but again no reason was given for their departure. Mayor to Overseers, March 29, 1751 (regarding Howell); August 6, 1751 (regarding Driver), box 7A, Society Miscellaneous Collection, HSP.

35. Box 7A, Society Miscellaneous Collection, HSP.

36. Gratz Collection, case 3, box 9, HSP.

37. Balch-Shippen Papers, vol. 1, p. 33, HSP.

38. Society Collection, HSP.

39. List of almshouse inmates, box 7A, Society Miscellaneous Collection, HSP.

40. Ibid.

41. Ibid.

42. Nash, *Urban Crucible,* 160–61; Williams, *America's First Hospital,* 8–11.

43. Nash, *Urban Crucible,* 116–17; Williams, *America's First Hospital,* 11–14.

44. Ibid., 48–60.

45. See Alexander, *Render Them Submissive*, 49–53 and 86–102, for a good description, albeit a different interpretation than that presented here, of the developing categories of the "idle" and the "industrious" poor.

46. On the impact of emerging ideas about masculinity and independence, see Kathleen M. Brown, *Good Wives, Nasty Wenches, and Anxious Patriarchs: Gender, Race, and Power in Colonial Virginia* (Chapel Hill: University of North Carolina Press, 1996); Mary Beth Norton, *Founding Mothers and Fathers: Gendered Power and the Forming of American Society* (New York: Alfred A. Knopf, 1996); Lisa Wilson, *Ye Heart of Ye Man: The Domestic Life of Men in Colonial New England* (New Haven: Yale University Press, 1999).

47. Benjamin Franklin, *Some Account of the Pennsylvania Hospital*, ed. I. Bernard Cohen (Baltimore: Johns Hopkins University Press, 1954), 3.

48. Board of Managers Minutes, 1751–1860 in 10 vols., vol. 1, Archives of the Pennsylvania Hospital (microfilm, American Philosophical Society, Philadelphia).

49. "CHARITY, or Tenderness for the Poor . . . ," *Pennsylvania Gazette*, July 19, 1764.

50. "The Act to Encourage the Establishing of a Hospital for the Relief of the Sick Poor," in Franklin, *Some Account*, 5. Board of Managers Minutes, Archives of the Pennsylvania Hospital, American Philosophical Society (microfilm), vol. 1, p. 38. The hospital also accepted some paying patients, although I have not disaggregated this group in the figures below. The number of paying patients admitted was related to the capital stock of the hospital; in more flush times, the number of paying patients was reduced. Most paying patients were either slaves or servants whose employers paid their fees, mentally disabled, or a few paupers whose fees were paid by the overseers of the poor. Williams, *America's First Hospital*. There was not any significant difference in the proportion of men and women who were paying as opposed to poor patients. The total of paying patients ranged from 6 to 18 percent of all patients between 1769 and 1775; an average of 10 percent of women were admitted as paying patients, while 13 percent of men were admitted as paying patients. The much larger number of male than female slaves whose owners paid for their medical care in the hospital undoubtedly affects these figures.

51. Out relief records show the significance of pregnant women among that population. See also the list of almshouse inmates and Bettering House inmates, contained within the records of each institution, among whom were always some pregnant women.

52. Nash, *Urban Crucible*, 322, and on postwar depression, 255–56, and rising unemployment, 260. On the material conditions faced by laboring families, see Smith, *"Lower Sort,"* esp. 92–125.

53. Public notices of charitable intentions, activities, and philosophies flooded into the newspapers after 1760. See among the many examples, notices of "charity sermons" preached, *Pennsylvania Gazette* for March 10, 1763, December 27, 1764, and March 26, 1772; a "public" evening for the benefit of the poor, January 8, 1767; ad hoc charitable relief societies January 7, 1761, January 31, 1765, February 7, 1765; religious organizations for poor relief, November 9, 1755; religious organizations for relief of their own ministers "their widows and children," June 5, 1760, November 27, 1760, March 19, 1761, July 22, 1762. On poor relief demand, see esp. Minutes of the Overseers of the Poor, July 20, 1768, PCA.

54. They raised the poor tax from 3 to 5 pence per pound of assessed wealth. Nash, *Urban Crucible*, 256; Nash, "Poverty and Poor Relief," 14.

55. Alexander, *Render Them Submissive*, 87.

56. Ibid., 89.

57. Nash, "Poverty and Poor Relief," 19. See also the description of the 1766 law "for the Better Employment, Relief and Support of the Poor . . . " establishing the new system in Alexander, *Render Them Submissive*, 88–90. Eventually private funds paid for less than 20 percent of the new institution's start-up costs. Initial projections of a self-sustaining operation gave way to reality— and another hike in the poor tax to 6 pence per pound in 1768. To the almshouse managers the solution to the money shortage was quite obvious. The overseers should "withhold the out pensions," both to save money and as "the Means of Obliging the Poor to come into the House of

Employment" and the almshouse. The overseers argued vociferously against this tact. Nash, "Poverty and Poor Relief," 20. Illustrating the sense of crisis surrounding the growing numbers of poor and the taxes levied to care for them, a great dispute took place in 1767–68 between the city proper and its neighboring environs, including the suburbs of Southwark and the Northern Liberties. See Edward Wharton Smith Papers, Society Miscellaneous Collection, HSP.

58. It may be that the different class backgrounds of the overseers (middling men) and the managers of the almshouse (wealthier merchants) informed their dispute. See Alexander, *Render Them Submissive*, 92–94. For an example of turf battles carried out largely in the name of pride and ambition in the postrevolutionary era, see Alexander, "Institutional Imperialism and the Sick Poor in Late Eighteenth-Century Philadelphia: The House of Employment vs. the Pennsylvania Hospital," *Pennsylvania History* 51 (April 1984): 101–17.

59. Visits like the one proposed by the managers of the almshouse were not unprecedented. In May 1768, a meeting of the overseers directed a committee to "attend the House of Employ ment" and "acquaint the Managers that the Overseers of the Poor of this City Proposed to Visit the Out Pensioners, in order to inquire into their Present circumstances." Minutes of the Overseers of the Poor, 1768–74, May 19, 1768, PCA.

60. For an account of the legal wrangling over funding for out relief, which resulted in irregularly dispensing very small, much-reduced amounts of out relief, see Alexander, *Render Them Submissive*, 96–97. See also "Accounts of Contributors to the Relief and Employment of the Poor" for May 1773–May 1774, in which small sums or weekly allowances were paid for those "whose circumstances rendered it less expensive than to be admitted into the House." *Pennsylvania Gazette*, May 18, 1774.

61. Ibid.

62. Ibid.

63. Ibid.

64. Wulf, *Not All Wives*; Grigg, *Dependent Poor of Newburyport*, 20–26.

65. Of two "mulatto" girls bound by the guardians of the poor in the 1750s, for example, Hester (no last name given) was bound for just over twenty-one years, while Abigail Rice was bound for just over twenty-four years. Their racial identity guaranteed that Hester and Abigail would be bound for longer terms than was usual for white children, but the poverty of most freed African Americans also connotes the close connection between childhood poverty and long periods of servitude. Guardians of the Poor Memorandum Book and Indentures Made, 1751–97, PCA.

66. Ibid.

67. Ten women and five men ran away from the Bettering House in December 1770. Almshouse Managers Minutes, PCA. Runaways also were reported in February, March, and September 1771. Runaways, but not their sex, were reported also in July and October 1772 and May 1773.

68. Quoted in Nash, "Poverty and Poor Relief," 27.

69. Between June 1769 and December 1771, 131 women and 58 men were committed to the Bettering House. Almshouse Managers Minutes, PCA.

70. Nash, "Poverty and Poor Relief," 26; James T. Mitchell and Henry Flanders, comps., *The Statutes at Large of Pennsylvania from 1682 to 1801* (Philadelphia, 1896–1911), chap. 552.

71. Minutes of the Almshouse Managers for December 5, 1770, and January 3, 1771, PCA; petition to the assembly as quoted in Robert J. Hunter, M.D., "The Origin of the Philadelphia General Hospital, Blockley Division," *Pennsylvania Magazine of History and Biography* 57 (January 1933): 15. Note that this was an overstatement; see n66.

72. See also Smith, *"Lower Sort,"* 170n68.

73. For example, about half of the "lunaticks" (who regularly comprised about one-third of the patients at the hospital, and a disproportionately large number of the paying patients) were female. In that case, the hospital had a clear mandate for their admission, and no discrimination was practiced. Also, the hospital treated a large number of out patients, but the lists of such

patients only very infrequently appear in the hospital's records. Some of those outpatients may have been women who could not accept residence because of their children.

74. For a cogent review of these developments, see Michael Meranze, *Laboratories of Virtue: Punishment, Revolution, and Authority in Philadelphia, 1760–1835* (Chapel Hill: University of North Carolina Press, 1996), 3.

# *Seven*

## Poor Relief "Without Violating the Rights of Humanity"

*Almshouse Administration in the Philadelphia Region, 1790–1860*

MONIQUE BOURQUE

Between 1790 and 1820, most of Philadelphia's outlying counties, including those in New Jersey and Delaware as well as those in Pennsylvania, moved to a county- and institution-based system of poor relief.[1] County poorhouses replaced a patchwork of outdoor relief, boarding arrangements, and (in the case of Wilmington, Delaware) a city poorhouse. The adoption of a county almshouse system resulted from concern for efficient administration of relief funds and the intention to provide better and more consistent care for paupers either abused or pampered by private households where they were boarded. Administrators proclaimed an intent to better categorize the institutionalized poor, dividing them into "worthy" and "unworthy" objects for charity to more effectively relieve those found deserving and to reform those who were undeserving. Inmates' lives were accordingly arranged in such a way as to prevent too much social intercourse (and any sexual intercourse), to provide work and define rigid schedules for performing tasks, and to teach the institutionalized poor the "habits of industry" necessary for success in an increasingly commercial economy.[2]

Far from being monolithic, menacing institutions that removed the unfortunate from their communities and isolated them in asylums designed to dominate them and to mold their behavior and values, the boundaries of almshouses were porous in both physical and administrative terms. A constant stream of inmates, hired workers, visitors (both inmates' relatives and the public), official committees, and local merchants and storekeepers flowed through the poorhouse buildings and grounds.[3] Connections between inmates and the people and markets in the surrounding communities made total control over internees a practical impossibility. Relationships between the administrators and the public, particularly financial transactions, made the asylums' daily functions vulnerable to public scrutiny. Simultaneously, the interaction between town and poorhouse encouraged the overseers to be flexible in handling individual cases, especially where work arrangements were involved. One striking aspect of the interdependence between administrators and inmates was the commitment to a social contract understood by both groups, an agreement that both aid and authority had limits.

Poor relief in antebellum America was never as simple as some historians have suggested—a matter of controlling the poor and establishing the moral authority of an expanding middle class.[4] Relief instead was administered in the context of complex social, political, and economic relations that bound together almshouse officials, relief recipients, and the local community, so that all three groups helped shape the emerging social welfare system. Community members established the legislation, rules, and regulations that governed care of the poor; they regularly assessed the success of those who administered those regulations; and they participated in the life of the almshouse by supplying goods or services or by employing inmates. Almshouse administrators freely adapted policy to fit the needs of individual cases and granted outdoor relief in some form to many of the "virtuous" poor who did not require constant supervision. The working poor played an active role in institution life both as relief recipients and as poorhouse employees. Members of all three groups recognized that the social boundaries between them shaded into one another and were porous, much like the physical boundaries of the almshouse grounds. Ambivalence about the administration of assistance was inherent in the language of both enabling legislation and almshouse regulations, reflecting the structure of relief itself.

This essay examines the disjunction between poor relief policy, as outlined in enabling legislation and almshouse rules and regulations, and actual practice at the local level. As in the eighteenth century, nineteenth-century almshouse officials struggled to balance Christian charity with fiscal prudence, to separate the "virtuous" and unlucky from the lazy and "vicious," and to understand what poverty meant in a changing society with an entrenched belief in American abundance.[5] Limitations on the power of administrators curtailed their ability to reshape the poor in a middle-class image. In addition, officials used their discretion to temper regulations, thereby disclosing that they clung to more humane aspects of traditional relief while adjusting to the new age of institutions. Moreover, indigents assumed an active role in shaping the welfare system to their own needs.

The transition to an institution-based system of relief during the late eighteenth and early nineteenth centuries was neither sudden nor smooth for most communities in the Philadelphia region. Planners recognized from the outset that the construction and operation of almshouses—much like the creation of prisons in our own times—would have broad impact on the communities in which they were located through the creation of jobs and supply contracts. The most heated debates within counties did not center on whether the almshouse would effectively shape the behavior of its inmates, however. Communities most often argued about whether institutionalizing the poor would be a financially more efficient system of assistance than traditional methods of supporting the destitute in private homes or in houses rented for the purpose and run by paid overseers.[6]

Directors of the new institutions wanted to aid the indigent and to recast their morality. They found, however, that numerous social and economic factors limited their ability to carry out their program. Indeed, their view of the poor as belonging to the community rather than as being outcast from it undermined the efforts of almshouse officials. Their reluctance to institutionalize people who had family to help them or when work arrangements could be made resulted from three separate but closely intertwined considerations. First, institutional life could be harmful to all but the most hardened reprobates; second, the community should continue to bear a significant responsibility in the support of its poor; and third, institutionalizing a significant proportion of the population could be disruptive for the community both by removing potentially useful citizens and by encouraging the creation of a group of permanent dependents. At the same time, almshouse administrators pursued a social agenda that included the modification of undesirable behavior by relief recipients.

Administrators used institutions and outdoor relief in attempting to change the behavior and to shape the morality of the needy. Officials hoped to exert both physical and moral influence by controlling paupers' diets, dictating regular schedules for all activities, and specifying that inmates "behave with decency and good manners toward each other" and "conduct themselves in an orderly, sober, and submissive manner."[7] The earliest almshouse rules condemn and specify punishments for such unacceptable behavior as idleness and intemperance. Administrators used outdoor support to reward the especially deserving, infirm, or otherwise particularly needy; they allowed some paupers to participate in the disposition of their cases; and they used the regimens of institutional life (diet, work assignments) and rewards (food, liquor, small sums of cash, or clothing) to modify inmates' behavior. Surprisingly, administrators did not generally rely on religious instruction to shape inmates' morality. Although most almshouses encouraged or at least allowed clergymen of various denominations to preach on the premises, few provided regular services and several even resisted attempts by local groups to provide Bibles or spiritual instruction to the destitute.[8]

These certainly were attempts to mold the conduct and values of the poor, as many historians have noted. But the efforts of institutional administrators to reform the indigent were largely ineffectual since administrators were constrained by a host of factors: insufficient legislative appropriations, chronic funding shortages, community observation and involvement, the burden of outside official examinations, and, perhaps most important, resistance by paupers themselves as they attempted to manipulate their admission, their tasks within the institution, and their discharge. The skill with which overseers and staff balanced adequate care for the deserving poor without seeming either to coddle them (thus supposedly stimulating permanent dependence) or to encourage the undeserving to seek assistance was an important component in public judgment of the welfare system. In this sense, little has changed in America during the past two centuries.

The poorhouse was a material expression of fiscal responsibility as well as civic benevolence, and administrators labored under a public scrutiny that grew particularly intense during periods of economic crisis. The county poorhouse was a prominent architectural feature in the landscape, but the community involvement necessary to keep it running efficiently made the almshouse an important characteristic of the social, political, and economic landscape as well. Public assessment of relief administrators' efficacy included opinions about the operation and physical features of the buildings, ranging from the internal arrangement of space, plumbing, heating, cooking, the circulation of air, and ornamentation both of interior rooms and the building's facade.[9] Newspaper commentators and reformers, such as Dorothea Dix, warned boards of overseers to avoid excessive expenditures on structures and grounds as ethically questionable and financially wasteful. "Expend not one dollar on tasteful architectural decoration," Dix advised. "Let nothing be for ornament, but every thing for use. Every dollar indiscreetly applied, is a robbery of the poor and needy, and adds a darker shade to the vice of extravagance in misappropriation of the public funds."[10]

The social and economic relations between relief institutions and their communities were as complex and as flexible as those among neighbors, precisely because they were relationships among neighbors. County poorhouses served a series of purposes within their communities regardless of the size of the town in which they were located. In addition to arranging for and

*Fig 6.*   Chester County Poorhouse, ca. 1800. Artist unknown. Courtesy of the Chester County Historical Society.

supervising the housing of the poor and outdoor relief, overseers sold or exchanged surplus foodstuffs and items manufactured in the institutions, found jobs in the almshouse and in the community for the able-bodied unemployed, indentured and monitored younger indigents, and hired local labor for tasks in and around the institution. The almshouses thus functioned as employers, consumers, and providers of cheap labor in the form of apprentices, proving grounds for young physicians, and lucrative sources of supply contracts.[11] These transactions were conducted using a mixture of cash, credit, and exchange of goods and labor between the institutions and their surrounding communities. For these reasons, almshouse administrators had a stake in continuing to regard the poor as members of the community rather than as outcasts who should be segregated from society.[12]

For the poor of the Philadelphia region in the eighteenth and early nineteenth centuries, as Gary Nash argues in this volume, all that was required to push many people into destitution was illness, injury, pregnancy, temporary unemployment, an economic downturn, or a bad harvest.[13] The working poor, in particular, suffered from the major reorientation of the region's economy in the first half of the nineteenth century, a transition that requires further discussion. Philadelphia's economic focus shifted from commerce to manufacturing as the city's status as a port for foreign trade declined while New York and Baltimore flourished. Industrial expansion after 1840 depended in part on the growth of a market for manufactured goods in the nearby rural counties. In these counties, household production correspondingly declined after 1815 while both industrial manufacturing and agricultural specialization increased dramatically. These eastern counties experienced waning jobs in agriculture between 1815 and 1840 and a concentration of workers in such enterprises as milling, paper, glass, textiles, and powder production. In the region's western counties—Chester, Bucks, Lancaster, and York—commercial agriculture intensified, especially the production of wheat and livestock (see figure 7).

The growth of interregional trade, stimulated by the construction of the nation's first stone turnpike between Lancaster and Philadelphia in the

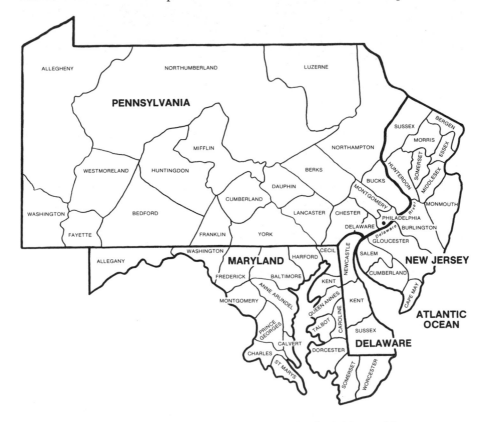

*Fig. 7*    Counties of the Mid-Atlantic Region. Drawing by Adrienne Mayor.

1790s and by new canals and railroads in the 1820s and 1830s, promoted iron production and opened up the anthracite coalfields. Much of the region's commercial agricultural output occurred on a small scale as individual households experimented with production for local and regional markets for cloth, thread, and dairy products. Depressions after the War of 1812 and again in the early 1840s, rapid growth of Philadelphia's population, and accelerating rates of migration to the city from the neighboring counties before 1840, all contributed to transforming the region's nonurban areas and creating difficult conditions for those who lived close to the financial margin. In the 1840s and 1850s, the population of western counties grew sharply, accompanied by an increase in the number of unskilled and lesser-skilled laborers; simultaneously, rural migration to the city decreased.[14]

Neither the number nor the demographic profile of relief recipients changed significantly during this era. Some of the overall population growth resulted from foreign-born migrants out of Philadelphia. Nevertheless, in spite of exaggerated fears about an influx of foreign-born indigents to rural areas, the major proportion of relief applicants was born in the Philadelphia region. Critiques of the evolving county-based system of poor relief resembled criticism of welfare common in our own time. The poorhouse population, it was asserted, was composed primarily of lazy drunkards, unwed mothers, feckless immigrants, and the aged, crippled, and mentally defective. In this view, urban and rural almshouses too frequently sheltered "regular customers" who cheated the system, entering the house when the weather grew too cold to sleep outside and leaving when the weather warmed sufficiently to live outdoors without danger of freezing.

As in modern America, analysis of relief recipients shows a clear disjunction between the actual population receiving aid and the one often depicted by newspaper editorials and public accounts. In fact, relatively few paupers registered in the Philadelphia region's poorhouse records in the first half of the nineteenth century suffered from disease, drunkenness, and accident; fewer than half had any physical ailment noted in the record. Paupers who were admitted more than once composed only about 15 percent of the poorhouse population in the same period.[15] These findings support the argument that on the level of local practice, and in spite of official prescription, individual paupers were generally judged by very different criteria than those specified in relief legislation.

Published commentaries on the poor increasingly emphasized a moral component to poverty beginning in the 1830s, and a trend toward blaming the poor for their situation is discernible in public discussion of relief costs and their objects. But practice did not conform to the harsh sentiments often printed in the local newspapers: administrators remained willing to work out flexible relief arrangements and to relay information between inmates and families outside. Why were officials in Philadelphia's satellite counties often lenient with their charges, and why did they persist in evaluating cases on an individual basis even as they publicly expressed much stricter views about the proper operation of the region's poorhouses? Administrators' interactions were by definition more intimate than relief transactions in larger urban institutions because rural institutions were closely involved in the economic lives of their communities as employers and as both suppliers and consumers of local goods. Moreover, many if not most applicants were known to overseers. Administrators felt a strong sense of obligation based on these factors.

In Philadelphia's satellite counties, relief was never a simple matter of substantial citizens looking after the less fortunate. In the outlying counties, poorhouse planners and administrators represented a wider variety of social groups than in the city, though all were white male landholders: overseers of the poor and almshouse clerks included comparatively wealthy men, farmers as well as merchants, artisans, and men whose families included applicants for relief.[16] Chester County's Joshua Weaver was clerk to the almshouse for some twenty-nine years. Weaver's belongings when he died in office included four looking glasses, three paintings, silver teaspoons, and twenty-four shares in the Bank of Chester County. Members of the Titus family appear on the lists of both overseers of the poor and of those relieved in Hopewell Township, Hunterdon County, New Jersey. Stewards included men like Gibbons Gray, whose finances were substantial enough for him to maintain a "plantation" while he and his wife resided at the Chester County almshouse as steward and matron.[17] Farmers and artisans also aspired to the steward's position, however. The nature of the community was such that relief administrators were likely to be acquaintances, neighbors, employers, or friends.

Relief administrators in Philadelphia's outlying counties were often not much wealthier than relief applicants, and poorhouse records show that most understood that the line between independence and indigence was easy to cross. In Chester County during the 1840s, officials had an especially good example of the fragility of material prosperity: Samuel Stringfellow, who had served as one of the trustees of the poor in 1802, declared bankruptcy in 1826 and found himself on Chester County's outdoor relief list in 1842.[18] Samuel Stringfellow's story illustrates the most basic moral inherent in antebellum poor relief: anyone could find himself or herself in the position of seeking public assistance. One of the most important lessons that relief institutions could teach, then, was humility, and accounts of visitors touring the region's poorhouses in the first half of the nineteenth century recommended it.[19]

Officials often fell short of their goal of transforming the inmates of institutions. One way to evaluate the function of almshouses as agents of social control is to examine their records for indications of autocratic or punitive conditions. Such conditions could include characteristics of other institutions such as prisons: incarceration, solitary confinement, hard labor, and a regulated appearance. Any list of institutional controls should also include less concrete requirements: loss of privacy, the confiscation of personal belongings, and regulation of behavior. Enabling legislation and rules for governance of the almshouses of the mid-Atlantic region specifically provide for most of these conditions, and some of them were enacted within the region's poorhouses. For example, paupers generally were not allowed private rooms; even married couples were frequently quartered separately in the wards.

Regulations required all paupers to wash regularly and change their linen weekly, and enjoined all inmates not to "swear, strike, abuse, or give ill language to one another, or to be clamorous" and to "behave themselves soberly, decently, and courteously to each other, and submissively to their superiors."[20] Poorhouse diets were planned to provide appropriate nourishment but not to be so lavish as to "operate as an inducement for others to envy the condition of a pauper."[21] Labor in the institutions was to be conducted on a strict schedule. All were to have work suited to their capabilities and were to perform their tasks when and in the manner directed by the steward or matron.

Both enabling legislation and most almshouse rules and regulations provided for the confiscation and institutional use or sale of paupers' possessions when they entered the institution. These appropriations, along with the labor provided by the individual while an inmate, were intended to defray at least a portion of the expense for maintaining the inmate within the institution. Salem County's poorhouse bylaws, for example, provided that paupers admitted to the house would "bring all their clothing and goods." Almshouse staff accordingly took stock of the new inmates' possessions. These might include household goods like Elizabeth Simpson's "Meal Sive & Bread Boll," personal items such as Margaret Bowman's tea box and fur hat, ornaments like Ann Mclure's pair of "old gold ear rings," or clothing such as Samuel Lewis's pantaloons and "stockins."[22] The inventories were often used to return the same or similar items to inmates when they left the poorhouse or if they died, were returned to family outside.[23]

Abandoned wives in Chester County used the opportunity of entering the house to appeal to the trustees of the poor for support in forcing husbands to maintain them. These appeals allowed the trustees to inventory the husband's property and, if allowed by the Court of Quarter Sessions, to appropriate some of it for the jilted spouse's support. Administrators did occasionally pursue a pauper's inheritance or pension for the purpose of paying for her or his upkeep, but generally they hoped to induce inmates to labor toward their own support around the institutions' grounds, in the poorhouse "manufactories" or outbuildings, and on the poorhouse farms.

Almshouse rules and regulations, often copied wholesale from other institutions, strongly suggest a punitive intent on the part of legislators and relief officials, that is, an effort to make institutional life so unpleasant that most poor folk would take pains to avoid it. In New Castle County, Delaware, the rules and regulations recommended solitary confinement in the "Dark Cell" for up to forty-eight hours with only bread and water for a wide variety of offenses, including feigning illness or otherwise refusing to work, smuggling alcohol onto the premises, or smoking in bed. The rules and bylaws of Salem County, New Jersey, promoted solitary confinement on bread and water for the same offenses nearly fifty years later. The rules for New Castle County also included a provision for causing recalcitrant paupers "to wear an Iron Ring around their Leg with a Chain and wooden Clog fixed thereto." Punishments common to all of the institutions included denial of a meal or of a whole day's meals and additional labor added to offenders' daily obligations.[24]

The records of individual institutions show, however, that administrators routinely failed to enact the harsh official provisions to their full extent. The rules left some latitude for punishment: those for New Castle and Salem counties required that the steward prove a serious offense in the presence of three overseers before a punishment could be levied. The minutes for the almshouses of Lancaster and New Castle counties contain no reference to paupers being placed in the dark cells for any reason, though the minutes do mention other punishments. Visitors' reports to the boards of directors do not mention solitary confinement (other than for the violently insane) in their complaints about the institutions. Failure to mention the harsher punishments does not necessarily mean that solitary confinement did not take place, but it suggests that this type of punishment was not common. The catalogue of the misdeeds of the directors of the poor for Bucks County instead reflects subtler mistreatment of the inmates, for example, charges that the matron had behaved callously to the sick.[25]

Some enabling legislation recognized the disjunction between prescription and practice and provided administrators liberty to bend the rules for special cases. Bucks County overseers of the poor were to "receive, provide and employ *according to the true intent and meaning of this act,* all such poor and indigent persons as shall be entitled to relief, or shall have gained a legal settlement."[26] Impoverished residents of Salem County who could not "without violating the rights of humanity, be removed to the poor-house" were to "receive *such support as the nature of the case requires, wherever they may be,* at the discretion of the overseers of the poor of the township in which their settlement may be."[27] The trustees of the poor for New Castle County justified the extension of outdoor relief to the sick, rather than moving them into the poorhouse, in order to avoid "Violating the Rights of Humanity."[28]

The regulations also provided specific restrictions on administrators' use of force in controlling inmates. The rules and bylaws of Salem County's almshouse forbade any corporal punishment "by any officer or agent of the Institution, on any inmates over twelve years of age, under penalties of dismissal, Unless by Order of the Board of Trustees."[29] Separate logs of offenses and punishments were supposed to be kept, but no such log has become known for any of the institutions in the Philadelphia region. Hard labor, however, does not appear in any of the rules or legislation either as part of the regular routine or as punishment for misbehavior.[30] Overseers recognized that unlike prison inmates, a pauper's presence in the almshouse was in the strictest sense voluntary; despite the presence of walls, poorhouse residents could and did leave when it suited them to do so. Almshouse inmates, like those of insane asylums, could to a limited extent employ the resources of the institution for their own purposes.[31] It is therefore unrealistic to view the almshouse as an institution either capable of, or intended for, imposing complete control on its inmates. Consequently, recent scholarship has been increasingly concerned with examining the local social and economic context of the relationships between administrators and aid recipients.[32]

Overseers' paternalistic attitudes were reflected in their language. Administrators often employed the metaphor of the family to describe almshouse residents. Visitors to the Chester County almshouse in 1831 praised the "industry, economy, the care and the kindness of the present Matron in the management of her numerous and afflicted, and exceedingly troublesome family," and were "gratified . . . to say that the Steward seems to feel and act toward the unfortunate Paupers as a wise and tender Father feels and acts toward his family."[33] At the same time, the often harsh personal notes added by clerks to admission records and annual reports ("an ungovernable temper," "a regular breeder") highlight the tensions inherent in the relief process and underscore that community generosity had limits.

The persistent use of the word "family" to describe the institutionalized poor in the Philadelphia region, and descriptions of the poorhouses as vital parts of a "Christian community," underscores the commitment of relief officials to a larger vision of civic generosity. Administrators had long presented the process of aiding the poor in terms of Christian duty and communal responsibility, and their language included concern that the virtuous poor should not be stigmatized by receiving relief. The *Pennsylvania Gazette,* for example, urged the "secrecy and delicacy enjoined by Christianity" in relieving the indigent sick.[34] In Philadelphia's satellite counties, this language was not mere window dressing. Although effective management of funds was of enormous concern to administrators, and most of the institutions borrowed money and pled for donations in addition to attempting a wide variety of money-making endeavors, cutting the services to the poor was a last resort rather than a first decision. In Lancaster County in 1821, the directors of the poor combined some reductions in the quarterly payments to paupers on outdoor relief with (voluntarily taken) salary cuts for the steward, the clerk, and the almshouse physician, before the board finally voted to abolish outdoor relief in 1826.[35]

The "family" within any given almshouse included inmates from outside the township, outside the county, and even outside the region, forcing administrators to function within a working definition of family and community that was very broad indeed. The interactions between overseers of the poor and poorhouse residents thus have important implications for how historians of poverty think about the impact of economic change on communities as well as on individuals.

The poorhouse was in many respects a large household, and the records reflect some priorities appropriate to that vision of the institution: the primary qualifications for the post of steward were those of a practical farmer, and the performance of each steward was evaluated against that standard. Samuel Kirby's neighbors wrote in support of his application for steward, describing him as "well acquainted with farming business, a good accountant" who "is well known to us to be a man of Honesty Integrity and Temperance" and whose wife was also "well qualified in all respects as a matron."[36] When the Bucks County Court of Quarter Sessions held special hearings in 1819 inquiring into charges of mismanagement at the county almshouse, much of the testimony focused on the steward's management of the farm.[37] Hopeful stewards also promised to use their "best endeavors to promote the interest of the county and the comfort of the paupers."[38] Weaver Nathan Clifton presented his weaving skills as an additional savings for the Gloucester County almshouse, proposing to "do all the weaving Manufactord in that House" for his term of service.[39] Daniel and Amey Wills presented themselves as candidates for steward and matron and promised to perform the shoemaking and "tayloring" in addition to their administrative duties.[40] Poorhouses required of administrators and staff a commitment to the institution's welfare that was more than mere rhetoric.

Paupers expressed in labor and other transactions a clear sense of the extent to which they would accept the authority of administrators, and of their due both as inmates and as human beings. Applicants for relief had their own ideas about the role of the poorhouse in the community and in their lives, and they attempted to influence the relief process at all stages. Paupers accepted administrative authority in some areas and challenged it in others, and administrators recognized that their power had both moral and practical limits.

Admission interviews were a first opportunity for the poor to manipulate officials' perceptions as relief applicants presented their life and work histories. Paupers who were not immediately identifiable as members of the community could use admission interviews to present themselves in the most favorable light. Many took the opportunity to present plausible stories that would be likely to obtain assistance if the details were not checked too closely.[41] Transients used these examinations to place themselves in the community by detailing work histories and employers, landlords, and neighbors and to establish their inability to achieve a financial foothold through the usual residency requirements of long-term employment, property ownership, and the qualification to vote.

Previous acquaintance with members of the overseers or with the stewards was helpful in obtaining aid, though not necessary as long as the applicant could present a credible and verifiable life history. In Philadelphia's outlying counties, where the administrators of the county poorhouses were in frequent contact with one another and where the working poor routinely traveled between counties in search of work, many paupers were well known to the house stewards. When Eliza Passmore was admitted to the poorhouse in Chester County, the steward informed the Lancaster County almshouse that he was well acquainted with her father and had known both Eliza and her mother for twenty years.[42]

The real tension over relief decisions was not between administrators and paupers, but between administrators from different counties; the issue at the center of conflict was not whether an individual should be helped, but rather who would shoulder the financial responsibility. There was a steady stream of inmates being transferred between institutions at any given time, and the region's overseers of the poor met periodically to settle accounts with one another. Administrators had every reason to believe that if any given pauper was established properly as a resident of another county, the cost of that person's board could be settled with the appropriate institution either by cash payment or a credit against the account between the institutions.[43] Administrators therefore had no great incentive to deny aid to any single applicant unless that person seemed clearly undeserving, and even clear character flaws did not keep "regular customers" off the rolls. The records are full of harsh descriptions of applicants and inmates clearly lacking in moral fiber yet given assistance: James Stewart, "intemperate and lazy"; James Greer, "intemperate"; Nancy Winger, "good at breeding."[44] Moral judgments were certainly a part of the admission process and of inmates' experience of the institution after admission.

Paupers and their families recognized the importance of conforming to administrators' expectations of them and attempted to make use of these expectations. Stewards helped maintain contact between the institutionalized poor and family members outside. Families wrote to stewards to inquire about their relatives and to pass on information from those at home. The poor understood that the steward could both facilitate the exchange of information and prevent it, and they were careful to consider his power when exchanging information or appealing for the discharge of an institutionalized family member. When Debbie Ann Baitzel asked the steward of the Chester County poorhouse to release her son George upon payment of the cost of his board while in the house, she added, "My husband has reformed and is doing well and we are able and willing to provide for him at our own expense."[45]

Stewards also recognized that appearances were malleable and that the poor attempted to manipulate the system. Refusing the account for support of Sarah Besely, an insane woman in the Schuylkill County poorhouse, the steward of the Chester County almshouse wrote to the directors of the poor for Schuylkill County. "That she knows the name of the Steward of this institution is not surprising and, no doubt, she knows the names of the Stewards of many more," he remarked tartly. "People, even insane, wandering about the country, would very likely pick up such important intelligence."[46]

Stewards used power and realized its limits. Thomas Baker refused to reveal the whereabouts of apprentice Ellen Pyles to her half brother, James Courtney, possibly fearing that Courtney would remove the girl from her indenture.[47] Baker, however, also recognized that power over inmates should be exercised with some restraint. In response to a husband's inquiry after his insane wife, the steward explained that he hoped to avoid confining her, though her condition was not improving: "I don't wish to do so, if I can get along without it. She is very noisy at times, & we bear with her because I am very much opposed to keeping her in a Cell or of anyone else, if it be possible with safety to avoid taking such a step."[48]

The poor were well aware of the workings of the system and clearly understood that their lives were not entirely in the hands of officials. Work assignments and details of daily life were negotiable depending on the inmate's relationship with the steward or matron. It was not unusual for paupers to have some voice in their welfare, particularly concerning medical treatment. When the attending physician of New Castle County's almshouse pronounced Jane Eccles's ulcers "incurable," and Andrew Crips "appeared and made a Proposal of Curing her for the sum of Three Pounds, but if not cured to receive no Pay," Eccles and her husband were consulted. They "being content with the Proposal, the Trustees agreed to it."[49] Less dramatic situations like boarding of the insane also required administrative creativity. The attending physicians of the Lancaster County almshouse often negotiated with relatives and friends over the financial arrangements for inmates transferred to other institutions, including the Pennsylvania Hospital for the Insane and the Pennsylvania Institution for the Deaf and Dumb in Philadelphia.[50] The nonviolent insane were often supported first on outdoor relief, then within the almshouse, and then moved to the state facilities when they became available.[51]

The complex personal relationships between officials and paupers are the most poorly documented area of institutional life. Some aspects may be guessed at since daily interactions drew public scrutiny when things went wrong, and inmates occasionally brought problems to public attention. The inmates of the New Castle County almshouse presented the directors in 1791 (almost immediately after its inception as a county poorhouse) with a signed complaint about conditions in the house and their diet in particular.[52] Paupers were among the witnesses testifying in hearings concerning possible mismanagement of the Bucks County almshouse in 1819.[53] Individual paupers also approached the stewards or appeared before boards of overseers to complain of poor food or poor treatment by the staff; Alexander Curry, for example, presented an address to the board of trustees for New Castle County's poorhouse complaining of ill treatment by the steward and the matron.[54] It is true that paupers' complaints generally were dismissed as being without foundation, but it is significant that inmates felt they could make complaints and have their charges investigated.

Both inmates and overseers described paupers' claims to reasonable treatment in terms of society's moral obligation to care for the unfortunate. Both groups, however, understood that the right to assistance was based at least in part on individuals' past productivity or potential for future usefulness to society. Inmates understood that if they wished to disassociate themselves from the unworthy poor, it was necessary to demonstrate either willingness or inability to work. The support of more prosperous neighbors could be valuable in this process of justifying assistance, particularly if the applicant wished to receive outdoor relief. John Sleesman presented a testimonial "certifying his conduct through life much in his favor" to the trustees of the poor for Chester County as part of his plea that his outdoor payments be continued. Substantial citizens of his town of origin signed the petition, portraying him as a man who had been a productive citizen before his leg was broken in an accident.[55]

Paupers understood that some of their entitlement was based on their expressed willingness to perform useful tasks around the institution; inmates' valuation as "deserving" or "undeserving" members of the lower sort was shaped in part by the issue of work. It was no accident that the device on the official seal for Chester County's trustees of the poor included a spinning wheel.[56] Failure to perform work adequately, feigning illness, and refusal to work were all ways inmates could, and did, express dissatisfaction with their situation. Labor relations may thus have been the clearest expressions of institutional authority and individual resistance.

Resistance to the most coercive form of labor relations, the binding out of the children of the poor, was common. Parents absconded with their children if both were institutionalized; they kept track of children's lives as apprentices; and some parents prodded administrators into canceling the indentures in cases where the child was being ill used or the parent felt capable of convincing trustees of their ability to support the child adequately.[57] The institution's position as source of (and mediator for) apprentices required maintenance of a complicated network of social contacts and a web of labor and financial transactions upon which the farm and manufactures depended. In addition to arranging and monitoring indentures, responding to inquiries from apprentices' families, and handling charges of misbehavior on the part of masters or apprentices, overseers sometimes placed apprentices in multiple indentures before they settled into a stable situation. Temperance Howard, an African-American girl, was in the Chester County poorhouse at least four times during her childhood and adolescence. In 1824, at age nine, she entered the institution "in Exchange," probably for another apprentice; four months later, a cryptic note in the steward's book notes that her "Leg [was] taken off by Doct[or] Taylor and his associates." Taken out on a month's trial in June 1827, she was returned two days later, stating to the steward by way of explanation that "her mistress was a Quaker woman and could not Bare the noise of her wooden leg on the floor." This was the girl's second placement from the almshouse, and it appears that the overseers may never have successfully bound her out.[58]

The most effective resistance to institutional life was simply to abscond, and many paupers either did or threatened to. When Samuel Riley, "A Saucy Black Man," did not want to perform the tasks assigned him, he threatened to apply for admission to the Philadelphia almshouse, a measure that would make the Chester County officials responsible for paying the Philadelphia overseers for Riley's room and board.[59]

But labor in the almshouses of the region was not entirely about succumbing to or resisting authority; inmates could negotiate both for work done and for its compensation. These institutions functioned much as the smaller farms around them did in the antebellum period: residents' tasks included artisanal production and agricultural activities, and stewards used a complex and flexible system of accounting for exchanges of labor and goods. Administrators used a system of rewards and of occasional cash wages to induce paupers to labor cheerfully. Individual tasks performed well merited occasional gifts of a small sum of money or a piece of clothing: Hanna Anderson was allowed "a New Suit of Wearing apparel as a reward for her exemplary Industry for a Sunday Suit." Dedicated service over time might merit the granting of an official post within the institution and an accompanying salary: Mary Franklin was promoted to wage-earning status as a nurse for her "careful" attendance on the sick in the New Castle County almshouse. John Atkinson, who labored on the Lancaster County almshouse farm to fulfill the debt for his support, was eventually "discharged as a pauper" and hired to do the same labor for $8.00 per month.[60]

The working poor of the Philadelphia region realized that the institutional labor system could be manipulated in very basic ways: to gain goods, to acquire cash, and perhaps most fundamental, to avoid having to officially enter the almshouse. This could be especially important for unskilled men, whose most likely employment would be seasonal in nature. Women were employed doing spinning as outwork, supplying the institution's inmates with fabric for clothing, or as midwives for the babies born in the institution.[61] Skilled artisans had more influence with directors and were at least occasionally able to make arrangements to their advantage. When James Laughlin was discharged from the Lancaster County poorhouse, the directors of the poor furnished him with "a side of upper leather of the value of 2.50 and a side of sole leather of the value of 5.70 as a beginning for him to follow his trade of Shoemaking." In exchange, he promised to repay the loan "in a reasonable length of time."[62]

For their part, administrators made arrangements wherever possible that would encourage relief applicants to work, whether or not they worked on the institutions' grounds. The willingness of administrators in outlying counties to be creative with work arrangements did not mean that life for the nonurban artisan was any easier than for his urban counterparts, however. Shoemaker Thomas McFall appears to have entered the Chester County almshouse thirteen times between 1810 and 1821, and weaver William Jackson was apparently an inmate five times between 1835 and his death in the poorhouse in 1841.[63] The sheer complexity of individual applicant's situations must have contributed to almshouse administrators' willingness to make flexible relief decisions.

Individualized solutions to the problems of the poor continued to be integral to relief administration after counties adopted a poorhouse-based relief system precisely because relief was allotted within the larger context of the institution's relation with the community. Officials formulated relief strategies in individual poorhouses in contradiction to the harsh provisions of relief legislation. This disjunction between policy and practice arose from officials' recognition that the relief structure could be dehumanizing, and from their efforts to conserve funds and discourage chronic dependency. The poor understood how the relief system worked and actively shaped their relief experience when they could.

When overseers judged relief applicants or recipients to be morally lacking, their treatment could be harsh, and living conditions in the poorhouses were always far from ideal. The shift to institutional relief, however, did not necessarily result in less humane care of the poor because the new county poorhouses remained part of the community. The almshouse system naturalized the division between residents who were unfortunate and "strangers" who required scrutiny. Strangers still received relief, but discussion centered on whether they were entitled to it in the county where they applied or whether they belonged elsewhere.

The metaphor of almshouse inmates as a family was a reference point for concern about isolating relief recipients and creating a permanent class of dependent poor folk; those down on their luck might not later contribute to society if when seeking aid they were removed from the community. The persistence of the family or household as a metaphor for the institution suggests a continuing belief in the poor as reclaimable members of society. The extension of such domestic terminology to the description of the poor indicates that the boundaries of community were still negotiable in spite of the tremendous economic and social changes in the Philadelphia region between the turn of the century and the beginning of the Civil War.

## Notes

1. I thank Ruth Herndon, Thomas Valente, Seth Rockman, and Billy Smith for commenting on earlier versions of this essay.

2. Outdoor relief, also called out relief, was a system of cash payments for "worthy" applicants, made in lieu of admission to the almshouse. Usually paid quarterly, they were given either

directly to the applicant or to a relative or other adult (sometimes an overseer of the poor) to be spent on the pauper's care.

Bells, usually situated in cupolas on top of the main residential buildings, regulated schedules in the institutions. Regulations specified when paupers rose and went to bed, what they wore, how often they changed and washed their clothing, and how long they took to eat meals. No distinction was made between farm work as seasonal or task-oriented and schedule-oriented manufacturing work as it emerged in nineteenth-century America. This reflected administrators' belief that regular labor was more important than the work actually performed. Routine work habits did not necessarily mean laboring for the same length of time each day or at the same hours. Almshouse regulations specified when to begin and stop work, but these times varied seasonally and included rough descriptions, like "dusk," as well as specific hours.

3. Informal visits from tourists or visiting relatives of local residents could at times be so disruptive to the institutions' daily functioning that early in the almshouse's lifetime Chester County's trustees of the poor restricted visits from all persons "not having business" to Sundays and Mondays. Minutes, Trustees of the Poor, Chester County, February 27, 1809, Chester County Archives, West Chester, Pa. (hereafter CCA).

4. Numerous historians have discussed the emergence of an institution-based antebellum social welfare system, interpreting it as part of a process of "naturalizing" an emerging social order, establishing the moral authority of the middle class over the lower classes, and solidifying unequal relations of economic and social power. Class conflict was an integral part of social change in antebellum America for the following three historians who document conflicts over control of workers' time, alcohol use, and religious observance as critical in early industrial development, themes that are still being explored: Paul Johnson, *A Shopkeeper's Millennium: Society and Revivals in Rochester, New York, 1815–1837* (New York: Hill and Wang, 1978); Herbert Gutman, *Work, Culture, and Society in Industrializing America: Essays in American Working-Class and Social History* (New York: Vintage Books, 1976); and Bruce Laurie, *Working People of Philadelphia, 1800–1850* (Philadelphia: Temple University Press, 1980). Michael B. Katz's well-known books *Poverty and Policy in American History* (New York: Academic Press, 1981) and *In the Shadow of the Poorhouse: A Social History of Welfare in America* (New York: Basic Books, 1986) and David J. Rothman's landmark *The Discovery of the Asylum: Social Order and Disorder in the New Republic* (Boston: Little, Brown, 1971) have shaped later studies of the resistance of the poor population to reformers' and administrators' attempts to classify and control them.

5. On the enduring myth of abundance and the ways in which it obscures understanding of poverty in America, see Gary Nash's essay in this volume.

6. That administrators' commitment to efficiency outweighed other considerations is evident in their willingness to experiment with specific types of solutions. For example, they provided individual paupers with the means for their own support, such as a cow or a loom. In addition, they changed from boarding paupers in households to institutionalizing them in poorhouses, then returned to boarding in households, as in Hunterdon County, New Jersey. These patterns are not unique to this region or to the first half of the nineteenth century. For similar solutions in eighteenth-century Rhode Island and New York, see Ruth Herndon, "Continuity and Change in Rhode Island, 1750–1800" (Ph.D. diss., American University, 1992); and Robert E. Cray Jr., *Paupers and Poor Relief in New York City and Its Rural Environs, 1700–1830* (Philadelphia: Temple University Press, 1988).

7. The wording of such regulations was standard almost everywhere; see, e.g., *Rules and Bylaws Ordained and Established by the Board of Trustees of the Poor of the County of Salem, New Jersey, February, 1846* (Salem: R. Gwynne, 1859).

8. The irregularity in religious services resulted from the practical difficulty of providing for the needs of multiple denominations and from the problem of arranging attendance. The directors of the almshouse for Lancaster County did not appoint a regular religious instructor for the inmates until 1864; Henry A. Showalter, *Sesquicentennial of the Lancaster County (P) Hospital* . . . (Lancaster, Pa.: Lancaster County Historical Society, 1951), 105. In 1854 the directors of

the poor for Lancaster County rejected the proposal of the president of the Bible Society to appoint a chaplain to the almshouse; Records of the Lancaster County Board of Commissioners, Minutes, February 4, 1854, Lancaster County Historical Society, Lancaster, Pa. (hereafter LCHS). When asked during the 1819 hearings about preaching at the Bucks County almshouse, the Reverend Dubois and the Reverend Belville were confused about whether they should make appointments or were even welcome to preach at the almshouse; *Minutes of the Almshouse Visitation* (Doylestown, Pa.: Published by Simeon Siegfried, August 1819), 60–64.

9. The *Delaware County Republican* praised Delaware County's second almshouse, for example, both for its internal arrangements, which included "Julius Fink's patent ranges with water back and circulating boiler attached" and a bathtub and "shower bath" in the paupers' bathroom, and for its external appearance. The article noted the connection between cleanliness and reform, commenting on the existence on the first floor of "a bath room intended for the punishment of refractory paupers" (April 3, 1857). The second Chester County almshouse drew praise as a "plain, substantial, and commodious building, imposing from its size and the fine position it will occupy, but without unnecessary ornament" (*American Republican,* January 31, 1854).

10. *Memorial Soliciting a State Hospital for the Insane (PA)* in *The Almshouse Experience: Collected Reports* (New York: Arno Press, 1971)), 53–54. Ornamental trees and shrubbery were also frowned upon as extravagant; a defender of the Delaware County trustees of the poor argued that the directors had never considered such an expenditure. See *Delaware County Republican,* September 28, 1855.

11. Several of the poorhouses in Philadelphia's outlying counties attempted to attract medical students to their institutions to provide up-to-date medical care to the inmates more cheaply. See Monique Bourque, "Liberty, Industry, and Independence: Almshouses and Labor in the Philadelphia Region, 1791–1860" (Ph.D. diss., University of Delaware, 1995), chaps. 1, 3. For physicians' own accounts of their motives for institution practice, see Applications for Almshouse Physician, 1823–42, Records of the Overseers of the Poor, Gloucester County, N.J., Gloucester County Historical Society, Woodbury, N.J. (hereafter GCHS).

12. Other scholars have begun to examine the ways in which individual nonurban institutions figured in local political battles. See Glenn Altschuler and Jan Salzgaber, "Clearinghouse for Paupers: The Poorfarm of Seneca County, New York, 1830–1860," *Journal of Social History* 17 (1984): 573–600; and Altschuler and Salzgaber, "The Limits of Responsibility: Social Welfare and Local Government in Seneca County, New York, 1860–1875," *Journal of Social History* 21 (1988): 515–37. For Philadelphia, see John K. Alexander, *Render Them Submissive: Responses to Poverty in Philadelphia, 1760–1800* (Amherst: University of Massachusetts Press, 1980); Priscilla Clement, *Welfare and the Poor in the Nineteenth-Century City: Philadelphia, 1800–1854* (London: Associated University Presses, 1985); Clement, "The Philadelphia Welfare Crisis of the 1820s," *Philadelphia Magazine of History and Biography* 105 (1981): 150–65; and Clement, "Nineteenth-Century Welfare Policy, Programs, and Poor Women: Philadelphia as a Case Study," *Feminist Studies* 18, no. 1 (1992): 35–58.

13. On poverty in Philadelphia, see Billy G. Smith, *The "Lower Sort": Philadelphia's Laboring People, 1750–1800* (Ithaca: Cornell University Press, 1990); and Clement, *Welfare and the Poor.* Much less is available on the outlying counties, but Lucy Simler found a growing class of landless, wage-dependent laborers in Chester County; see "The Landless Chester County Worker: An Index of Economic and Social Change in Chester County, Pennsylvania, 1750–1820," *Pennsylvania Magazine of History and Biography* 114, no. 2 (April 1990): 163–99. See also Joan Jensen, *Loosening the Bonds: Mid-Atlantic Farm Women, 1750–1850* (New Haven: Yale University Press, 1986).

14. This and the preceding paragraph are based on Diane Lindstrom, *Economic Development of the Philadelphia Region, 1810–1850* (New York: Columbia University Press, 1978). On women's participation in the household economy, see Joan Jensen, "Cloth, Butter, and Boarders: Household Production for the Market," *Review of Radical Political Economics* 12 (1980): 14–24; Jensen, *Loosening the Bonds,* and Jeanne Boydston, *Home and Work: Housework, Wages, and the Ideology of Labor in the Early Republic* (New York: Oxford University Press, 1990).

15. This is based on a sample of 2,656 admissions to six institutions in 1810, 1820, 1830, 1840, 1850, and 1860. For detailed analysis of demographic data on the institutionalized poor in antebellum Philadelphia's outlying counties, see Bourque, "Populating the Poorhouse: A Reassessment of Poor Relief in the Antebellum Deleware Valley," *Pennsylvania History* 70:3 (2003). While recidivist paupers and the chronically dependent were a matter of considerable concern to administrators, paupers who entered the house more than once were probably more visible rather than more numerous.

16. This resulted in part from Pennsylvania and New Jersey legislation in requiring all male landholders to serve on township committees and boards of county freeholders.

17. Weaver died in 1827 at the age of seventy-three. See Minutes, Trustees of the Poor, Chester County, August 8, 1827, CCA. For Titus family, see Hopewell Township Committee Poor Book, ca. 1799–1850, Hopewell Museum, Hopewell, N.J. For Gray, see Minutes, Trustees of the Poor, Chester County, February 25, 1823, CCA. Averaging between $300 and $400 annually, wages for stewards were about the same throughout the region, regardless of the institution's size. In Philadelphia, the stewards for the almshouse received a higher salary; the superintendent of the manufactory received a salary comparable to that of the stewards of the outlying county almshouses. Maintaining a farm or business while in residence as an officer was common. See examples in Frank Stewart, *Notes on Old Gloucester County* (Camden: New Jersey Society of Pennsylvania, 1917), 40.

18. Samuel Stringfellow petitioned the Chester County Common Pleas Court as an insolvent debtor in 1826. In 1801 or thereabouts, his petition states, he agreed to act as security for one P. Hart, pledging his responsibility to pay Caleb Brinton $533.33 should Hart be unable to do so. Shortly afterward, Hart defected and left Stringfellow to pay the bond. Stringfellow was at that time the owner of a "plantation" in West Goshen and had improved the land and added "large and extensive buildings" to the property. He took out additional loans to cover the extra debt and struggled for twenty-five years before giving in and declaring bankruptcy. For Stringfellow's service on the board of trustees for the poorhouse, see J. Smith Futhey and Gilbert Cope, *History of Chester County, Pennsylvania, with Geological and Biographical Sketches* (Philadelphia: Louis J. Everts, 1881), 405; Common Pleas, Insolvent Debtors' Petitions, December 1826, no. 7, CCA; Annual Report, Trustees of the Poor, Chester County, 1843, CCA.

19. See Anne Royal, *Mrs. Royall's Pennsylvania, or Travels Continued in the United States* (Washington: printed for the author, 1829); Edward Strutt Abdy, *Journal of a Residence and Tour in the United States of America, From April, 1833, to October, 1834* (London: J. Murray, 1835), 3 vols.; and Sidney George Fisher, *A Philadelphia Perspective: The Diary of Sidney George Fisher Covering the Years 1834–1871* (Philadelphia: Historical Society of Pennsylvania, 1967).

20. Eighteenth century legislation in Delaware and New Jersey also included such measures as marking inmates' clothing with a "P." In Delaware the badge rule was only in effect until 1802, and there is no evidence of paupers being forced to wear them. Nonetheless, the cheap fabric, possibly poor fit, and presumably unstylish cut of institutional clothing appears to have been distinctive enough to make a relief recipient easily identifiable. When Edward Heaton was admitted to the Philadelphia almshouse in 1856 and could give no information other than that he was born in Pennsylvania, the almshouse clerk noted that "his clothes would indicate, that he has been in some Public Institution." See Daniel Smith to Thomas Baker, March 26, 1856, Directors Correspondence, Trustees of the Poor, Chester County, box 3, CCA.

21. Minutes, Directors of the Poor, Lancaster County, Pennsylvania, April 9, 1811, LCHS.

22. For Simpson, see Trustees of the Poor, Kent County, Delaware, Inventories, August 3, 1836, DSA. Bowman, Mclure, and Lewis are noted in Inmates' Property at Death, December 1811, February 1812, October 1811, respectively, PCA.

23. When Catherine Curry left the Lancaster County almshouse in 1828, the overseers allowed her three dollars "for sundry articles which were of her property and were used and worn out in the house of employment during the time she resided therein"; see Minutes of the Directors of the Poor and House of Employment, Lancaster County, March 23, 1828, LCHS.

24. Minutes, Trustees of the Poor of New Castle County, April 18, 1791, DSA. The Lancaster County rules provided for the same penalties in 1799; see Minutes, Directors of the Poor and House of Employment, Lancaster County, December 12, 1799, LCHS. See also Salem County, *Rules and Bylaws*.

25. *Minutes of the Almshouse Visitation*, 71–74, 82, 100.

26. *Pennsylvania Correspondent and Farmers Advertiser*, June 25, 1807. This statement is from the enabling legislation for Bucks County, printed in this issue (emphasis mine).

27. *Rules and Bylaws Ordained and Established by the Board of Trustees of the Poor of the County of Salem, New Jersey, February, 1846*, Supplement, 1855 (Salem, N.J.: R. Gwynne, 1859) (emphasis mine).

28. Minutes, Trustees of the Poor, New Castle County, November 16, 1803, DSA.

29. *Rules and Bylaws*, 7.

30. Adam Hirsch's survey of the literature on the development of penitentiaries suggests that in antebellum America "hard labor" was distinctly different than the increases in daily tasks advised as punishment for rebellious or lazy paupers. Instead, it consisted of difficult physical labor, such as stone breaking or road construction. The existence of quarries on the properties of the almshouses of Chester and Lancaster counties suggests that hard labor could have been used as punishment. The majority of quarry work, however, was performed by individuals paid for that work (possibly inmates) or by locals who had bought "quarry rights" in order to obtain stone for use in construction. Quarry transactions were part of the labor structure within counties, and administrators regarded the quarries as potential sources of materials and income rather than as opportunities to punish the unruly. Adam Hirsch, *The Rise of the Penitentiary: Prisons and Punishment in Early America* (New Haven: Yale University Press, 1992), chap. 1. For institutional use of quarries, see Minutes, Directors of the Poor and House of Employment, Lancaster County, May 1, 1826, March 5, 1827, LCHS.

31. See Constance M. McGovern, "The Community, the Hospital, and the Working-Class Patient: The Multiple Uses of Asylum in Nineteenth-Century America," *Pennsylvania History* 54, no. 1 (1987): 17–33. The striking similarities in images (paintings, for example) and in physical arrangement of interior spaces in almshouses, colleges, and other residential institutions also reflect the constraints of providing for the needs of any population not contained by force.

32. See Stephen J. Ross, "'Objects of Charity': Poor Relief, Poverty, and the Rise of the Almshouse in Early Eighteenth-Century New York City," in *Authority and Resistance in Early New York*, ed. William Pencak and Conrad Edick Wright (New York: New-York Historical Society, 1988).

33. Visitors Report, 1831 (filed January 25, 1832), Records, Trustees of the Poor, Chester County, CCA.

34. *Pennsylvania Gazette*, January 3, 1787.

35. Minutes, Lancaster County Directors of the Poor, January 5, 1821, LCHS.

36. William Rine et al., to the Board of Chosen Freeholders of Gloucester County, December 27, 1827, GCHS. Applying for reappointment two years later, Kirby cited growth in his farm labors and "tayloring" for the almshouse to justify an increase in salary; see Kirby to the Board of Chosen Freeholders of Gloucester County, December 26, 1829, GCHS. More than fifteen years later, when Kirby applied for his old job, Joseph Dilkes's letter supporting his application stressed the author's personal knowledge of past stewards and the current applicant pool. It also asserted that Kirby was "the best farmer that had ever had the care of that place." Dilkes to the Board of Chosen Freeholders of Gloucester County, January 1, 1845, GCHS.

37. See *Minutes of the Almshouse Visitation*, esp. 28–33. When public attention focused on almshouse farm operations, discussion centered on whether the steward managed the farm effectively and productively, rather than whether the farms were profitable. Visiting and investigative committees invited testimony from neighborhood farmers about the appropriateness of the amount of manure purchased and the ages and types of stock maintained. Increases in production were important, but the word of the steward and of the institution's neighbors could be

as vital to investigators as audits of the Trustees' accounts in evaluating the success of almshouse farms.

38. Robert Jaggard to the Board of Overseers, December 24, 1841, Applications for Almshouse Steward, 1822–45, GCHS. Jaggard served as steward for at least three years.

39. Clifton to the Board of Chosen Freeholders of Gloucester County, December 23, 1822, GCHS.

40. Wills to the Board of Chosen Freeholders of Gloucester County, December 21, 1822, GCHS. Stewards' wives commonly served as matrons for the institutions; the Willses' application is unusual in that Amey was presented as an applicant in her own right rather than as an adjunct to her husband's application, and she appended her signature to the letter.

41. Robert Derry explained when admitted to the Philadelphia almshouse that he had been born in West Chester and was bound at age three to Jasper Wilcox, who owned a paper mill in West Chester. Derry left Wilcox's service after his indenture and supported himself "doing small Jobbs" in Philadelphia until admitted to the almshouse for a medical problem. But Chester County's almshouse steward checked the story and refused to acknowledge Derry's claim of residency in Chester County, noting that "I have been to find out Robert Derry . . . there is not one word of truth in it." Directors of the Poor, Philadelphia Almshouse, to Thomas Baker, January 21, 1860, and his reply, n.d., CCA.

42. Thomas Baker, Steward, Chester County Almshouse, to Directors of the Poor and House of Employment, Lancaster County, February 12, 1855; Directors Correspondence, Trustees of the Poor, Chester County, box 3, CCA.

43. Administrators often disagreed about the responsibility for paupers; arguments about their legal residence at times became acrimonious, and even resulted in lawsuits; see, e.g., Minutes, Directors of the Poor and House of Employment, Lancaster County, November 21, 1825.

44. Trustees of the Poor, Chester County, Annual Report, 1841.

45. Baitzel to Thomas Baker, Steward, Chester County Poorhouse, February 21, 1860; Directors Letter Book, CCA.

46. Thomas Baker to Directors of the Poor, Schuylkill County, October 23, 1860, CCA.

47. Courtney to Baker, January 24, 1860, and reply, February 10, 1860, CCA.

48. Baker to Robert Wilkinson, June 20, 1856, CCA.

49. Minutes, Trustees of the Poor, New Castle County, June 20, 1792, DSA.

50. These negotiations included who would pay for the inmates' board at the institution, how long they would stay, and whose responsibility the inmates would be at the expiration of their stay.

51. Thomas Sheward, a deranged inmate of the Chester County almshouse, was first boarded at the expense of his nephew beginning in 1812, then transferred to the Pennsylvania Hospital for the Insane in 1817; Minutes, Trustees of the Poor, Chester County, May 25, 1812, CCA. Samuel Moris was transferred from the Delaware County almshouse, where his father had paid to have him boarded since 1850, to the "State Lunatic Hospittle" in Harrisburg in 1853. After his removal to the hospital, his family continued to pay the quarterly expenses for his board to the overseers of Delaware County, who presumably routed the payments to the administrators of the hospital. Day Book, 1852–60, Records, Delaware County Home, Historical Society of Pennsylvania, Philadelphia (hereafter HSP).

52. Minutes, Trustees of the Poor, New Castle County, Delaware, July 26, 1791, DSA.

53. *Minutes of the Almshouse Visitation*, 49–53.

54. Minutes, Trustees of the Poor, New Castle County, Delaware, April 4, 1798, DSA.

55. Minutes, Trustees of the Poor, Chester County, September 3, 1804, CCA.

56. Ibid., December 26, 1808.

57. Moses Pyle "stole" his children from the Chester County almshouse, apparently to prevent them from being bound out; Annual Report, Trustees of the Poor, Chester County, filed 1808, CCA. William McGinnes's indentures were canceled when the overseers of the poor for Hunterdon County determined that his master had abused him; Hopewell Township Poor Book, Hunterdon County, December 5, 1826, Hopewell Museum, Hopewell, N.J.

58. Steward's Book, Trustees of the Poor, Chester County, December 28, 1824, April 4, 1825, CCA; Admission and Discharge Book, Chester County Poorhouse, June 28, 1827; Steward's Book, June 28, 1827, CCA. Howard appears in the annual reports for 1824, 1826, 1832, and 1835, in addition to the 1827 entry for her return.

59. The steward of the Chester County almshouse explained the situation in a letter to Philadelphia's guardians of the poor. See Walter Yarnall to the Philadelphia Guardians of the Poor, January 21, 1842; Directors Correspondence, Trustees of the Poor, Chester County, box 3, CCA.

60. For Anderson and Franklin, see Minutes, Trustees of the Poor, New Castle County, December 30, 1808, and November 16, 1803, DSA. For Atkinson see Minutes, Directors of the Poor and House of Employment, Lancaster County, January 7, 1811, LCHS.

61. Like the Philadelphia almshouse, the almshouses of Bucks, Chester, Delaware, and New Castle counties maintained employment logs. A few women spun and a handful of men wove in the house, but most was done as outwork intended to be an alternative to relief in the house.

62. He repaid the directors two years later. Minutes, Directors of the Poor and House of Employment, Lancaster County, April 4, 1825, and October 2, 1827, LCHS.

63. Admission Index, Trustees of the Poor, Chester County, CCA. Transactions for work performed appear in the institution's Pay Books. Tentativeness about the number of admissions is due to the possibility of two men with the same name being in the institution at the same time.

# *Eight*

## Bound by Charity

### *The Abandoned Children of Late Eighteenth-Century Charleston*

JOHN E. MURRAY

> Daughters of Carolina! . . .
> you whose little prattlers are yet but tottering around your feet;
> when you press them to your bosom . . .
> thank God that they are not orphans,
> cast upon the care and bounty of strangers,
> bound to them by no stronger a tie than charity.
> —The Reverend William Hollinshead, "An Oration
> Delivered at the Orphan-House of Charleston,
> South Carolina, October 18, 1797 Being
> the Eighth Anniversary of the Institution"

Orphaned and abandoned children in early America endured various fates. Extended family members raised many orphans.[1] Children who lacked family, as well as those abandoned by parents too impoverished to care for them, depended upon the kindness of local officials. Typically, these administrators had two goals: to minimize the burden on the public purse and to prepare children to become productive, self-supporting adults. A common process that achieved the former and provided some hope of the latter was to bind the orphaned child to an adult who became the child's master or mistress.[2] An auction similar to those used to bind paupers or debtors or a more bureaucratized procedure through the local almshouse connected masters and mistresses with orphans in some areas.[3] In 1790, the largest city in the South, Charleston, transformed this process by opening the first municipal, public-funded orphanage in the United States, the Charleston Orphan House. Rather than living in the harrowing conditions of an almshouse, orphans and abandoned youth were raised in an institution dedicated to the care of youngsters until they were old enough to work. This essay documents both the operations of the Orphan House and the experiences of the children who lived there during its first decade. Given social and economic constraints on the Orphan House's activities and the experiences of orphans and poor children elsewhere in early America, the Charleston Orphan House apparently provided a decent home and an effective education for young people with few happy alternatives.

Orphanages have become a policy issue in recent years as Americans have struggled, largely unsuccessfully, to deal with the great number of children living in poverty.[4] An institution today that bears some resemblance to the Charleston Orphan House is foster care—a temporary home with no legal commitment to permanency by either party, before a permanent legal arrangement is made with another family. Currently more than half a million American children live in foster care, at a cost of about $20,000 per year for each child.[5] As in the present, so in the past: the expense of caring for children unable to reside with their parents constrained public efforts in Charleston. Still, efforts in a society much poorer than our own provide an additional perspective on present dilemmas and suggestions to revive past institutions.[6]

Earlier methods to care for orphans indicate that Charlestonians were willing to spend their money to provide for these waifs—but not too much of it. Before the Orphan House was founded, Charleston supported destitute children through its two Anglican parishes, St. Philip's (founded in 1683) and its daughter congregation St. Michael's (first building dedicated in 1761). As local agencies of the established church, they had legal authority to collect taxes for poor relief and to distribute the proceeds. The churchwardens of St. Philip's gave cash grants to mothers of "bastard" children, but only until the fathers were identified and made to support their offspring. Men who abandoned their families were likewise ordered by the church to deliver funds to their dependents. The parish financially sustained women who cared for orphaned and abandoned children in their homes, which included support for wet nurses for the very young. The city maintained other children at the workhouse, in a hospital, and at the Provincial Free School, established specifically for poor and orphaned children.[7] Foreshadowing the Orphan House's policies, churchwardens bound out several older adolescents directly as apprentices.[8]

As early as the 1750s churchwardens began casting about for ways to maintain the children at lesser expense. Wardens observed that the older children whom they had bound out as apprentices were cared for with few "expenses on the parish."[9] When Charleston was incorporated in 1783, responsibility for these children shifted from the now-disestablished Anglican parishes to the city itself, which soon sought to reduce expenditures on poor children. One way was to centralize care of orphans in a single location, as at Bethesda, the orphanage founded by George Whitefield in nearby Savannah, which the city council studied closely. In 1790 the council passed an ordinance that established the Charleston Orphan House.[10] The measure began by noting the "heavy expense" that attended the previous system of "supporting and educating poor children."[11] By the end of the year, forty-two new children had been legally bound into the Orphan House, and many more were to follow.

Children entering the Orphan House, their parent or guardian, Orphan House officials, and the master to whom the child was ultimately bound all signed a legal document called an indenture.[12] Surviving indentures offer a wealth of information on the abandoned children of Charleston. The first part of the document was filled in when the child entered the Orphan House. It describes the age of the child, his or her natal family structure or whether the child had no living parents, the ability of the parent(s) or guardian to sign his or her name, and if the child had received some education, as indicated by whether the child could sign his or her name rather than mark with an *X*. The second part of the indenture was completed when the child was bound apprentice to the new master. It provides information about the child's experience in the Orphan House. Comparison of the dates on the two parts shows how long the child spent in the House; signing or marking the second half of the document indicates the effectiveness of the orphanage's basic literacy training. The bottom of the indenture outlined the young apprentice's prospects for the future: what kind of training and education his or her master was supposed to provide. Careful examination of this information yields a picture of the early lives of poor children, which otherwise is obscured in the written historical record.

The chances of a child being orphaned in Charleston or elsewhere in the South Carolina lowcountry were considerable, owing to elevated levels of adult mortality there. In nearby Berkeley County, adults who were about the same age as the parents of the Orphan House inmates suffered severely.[13] Among white men born there between 1761 and 1800, approximately 33 percent of those who reached the age of twenty died before their fortieth birthday, a startling figure even for a preindustrial society. Although the corresponding proportion for women was much smaller, at only 7 percent, the proportion of women in the previous generation dying before age forty was also about a third.[14] Since marriage and childbearing among adults was common, the number of children who lost one or both parents must have been exorbitant. As discussed below, children of single parents accounted for the greatest number of youths admitted to the Orphan House.

Few children of property-owning families and no offspring of black families were admitted into the Orphan House. Among affluent families, widowers and especially widows could generally expect to remarry fairly comfortably, and stepparenthood was anticipated as part of the obligation in the new marriage. Legal institutions, such as marriage settlements and wills, were specifically intended to direct the distribution of property and the care of children following the almost expected demise of one or both parents during their offspring's childhood.[15] The serial monogamy that followed the frequent deaths of spouses and parents gave the Carolina elite the appearance of being "one great tangled cousinry."[16] Orphans typically remained within these wealthier extended families. Skilled white artisans in Charleston provided for their own and their colleagues' surviving children through such organizations as the Mechanics' Society, the Barbers' Society, and the Coopers' Society, which aided and schooled orphans of members.[17]

The racist views of Charleston officials meant that African Americans, who formed a slight majority in late eighteenth-century Charleston, were not welcomed in the Orphan House. Free or slave, families of blacks lost parents and spouses to the agues and fevers common to the lowcountry. Orphaned slave children must have been numerous, given the harsh disease environment and the heavy workload of the slaves. Grandparents and other kin, both real and "fictive," raised many orphaned black children. Occasionally, the mistress took the slave orphan into the "Big House" and raised the child jointly with her extended family, although black children soon realized they were slaves rather than free.[18] Slave orphans were ultimately the responsibility of the master, not the local government. We know very little about the fate of free black orphans, although free African Americans obviously tried to care for them. Early in the nineteenth century, Charleston's free black elite launched the Minors' Moralist Society, a charity specifically intended to care for free black orphans. Later, the Brown Fellowship Society provided for widows and orphans of members. How effective these efforts were relative to need is unknown.[19]

The death or impoverishment of a parent made white children, especially those from the lower classes, eligible for the Orphan House. The Orphan House must have cared for a large share of the orphans of poorer inhabitants of Charleston. By the 1790 census, whites comprised just less than half the population of Charleston, at 49.5 percent.[20] Historian Robert Olwell estimated that one-fifth of Charleston's white population in the revolutionary era was non-slave-owning, working poor, the population from which the House's inmates were likely to be drawn.[21] Thus, since black children were excluded, the Orphan House drew potential inmates from approximately one-tenth of the city's residents, a population of about 1,600. By the late eighteenth century, white mortality rates appear to have declined from the brutal 50 or 60 per thousand that Peter Coclanis estimated for Charleston in the 1730s. If the force of mortality fell more heavily upon the very young and very old than upon those of child-raising age (as it did in Berkeley County), then perhaps 30 or 40 children were eligible for admission each year to the House. Since the Orphan House admitted an average 26 children per year in this period, it apparently accepted most of the poor white children in Charleston who had lost one or both parents.[22]

Throughout the 1790s the population of the Orphan House averaged slightly more than 100 children at any one time. At the beginning of the decade it consisted of children who had been in the charge of the previous orphan house and other outdoor arrangements, as well as children who had just been admitted as inmates of the newly chartered Orphan House. One unique event caused a spike in the number of children admitted: the slave revolt in Saint Domingue (Haiti), which alarmed the lowcountry's white elite. After France recognized the rebel government in autumn 1793, seventeen children of refugees who had come to Charleston applied for admission to the Orphan House. The board of commissioners agreed that children from Cap Francois should be admitted immediately without any of the usual investigations into claims of poverty.[23] In each year there were more boys than girls, although this ratio was greater in the middle of the decade than at the beginning or end. Some information is available for nearly all 265 children who entered the Orphan House during this decade. Due to death, running away, and returning to parents, later information is available for smaller numbers of children, as noted below.

The children bound into the Charleston Orphan House came from a variety of family arrangements (see table 13), with little difference between boys and girls. Two parents together bound only 4 percent of children, suggesting that these families had become impoverished and thus unable to support the new inmate. The child's mother authorized the binding in more than half of cases. Given the legal inability of women to sign contracts, endorsement of the indenture by the child's mother alone almost certainly meant that the child had no living or known father.[24] In general, single, abandoned, and widowed women must have found it difficult to earn an income sufficient to care for their progeny, whether due to traditional restrictions on women in labor markets or gender differences in productivity.[25] The 16 percent of children bound solely by their fathers may have come from intact families, but we cannot know for sure without further information. Nor can we differentiate between father-headed families in financial distress and those in which new

TABLE 13. Family Structure of Children Admitted to Charleston Orphan House, 1790–1799

| Child Admitted | Boys (%) | Girls (%) | Total (%) |
| --- | --- | --- | --- |
| Bound by both parents | 4.6 | 2.7 | 3.8 |
| Bound by mother | 50.3 | 54.5 | 52.1 |
| Bound by father | 16.3 | 14.3 | 15.5 |
| Bound by other relative | 3.9 | 5.4 | 4.5 |
| Bound by non-relative | 13.1 | 13.4 | 13.2 |
| Orphan | 11.1 | 9.8 | 10.6 |
| TOTAL | 99.3 | 100.1 | 99.7 |
| Number of cases | 153 | 112 | 265 |

Source: Indenture books Charleston Orphan House Records, South Carolina Room, Charleston Public Library.
Note: "Other relatives" included aunt, grandmother, sister, cousin, brother, and stepfather; "non-relatives" consisted of churchwardens, a friend, the poorhouse, and unspecified or unknown others; "orphan" refers to children described only as orphan on their indenture. Columns may not add to 100 percent due to rounding.

stepmothers wanted to distance themselves from their husband's children. Combining the cases of children bound by more distant relatives, such as much older siblings or grandparents, with those bound by nonrelatives, such as church wardens and poorhouse officials, in addition to those whom the indenture explicitly described as orphans, yields an estimate that approximately one-fourth of the youngsters admitted to the House were "full orphans" (lacking both parents). Later in the nineteenth century, relatively few residents of orphanages were full orphans. Since the Charleston Orphan House was one of the earliest orphanages in the country, full orphans always may have constituted a minority in American orphanages.[26]

The Orphan House accepted children at a variety of ages. A small number were infants and toddlers, and an even tinier number of teenagers were admitted. The typical child bound into the House was just shy of his or her eighth birthday (see table 14). Although age at binding to the orphanage differed little by sex, family circumstances affected the age of new inmates. Children of both sexes who were bound by one parent tended to be just past their seventh birthday. Children who were full orphans (bound by someone other than their parents) were older by a year, or around eight years old. Those few bound by both parents were a year older again, or nine years of age. The evidence is limited, but it is nevertheless suggestive. Children bound by a single parent may have come from the poorest and most desperate homes and thus were most in need of institutional care. Full orphans might have received assistance from the Provincial Free School, allowing them to stay out of the House for a longer time.

TABLE 14. Average Age of Children Admitted to Charleston Orphan House, 1790–1799

| Child Admitted | Boys (age in years) | Girls (age in years) | Total (age in years) |
|---|---|---|---|
| Bound by both parents | 9.2 | 9.8 | 9.4 |
| Bound by mother | 7.3 | 7.5 | 7.4 |
| Bound by father | 7.0 | 6.9 | 7.0 |
| Orphan | 8.4 | 8.5 | 8.4 |
| All children | 7.7 | 7.8 | 7.7 |
| Number of cases | 150 | 104 | 254 |

*Source:* Indenture books Charleston Orphan House Records, South Carolina Room, Charleston Public Library.
*Note:* "Orphan" refers to children bound by someone other than a parent or described as orphan on their indenture. Ages for 11 of the 265 total children admitted to the House were not indicated.

The child's endorsement on the indenture document lets us evaluate his or her exposure to basic education both prior to and while in the orphanage (see table 15). Scholars have closely studied the meaning of the ability to sign, as it is often the only education-related characteristic that is known about people of small means in the past. Children who could sign the indenture at entrance rather than make a mark likely learned to do so either in school or from their parents. Typically, schools taught reading before writing, and writing instruction may not have begun until the age of five or six. Thus, the ability to sign after age five indicates a medium level of education: most of those who could sign probably were reasonably good readers, and most markers presumably could not read. Some who signed, however, could write no more than their names, and a marker might well be able to read at least simple Scripture.[27]

Overall, less than a quarter of the children were able to sign, rather than mark, their names at entrance to the Orphan House. The ability of Charleston children to sign correlated with their age, sex, and their previous family situation. One-quarter of boys and only 18 percent of girls signed their name, suggesting, not surprisingly, that boys received better literacy education. The children bound by both parents were much more likely to sign than were orphans or those bound by just one parent. But caution is in order before inferring the effects of family structure on child literacy. The pattern for literacy is similar to that for age at entrance in table 14: high age and literacy levels among those bound by both parents, low age and literacy among those bound by one parent, and intermediate age and literacy for full orphans. About the same level of literacy existed among children bound by

TABLE 15. Signature Literacy of Children Admitted to Charleston Orphan House, 1790–1799

| Child | Boys (% who signed name) | Girls (% who signed name) | Total (% who signed name) |
|---|---|---|---|
| Bound by both parents | 42.9 | 66.6 | 50.0 |
| Bound by mother | 18.7 | 13.1 | 16.2 |
| Bound by father | 17.4 | 13.3 | 15.8 |
| Orphan | 36.4 | 25.8 | 32.0 |
| TOTAL | 24.8 | 18.2 | 22.0 |
| Number of cases | 149 | 110 | 259 |

*Source:* Indenture books Charleston Orphan House Records, South Carolina Room, Charleston Public Library.
*Note:* "Orphan" refers to children bound by someone other than a parent or described as orphan on their indenture. "Signature literacy" is calculated as the proportion of children who signed their indenture to the Orphan House. Six of the indentures for the 265 total children admitted to the House were not signed.

only one parent, without regard to whether that parent was the mother or father, a point explained more fully below.

The timing of signature literacy acquisition can also be estimated. Graph 8 illustrates the likelihood that boys and girls could sign at each age. Small sample sizes hamper our ability to assess older children's literacy, but the story among the younger children is straightforward. Boys apparently learned to write roughly two years before girls, and this initial difference in probability of signing persisted through age nine. This literacy differential appears to date from a very young age; a handful of boys could write their name as early as six years of age, but no girls could sign until age eight. Some of the children may have learned to write at the Provincial Free School, which St. Philip's operated for the poor, while others learned at home.[28] In any case, even before receiving formal schooling at the Orphan House, boys began learning to write around age six, two years before girls.

Parental literacy seemingly influenced whether youngsters learned to sign. Relatively few parents and guardians were literate. Only 32 percent of mothers and female guardians could write their names, whereas 74 percent of fathers and male guardians could sign. The adults who bound the children were far less literate than the masters (97 percent literate) and mistresses (93 percent) who ultimately took them in. One interpretation is that the Orphan House acted as a conduit to transfer children of the poor into houses of the rich.[29] Among children bound by one parent, the gender difference in parental literacy did not translate into variation in child literacy by the

GRAPH 8  Signature Literacy by Sex, Charleston, 1790–1800

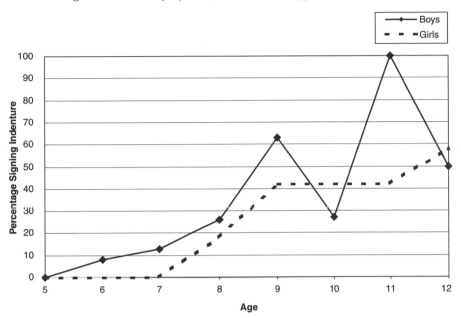

*Source:* Indenture books, Charleston Orphan House Records, South Carolina Room, Charleston County Public Library.

gender of their parent. That is, children bound by fathers did not benefit from the greater average rates of fathers' literacy; children bound by mothers just as often signed their names even though the mothers were far less likely to be literate. The Orphan House indentures thus indirectly support the hypothesis, consistent with other studies of past and present populations, that the literacy of mothers is more important than that of fathers in inducing literacy among children.[30]

The indentures of the Charleston Orphan House reveal some of the experiences of the children while they were inmates. In particular, we can learn from these documents how long the children lived at the Orphan House, some of their educational experiences while there, and the circumstances of their departure. On average, both boys and girls lived at the Orphan House for more than five years before binding to their new master. This exceeded the typical two-to-four-year stays documented by Timothy Hacsi in mid- to late-nineteenth-century orphanages. It resembled the six years spent by girls in the Boston Female Asylum in the 1840s, however, in part because both institutions waited to indenture their inmates until the girls were somewhat older adolescents.[31]

The age at which commissioners believed the children were old enough to work can be seen in Orphan House policy. Commissioners named boys who had turned fourteen years old and girls who had turned twelve on a list that circulated among prospective masters.[32] Among the children for whom precise age at entry and exit are known, children of both sexes typically were bound out just before their thirteenth birthday. But the House did bind out children as early as age nine, and it was common for both boys and girls to be indentured before age twelve. In the mid-nineteenth century, lady commissioners who oversaw treatment of girl inmates argued to no avail that the Orphan House should raise the age of indenturing girls from twelve to fifteen because they feared that younger children were being overworked by masters and mistresses. The eighteenth-century indentures suggest that what appeared to be a minimum age for indenturing was really a minimum age for children to be advertised as available for indenturing. If girls younger than twelve had been bound out all along, then the lady commissioners' pleas may have understated the exploitation of young girls.[33]

Another Orphan House policy was to provide religious training in Christianity, mostly of the Protestant sort. Initially, conducting Sunday morning prayer services was a duty that rotated among the commissioners. Later the children marched through the streets of Charleston each Sunday to attend a nearby Protestant church, including two Episcopal, two Independent (Congregational), a Presbyterian, and a Baptist church. The early Carolina historian David Ramsay remarked on the good feelings generated by the variety of ministers who preached at the Orphan House, noting less the effect of the sermons on the children than on the cohesiveness of white Charleston society in general.[34] After 1802, commissioners allowed Catholic inmates to worship in a nearby Catholic church. Also in that year a chapel was constructed on orphanage grounds, where visiting Protestant ministers conducted services. Not until 1825, after vigorous protest by the redoubtable Bishop John England, were Catholic priests admitted to catechize Catholic children and offer Mass. Optional daily prayer was in the Anglican tradition.[35]

Patterns of children's signature literacy suggest that the Orphan House effectively taught basic writing to the earliest cohort of children. From the start, educating inmates was an important priority. At the founding of the Orphan House, commissioners appointed a schoolmaster to oversee the education of the inmates, and beginning in 1799 a schoolmistress had special responsibility for the girls. Historian Jennifer Monaghan discovered a division of labor by gender in literacy instruction, in which teaching reading was women's work and teaching writing was men's work, at least in New England.[36] Such may have been the case at the Charleston Orphan House as well since the Rules of 1806 specified that the schoolmistress was to teach the children to read.[37] Regarding the most basic of writing skills, as evident in

TABLE 16.  Signature Literacy of Children at the Charleston Orphan House, 1790–1807

| Child's Age When Admitted | Percentage Signing Name | | | | | |
|---|---|---|---|---|---|---|
| | When Admitted | After 1 Year | After 2 Years | After 3 Years | After 4 Years | After 5+ Years |
| 5–8 years | 12 | — | 100 | 83 | 100 | 100 |
| 9–12 years | 49 | 88 | 93 | 100 | 100 | 83 |
| 13+ years | 80 | 100 | 100 | — | — | — |
| All children | 30 | 91 | 94 | 92 | 100 | 98 |
| Number of cases | 191 | 11 | 18 | 26 | 26 | 49 |

*Source:* Indenture books Charleston Orphan House Records, South Carolina Room, Charleston Public Library.
*Note:* "Signature literacy" is calculated as the proportion of children who signed their indenture to the Orphan House.

table 16, few children left the orphanage unable to sign their names, even though the vast majority of children admitted to the institution could not sign. This was probably no accident. It was common for commissioners to deny applications from masters for specific children on the grounds that the child had not made sufficient progress in his or her education. Although a few children left the Orphan House illiterate, it must have been a practice that the commissioners, with final say on who left and who stayed, frowned upon.[38]

Literacy acquisition must have occurred relatively quickly after entrance into the Orphan House. Comparison of children's endorsements upon entrance and exit shows signature literacy before and after attending the Orphan House school, while holding the critical factor of age constant. Among children nine to twelve years old, 49 percent could write their names at entrance but 88 percent could sign after one year in the Orphan House, a figure that continued to rise with each additional year in the House. Although apparently every child received literacy training, other sorts of education may have been influenced in part when the surviving parent persisted in advocating for the youngster, which occurred at the Orphan House later in the nineteenth century.[39] Given relatively low rates of literacy among the parents of these children and the low quality of the free schools, it is unlikely that the near universal literacy among departing inmates would have occurred without the Orphan House's efforts.

Children departed the orphanage in several ways (see table 17).[40] By far the most common outcome for boys was to stay at the orphanage until they

TABLE 17. Fate of Children Admitted to Charleston Orphan House, 1790–1799

| Child's Experience | Boys (%) | Girls (%) |
| --- | --- | --- |
| Bound to master or mistress | 71.2 | 54.5 |
| Ran away from House | 5.2 | 5.4 |
| Returned to parent(s) | 7.8 | 17.9 |
| Died | 7.8 | 8.9 |
| Other/unknown | 7.8 | 13.4 |
| TOTAL | 99.8 | 100.1 |
| Number of cases | 153 | 112 |

*Source:* Indenture books Charleston Orphan House Records, South Carolina Room, Charleston Public Library.
*Note:* Columns may not add to 100% due to rounding.

were bound out to a new master, which happened to 71 percent of those admitted in the 1790s. About 54 percent of girls eventually were bound out. But 18 percent of girls returned to their natal family; typically the mother who bound the child initially had reestablished herself, often by remarrying, and was able to resume her parental role. Indeed, the sole surviving parent of children throughout early America often maintained an interest in their institutionalized child's welfare.[41] The Orphan House expelled very few children for being troublemakers, although about 5 percent of youths fled the institution.

Disease and death among children were an inescapable part of lowcountry life. Infectious disease spread quickly and virulently within the House. Inmates suffered from epidemics of whooping cough (1809), conjunctivitis (1810), and measles (1813). About 8 percent of the children died in the Orphan House. Among the six children for whom cause of death was reported, two died of consumption and the others from measles, yellow fever, croup, and dropsy. Deaths were distributed evenly over the years except in 1794, when five children died, one each in April, May, July, August, and September. The cause of these five deaths is unknown, but they may well have been the victims of the yellow fever epidemics that afflicted the city that year.[42] Corresponding to the seasonality of deaths among Charleston's whites earlier in the eighteenth century, child deaths also tended to occur in the hot season of July through October.[43] Another peak in child mortality occurred in March through May, when five deaths of the sixteen with known dates occurred. These deaths may have been related to the diarrheal "April and May Disease," which recurred each spring in the Orphan House.[44] Smallpox was a relatively unimportant problem, and inmates routinely were inoculated beginning in 1811.[45]

Mortality among children in the Orphan House was relatively high, perhaps reflecting difficult conditions of daily life there. Death rates among the institution's inmates were approximately 20 per thousand. One estimate for contemporary rural Massachusetts found death rates among children younger than ten to have been around 30 per thousand, but only 1 or 2 per thousand among ten- to fifteen-year-olds.[46] Similarly, a study of relatively wealthy Philadelphia children of the eighteenth and nineteenth centuries estimated death rates of about 4 per thousand for five- to nineteen-year-old boys and girls.[47]

If all went well, after some years in the Orphan House the child faced another great change in his or her life: binding out to a master or mistress. Typically, adults visited the Orphan House and talked with children after having seen the child's name on the binding-out list. Once interested, potential masters and mistresses discussed the contract's specifications with the commissioners. Similar to apprenticeships throughout early America, the indenture expired at age twenty-one for boys and eighteen for girls. Most children were to learn their masters' trade, although a few were not promised training in a particular craft. Mistresses had discretion as to whether girls they took in would become seamstresses or domestics. Many terms in the indenture were open to negotiation. Some documents promised three months of schooling during each of the first three or four years of the indenture, while others contained no such assurances.

All contracts promised some kind of payment at the end; the boilerplate on every document required the master or mistress to supply a new suit of clothing and other personal items. Some additional clauses written in by hand described a cash payment, typically to be made to the "Commissioners of the Orphan House for his [her] use." These payments appear to have ended up in the orphans' hands. The indenture of Michael Lowry included this statement on the back: "Recd from Benjamin Cudsworth, Steward [manager of the Orphan House] forty three dollars in full of my apprenticeship as mentioned in the within indentures [signed] Michael Lowry." Further, some indentures specified that payments promised to apprentice mariners, such as John Bates, were to be made directly to the child since presumably it was impossible to know when the ship would again be in Charleston where the captain could pay the Orphan House. All indentures required the master to pay the orphanage in two cases: a larger sum if he returned the apprentice to the Orphan House before the indenture expired, and a smaller amount if the apprentice completed the indenture. Orphan House financial records suggest that payments made in cases of broken indentures constituted a small but important source of income for the Orphan House, but no comments were made regarding payments for completed indentures that were retained by the commissioners.[48]

The promises of education, skill training, and payments at the end of the apprenticeship varied by the child's gender. The indentures made sharp distinctions between boys and girls in most of these terms (see table 18).[49] Boys received assurances of considerably larger freedom dues (payments at the end of the indenture) than did girls, although compensation to both sexes were made with about equal frequency. One reason for this gender differential may have been that masters were especially keen to discourage boys from running away toward the end of their apprenticeship, whereas girls may have been less likely to abscond. Moreover, the work of males was rewarded more highly in financial terms than was the work of females in early America, and the crafts children learned differed by gender. Typically, boys learned the skills of laboring people: two-thirds of boys were to acquire proficiency for jobs in seafaring and shipping, transportation, construction, metal working, and making textiles and clothing. Another 13 percent of boys were not assured of learning any job skills, perhaps suggesting that they would toil as unskilled laborers. Highly skilled and richly remunerated professional trades, such as architect, attorney, insurer, merchant, and even a planter, were specified in 11 percent of the indentures. Girls' trades included low-paying ones traditionally associated with their gender: mantua making, millinery, upholstering, and domestic service. The provision of such skill training to white children might be viewed as remarkable in a society that knew what increased labor supply would do to wage levels. The few free black artisans in Charleston, whose children could not enter the Orphan House, were thought to be a perpetual threat to the employment of white artisans and were heavily regulated.[50] Cheap child labor, on the other hand, was apparently seen as far less of a threat and so was allowed to continue.

Perceptions of class and gender shaped the commitments to education for apprentices. A quarter of boys but only 6 percent of girls could expect their masters to provide schooling. Education, of course, cost time and money, which masters and mistresses were loath to spend. Moreover, they perhaps believed that much book learning would be wasted on poorer girls, especially since many of them had acquired the basics in the Orphan House. The small proportion of boys who received further schooling suggests that masters and mistresses held similar beliefs about the necessity of schooling for poor boys as well. Tellingly, orphan and poor apprentices elsewhere in America were far more likely to be assured education. The proportion of Philadelphia

TABLE 18. Terms of Indentures of Children Bound Out of the Charleston Orphan House

| Terms of Indenture | Boys (%) | Girls (%) |
| --- | --- | --- |
| **Education** (literacy, counting) | 25 | 6 |
| **Skill training** | | |
| domestic ("housewifery") | 0 | 38 |
| textiles manufacturing | 9 | 5 |
| dressmaking | 0 | 29 |
| maritime, seamen | 9 | 0 |
| shipping | 5 | 0 |
| construction | 22 | 0 |
| transportation | 11 | 0 |
| metal working | 8 | 0 |
| "professional" skills | 11 | 0 |
| other trades | 13 | 0 |
| unspecified trade | 13 | 28 |
| Promised freedom dues | 61 | 68 |
| Value of freedom dues | $4.64 | $2.85 |
| Number of cases | 127 | 84 |

*Source:* Indenture books Charleston Orphan House Records, South Carolina Room, Charleston Public Library.
*Note:* The value of the freedom dues has been translated into 1791 dollars based on the price series E-90 for Charleston in the U.S. Bureau of the Census, *Historical Statistics of the United States* (Washington: Government Printing Office, 1975), 204, with values for missing years calculated by linear interpolation.

indentures that promised education grew from a third in the 1770s to two-thirds in the 1810s. Among those children promised education, a shift from informal offers to teach reading, writing, and counting to more formal schooling was evident.[51] In New England, nearly every child bound out from the Boston almshouse carried some kind of educational clause in his or her indenture, nearly all of which were promises of informal training in reading, writing, and (for boys) arithmetic.[52] In Louisa and Prince William counties, Virginia, at mid-century, some 83 percent of white public apprentices were promised further education; about a fifth of such promises took the form of schooling.[53] The scarcity of further educational opportunities for the Orphan House children was similar to those facing other poor white children in the South, a region that lagged far behind other areas of America in establishing a public educational system. Well into the nineteenth century, free schools for Charleston's poor continued to teach nothing more than reading, writing, and arithmetic through the rule of three and remained an option only for those who could not afford any better.[54]

No poor orphan had it easy in eighteenth-century America, and many aspects of orphanage life must have been very difficult. One early nineteenth-century steward, Benjamin Cudsworth, complained upon his resignation that while the girls were generally of "very good" character, the boys tended toward "malignant" behavior. Life in the Orphan House, he concluded, "was Hell."[55] We should note, however, the experiences of other contemporary children before accepting these harsh judgments uncritically. In most of the North, binding poor orphans to local masters was a common practice with potentially grim consequences for the children. Barry Levy characterized the Massachusetts system of binding out abandoned or destitute children as "unsentimental, often abusive, [and] exploitative."[56] Town fathers had the power to remove a child from the master's household upon proof of abuse, but how often that happened and how effective it was in preventing abuse cannot be determined.[57] Some orphans who were bound at a very young age were treated primarily as a cheap source of hard labor.[58]

The Charleston Orphan House may have been an improvement on out-door methods of orphan care in which the child's well-being was monitored only to the extent that neighbors or surviving parents complained about abuses.[59] Unlike the New England practice of using outdoor poor relief as orphan care, in Charleston "vicious" children stood some chance of being corrected, adult supervisors were reasonably closely monitored, and educational efforts provided some minimal level of training. Children who passed through the Charleston Orphan House received an average five years of care that included reasonably effective basic education. Had they been bound directly to their masters at age eight or so, their prospects for exploitation would have been greater and prospects for basic literacy training less promising.

At the same time, the Orphan House paradoxically benefited in economic terms from its racial admission restrictions. Given its charge to accept only the relatively few white orphans and destitute children, it probably cared for most of the eligible white children in Charleston. Even within this constraint, commissioners desired to minimize their expenditures; hence their refusal to keep girls in the Orphan House until age fifteen, as the lady commissioners had desired. These economic constraints undoubtedly had an adverse impact on children in the House.

This awareness of the costs of child raising suggests an important barrier to the revival of orphanages: institutions are an expensive way to care for abandoned children. The Charleston Orphan House was funded by taxing those who held nearly all of the city's wealth to pay for the care of few of Charleston's orphaned children. Given that limitation, the Orphan House cared for most of the white children in need of its services, but the city's ratepayers were not prepared adequately to fund an institution that would care for all orphans, nor would they have allowed the Orphan House to keep children after they had reached working age. There is little reason to expect that present-day taxpayers would feel differently about funding a revived system of orphanages. The effect of underfunding such hypothetical institutions might well be that the children who emerged from such a system would face about the same likelihood of dropping out of school, becoming parents out-of-wedlock, and earning relatively low incomes in adulthood as children in the present system of foster care and welfare for single mothers.[60]

The establishment of the Charleston Orphan House as a charity for white children was a rich act of irony, given its location in one of the most densely slave-populated areas of the South.[61] Civic-minded Charlestonians were immensely proud of their benevolent charities in general and the Orphan House in particular. When George Washington visited Charleston in 1791, his hosts directed him to the Orphan House to show how committed the city was to the care of indigent whites.[62] The racial composition of its inmates suggests that the Orphan House was one of those charities that enraged reformers like Sarah and Angelina Grimké, in the 1830s: some of the same citizens who kindly provided for dispossessed whites administered beatings to enslaved blacks. Designed as an "institution of national virtue," the Charleston Orphan House probably did provide a level of care for its children that was an improvement on previous arrangements for homeless youth and better than contemporary outdoor, noninstitutional alternatives.[63] Although it is anachronistic to expect Charleston to have provided such care to the poor of all races, it is appropriate to conclude this essay by noting this bitter paradox of history since so many of America's poverty-related problems today are linked inextricably with the issue of race.

## Notes

1. I thank Monique Bourque, Ruth Herndon, Robert Olwell, and Billy Smith for comments and suggestions.

2. Some girls were bound to adult women.

3. Auctions were common in New England; see Benjamin J. Klebaner, "Pauper Auctions: The 'New England' Method of Poor Relief," *Essex Institute Historical Collections* 91 (1955): 195–210. In particular, Robert W. Kelso, *The History of Public Poor Relief in Massachusetts, 1620–1920* (Boston: Houghton Mifflin, 1922), 96–97, describes an auction of family members in Gardner, Massachusetts, in which the subsidy from the town decreased with the age (and hence usefulness) of the child. Marcus Wilson Jernegan, *Laboring and Dependent Classes in Colonial America, 1606–1783* (New York: Frederick Ungar, 1922), 182, noted that auctions of the poor in Virginia were occasionally proposed but seldom carried out. On northern children in

almshouses, see Lawrence William Towner, "The Indentures of Boston's Poor Apprentices, 1734–1805," in *Past Imperfect: Essays on History, Libraries, and the Humanities,* ed. Robert W. Karrow Jr. and Alfred F. Young (Chicago: University of Chicago Press, 1993), 36–55; and Billy G. Smith, *The "Lower Sort": Philadelphia's Laboring People, 1750–1800* (Ithaca: Cornell University Press, 1990), 165–71.

4. E. Wayne Carp, "Two Cheers for Orphanages," *Reviews in American History* 24 (1996): 277–84.

5. Conna Craig and Derek Herbert, "The State of the Children: An Examination of Government-Run Foster Care," National Center for Policy Analysis Policy Report no. 210, August 1997; General Accounting Office, "Foster Care: Agencies Face Challenges Securing Stable Homes for Children of Substance Abusers," GAO/DHHS-98–182, September 30, 1998.

6. This verdict is similar to that of Timothy A. Hacsi, *Second Home: Orphan Asylums and Poor Families in America* (Cambridge: Harvard University Press, 1997).

7. Nita Katherine Pyburn, "The Public School System of Charleston Before 1860," *South Carolina Historical Magazine* 61 (1960): 86.

8. Walter J. Fraser, "The City Elite, 'Disorder,' and the Poor Children of Pre-Revolutionary Charleston," *South Carolina Historical Magazine* 84 (1983): 175.

9. Ibid., 178, quoting St. Philip's Vestry Book.

10. The Charleston Orphan House was the first public orphanage in the country; the privately funded Bethesda was older by a half century.

11. Copy of ordinance in Minutes of Commissioners' Meetings, vol. 1, Charleston Orphan House records, South Carolina Room, Charleston County Public Library.

12. Indenture Book for Boys and Girls, Records of Commissioners of the Charleston Orphan House, City of Charleston Archives; partial transcriptions appear in Susan L. King, *History and Records of the Charleston Orphan House, 1790–1860* (Easley, S.C.: Southern Historical Press, 1984).

13. "Inmate" was the Orphan House's term for the children who lived there. It was used without prejudice locally and in subsequent scholarly writings.

14. H. Roy Merrens and George D. Terry, "Dying in Paradise: Malaria, Mortality, and the Perceptual Environment in Colonial South Carolina," *Journal of Southern History* 50 (1984): 533–50.

15. John E. Crowley, "The Importance of Kinship: Testamentary Evidence from South Carolina," *Journal of Interdisciplinary History* 16 (1986): 559–77; Marylynn Salmon, "Women and Property in South Carolina: The Evidence from Marriage Records," *William and Mary Quarterly,* 3d ser., 39 (1982): 655–85.

16. Bernard Bailyn, as quoted in Robert M. Weir, *Colonial South Carolina: A History* (Columbia: University of South Carolina Press, 1997), 235.

17. Richard Walsh, *Charleston's Sons of Liberty: A Study of the Artisans, 1763–1789* (Columbia: University of South Carolina Press, 1959), 133–34.

18. Larry E. Hudson, *To Have and To Hold: Slave Work and Family Life in Antebellum South Carolina* (Athens: University of Georgia Press, 1997), 81.

19. Marina Wikramanayake, *A World in Shadow: The Free Black in Antebellum South Carolina* (Columbia: University of South Carolina Press, 1973), 85.

20. Peter A. Coclanis, *The Shadow of a Dream: Economic Life and Death in the South Carolina Low Country, 1670–1920* (New York: Oxford University Press, 1989), 112, 116.

21. Robert Olwell, *Masters, Slaves, and Subjects: The Culture of Power in the South Carolina Low Country, 1740–1790* (Ithaca: Cornell University Press, 1998), 45.

22. Coclanis, *Shadow of a Dream,* 166–74; Merrens and Terry, "Dying in Paradise," 542–46. If the crude mortality rate was 40 per thousand, with infants, children, and those over fifty accounting for 30 to 35 of those deaths, then between 10 and 20 poor white Charlestonians of child-raising ages died each year. Not all of these people were in fact parents, and not all who were needed the Orphan House's help. Among the young adult and middle-aged deceased who were parents, each may have left four children, totaling three dozen or so orphans each year. These figures are

reasonable, if speculative. The point is that in its first decade, the Orphan House accepted a great proportion of that small minority eligible for its services.

23. Minutes of Commissioners Meetings, vol. 1, September 26, 1793, Charleston Orphan House records, South Carolina Room, Charleston County Public Library.

24. On the different legal limitations endured by single ("feme sole") and married ("feme covert") women in colonial South Carolina, see Weir, *Colonial South Carolina*, 282.

25. On gender issues, see the essay by Karin Wolf in this volume; on productivity differences, see the discussion below on varying levels of literacy by sex among relatively poor South Carolinians.

26. Hacsi, *Second Home*, 105–6.

27. Kenneth A. Lockridge, *Literacy in Colonial New England: An Enquiry into the Social Context of Literacy in the Early Modern West* (New York: W. W. Norton, 1974), 7; see also John E. Murray, "Generation(s) of Human Capital: Literacy in American Families, 1830–1875," *Journal of Interdisciplinary History* 27 (1997): 413–35, about literacy of children in particular. Olwell, *Masters*, chap. 3, discusses scriptural literacy among lowcountry slaves.

28. Walter J. Fraser Jr., *Charleston! Charleston! The History of a Southern City* (Columbia: University of South Carolina Press, 1989), 203.

29. These percentages are based on 102 mothers and female guardians, 31 fathers and male guardians, 70 masters, and 27 mistresses. Elsewhere in the South, Lockridge, *Literacy*, reported literacy rates of about 70 percent among mid-eighteenth-century male Virginia wealth holders and about 50 percent among Virginia women (pp. 79, 92); Robert E. Gallman, "Changes in the Level of Literacy in a New Community of Early America," *Journal of Economic History* 48 (1988): 567–82, found male literacy rates of 79 percent and female rates of 35 percent among property holders in mid-eighteenth-century Perquimans County, North Carolina.

30. Murray, "Generation(s)."

31. Hacsi, *Second Home*, 130–31.

32. King, *History and Records*, 17.

33. Gail S. Murray, "Charity Within the Bounds of Race and Class: Female Benevolence in the Old South," *South Carolina Historical Magazine* 96 (1995): 54–70.

34. David Ramsay, *History of South Carolina from Its First Settlement in 1670 to the Year 1808* (Newberry, S.C.: W. J. Duffie, 1858), 2:25–26.

35. King, *History and Records*, 7–8; Alan Keith-Lucas, *A Legacy of Caring: The Charleston Orphan House, 1790–1990* (Charleston: Charleston Orphan House, 1991), 7. Compare the strenuous efforts of Philadelphia area almshouses to prevent regular religious services or instruction from occurring on the grounds in Monique Bourque's essay in this volume. Perhaps the Carolinian approach reflected the desire of the white elite to keep the white lower classes content in order to maintain a unified facade among the white minority. On elite white unity in the mid-eighteenth century, see Weir, *Colonial South Carolina*, 122–38. On the refusal to allow two Jewish inmates to meet with a rabbi in 1857, see Susan L. King, "The Charleston Orphan House: The First Hundred Years," *Proceedings of the South Carolina Historical Association* (1998): 107.

36. E. Jennifer Monaghan, "Literacy Instruction and Gender in Colonial New England," *American Quarterly* 40 (1988): 18–41.

37. *Rules for the Government of the Orphan-House, at Charleston, South-Carolina* (Charleston: W. P. Young, 1806).

38. See, e.g., Charleston Orphan House, Minutes of Commissioners' Meetings, vol. 1, December 11, 1794, Charleston Orphan House records, South Carolina Room, Charleston County Public Library.

39. Barbara Bellows, "'My Children, Gentlemen, Are My Own': Poor Women, the Urban Elite, and the Bonds of Obligation in Antebellum Charleston," in *The Web of Southern Social Relations: Women, Family, and Education*, ed. Walter J. Fraser, Frank Saunders, and Jon Wakelyn (Athens: University of Georgia Press, 1985), 52–71.

40. On this topic, see John E. Murray, "Fates of Orphans: Poor Children in Antebellum Charleston," *Journal of Interdisciplinary History* 33 (2003): 519–45.

41. See Monique Bourque's essay in this volume. One Maryland county is analyzed in Lorena S. Walsh, "Child Custody in the Early Colonial Chesapeake: A Case Study," unpub. paper, 1981. See also Ruth Herndon's essay in this volume.

42. Joseph I. Waring, *A History of Medicine in South Carolina, 1670–1825* (Columbia: South Carolina Medical Association, 1964), 113, 149.

43. Coclanis, *Shadow of a Dream*, 42.

44. Waring, *History of Medicine*, 154.

45. King, "Charleston Orphan House," 109.

46. In rough terms, there were about one hundred children in the orphanage at any given time. Thus, the 22 deaths spread out over a decade plus (the last death among this cohort occurred in 1802) indicated a death rate of about 20 per thousand life-years of children aged between five and fifteen. The Massachusetts death rate is in R. S. Meindl and A. C. Swedlund, "Secular Trends in Mortality in the Connecticut Valley, 1700–1850," *Human Biology* 49 (1977): 396.

47. Louise Kantrow, "Life Expectancy of the Gentry in Eighteenth and Nineteenth Century Philadelphia," *Proceedings of the American Philosophical Society* 133 (1989): 312–27.

48. Indentures of Michael Lowry, admitted October 16, 1798, and John Bates, admitted August 8, 1793, Indenture Book for Boys and Girls, Records of Commissioners of the Charleston Orphan House, South Carolina Room, Charleston County Public Library.

49. John E. Murray and Ruth Wallis Herndon, "Markets for Children in Early America: A Political Economy of Pauper Apprenticeship," *Journal of Economic History* 62 (2002): 356–82.

50. Wikramanayake, *World in Shadow*, 101.

51. Farley W. Grubb, "Educational Choice in the Era Before Free Public Schooling: Evidence from German Immigrant Children in Pennsylvania, 1771–1817," *Journal of Economic History* 52 (1992): 363–75.

52. W. Graham Millar, "The Poor Apprentices of Boston: Indentures of Poor Children Bound Out Apprentice by the Overseers of the Poor of Boston, 1734–1776" (M.A. thesis, College of William and Mary, 1958).

53. Jernegan, *Laboring and Dependent Classes*, 167. He examined 139 indentures.

54. Laylon Wayne Jordan, "Education for Community: C. G. Memminger and the Origination of Common Schools in Antebellum Charleston," *South Carolina Historical Magazine* 83 (1982): 105.

55. Keith-Lucas, *Legacy of Caring*, 9.

56. Barry Levy, "Girls and Boys: Poor Children and the Labor Market in Colonial Massachusetts," *Pennsylvania History* 64 (1997): 303.

57. See Ruth Herndon's essay in this volume.

58. Walsh, "Child Custody."

59. Still, some historians have judged that this system, too, was about as humane as could be expected, given the general lack of resources and attitudes toward children and their labor. See Towner, "Boston's Poor Apprentices," 53.

60. Robert Haveman and Barbara Wolfe, "The Determinants of Children's Attainments: A Review of Methods and Findings," *Journal of Economic Literature* 33 (1995): 1829–78.

61. The theme of ironic benevolence is explored thoroughly in Barbara L. Bellows, *Benevolence Among Slaveholders: Assisting the Poor in Charleston, 1670–1860* (Baton Rouge: Louisiana State University Press, 1993), which examines the Orphan House primarily in the 1850s.

62. Fraser, *Charleston! Charleston!* 179.

63. Bellows, *Benevolence*, 46, 121.

# PART THREE

## Politics, Religion, and the Creation of Poverty

# *Nine*

# Poverty and Politics in the Hudson River Valley

THOMAS HUMPHREY

Politics in New York ran hot throughout the colonial period. In the late seventeenth century, Jacob Leisler resisted the Catholic influence of England's King James II. By the spring of 1689, he found some allies among inhabitants of New York City, Queens, Long Island, and Westchester who opposed the Stuart monarchy, putting Leisler and his followers at odds with men like Lieutenant Governor Francis Nicholson who supported the Catholic king. Although Nicholson had made Leisler a high ranking official, by May Leisler could no longer tolerate Nicholson's decisions. In June, Leisler agreed to help an armed group take over Fort James. When he tried to use his new-found position to foment more dramatic social and religious change, the new Protestant king, William II, denounced Leisler and made him a rebel. Leisler quickly found himself pitted against such landed opponents as Stephanus Van Cortlandt, Frederick Philipse, Robert Livingston, and Kiliaen Van Rensselaer, all of whom had carved out enormous estates in the Hudson Valley and intended to fill them with tenants who would improve the land and pay rent. What had started as a contest between political and religious opponents became a fight between landed men with official power and landless men without it. Leisler paid for leading the rebellion in May 1691 when he and an associate were taken to a public place, hanged, and decapitated.

Politics in New York remained the nearly exclusive playground of the rich throughout the rest of the colonial period. In the 1730s, John Thomas challenged the powerful Frederick Philipse for an assembly seat but lost, prompting Philipse to, in Edward Countryman's turn of phrase, give Thomas "a public reprimand." Thomas won the seat seven years later. In 1761, various men stood for election in Albany County, each believing they had the support of the enormously influential Robert Livingston Jr. The election turned when Livingston threw his support behind one candidate over the other. These

elections illustrate both how effectively landlords influenced politics by sway-
ing voters.[1]

How tenants on Livingston Manor and Rensselaerswyck voted demonstrates how wealthy landlords nearly completely controlled the political
actions of their much poorer tenants. In every election between 1700 and
1766, tenants on these two northern Hudson Valley manors elected either
their manor lord or his agent as the manor's representative to the colonial
assembly. The Livingstons owned approximately 160,000 acres on the east
side of the Hudson River in Dutchess County, and the Van Rensselaers owned
roughly one million acres in Albany County, New York. These and other land-
owning families earned income from the rents paid by tenants. The leases
they signed created a symbiotic but inherently unequal socioeconomic relationship that outlined their formal economic arrangement, and each party
implicitly expected the other to behave in ways that preserved that relationship. Tenants believed that landlords should allow them to miss an occasional
rent payment when they harvested poor crops because of extraordinary circumstances, such as bad weather, illness, injury, war, or floods; landlords
anticipated that their tenants would pay rent on time and vote them into
important colonial offices. Many tenants on these estates satisfied property
requirements for voting but did not fulfill the higher standards for office-
holding. Most landlords felt quite confident in that regard in a colony where
voters stood and announced their votes while agents of the landlords carefully recorded who voted for whom. Although tenants worried about the consequences of voting for the wrong candidate, landlords assumed themselves
to be more capable rulers than the voters. Under such a system, voters regularly elected men of superior social standing to offices most voters could not
occupy because they did not own sufficient property to qualify to hold more
than local offices.[2]

J. R. Pole explained this paradox of poorer people repeatedly electing
elites by introducing the notion of "deference" in the early 1960s when he
examined the voting patterns of colonial Virginians. He concluded that voters usually elected wealthy men to political office because voters deferred to
the political acumen and experience of their wealthier "superiors." Sung Bok
Kim applied that interpretation to voting patterns in colonial New York, arguing that the tenants on Livingston Manor and Rensselaerswyck accepted the
landlords' "leadership as natural."[3] Voters in early New York, however, chose
between candidates who rarely represented the voters' interests but who
more often symbolized feuding factions of the elite. Then, as today, the candidate supported by the community's wealthiest and most powerful members

*Fig. 8*    Hudson River Manors, ca. 1765. Drawing by Thomas Humphrey.

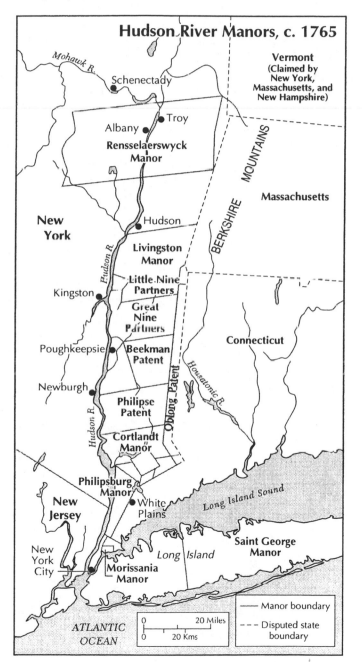

usually won, which explains why the Livingstons and Van Rensselaers consistently emerged victorious.

Since Pole first introduced the idea of deference, historians of early America have interwoven their analysis of deference with their interpretation of the American Revolution. On one side, historians such as Michael Zuckerman have argued that power struggles in the 1760s and 1770s resulted in part from egalitarian ideas that pervaded the colonists' perspective, prompting them overtly to reject hierarchical power structures. Most colonists thereby supported the Revolution because they embraced Jefferson's assertion that all men were equal as common sense. On the other side, scholars like John Murrin asserted that although colonial American society was politically deferential, the American Revolution unleashed a radical egalitarianism that eradicated deference to such an extent that the conservative attempt to restore it (in the form of the United States Constitution of 1789) ultimately failed. These radical attacks on hierarchy began in the 1760s when Parliament imposed the Stamp Tax on colonists, and those assaults intensified throughout the revolutionary period. Although disparate at the beginning, these various strains of radicalism coalesced during the Revolution to form the foundation of the revolutionary perspective, informing the revolutionaries' vision of equality, republicanism, independence, and freedom. By the end of the era, however, people who espoused these views divided over the meanings they ascribed to these tumultuous events. Ultimately, both schools of scholars have agreed that the Revolution was radical, either because it accepted an antihierarchical agenda from the beginning or because it unleashed one.[4]

The rural rebels who attacked deference in the Hudson Valley were not allied with the people who protested the Stamp Tax and other British imperial acts. Indeed, rural rioters struggled over land with the very men who comprised the Sons of Liberty because many of the latter were landlords in the northern Hudson Valley. These landlords, in turn, used their considerable political, economic, and military power to resist poorer people who challenged the distribution of land and the traditional political hierarchy. Landlords occupied the top of that hierarchy primarily because of the wealth and power derived from their vast estates. The conflict over land and power was a zero sum game with political implications: landlords lost whatever rioters gained. During the Revolution, the Livingstons and Van Rensselaers staunchly supported the revolutionaries, in part to protect their property and the political power that guaranteed. Meanwhile, tenants took advantage of the upheaval of the Revolution to redefine their society. After the Revolution, tenants and landlords continued their disputes over land. As a result, from the 1750s through the 1790s, the socially subversive activities of lower sort land rioters sometimes paralleled but more often conflicted with the political rebellion waged by revolutionary landlords.

The conflicts over land between rural rebels and revolutionary landlords indicate that the radicalism unleashed in the Hudson Valley in the 1760s that attacked hierarchy and deference was not always, or even necessarily, part of the agenda of the men who waged political rebellion against the British at the same time.[5] That they and other Americans of different social status looked at the Revolution in vastly different ways suggests that historians need to examine the various strains of radicalism without necessarily placing them into the overall construction of the revolutionary movement.[6] Not everybody participated in the Revolution in the same way or even at all. Such an approach might inspire Americans of the twenty-first century to see that the foundation for their political and cultural heritage, the American Revolution, was not the homogenous and ultimately beneficial event historians such as Bernard Bailyn and Gordon Wood have described. Americans then might use that perspective to reexamine their own society to discover their own culturally diverse community—and the challenges they face.[7]

Hudson Valley tenants were not generally as destitute as many of the other people discussed in this volume. For instance, Ruth Herndon examines how community leaders in Rhode Island warned out poor women and others, too, yet New York officials rarely warned out tenants. Still, tenants, like indigents throughout early America, lived fundamentally as dependent people and they frequently experienced conditions similar to those of the poor and the near poor. Like the poorer Philadelphians analyzed by Simon Newman, rural residents in the Hudson Valley died more often because of poor diets and hard work under tough conditions than from old age. At the same time, while tenants usually lived above the contemporary poverty line, they still lived very close to the financial margin and often feared falling into poverty at some point in their lives. In that regard, the reality and the fear of at times falling into destitution were as important a part of tenants' lives as poverty was for others discussed in this volume. Many farmers became tenants precisely because they were too poor to buy land in a region dominated by landlords. Although tenancy offered people without capital the chance to obtain good land at low rates, tenants accepted their subordinated status in an America supposedly characterized by white freeholders because it was one of the few ways to provide for their families. Their dual condition as tenants and farmers left them, as Gary Nash points out, precariously perched on the brink of poverty and living in insecure economic environments where a number of factors—including disease, injury, poor weather, war, and the like—

could drive them into destitution. Like tenants elsewhere in the colonies, tenants on Livingston Manor and Rensselaerswyck did not enjoy the same political and economic freedoms as their freeholder neighbors. Moreover, tenants' economic dependence and their weak political position were compounded by their instability on the land and by their inability to will land to their heirs. To that end, Gary Nash rightly identifies tenancy as an indicator of poverty in eighteenth-century British North America.[8]

The immense gap between rich and poor in the northern Hudson Valley reflected the difference between landlords and tenants. Landlords owned most of the arable land in the northern Hudson Valley. Both the Livingstons and the Van Rensselaers grew rich by selling and trading the agricultural products, cash, and labor tenants paid in rent. These families translated their wealth into political power during the eighteenth century and, on the eve of the Revolution, sat at the top of New York's hierarchy. Tenants, in contrast, generally could not afford to buy land or to move out of the region. The landlords capitalized on these circumstances. In 1749, Robert R. Livingston advertised that he owned a "large Tract of Land Laying in the Province of New York." He wanted to settle the land with German immigrants who could afford to make the trip to the Hudson Valley but who could not afford to buy land after they arrived. Fifteen years later, Robert R. Livingston and his cousin Robert Livingston Jr., the manor lord, again targeted poor immigrants who might become tenants. They knew that a "Number of Fresh Families" who could not afford to buy land had recently landed in New York City. The two men proposed to purchase 10,000 acres more and rent it to these immigrants. Once they became tenants, most families struggled to make their farms productive and all labored under the instability of tenancy. Those few tenants who fared well never rivaled the wealth and power of their landlords.[9]

Statistical evidence gathered in the 1760s and 1770s shows that the majority of tenants on both manors lived near or at the bottom of the social hierarchy. The assessment rolls of the mid-1760s record the taxes paid on realty, which included all improved lands and unimproved land deemed part of an improved farm. Real estate also consisted of houses, barns, mills, stores, and other outbuildings. Tenants on both manors agreed to pay taxes and assessments levied on their leaseholds when they signed leases with the Van Rensselaers and Livingstons. Landlords paid the assessments on their mansions and the improved parts of the land they operated. In the colonial period, landlords fought hard and largely successfully against a tax on unimproved land for the very simple reason that a good portion of the land they owned was uninhabited and unimproved even in the late colonial period.[10] For Rensselaerswyck, 88 percent of the 561 people on the list were assessed at £10 or less. The remaining 12 percent included such affluent men as Stephen Van Rensselaer, who was assessed £270, and his relative John Van Rensselaer, who was assessed £125; these men possessed property worth ten to twenty times that of the majority of their tenants. The figures for Livingston Manor resemble those of Rensselaerswyck: Robert Livingston Jr. was assessed £300 and his cousin Robert R. Livingston, Esquire, was assessed £110. As on Rensselaerswyck, nearly 90 percent of the 464 people rated were assessed £10 or less.[11]

In 1779, the New York state legislature taxed the inhabitants of the state to generate income to pay war expenses.[12] The 1779 tax valuations reveal the significant gap between rich and poor and the comparative distress of tenants compared to other New York farmers. The tax rolls likewise show that even if most tenants were not impoverished, many teetered on the brink of indigence and not infrequently sank into the depths of monetary despair. While the typical freeholder in the Hudson Valley owned roughly £270 in realty, tenants were assessed on average £132 on Livingston Manor and £255 on Rensselaerswyck. Moreover, approximately 70 percent of all tenants on both manors lived on leaseholds assessed at less than £150, approximately half the value of the farms of most freeholders in New York.[13] Assessors also rated the realty of the landlords, who possessed considerably more realty than their tenants. They rated the realty of John Van Rensselaer at £10,000, indicating that he held nearly forty times the realty of two-thirds of the tenants on Rensselaerswyck. Similarly, the realty of the executors of the estate of Stephen Van Rensselaer, who died as manor lord in 1769, was rated at £19,000, nearly eighty times the value of the holdings of the wealthiest tenants and more than one hundred times the holdings of most of the tenants. The realty of Robert Livingston Jr., the manor lord of Livingston Manor, was rated at approximately £30,000, although that did not include his property in Albany and New York City. These figures demonstrate the extraordinary polarization of wealth in the region on the eve of the Revolution.[14]

But these comparisons of the wealth of tenants, their landlords, and freeholders miss the basic doctrine of tenancy. Although they lived in houses and on farms that resembled in size and composition the farms of freeholders in the region, and although they paid taxes assessed on their leaseholds, tenants on Livingston Manor and Rensselaerswyck could never fully reap the benefits or the value of their land because they did not own it.[15] When their leases expired or when a tenant died and the others named on the lease could not pay to have the lease reassigned, the improved land, the orchards, and the buildings all returned to the landlord. The landlord, not the tenant, thus enjoyed the ultimate reward of the tenants' labor because improved land was always more valuable than unimproved land. Consequently, not all tenants were necessarily poor, but they all lived on land temporarily, and they could not will it to heirs. This instability greatly undermined their ability to provide for their families and heirs. Worse, they lived in fear that one small miscue— disease, injury, bad weather, poor crops, fluctuating prices, improper voting, or war—could throw them into poverty. In this agrarian society, few were richer than the landlords and few were poorer than the tenants.[16]

Despite the disparities in wealth, most tenants in the region lived on their leaseholds for a long time, and potential or actual poverty brought on by poor harvests shaped their lives. The length of tenure also indicates that although some tenants likely moved on to own land, many others decided to stay on their leaseholds. Tenants on Livingston Manor usually rented land for three lives, and 190 of the 377 tenants, or roughly 50 percent, listed as residents of the manor between 1767 and 1784 lived on their leaseholds the entire period. On Rensselaerswyck, tenants signed leases that lasted ostensibly "for ever." Although the leases look like permanent transfers of the land, the Van Rensselaers never relinquished their right to re-enter the land if a tenant failed to fulfill his or her end of the contract. Regardless, roughly two-thirds of the tenants stayed on the land for approximately twenty years, and as many as half of the leaseholds may have remained with the heirs of the tenant who signed the lease.[17]

Nearly every one of these tenants missed some rent payments, and most owed at least two years' rent and many owed much more. Although tenants might have used their debt to bargain for lower rents or longer leases, most already had long leases and they stayed on their leaseholds for many years. Landlords pragmatically sought to avoid evicting even deeply indebted tenants. An eviction was a legal process initiated by the landlords and carried out against the impoverished tenant, making evictions highly charged affairs that might likely turn violent. Eviction demonstrated quite plainly to tenants how close they lived to the edge of subsistence. As a result, tenants sometimes attacked landlords and officials who coldly threw a tenant and his family out of his house over money. However profit-driven landlords may have been, they knew they had to keep the peace if they wanted to continue to collect rent from tenants. Thus, landlords tolerated some debt for the sake of peace, and tenants breathed a bit easier knowing that they could miss a rent payment or two before facing eviction, poverty, and starvation.[18]

To escape these conditions and to secure their livelihoods, rural people sometimes rioted to obtain land, and increasingly they argued that they had earned the right to own the land by living and working on it.[19] These poorer people were politically active, especially when they thought they had a chance of achieving change. The disputes resulted in numerous skirmishes between landlords and rural rioters, and rebellion peaked in colonial New York in 1765 and 1766, at the same time protesters in Albany and New York City were demonstrating against the British Parliament's attempt to impose the Stamp Tax.[20] Although rural rioting peaked at the time of the Stamp Act crisis, the domestic struggle between wealthy landlords and poorer rural insurgents both predated and superseded the struggles with Great Britain in the 1760s. Land rioting in the region began in the 1750s when disgruntled tenants joined forces with New York and New England squatters and Native Americans. Conflict arose out of disputes over colonial borders, proper boundaries of the estates in question, and conflicting European and Native American claims to land. Landlords wanted to preserve their tenanted estates. Rioters wanted to be freeholders because that status offered them better economic and political stability. By the early 1760s, dissidents had waged several court battles and small skirmishes against the Livingstons and Van Rensselaers but lost every time. Their desire for land could not overcome the power of their opponents. By 1765, both sides had reached a critical point. Insurgents decided that only a massive and violent rebellion would succeed. Landlords, on the other side, struggled to preserve order, and they prepared to use British military force to defeat the insurgents once and for all.[21]

In late 1765, Rensselaerswyck tenant Robert Noble led the rioters as they marauded through the countryside, attacking people who refused to support them. The crowds included disgruntled tenants and many of the inhabitants of nearby Spencertown, who had voted to join the rebels, to defend their "Lands against other Claimants," to raise money to "defray charges in Defence" of their land and towns. In June 1766, at the peak of the rioting, Noble led approximately 250 men on raids against tenants who had refused to join the rioters or who had taken over the leaseholds of rebellious tenants. The demonstrators also marched to Robert Livingston Jr.'s manor house, threatening to pull it down and to "murther the Lord of the Manor" if he did not give the tenants the land on which they lived. They demanded freehold possession of the land and rejected any remnants of tenancy.[22]

John Van Rensselaer, joined by members of his family and by the Livingstons, organized a posse to arrest Noble. Some members of the posse may have lived on the farms of rioters who had been evicted, or they may have simply sided with the landlords to preserve the stability of their rural lives. Others presumably served the landlord reluctantly, joining the posse to satisfy rent obligations and not because they felt strongly one way or the other. In any case, the order to join the posse was not a demand these tenants could refuse. On June 26, 1766, Van Rensselaer and Walter Livingston headed the force of approximately 130 men who marched to Noble's farm. They wanted either to force the insurgents off the manor or to arrest them for stealing land. Several members of that posse—Dirck Ten Broeck, Abraham Ten Broeck, Thomas Hun, and Walter Livingston—had recently objected to the Stamp Tax on the grounds that it provided the British Parliament with a method to usurp their liberties by jeopardizing their property and economic freedom. These wealthy men feared Parliament's tyrannical abuses of power as much as they loathed the anarchy of a lower sort mob. What constituted legitimate and illegitimate exercise of power apparently depended on whose authority was threatened and by whom. These Sons of Liberty thought "no [one] is entitle[d] to Riot but themselves."[23]

That afternoon, Van Rensselaer and his men confronted the resisters at a fence the rebels constructed across the road leading to Noble's farm. Noble and approximately thirty rioters met the posse at the fence. Albany County Sheriff Harmanus Schuyler demanded that Noble and his followers become Van Rensselaer's tenants or leave. The rebels refused to do either. After a heated debate between Noble and Van Rensselaer, Schuyler pushed the top rail of the fence off and climbed over. When he "got over" the fence, rebels with clubs immediately "assaulted" him. The sheriff, who held no warrant for Noble's arrest, fired his pistol into or above the crowd and the posse began firing into the crowd. The rebels retreated to Noble's house, retrieved their guns, and shot back. The two sides shot at each other for approximately forty-five minutes, during which at least three rioters and one member of the posse were killed and several others on both sides were wounded. In the end, the posse fled and when Walter Livingston tried to rally the men after they regrouped, many refused and went home.[24]

The landlords wanted a resolute victory over the rioters. They knew, however, that they could realize it only with aid from the British army, but the army initially refused. John Van Rensselaer renewed his pleas a few days after the shooting at Noble's house. The rebels had opened fire on colonial officials, which was tantamount to treason, so the army complied with Van Rensselaer's request. On July 26, Jeremiah Van Rensselaer and Sheriff Harmanus Schuyler marched with approximately 250 British regulars to rout insurgents on Livingston Manor, Rensselaerswyck, and Claverack—the southern portion of the Van Rensselaers' estate. Over three days in late July and early August, British troops marched through the countryside, stealing and killing livestock and harassing people regardless of their allegiances. Under the landlords' directions, the troops destroyed Nobletown and Spencertown. Most of the two hundred families who lived in the region fled into nearby woods or to Massachusetts or Connecticut. By the first of August, British troops had arrested thirty-two rioters and most of the others had left.[25]

The landlords' willingness to use force angered many of the tenants of Livingston Manor, who had voted for their landlord or his agent in every election from the beginning of the century to 1766. In response to the landlords' use of excessive force, tenants refused to vote for them after 1767. William Moore, a twelve-year-old boy who lived with his family as tenants on the manor, supposedly wrote a poem in which he told the Livingstons that they "can't be assemblymen" anymore, warning them that they would not have obtained political power at all if "it wasn't for your land." Moore probably did not write the poem; someone most likely signed the boy's name to avoid persecution. Nevertheless, the message was prophetic and both reflected and perpetuated the widening chasm between rich and poor. Without support from tenants, the Livingstons did not win an election after 1767. In 1768, Justice Robert R. Livingston complained that he lost his assembly seat although he "had everything in his favour, which power could give him." He attributed his loss the following year directly to the tenants who refused to vote, "notwithstanding all the pains [he] was taking." Worse, he lost the election to Dirck Brinkerhoff, who was popular with the tenants in the region and who represented their interests in the assembly through the end of the Revolutionary War. The Van Rensselaers, equally responsible for setting the British army on the rioters, did not face the same kind of backlash. Perhaps enough of their tenants remained unaffected by the rioting, or perhaps the Van Rensselaers exercised more control over their tenants' voting patterns. The evidence remains unclear.[26]

Land rioters resumed their struggle for property at much the same time that the imperial crisis became a conflict over independence, and they used the upheaval to obtain property. To say they fought during the war is not to say they fought for revolution. Indeed, historians have alternately considered tenants and rural New Yorkers as either openly hostile to the revolutionary cause or as vital supporters of the Revolution. Most tenants, however, refused to join either side primarily because they wanted to remain on their farms and tend their crops. Like a great many white Americans, farmers in the Hudson Valley were more concerned with providing for their families and meeting more pressing production obligations than they were with the political rebellion waged by the revolutionaries. Further, the uncertainty of the Revolution in New York and the regular appearance of both armies in the region during the first five years of the war induced people in the countryside to resist allying too strongly with either side. The rural people remained largely indifferent to the Revolution and generally unconvinced by the republican rhetoric that revolutionaries used to prompt other colonists to join their cause.[27]

In large part, landlords chose sides in the Revolution based on whom they thought might protect their existing claims to land. That said, they did not make these decisions easily. Robert R. Livingston of Clermont, for instance, deeply distrusted his tenants, lamenting that they refused to serve in local militias. They worried more that their families must "want when they are killed." Livingston also feared that some tenants resolved to "stand by the King as they have called it, in hopes that if he succeeded they should have their Lands." He urged fellow revolutionaries to discourage tenants from opposing their landlords purely for material reasons because if "they meet with the least encouragement," they might "throw the whole country into confusion."[28] Loyalists such as John Watts and disgruntled Livingston Manor tenants Nicholas Rouwe and Christian Cooper confirmed Livingston's fears. While Watts advised the British ministry that all "present tenants" would fight for the British for a "freehold," Rouwe and Cooper attested that the "Farmers, & Inhabitants of the Manor of Livingston" would fight to escape the "cursed tyrannical proceedings" of their landlords and that tenants would "chearfully turn out to Cooperate with" the British to get land.[29]

Tenants and farmers in the region made similarly difficult choices, sometimes allying with both sides to ensure their safety. In January 1776, approximately fifty residents of Rhinebeck, a town near Livingston Manor, signed a "List of the Kings true" subjects, and they all signed a similar list five months later. In the second list, the signers noted that signing an oath of loyalty to the king was better done privately because they had "seen a few days ago" how their neighbors were "used and punished because they would not sine" the revolutionary's oath. According to the signers, the local "commite cald there menite men to gether from all parts to compel" people to sign oaths of loyalty to the revolutionary cause. The committee threatened to fine them and to throw them in "preson" if they refused. "So," the Rhinebeck loyalists continued, "we thought it best to sine for we could see no way to ascape for if we hat not [signed] we would constaintly ben ruined." They finally signed the oath of loyalty to the Revolution, swearing that "no allegiance is due from us to the King and crown of great britain and we do accordingly disclaim and renounce all allegiances to the said king and crown." Further, they vowed to act as "good subjects of the state of new york[.] we will do our duty in supporting the measures of the general congress of united states of America [to the] further establishment of liberty and Independency of the said states in opposition to the arbitrary claims, wiked usurpations and hostle invasions of the king and partliament" into the states. Although they swore that they took the "oath voluntarily" and that they would perform their duties "without any mental reservatioins or equivocation whatsoever," these poorer rural people had few alternatives.[30]

Tenants on Livingston Manor faced just that kind of pressure to sign oaths of loyalty to the Revolution and similar consequences if they refused. If someone signed the bond or swore the oath and then violated it, that person had to pay a fine or might have his house pulled down. Tenants, however, faced the additional penalty of losing their leaseholds and personal property to frightened and vengeful revolutionary landlords. Between May and October of 1776, the Livingston Manor Committee of Correspondence demanded that approximately 100 of the roughly 475 leaseholders on the manor sign bonds of surety for their good behavior. Although these disaffected tenants signed the oaths, they did not necessarily thereafter support the revolutionary cause.[31] Most of these disgruntled tenants, like others labeled "disaffected," were much poorer than the revolutionaries they faced.[32] Of the 54 people ordered to appear before the Committee of Safety for Livingston Manor in fall 1776 and spring 1777, for instance, 24 lived on leaseholds with realty valued at an average of £95 in 1779, approximately one-third the value of the average realty of freeholders and well below the mean for the manor.[33]

Some tenants stood before the committee for political reasons not necessarily tied to independence from Britain. In September 1776, Jury Wheeler informed the committee that he would shoot John Elliot, the captain of his local militia unit, rather than serve under him. Wheeler did not openly oppose either group. His concerns were more personal. He wondered what might happen to his family if he supported either side, and he worried how his family might survive if he was called to fight for an extended period of time or, worse, was killed in the fighting. Moreover, he knew the committee already suspected him of being a loyalist because his relative George Wheeler had joined the British. When the committee investigated Wheeler's threat, his kinsman Nicholas Wheeler threatened to beat and kill John Decker Robinson if he testified before the committee. Robinson, who had evidently heard Jury Wheeler threaten to shoot Captain Elliot, lived near the Wheelers on the southeast portion of Livingston Manor near the towns of Hillsdale and Spencertown. On the first of October, Jacob Miller informed the committee that a "Number of Disaffectd persons" in the same area where the Wheelers lived intended to strike "some Blow, [at] the Very first Favourable Opportunity." The region was a hot spot of opposition to the Revolution.[34]

Other tenants faced the committee because they had joined previous attacks on the landlords. They might, the committee reasoned, know something about potential insurgency. In October 1776, the committee ordered Andries Reese to appear to divulge what he knew of plans for new riots. Tellingly, Reese's relative William Reese had been shot in the back by a member of a posse organized by the Van Rensselaers to stop rioting in 1755. Reese told the committee that he had heard Adam Kilmer announce that "if the Regulars should come up in the Country they would be rejoiced" because many of the dissident tenants had signed a "Kings Book," in which they had proclaimed their loyalty to the king. Perhaps Reese referred to a version of the letter signed by some of the residents of Rhinebeck in June 1776, but the people who signed the "Kings Book"—Kilmer, John Pulver, Peter Butler, Casparus Lantman, and "Several More"—were all tenants in the southeastern portion of the manor, where they had lived for more than a decade and where rural rebellion had erupted in the 1760s. Kilmer, for his part, swore that he had no knowledge of a "Kings Book" or about anyone in the countryside trying to rouse people to fight for the king.

Regardless of Kilmer's assertions, so many disaffected people lived in the region in 1776 that their sheer number disrupted the revolutionaries' ability to muster the local militia. Henry Livingston, a relative of the manor lord, considered this when he defied an order to muster fifty men to march to Lake Champlain. He did not think he could find fifty men willing to risk their lives and their farms to fight for independence. Livingston responded that he feared a general rising of disgruntled rural people "if the Whigs go all ag[ains]t their Families."[35]

The class divisions between landlord and tenant saturated these ostensibly political confrontations. What Jonathon Clark found for Poughkeepsie, New York, also characterized Livingston Manor. The revolutionaries were invariably wealthier than the people who sided with the British or who remained neutral. Such differences between wealthy revolutionaries and poorer, disaffected tenants strongly suggest that the political Revolution in New York was infused with powerful elements of class conflict.[36]

Scattered insurgency among the disaffected poor coalesced into tenant rebellion early in the war. In the last months of 1776, more than four hundred tenants on Rensselaerswyck marched in arms about the countryside to join other rebellious tenants in a general war against revolutionary landlords. Like tenants on Livingston Manor, they refused to serve in locally organized militia units because they feared they might lose their land and that their families would be thrown into irrevocable poverty if they were killed. Although these rebels preferred to "skulk" in the woods rather than fight for the revolutionaries' brand of independence, they also armed themselves and gathered at the base of the Helderberg Mountains in the western portion of Rensselaerswyck to oppose revolutionary forces. Once there, they planned how they might best protect their lands. A small group of revolutionaries marched into the region to capture as many of the discontented tenants as possible; they managed to seize only John Van Den Bergh, who confessed that many tenants had decided that they would not fight for either side "if they can help it." They had also vowed to resist all comers, loyalist or revolutionary, who tried to take their land.[37]

When riots broke out on Livingston Manor in spring 1777, the insurgents stated their aspirations clearly. They combined long-standing grievances over land with disputes that stemmed directly from the Revolution. As in the 1750s and 1760s, lower sort rioters in 1777 hoped to obtain land; some had been fighting for the same land for twenty years. Some expressed anger that they and their neighbors were drafted for the revolutionary militia and others hoped that the new state constitution might democratize politics and land owning in New York. One observer noted that a state constitution favorable to tenants might "give the finishing strokes to pacify all opposition" to the revolutionary cause in the state. In April 1777, however, state legislators agreed on a constitution that reduced property qualifications for voting but retained high property qualifications for holding office. Moreover, the new constitution did not make provisions for secret ballots, long a topic of contention in New York and obviously a concern to tenants, nor did it address land ownership or tenancy. Most, however, rioted for land. British officials apparently had agreed to reward each rioter two hundred acres for fighting against the revolutionaries, prompting revolutionaries to accuse the rioters of being loyalists.[38]

Tenants timed their rebellion in 1777 at the moment when a strongly defined government did not exist in New York. The rioters had lost in courts and on the field in the 1750s and 1760s, but the Revolution temporarily upset the traditional power structure in New York and the question of who was going to rule at home remained unresolved. When the landlords' power in the community appeared tenuous and with rumored support from a strong military power, rural people in the northern Hudson Valley mounted a serious attack on New York's political and social hierarchy. If they won, they would have certainly turned their world upside down.[39]

Despite the rumored support of the British army and the strength of four to five hundred dissidents marching throughout Livingston Manor, the rebellion was at best a precarious undertaking. The insurgents were poorly prepared, inadequately armed, and faced an enemy who knew their plans. They obtained guns, powder, and ball from neighbors, borrowed under the pretext of hunting deer. So many people knew of the rumored rebellion that those who lent guns and munitions must have been aware of the real intentions of their neighbors. The rioters also stole powder that the Livingstons had stored for the militia and Continental Army, and some even scraped lead for musket balls from the nets strewn across the Hudson River to block passage of British ships.[40] The rebels timed their rebellion to coincide with a British invasion of the lower Hudson Valley. The attack appeared imminent because of the British presence in the north, but it came several months too late to help the land rioters. The revolutionaries, for their part, had heard rumors of the rebellion for weeks and were hardly surprised by the uprising. Margaret Livingston, sister-in-law of the manor lord, knew of the "most Diabolical Intentions" of the "Internal foes" a week before the rioting started. Besides, the committee of the manor had already learned of the plot from a "Dying Man in Ulster County who could not Die till he had communicated it to one of the Committee."[41]

Although the Committee of Safety for the Manor reported that "almost everybody in the upper manor . . . appears to have engaged with the enemy," the rebellion did not last long. By early May, after only a few weeks of insurrection, the rioters realized that the British were not going to invade, and many offered to surrender if they could remain on their leaseholds. The revolutionaries jailed more than three hundred insurgents in Albany and Dutchess counties and ordered all the prisoners to sign oaths of loyalty to the revolutionary cause and to agree to bonds of surety for future good behavior. The wives of dissidents who remained at large flooded the Livingston Manor Committee of Correspondence with requests for amnesty for their husbands, who presumably were still hiding in the woods to avoid capture. Tenants did not organize a similar uprising for the remainder of the war.[42]

But disgruntled rural people continued to resist anyone who threatened to take their land. In 1778 and 1779, groups of tenants from both Livingston Manor and Rensselaerswyck, including some military deserters, roamed the countryside and attacked people perceived as jeopardizing their welfare. The revolutionaries often referred to these brigands as "wicked tories" and accused them of provoking Indians to attack the inhabitants of the region under the pretense of being loyalists.[43] The rioters, for their part, attacked people from either political side who harassed farmers and tenants; they particularly targeted revolutionary militia officers who fined tenants for failing to join the militia.[44] By summer 1778, the rebels began choosing their victims based more on their wealth than on their political persuasion, again turning political rebellion into social conflict between rich and poor. Peter R. Livingston complained that several of the "well Affected and most Loyal Inhabitants" of the region had been "despoiled and Plundered of all their arms and great part of their Ready money cloathing and Valuable Effects" by the robbers. "Every man," Livingston lamented, "fears it will be his turn next."[45] Many of the revolutionaries wanted to wage only a political rebellion. But the insurgents about whom Livingston complained kept trying to make the Revolution a social rebellion as well, in part because the war and tenancy had combined to reduce these people to "the most necessitous circumstances." The dissidents, however, remained unsuccessful and rural rebellion waned after 1780.[46]

Immediately following the Revolution, rural rebels renewed their attempts to escape tenancy. They initially petitioned the new state government for land, claiming, as they had in the 1760s and 1770s, that they were entitled to own the land they had lived and labored on for decades. Such a redistribution of property would have significantly altered the political and economic power structure of New York to the detriment of landlords. Those landed tycoons who had survived the Revolution with their estates intact began reasserting their control over the people who lived on their land. They required squatters either to become tenants or to evacuate the land, and they demanded that tenants resume paying rent. Many tenants had stopped paying rent during the war because the war and poor weather thrust many of them into grinding poverty, but others had stopped to protest their landlord's authority. Both groups also infused their long-standing grievance with revolutionary rhetoric, making conflicts over land an important part of the contentious revolutionary settlement in New York.[47]

In 1790, Philip Schuyler, who administered part of the Van Rensselaer estate after he married into the family, responded to the rebels' petitions for land by requiring tenants in the region to pay their back rent or leave. The former army general also ordered squatters to sign tenant leases or move. To his credit, Schuyler recognized the limited benefits of squeezing the rural poor. He knew he could not get all of the money and rent they owed, but he hoped to avoid widespread Shaysite-style rebellion in the Hudson Valley. To limit his losses, to quiet disruptive farmers, and to avoid rural revolt, Schuyler offered to sell the tenants and squatters land for 18 shillings per acre with a five-year mortgage; if they agreed, their outstanding debts would be canceled. Schuyler also announced that those people who wished to remain tenants, or who could not raise the money for a down payment on their farms, could eradicate their debt by paying one year's full rent. Schuyler thought that he made a fair offer, and in many respects he had. Improved land in the Hudson Valley sold for between £3 and £7 an acre depending on location, and unimproved land in Maine, New York, and Pennsylvania sold for between £1 and £3 per acre. Much to his surprise, nearly all of the people refused his offer. The insurgents did not think they should have to purchase land their labor entitled them to own.[48]

Angry that these disgruntled people rebuked him so completely, Schuyler tried to evict them so he could sell the improved and now more valuable leaseholds. In October 1791, under Schuyler's direction, the deputy sheriff of

Columbia County traveled to evict John Arnold from his farm so it could be sold. Arnold had grown increasingly unruly, had fallen hopelessly in debt, and apparently had no intentions of paying what he owed. Here was the tenants' worst fear come true: an indebted tenant thrown into the wilderness so a rich man could make more money. More than that, the confrontation epitomized the struggle for autonomy and equality that pitted a landlord who sought peace and profit from his tenants against a landless tenant who wanted the freedom to keep the land he and his family had improved. In this case, success for the first meant poverty for the second.

Sympathetic tenants rallied to support Arnold. When the deputy arrived, people "assembled and with threats deterred the deputy from proceeding with" the sale of the farm. A few days later, the sheriff, Cornelius Hogeboom, visited Arnold's farm accompanied by a county judge, Stephen Hogeboom, and the admonished deputy sheriff. While these men waited for another deputy to arrive with the papers necessary to conduct the sale, a number of known rebels began to congregate ominously in the nearby woods. The sheriff and his party wisely tried to leave, but Arnold, incensed that his house was being sold from underneath his feet, drew his pistol and fired into the air. At the signal, thirty to forty men painted and dressed to look like Native Americans ran from a nearby farm and chased the sheriff and his companions. Apparently, most of the protesters intended only to scare the officials and to prevent the auction of the farm. Arnold and Thomas Southward, however, trapped the sheriff, and Southward shot him fatally in the chest. The deputies and Stephen Hogeboom retreated to the nearby town of Hudson where they organized a posse to capture the rioters, who fled into the countryside or hid at Peter Showerman's farm. The posse captured thirteen of the rebels, charging all but two with felonious rioting. John Arnold was accused of murder and Thomas Southward with capital murder because he had killed the sheriff.[49]

New Yorkers split over the attack, and the division suggests how they wanted to define their new state. Outside Columbia County, men who supported Governor George Clinton castigated the rioters for challenging the legitimacy of the new government. Clinton criticized the dissidents for daring to threaten the "laws and authority of the government." With the memory of Shays's Rebellion firmly in mind, wealthy men set aside their political differences to restore order in their state. Inside the county, pro-Clinton judges who heard the case rang a compassionate note for the dissidents and, in doing so, expressed their contempt for landlords. The jury proved even more lenient. Many of the jurors were poorer farmers, while others were tenants or had been tenants. They set aside political considerations between Federalists and Anti-Federalists to side with their neighbors who were trying to obtain control of the land for their families. The jury acquitted all thirteen men, including Arnold and Southward.

This verdict clearly reflected how dissatisfied many poorer rural folk had grown with the outcome of the Revolution in New York and with the increasing polarization of power and wealth in the state. They thought the Revolution entitled them to greater political and economic equality and independence, but wealthy New Yorkers, regardless of their political affiliation, used their power to suppress social change orchestrated from below. Like the tenants of Livingston Manor who refused to vote deferentially after landlords employed British military force against the rioters in the 1760s, the jurors used their power to announce their dissatisfaction with the revolutionary settlement and with the persistent rule of landlords. The decision outraged New York landlords and state officials in part because Arnold and Southward appeared to be so clearly guilty. Moreover, the elite thought the jury had ignored moral and legal calls for justice to express their displeasure with the economic and political power of the landlords.[50]

The insurgents were badly shaken by the severity of the proceedings, but the decision bolstered their resolve to push for the social changes they thought the American Revolution had promised. In 1793, disgruntled rural people submitted at least four petitions to the state legislature, arguing that they had earned the right to own land because they had lived and labored on it for years. They had bought the land with their sweat and occupancy. Pelatiah Hunt, James Savage, Stephen Miller, and Seldon Curtice headed the lists of petitioners who submitted claims to land in four towns in the eastern part of Rensselaerswyck—Kinderhook, New Canaan, Hillsdale, and Claverack. People in all of these regions had engaged in rioting to secure land since the mid-1750s. In 1793, they received some official support from members of the state assembly, who asked for further justification of the petitioners' claims. The members of the assembly, however, also sought to keep these rural people from killing more sheriffs. On February 13, 1793, Jonathon Havens read a bill in the assembly designed to grant the people in Hillsdale land, but the bill was put down and a second reading ordered. Two weeks later, on March 2, Havens read the new bill before the legislature but announced that there was "little prospect of having the said controversies determined in the ordinary course of law." Other assemblymen concurred, declaring that although the petitions were of a "nature so alarming, as to require the serious attention of the Legislature," they could not agree on a course of action. Instead, they did nothing.[51]

A short time later, in March 1794, Andrew Wheeler headed a list of tenants who asked the state assembly to review their ongoing, now four-decade-old land dispute with the Livingstons. Wheeler had been a tenant on the manor for twenty years and had rioted against the Livingstons in 1777. Although the committee that reviewed the case declared the petitioners had a "title to a considerable portion of the said lands," the members could not determine the proper boundaries of Livingston Manor to thereby outline which land the petitioners might claim. Less than a year later, Petrus Pulver submitted a similar appeal to the assembly in which he and the 214 other signers again requested that the assembly review their case against the Livingstons. Although he headed the list of petitioners, Pulver was not unique. Of the 214 petitioners, 98 demonstrated their low status by placing their mark, including Catrina Michel. Almost all were tenants. Fifty of the signers were listed as inhabitants of Livingston Manor on the assessment rolls of 1779. These signers held property valued at as much as £225 and as little as £10. The average signer was assessed £119, below the mean wealth of the manor's other tenants. At least forty-seven shared family names with known tenants, and twelve more had been squatters before becoming tenants. Further, Pulver asserted that "a great part of Your Petitioners are Tenants holding under the Descendants of the said Robert Livingston upon Terms and Conditions oppressive and burthensome to the last degree." The petition recapitulated the ongoing dispute with the Livingstons, charging that they had bought their land under "false and fraudulent pretences" from Native Americans and that they expanded the boundaries of their estate illegally.

Most important, these petitioners wanted to escape tenancy to obtain the independence promised during the American Revolution. The legislature concurred but the landlords disagreed. The legislature, for its part, reviewed Pulver's petition but determined that the Livingstons should continue to claim the land because they had lived on it for more than a century. In rendering that decision, the legislature invoked the reasoning of lower sort rural rebels to secure the land claims of the wealthiest members of the state, making institutional what had been subversive. The Livingstons, for their part, preserved their property for the remainder of the eighteenth century. The Van Rensselaers kept their estate until Anti-Renters successfully overturned the great estate in the middle of the nineteenth century.[52]

Landlords and tenants in the northern Hudson Valley thus participated in and experienced the revolutionary era quite differently. Each strove for distinct, and often conflicting, types of change. Rural rebels on Livingston Manor and Rensselaerswyck generally lost the struggle and realized few significant gains during the Revolution. Independence for them meant freehold possession of land, entitling them to increased political autonomy and participation. To landlords in the 1790s, the political revolution they hoped to control had moved too close to the social rebellion they feared. Independence for them meant freedom from the political oppression of Parliament without relinquishing their position at the top of New York's political and social hierarchy. To achieve their goals, they had to crush the aspirations of poorer folk who dreamed of social revolution and political independence. These differences indicate that historians need to revise their traditional model of the Revolution as a distinct event that unleashed social and political radicalism that defeated deference and hierarchy.

Such a revision would make the Revolution part of a long-term battle between rich and poor over power and land that characterized New York in the eighteenth and early nineteenth centuries. In the colonial period, New Yorkers invoked various arguments as they fought over who owned land. Some were subversive. Although some Revolutionaries appropriated aspects of the land rioters' arguments, the Revolutionary movement did not incorporate all or even most of the radical goals espoused by land rioters. Moreover, disputes over land that had started in the colonial period continued well into the nineteenth century in the Hudson Valley, and new combatants engaged in similar battles as people moved west. They all built on the rebellious agenda laid out by land rioters in the 1750s and 1760s when they strove to upend New York's political and economic hierarchy. The longevity and persistence of these conflicts suggest that historians need to make the Revolution in New York one part, albeit an important one, of a battle waged by people who lived on the economic, and therefore political, margins as they struggled throughout the last fifty years of the eighteenth century to win their rights and to establish their economic stability and political independence.

# Notes

1. Sung Bok Kim, *Landlord and Tenant in Colonial New York: Manorial Society, 1644–1775* (Chapel Hill: University of North Carolina Press, 1978), 49–54, 210–12; Edward Countryman, *A People in Revolution: The American Revolution and Political Society in New York, 1760–1790* (New York: W. W. Norton, 1989), 77, and chaps. 1 and 2; Daniel W. Voorhees, "The 'Fervent Zeale' of Jacob Leisler," *William and Mary Quarterly*, 3d ser., 51 (1994): 447–72.

2. For an analysis of voting practices in colonial New York, see Roger Champagne, "Family Politics versus Constitutional Principles: The New York Assembly Elections of 1768 and 1769," *William and Mary Quarterly*, 3d ser., 20 (1963): 57–79; Robert J. Dinkin, *Voting in Provincial America: A Study of Elections in the Thirteen Colonies, 1689–1776* (Westport, Conn.: Greenwood Press, 1977), 133–36; Kim, *Landlord and Tenant*, 210–12; Countryman, *People in Revolution*, chaps. 1 and 2.

3. J. R. Pole, "Historians and the Problems of Early American Democracy," *American Historical Review* 67 (1962): 641; and Kim, *Landlord and Tenant*, 121. For two quite different interpretations of deference as political behavior, see John K. Alexander, "Deference in Colonial

Pennsylvania and That Man from New Jersey," *Pennsylvania Magazine of History and Biography* 1028 (1978): 422–36; and Richard Beeman, "Deference, Republicanism, and the Emergence of Popular Politics in Eighteenth-Century America," *William and Mary Quarterly,* 3d ser., 49 (1992): 401–30.

4. Michael Zuckerman, "Tocqueville, Turner, and Turds: Four Stories of Manners in Early America," *Journal of American History* 85 (1998): 13–42; John M. Murrin, "In the Land of the Free and Home of the Slave, Maybe There Was Room Even for Deference," ibid., 86–91. See also Aaron S. Fogleman, "From Slaves, Convicts, and Servants to Free Passengers: The Transformation of Immigration in the Era of the American Revolution," ibid., 43–76; Kathleen M. Brown, "Antiauthoritarianism and Freedom in Early America," ibid., 92–96; and Gary J. Kornblith and John M. Murrin, "The Making and Unmaking of an American Ruling Class," in *Beyond the American Revolution: Explorations in the History of American Radicalism,* ed. Alfred F. Young (DeKalb: Northern Illinois University Press, 1993), 27–79.

5. For a discussion of how land ownership dictated people's economic and political power, and for how property ownership determined New York's power structure, see Irving Mark, *Agrarian Conflicts in Colonial New York* (1940; repr., New York: Ira J. Friedman, 1965), chap. 2; Kim, *Landlord and Tenants,* chap. 3; and Countryman, *People in Revolution,* 74–85. The literature on the protests of the Stamp Act and involving the imperial crisis is rich, but these historians have argued that the Stamp Act protests began the political movement that became the American Revolution, see Edmund S. Morgan and Helen Morgan, *The Stamp Act Crisis* (Chapel Hill: University of North Carolina Press, 1953), 119–33; Bernard Bailyn, *The Ideological Origins of the American Revolution* (Cambridge: Belknap Press, 1967), 99–102; Morgan, *Inventing the People: The Rise of Popular Sovereignty in England and America* (New York: W. W. Norton, 1988), 239; and Gordon S. Wood, *The Radicalism of the American Revolution* (New York: Vintage Books, 1992), 172–75. For the attack on the Stamp Tax collector in Albany, New York, see "Henry Van Schaack's case respecting the abuse he met with from the traitors at Albany," Albany, New York, January 1766, Unsorted Lawsuits, V–Z, John Tabor Kempe Papers, New-York Historical Society, New York, N.Y. (hereafter NYHS); and Abraham Yates to Robert Livingston Jr., Albany, January 3, 1766, Livingston Papers, available at the Franklin Delano Roosevelt Library, Hyde Park, N.Y., 13 rolls, roll 1.

6. For a recent example of this approach, see Peter Linebaugh and Marcus Rediker, *The Many-Headed Hydra: Sailors, Slaves, Commoners, and the Hidden History of the Revolutionary Atlantic* (Boston: Beacon Press, 2000).

7. Bailyn, *Ideological Origins of the American Revolution,* 301–19; Wood, *Radicalism of the American Revolution,* 5–6.

8. See the essays by Ruth Wallis Herndon, Gary B. Nash, and Simon Newman in this volume. See also Gregory A. Stiverson, *Poverty in a Land of Plenty: Tenancy in Eighteenth-Century Maryland* (Baltimore: Johns Hopkins University Press, 1977). I explain more fully the instability of tenants on the land and their subordinated economic and political status in New York in "Agrarian Rioting in Albany County, New York: Tenants, Markets and Revolution in the Hudson Valley, 1751–1801" (Ph.D. diss., Northern Illinois University, 1996), chaps. 1 and 2. For tenancy in other colonies, see Willard F. Bliss, "The Rise of Tenancy in Virginia," *Virginia Magazine of History and Biography* 108 (1950): 427–41; Stephen Innes, *Labor in a New Land: Economy and Society in Seventeenth-Century Springfield* (Princeton: Princeton University Press, 1983), chaps. 2 and 3; Paul G. E. Clemens and Lucy Simler, "Rural Labor and the Farm Household in Chester County, Pennsylvania, 1750–1820," in Stephen Innes, ed., *Work and Labor in Early America* (Chapel Hill: University of North Carolina Press, 1988), 106–43; and Woody Holton, *Forced Founders: Indians, Debtors, Slaves, and the Making of the American Revolution in Virginia* (Chapel Hill: University of North Carolina Press, 1999), esp. chap. 7.

9. Robert R. Livingston and Bulien Verplank, "Immigration Advertisement," December 20, 1749, Robert R. Livingston Papers, roll 1 of 57 rolls of microfilm, New York State Library and Manuscripts Collections, Albany, N.Y. (hereafter NYSL); and Robert R. Livingston to Robert Livingston Jr., New York City, June 7, 1764, Robert R. Livingston Papers, roll 1, NYSL.

10. "Mr. Livingston's Reasons Against a Land Tax," ed. and intro. by Beverly McNear, *Journal of Political Economy* 48 (1940): 63–90; and Kim, *Landlord and Tenant*, 272–74.

11. For the figures, see Florence Christoph, *Upstate New York in the 1760s: Tax Lists and Selected Militia Rolls of Old Albany County, 1760–1768* (Camden, Maine: Picton Press, 1992), 36–81, and 83–89; and see Countryman, *People in Revolution*, 27.

12. "An Act for Raising Monies," Laws of New York, March 1779, in *Early American Imprints, First Series* (New York: Readex Microprint, 1985). For lease requirements, see Humphrey, "Agrarian Rioting in Albany County," chap. 1. See also the assessment rolls for Livingston Manor and Rensselaerswyck, 1779, A-FM, #71, NYSL. The act is restated on the top of the assessment rolls. Sung Bok Kim used these assessment rolls to show the lucrative nature of tenancy in the Hudson Valley and adequately explains the difficulties of these lists. Kim's analysis, however, contains two major problems. He assumes assessors adhered to the "colonial tax practice of not taxing unsettled and undeveloped lands," and he refers to colonial tax laws instead of the law passed by the New York State Assembly. See Kim, *Landlord and Tenant*, 270–80, and table 6.3, quote on 272–74.

13. Unless otherwise noted, all currency in the essay is New York currency because the assessors in 1779 rated realty and personalty in 1775 £NY. For New York currency in 1775, £100 sterling roughly equaled £165 NY, or £3 sterling to £5 NY. See John J. McCusker, *How Much Is That in Real Money? A Historical Price Index for Use as a Deflator of Money Values in the Economy of the United States* (Worcester, Mass.: American Antiquarian Society, 1992), appendix A and table A-2; Countryman, *People in Revolution*, 344n7.

14. Assessment rolls for Counties, 1778, A-FM, #71, NYSL. Personalty valuations are of little consequence because under the assessment law of 1779, personalty was rated and taxed only when it exceeded a person's outstanding debt.

15. During the revolutionary period, tenants on Livingston Manor leased, on average, 118 acres; those on Rensselaerswyck leased 136 acres; and tenants in Virginia on proprietary manors in 1767–68 leased 152 acres. Freeholders in Balltown, Maine, in 1791 and in Chester County, Pennsylvania, in 1782 leased 138 acres and 125 acres, respectively. See the records for Livingston Manor in rolls 6, 7, and 8 in the Livingston Family Papers, and in roll 52 in the Robert R. Livingston Papers; leases for Rensselaerswyck, including Claverack, in boxes 36, 84, and 86 in the Rensselaer Manor Papers, NYSL. For Virginia, see Stiverson, *Poverty in a Land of Plenty*, table 2.3; for Maine, see Alan Taylor, *Liberty Men and Great Proprietors: The Revolutionary Settlement on the Maine Frontier, 1760–1820* (Chapel Hill: University of North Carolina Press, 1990), tables 3 and 4; and for Pennsylvania, see James Lemon, *The Best Poor Man's Country* (Baltimore: Johns Hopkins University Press, 1972), 89–91.

16. Daniel Vickers constructs a model for an agrarian moral economy in the North American colonies in "Competency and Competition: Economic Culture in Early America," *William and Mary Quarterly*, 3d ser., 47 (1990): 3–29, in which he maintains that farmers and laborers sought to attain "competency," or economic subsistence for their families and for the next generation. He reiterates his argument in *Farmers and Fishermen: Two Centuries of Work in Essex County, Massachusetts, 1630–1850* (Chapel Hill: University of North Carolina Press, 1995), esp. chap. 5. Competency, the ability to provide for the household, and market participation that tied farmers to a capitalist market are not necessarily exclusive activities or ideas. Some farmers, and tenants, may have felt that they could best provide for their households by successfully trading in local and extralocal markets. Local trade and profit alone did not, and would not, make them capitalists. For rural market participation, see Allan Kulikoff, *Agrarian Origins of American Capitalism* (Charlottesville: University Press of Virginia, 1992), 20–34 and 132–40.

17. For Livingston Manor, see the leases in the Robert R. Livingston Papers, roll 52, NYSL; the leases in the Livingston Family Papers, rolls 6, 7, and 8, FDR Library; and the Livingston Manor Rent Ledger, 1767–84, NYHS. I base these conclusions on my survey of 768 specific leases issued in the second half of the eighteenth century for the manor that indicate how long tenants stayed on their leaseholds, and on the rent records for the estate found in Ledger A of Rents, Rensselaerswyck Manor, NYSL. Here I also want to refine Reeve Huston's interpretation of "for

ever," in *Land and Freedom: Rural Society, Popular Protest, and Party Politics in Antebellum New York* (New York: Oxford University Press, 2000), in which he argues that tenants on Rensselaerswyck with perpetual leases became "the legal owners of their farms, subject to rents and other restrictions" (p. 23). In a survey of these 768 leases, approximately 45 percent of the leaseholds, 348, changed hands. The land was re-leased, and the new tenants did not have the same surname as the original tenant. What happened to the rest remains a mystery. It is possible that the other 55 percent of the leaseholds stayed within the families of the original lessee, or that the sons or daughters of leaseholders may have sold the leasehold without the Van Rensselaers' consent. What remains clear, however, is that the Van Rensselaers did not relinquish their ownership of the land. See the leases for Rensselaerswyck Manor at the NYSL. See Huston, *Land and Freedom,* 25, for a discussion of how the Van Rensselaers handled tenants' debt. The issue is most clearly addressed in Charles W. McCurdy, *The Anti-Rent Era in New York Law and Politics: 1839–1865* (Chapel Hill: University of North Carolina Press, 2001), 22–31.

18. The literature on eviction and farmers' response to it is rich. See, e.g., John L. Brooke, *The Heart of the Commonwealth: Society and Political Culture in Worcester County, Massachusetts, 1713–1861* (New York: Cambridge University Press, 1989); and Terry Bouton, "A Road Closed: Rural Insurgency in Post-Independence Pennsylvania," *Journal of American History* 87 (December 2000): 855–87.

19. I explain these early events in more detail in Humphrey, "Agrarian Rioting in Albany County," chaps. 3 and 4. See also the accounts of the rioting in the 1750s in Kim, *Landlord and Tenant;* and in Mark, *Agrarian Conflicts.*

20. Robert R. Livingston to Robert Livingston Jr., Woodstock, May 1, 1766, Livingston Papers, roll 8; Robert Cambridge Livingston to Robert Livingston Jr., New York City, May 29 and 30, 1766, Livingston Papers, roll 8; "Constitution of the Sons of Liberty of Albany, and Names of the Signers," *American Historian and Quarterly Genealogical Record* 1 (1876), 142–52; and "Henry Van Schaack's case respecting the abuse he met with from the traitors at Albany," Unlisted Manuscripts and Lawsuits, V-Z, John Tabor Kempe Papers, NYHS.

21. See Morgan and Morgan, *Stamp Act Crisis,* 119–33; Wood, *Radicalism of the American Revolution,* 172–75; and Countryman, *People in Revolution,* chaps. 1 and 2.

22. For the decision of the inhabitants of Spencertown to join Noble, see the Minutes of the Spencertown Meeting, Spencertown Proprietors Book and Papers, 1755–63, NYSL; *Montresor Journals in Collections of the New-York Historical Society,* ed. G. D. Scull (New York, 1882), June 28, 1766, 375–76; and "Copy of a Warrant for the Justice of Albany against [Robert Noble] and others June 1766," Rensselaerswyck Miscellaneous Manuscripts, NYHS.

23. Captain John Montresor quoted in *Montresor Journals,* May 1, 1766, 363; "Albany City Records, 1753–1783," in *Collections on the History of Albany,* ed. Joel Monsell, 4 vols. (Albany: J. Munsell, 1876), 1:85–351; Countryman, *People in Revolution,* chap. 7; and Staughton Lynd, "The Revolution and the Common Man: Farm Tenants and Artisans in New York Politics, 1777–1788" (Ph.D. diss., Columbia University, 1962), 119–26.

24. "Copy of a Warrant for the Justice of Albany against [Robert Noble] and others June 1766," Rensselaerswyck Miscellaneous Manuscripts, NYHS; *Montresor's Journal,* July 2, 1766, 376; "Notes on the Trial of the Defs. For the Several Murthers vizt. of Cornelius Ten Broeck, Thomas Whitney, and John Bull," NYSL; and the trial transcripts for "The King agt Alex. McArthur, Daniel McArthur, Thomas Johnson, Levi Stockwell," August 1766, Miscellaneous Manuscripts, D, NYHS.

25. "Copy of a Warrant for the Justice of Albany against [Robert Noble] and others June 1766," Rensselaerswyck Miscellaneous Manuscripts, NYHS; the trial transcripts for "The King agt. Alex. McArthur, Daniel McArthur, Thomas Johnson, Levi Stockwell," August 1766, Miscellaneous Manuscripts, D, NYHS; and Kim, *Landlord and Tenant,* 405–9.

26. Cadwallader Colden to the Earl of Hillsborough, New York City, April 25, 1768, in E. B. O'Callaghan, ed., *Documents Relative to the Colonial History of the State of New York,* 15 vols. (Albany: Weed, Parsons Printers, 1857), 7:61; Peter R. Livingston to Philip Schuyler, New York

City, February 27, 1769, as quoted in George Dangerfield, *Chancellor Robert R. Livingston of New York, 1746–1813* (New York: Harcourt, Brace, 1960), 40; Kim, *Landlord and Tenant*, 212; and Countryman, *People in Revolution*, app. 2.

27. The two most influential works regarding the importance of republican ideology during the revolutionary period are Bailyn, *Ideological Origins of the American Revolution*, and Wood, *The Radicalism of the American Revolution*. Both authors posit that colonists absorbed republican rhetoric and that the colonists' developing ideology was the impetus for the American Revolution. These historians, however, rely on evidence produced primarily by people who were not representative of the rural people in New York or even of much of the colonial population. For discussions of the loyalty of rural people in New York to the revolutionary cause and reasons for those decisions, see Sung Bok Kim, "The Limits of Politicization in the American Revolution: The Experience of Westchester County, New York," *Journal of American History* 80 (1993): 868–89; Jonathon Clark, "The Problems of Allegiance in Revolutionary Poughkeepsie," in *Saints and Revolutionaries: Essays on Early American History*, ed. David D. Hall, John M. Murrin, and Thad W. Tate (New York: W. W. Norton, 1984), 285–317; and Michael A. Bellesiles, *Revolutionary Outlaws: Ethan Allen and the Struggle for Independence on the Early American Frontier* (Charlottesville: University Press of Virginia, 1993).

28. Robert R. Livingston to John Jay, July 17, 1775, as quoted in Staughton Lynd, "The Tenant Rising at Livingston Manor, May 1777," *New-York Historical Society Quarterly* 48 (1964): 167–68.

29. John Watts to the British Ministry, October 30, 1777, *Pennsylvania Evening Post*, reprinted in the *Morning Chronicle;* Nicholas Rouwe's Deposition, November 17, 1781, and that of Christian Cooper et al. to Henry Clinton, September 5, 1781, Livingston Manor, both in Samuel Hake's American Loyalist Claim, GB PR, AO 13, bundle 14, NYHS.

30. See the "List of the Kings true subjects in reinbeck," January 18, 1776, Travers Papers, box 5, Columbia County Historical Society, Kinderhook, N.Y.; Letter to the King, Rhinebeck, June 3, 1776, Travers Papers, box 5; and the Loyalty Oath, 1777, Travers Papers, box 5, Columbia County Historical Society.

31. Dirck Jansen to Abraham Yates Jr., District of the Manor of Livingston, May 19, 1776, Yates Papers, Manuscripts Room, New York Public Library (hereafter NYPL). The number of tenants on Livingston Manor during the Revolution is contained in the assessment rolls for Livingston Manor, 1779, roll A-FM, 71, NYSL. For the number of people who appeared before the Livingston Manor Committee of Safety in 1776, see "The Minutes of the Committee of Safety of the Manor of Livingston," *New York Genealogical and Biographical Record* 60 (1929): 239–43 and 325–41.

32. Ronald Hoffman, "The 'Disaffected' in the Revolutionary South," in *The American Revolution: Explorations in the History of American Radicalism*, ed. Alfred F. Young (DeKalb: Northern Illinois University Press, 1976), 275–316, quote on 285.

33. For the list of people brought before the Committee of Safety, see "Minutes of the Committee of Safety of Livingston Manor," 326–40. For assessment rolls, see the rolls of Livingston Manor, 1779, A-FM #71, NYSL. The 24 people described here do not include the 106 tenants who declined military service in late December 1776.

34. Thomas Humphrey, "'Poor Men were always oppressed by the rich': William Prendergast and the American Revolution in the Hudson Valley, 1727–1811," in *The Human Tradition in U.S. History: The American Revolution*, ed. Ian K. Steele and Nancy Rhoden (New York, 2000), 81–98.

35. For the incident involving Jury Wheeler, Jacob Miller, and Adam Kilmer, see "Minutes of the Committee of Safety of Livingston Manor," September 30, October 1, and October 7, 1776, 325–26, and 328–29; and *Historic Memoirs from 16 March 1763 to 25 July 1778 of William Smith*, ed. William Sabine, 2 vols. (New York: Arno Press, 1966), 2:19, October 1776, 26; and see the ratings of the Kilmers, Pulvers, Butlers, and Lantmans in the assessment rolls for Livingston Manor.

36. Clark, "Problem of Allegiance in Revolutionary Poughkeepsie," 300–301.

37. John Van Den Bergh quoted in Alice P. Kenney, "The Albany Dutch: Loyalists and Patriots," *New York History* 42 (1961): 340; and Lynd, "Tenant Rising at Livingston Manor," 169–70.

38. Philip Schuyler to the Continental Congress, Letterbook copy, January 7, 1777, Albany, and January 15, 1777, Fishkill, Schuyler Papers, reel 2, NYPL; "Minutes of the Committee of Safety of Livingston Manor," February 7, 1777, and March 11, 1777, pp. 338 and 340; John Wheelock to Gouvernor Morris, March 19, 1777, Hanover, Robert R. Livingston Papers, roll 1, NYSL. Robert R. Livingston knew that the tenants rioted for their land; see Livingston to John Jay, July 17, 1775, as quoted in Lynd, "Tenant Rising at Livingston Manor," 167–68; and *Historic Memoirs of William Smith*, 2:127–28. For the New York state constitution of 1777, see Abraham Yates's draft in the Yates Papers, box 4, NYPL; and Pierre Van Cortlandt to the New York Delegates of the Continental Congress, Kingston, July 17, 1777, *Correspondences of the Van Cortlandt Family of Cortlandt Manor, 1748–1800*, 2 vols. (Tarrytown, N.Y.: Sleepy Hollow Restorations, 1977), 2:213.

39. James Sullivan, ed., *Minutes of the Albany Committee of Correspondence, 1775–1778*, 2 vols. (Albany: University of the State of New York, 1923), 1:739, May 1, 1777; *Historic Memoirs of William Smith*, 2:130, May 7 and 8, 1777.

40. *Historic Memoirs of William Smith*, 2:127–34, May 3, 6, 10, and 12, 1777; *Journal of the Provincial Congress, Provincial Convention, Committee of Safety and Council of the State of New York*, 2 vols. (Albany: Thurlow Weed, 1842) 1:909–10, and 2:247; Lynd, "Tenant Rising at Livingston Manor," 171–75; and Cynthia Kierner, "Landlord and Tenant in Revolutionary New York: The Case of Livingston Manor," *New York History Quarterly* 70 (1989): 137–40.

41. Margaret Livingston to Reverend Westerlo, Clermont, May 10, 1777, Van Rensselaer Family Papers, Arnold Collection, Albany Institute of History and Art, Albany, N.Y. (hereafter AIHA); *Historic Memoirs of William Smith*, 2:132 and 134, May 10 and 12, 1777.

42. *Journals of the Provincial Congress*, 1:909–10, 912; Lynd, "Tenant Rising at Livingston Manor," 174; and *Historic Memoirs of William Smith*, 2:127–36.

43. Gouvernor Morris to Robert R. Livingston, Valley Forge, March 10, 1778, roll 1, Robert R. Livingston Papers, NYSL; The Trustees of Kingston to Robert R. Livingston, March 13, 1778, Kingston, and Livingston's letter to them dated March 1, 1778, Robert R. Livingston Papers, roll 1; and Philip Schuyler to the General Committee at Tryon County, Coghanewaga, March 17, 1778, Philip Schuyler Papers, NYSL.

44. *Historic Memoirs of William Smith*, 2:369–70 (May 6, 1778) and 404 (June 25, 1778); *Minutes of the Albany Committee of Correspondence*, 2:233–47 (September 5 and 15, 1778), 331–32 (October 16, 1778), 354–55 (April 25, 1779), and 388–89 (June 18, 1779); Countryman, *People in Revolution*, 151–52; John Barclay to the Albany Committee of Correspondence, Fort Edward, July 22, 1777, NYSL; and Philip Schuyler to Governor George Clinton, Stillwater, August 4, 1777, Schuyler Family Papers, AIHA.

45. Peter R. Livingston to George Clinton, Livingston Manor, June 12 and July 29, 1778, *Public Papers of George Clinton*, 4 vols. (New York: AMS Press, 1973), 3:452–53, 593–94.

46. Albany Committee of Correspondence, "A Letter to the Governor," September 12, 1778, *Collections on the History of Albany*, 1:288.

47. See, e.g., "The Petition of the subscribers [and] Inhabitants of the part of the County of Columbia and State of New York supposed to be included with the Lines of a Patent granted by the late Governor Tryon," January 9, 1789, Miscellaneous Manuscripts, Columbia County, New York, NYHS. The petitioners of 1789 quoted a petition they submitted in 1784, "The Petition of Simeon Roulee, Robert Mecker & Truman Powell in behalf of themselves and their Associates," January 25, 1789, Miscellaneous Manuscripts, Dutchess County, New York, NYHS. John Brooke graciously directed me to these documents.

48. The December 14, 1790 manuscript announcing Schuyler's intentions resides in the Philip Schuyler Papers, Manuscripts Room, NYPL; the speech was cited as the *Address of General Philip Schuyler to the Tenants of Lands at Hillsdale delivered Through his Wife from her Father, John Van Rensselaer*, November 12, 1790, in David M. Ellis, *Landlords and Farmers in the Hudson-Mohawk*

*Region, 1790–1850* (Ithaca: Cornell University Press, 1946), 34; and see Alfred F. Young, *The Democratic Republicans of New York: The Origins, 1763–1797* (Chapel Hill: University of North Carolina Press, 1967), 204. For land prices for Pennsylvania, see John J. McCusker and Russell R. Menard, *The Economy of British America, 1607–1789* (Chapel Hill: University of North Carolina Press, 1991), 204; for Maine, see Taylor, *Liberty Men and Great Proprietors,* 2–3; for western New York, see Alan Taylor, *William Cooper's Town: Power and Persuasion on the Frontier of the Early American Republic* (New York: Alfred A. Knopf, 1995), 71–72.

49. "A Letter," *Albany Gazette,* October 31, 1791, as quoted in Young, *Democratic Republicans,* 204–5; Ellis, *Landlords and Farmers,* 34–36; Alexander Coventry's Diary, October 25, 1791, NYSL. The minutes for *The People of the State of New York v. Thomas Southward, Jonathon Arnold, John West, Abel Hacket, Ebenezer Hatch, Robert Boze, John Boze, John Rodman, Joseph Fickner, and Jacob Virgil,* December 2, 1791, and *The People v. Peter Showerman,* February 8, 1792, both in the Court of Oyer and Terminer Minutes, 1788–1831, Columbia County Courthouse, Hudson, N.Y.

50. Governor George Clinton, January 1792, *Messages from the Governors,* ed. Charles Z. Lincoln, 2 vols. (Albany: J. B. Lyon Company, 1909), 2:319; Ellis, *Landlord and Farmers,* 35–36. See also Franklin Ellis, *History of Columbia County, New York* (Philadelphia: Everts and Ensign, 1878), 62.

51. *Journal of the Assembly of the State of New York,* 16th sess., pp. 54 (December 10, 1792), 83 (December 26, 1792), 179 (February 13, 1793), and 219–20 (March 2, 1793) in Clifford K. Shipton, ed., *Early American Imprints: 1st Series, 1639–1800* (Worcester, Mass.: American Antiquarian Society, 1956–83) (hereafter *Early American Imprints*), #25900.

52. *Journal of the Assembly of the State of New York,* 17th sess., pp. 135 and 157 (March 1794) in *Early American Imprints,* #27397; "Petition of Petrus Pulver & Others Demanding Investigations into the Livingston's Title," January 7, 1795; and see "A Map of the towns of Livingston, Germantown, and Clermont in the County of Columbia," 1798, in E. B. O'Callaghan, ed., *Documentary History of the State of New York,* 4 vols. (Albany: Weed Parsons and Company, Printers, 1857), 3:834–41, 491–92, insert. For the Anti-Rent movement, see Huston, *Land and Freedom.*

## Ten

# "God Helps Those Who Help Themselves"

*Religious Explanations of Poverty in Colonial Massachusetts, 1630–1776*

J. RICHARD OLIVAS

Historians have observed that between the seventeenth and eighteenth centuries American Puritanism became less Calvinistic and more Arminian in its doctrinal orientation. Religious explanations of salvation, for example, relied less upon predestination and more upon free will as time passed. If clergy and laity in the earlier period stressed God's omnipotent role in salvation, later generations emphasized the power of the individual who asked "What must I do to be saved?" A similar tendency also was at work in New England clerical explanations of human impoverishment. Throughout much of the seventeenth century, ministers of the "congregational way" taught that human poverty was a divinely foreordained condition. When biblical Job declaimed after the loss of his own riches, "the Lord gave, and the Lord hath taken away," he exemplified the dominant Puritan conception of poverty's origins. Not so much the rich and powerful but the Almighty intervened to appropriate a person's money and give it to another. Echoing this sentiment, Reverend Cotton Mather wrote in 1726, "'Tis the Lord who has *Taken away* from you, what He has *Given* to others." The small number of widows and orphans who constituted the "godly poor," according to Mather, could not escape God's "impoverishing blast." Since their condition was divinely predestined, an earthly trial whose purposes only God understood, congregational churches pledged themselves to care for their temporal needs.[1]

The manner in which Puritan ministers explained poverty in seventeenth-century America stemmed from their belief that God's relation to the physical world was literal and direct. Like Atlas of old who kept the sky from falling, the Puritan God intervened powerfully and miraculously to keep the sun, moon, stars, and planets from crashing into one another. The Almighty also interposed himself in human history to enrich and impoverish persons for his own inscrutable reasons. Poverty in the early Puritan mind, then, was a matter of divine appointment or fate. He had the whole world—and the material condition of all in it—in his hands.[2]

When Puritan ministers in the late seventeenth century embraced Newtonian ideas about a self-regulating universe, they abandoned religious teachings premised upon God's direct intervention in the physical realm. If laws like gravity and motion regulated creation's inner workings, God's relation to the physical world could not be as direct as clerics had once believed. By this logic, neither did God intervene in temporal affairs to enrich and impoverish people. Preachers like Cotton Mather occasionally claimed after 1700 that God made people poor, but these reflexive explanations sounded hollow and shorn of self-assurance. The God at the center of the cosmos had moved to the outer edges of the Puritans' conceptual universe.[3]

As the eighteenth century dawned, Puritan clerics understood what God's relation to the physical universe *was not*, but they were less certain what it *was*. If God did not make people poor, how did they get that way? Confident at a minimum that God did not intervene directly in temporal affairs, ministers between 1700 and 1750 searched diligently for indirect or secondary means to explain the divine relation to creation. Some religious thinkers theorized that Newton's physical laws were a fruitful starting point for investigation. If God used physical laws of motion and gravity to order the physical world, perhaps spiritual laws of some kind governed the unseen realm. Because of these theological and philosophical explorations, debate shifted from issues of predestination to those of provision. As the new century unfolded, ministers dwelt less on what God took away from His creatures and more on what He gave them.

Growing impoverishment in eighteenth-century Boston discredited any remaining notions that God caused poverty and increased pressure on clerics to explain how God provided for the material well-being of His creatures. As early as 1695, after residents of Massachusetts's "Head town" had felt the devastating effects of King William's War, Bostonians were questioning religious teachings that God had "wisely and justly" arranged their "*Temporal Affairs*." Cotton Mather conceded that the "*Providence* of God" was "too little Believed" in the Puritan heartland. In view of the misery in their city, Boston ministers did not dare assert that God caused poverty. Instead they looked for divinely ordained means—spiritual equivalents of motion and gravity—that would regulate their city's economic affairs and secure God's abundant blessings upon them.[4]

Clergymen before the mid-eighteenth century thought they discerned in Scripture two spiritual formulas through which God would provision the elect in the Bay Colony wilderness: the market and revivalism. Arguing in 1719 that the rise of cities in Massachusetts had ended the period of the Puritans' wilderness wanderings, Reverend Benjamin Colman declared that Bostonians should no longer look directly to God for food as if they were Israelites in the desert subsisting on manna and quail. Colman instead urged his fellow townspeople to trust in the emerging market economy as their "*living* and certain supply." Nevertheless, this suggestion offended many of Colman's coreligionists who believed that trusting in something other than God was improper or even idolatrous. City residents who might have been inclined to share Colman's faith in the market also understood that rich and powerful merchants could manipulate the market for their own advantage. Thus, Colman's hearers refused to accept uncritically a divinely appointed "method" that unscrupulous individuals could so easily subvert. Bostonians gradually embraced the market economy—but not as something with divine origins, especially since Colman's reasoning required people to believe that what God gave, man could take away. In 1740, Colman and other Boston-area ministers promoted revivalism as another divinely ordained formula through which divine blessing would descend upon the city's religious and commercial life. The Great Awakening's spiritual benefits were extensive, but economic blessings of the sort revivalist pastors had predicted never materialized, and commercial revivalism did not survive as a viable formula for explaining God's economic provision for humankind. Even if God did not cause their poverty directly, many Bostonians by the mid-eighteenth century may have wondered why He could not—or would not—cure it.[5]

Since ministers had failed in their attempts to find spiritual formulas for bringing down God's material abundance upon Boston and other cities in God's earthly Israel, they fashioned a religious teaching that placed the burden for poverty squarely on the individual. This doctrine, in short, stated that God helps those who help themselves. By explaining poverty's cause and continuance as the failure of individual initiative, ministers absolved God and the church for any responsibility in what, by the 1750s, was the intractable nature of urban impoverishment. Reverend Charles Chauncy of Boston argued in 1752 that human labor was the divinely appointed means through which God provisioned his earthly creatures. God's hand no longer caused earthly poverty; failure to work with one's own hands was now the culprit.[6]

In this essay I will explore attitudes about poverty that Puritan religious leaders brought with them to the British North American colonies, and how and why their ideas changed from the seventeenth century to the eve of the American Revolution. It focuses not on the poor themselves, nor on schemes of poor relief, nor on poverty as a social phenomenon, but on ministers' views about the resourceless among them. Boston preachers, in particular, are cited since poverty increased there disproportionately. Puritan explanations of human impoverishment passed through three discernible phases. An initial stage, lasting from 1630 to the 1690s, explained impoverishment as a fated result of divine intervention in human history. During a second stage, from the 1690s through the 1740s, ministers looked for spiritual formulas that would bring down God's material abundance upon their cities. During the third phase, lasting from the 1750s to the Revolution and beyond, congregational ministers anchored religious explanations of human impoverishment in a moral theory of labor. Joining providence with human effort, clerics explained that God provisioned humankind through the instrumentality of labor. At this divine-human nexus God gave daily bread to his creatures. Ministers by the 1750s had completely abandoned the idea that God caused poverty, believing instead that people were poor because they were unwilling to work.

The severity of this view collided with economic realities, however, especially when increasing numbers of New Englanders who wanted work could find none. Reverend Andrew Croswell of Boston, a minority of congregational ministers, and eventually even Charles Chauncy himself, noted that instrumental theories of divine providence discouraged liberality in giving and injected a coarseness into ecclesiastical and community life. Ministers and others in the early national period sought to increase private charity, but their task was complicated by religious explanations of human impoverishment developed in the eighteenth century.

From the beginning of the first settlements in Puritan New England to the 1690s, clerics believed that God interposed himself directly in the physical realm to impoverish human beings. How did congregational ministers come to believe that the Lord "made poor"? Perceptions that God impoverished persons flowed from a particular philosophical understanding of God's relationship to the world. This perception, in turn, affected the manner in which Puritan clerics interpreted history and religious texts. One's view of how God relates to the universe depends upon one's cosmology. As Simon J. Schaffer has written: "Seventeenth-century natural philosophers inherited two different concepts of God's relation with His Universe: (a) as supremely wise, God had constructed an orderly and rational world displaying evidence of design; (b) as supremely powerful, God was able to disrupt this order miraculously and was the source of activity in the world." The former cosmology was Cartesian in its philosophical underpinnings, exhibited mechanistic qualities, and needed no divine intervention to maintain its operations. The latter cosmology, despite its holding that the universe was orderly, ultimately needed God to superintend its organized workings. The latter view may be called Newtonian, since Sir Isaac Newton in his later years strenuously sought to subordinate the laws of gravity and matter to divine activity. A wide spectrum of natural philosophers who strongly disagreed over the nature and extent of God's relation to the universe gathered around its precepts of order and divine regulation, especially since they feared secular and deistic implications of the Cartesian view. Members of the clergy in Massachusetts, the vast majority of whom had been trained in natural philosophy or "philosophy of nature" at Harvard, subscribed to the notion that God regulated the physical universe.[7]

Only a small step separates the idea that God miraculously intervenes in the created realm to uphold its workings and the belief that God reaches into human affairs to impoverish human beings. To be sure, interventionist cosmologies differed vastly about the extent to which God invaded time and history. At one end of the continuum, adherents stressed God's power to penetrate the physical universe, while, at the other end, supporters stressed God's "continuous influence" upon nature's regular laws. This broad category included immediate interventionists like Reverend Increase Mather, a 1656 graduate of Harvard College, who in his early years believed that God spoke through thunder, sent comets and "monstrous" births as warnings, and punished people who violated the Sabbath. Yet it also encompassed English divines like Thomas Burnet and William Whiston who "developed a 'sacred physics' that explained biblical events in terms of physical law, such as the Deluge by the passage of a comet."[8]

Increase Mather's son Cotton, a Harvard graduate of 1678, embodied both of these cosmological tendencies, highlighting God's "continuous influence" over his awesome workings. But as he witnessed the growing intractability of poverty in eighteenth-century Boston, Cotton Mather invoked the older interventionist ethic to explain destitution. To a group of indigents, perhaps at Boston's almshouse, Mather explained the heavenly origins of their earthly plight: "'Tis the Lord who has *Taken away* from you, what He has *Given* to others." If they thought that a fundamental alteration in their condition was possible or that charity was unlimited, Mather admonished them to remember: "'Tis the GOD of Heaven who has Ordered your being found among the *Poor of the Earth. O Potsherd of the Earth,* Since 'tis the *work of His Hands,* which has made you to be what you are, and will have you to be a Vessel not guilded with some of the shining Dust that He has allowed unto others." Boston's poor, Mather concluded, "should Acquiesce" in their "Portion" and await the "Grave, the Grand Leveller" which "will quickly bring the Rich and the Poor to be on equal terms."[9]

Notions that the Lord "made poor and made rich" implied that moral accountability for poverty lay more in heaven than on earth. If God authored impoverishment, who was able to fight against Him? Thus, immediate interventionism fostered a measure of fatalism within ministerial thinking. And to the extent that clerics relied upon theories of divine-caused affliction, they were less likely to embrace alternative explications of worsening problems in their society. Although Puritan sermons sometimes inveighed against greed and merchant practices, such as engrossing of wheat and other staples, ministers saw inequitable social relations as a symptom of a larger, predestined scheme they were largely powerless to do anything about. To alter an indigent's condition was tantamount to tampering with a divinely sanctioned state. Because God was the immediate author of impoverishment, ministers encouraged the poor to accept their condition with humility, patience, and "a sweet *Submission* to the Will of God."[10]

Who were the poor in Puritan thought? Puritan clerics followed ecclesiastical traditions dating from the first century A.D. that regarded widows and orphans as main types of "the poor." Cotton Mather asserted that "in the List of, *The Poor,* be sure, *Poor Widows* are an Article." So, too, were orphans. In a virtually unbroken line from the apostles of Jesus through the Apostolic Fathers, the second- and third-century Apologists, Augustine, the Scholastics, and the Reformers, widows and orphans occupied a special place in church life. These patterns of thought, in turn, relied upon ancient admonitions from the Old Testament such as: "Ye shall not afflict any widow, or fatherless child." The New Testament likewise instructed Christians to "visit the fatherless and widows in their affliction." In mathematical terms, poor persons were the set; widows and orphans were the two primary subsets. Also included among the poor at different times and in different places were strangers, "shipwrecked mariners," "any who may be in mines, islands or prisons," and, more problematically, slaves.[11]

Eager to restore national church life along the lines of the primitive Christian community, English Puritans like Thomas Cartwright, William Perkins, and William Ames made elaborate preparations for poor relief in the sixteenth and seventeenth centuries. Leaders of the Puritan settlement in Massachusetts Bay imbibed many of these religious principles. John Winthrop read Cartwright and Perkins and exchanged correspondence with Ames; John Wilson and John Cotton, spiritual leaders of Boston's First Church, emphasized charity to widows, orphans, and others in need. As churches multiplied in Massachusetts's "Head town," especially under the leadership of Cotton Mather, Boston's clerics maintained concern for the "*Poor of the Earth*" in their midst. Congregational pastors believed that aid to widows and orphans fulfilled their primary scriptural obligation to the poor.[12]

But theirs was no mere perfunctory charity. From the very beginning of Massachusetts Bay, for instance, members of Boston's spiritual elite possessed a sincere and abiding concern for widows and orphans whom they regarded as the weakest members of society. Probate records and wills of Boston's religious leaders from 1630 to 1775 demonstrate that pastors, teachers, ruling elders, and deacons carried to their graves a concern for the poor in their midst. Nearly thirty years a deacon in First and Fourth churches, Isaiah Tay bequeathed "Fifteen Pounds to the Poor," and First Church deacon Zechariah Thayer willed "Twenty pounds like Bill of Credit" for the poor to draw upon when needed. Ruling Elder Caleb Lyman left the "Sum of Five hundred Pounds" and the "Interest thereof" for widows of Boston's Fifth Church. Boston's clerics built an enduring tradition of caring for their widows and orphans.[13]

Throughout his forty-three-year ministry at Boston's Second Congregational Church, Cotton Mather cultivated a special solicitousness for the needs of widows, orphans, and other needy Bostonians. Mather "deliberately involved himself to an unusual degree in the lives of his parishioners and devoted considerable time to catechetical work and regular visitation." Entries in his diary indicate that Mather cared deeply for widows and orphans, yet he extended help to other needy persons, even to those beyond the bounds of his own parish. Touched by concern for "a Family" in his "Neighbourhood, conflicting with much Poverty and Misery," Mather resolved: "I must make it an object of my peculiar Charity." As the winter of 1707 approached, Mather carried "some Releef of Money" to families that did not attend church and had "not a Character of Godliness upon them." By taking care of persons not counted among the "Godly Poor" that attended services at his church, Mather hoped that "in this way of treating such poor Creatures, there may be some of them won over to the Wayes of Piety!" Moreover, he sent money, books, and his wishes to the minister in Salem, encouraging him to do the same for "the *poor* and *bad* people" there. "Who can tell," Mather wrote, "how far the *good Angels* of Heaven, may co-operate in these proceedings!" Ecclesiastical tradition favored widows and orphans but in New England often extended to other needy persons within and without the church.[14]

Language both reflected and shaped how eighteenth-century religious leaders viewed the poor. English dictionaries of the period supply three primary meanings of the word "poor": needy, pitiable, and from the plural noun ("the poor") a collective denotation. In its adjectival forms, "poor" signified a state of "having few, or no, material possessions," lacking "means to procure the comforts, or the necessaries, of life." Poor meant needy, but the extent of need depended upon context. Applicable to varied social settings, poor could mean anything from "absolute want to straitened circumstances or limited means relatively to station." Literate religious leaders and their parishioners spoke both of a "poor gentleman" as well as a man "too poor to maintain a wife." Lack or want also applied to the natural realm, as in "poor soil" that yielded little or was entirely unproductive. When it concerned material and spiritual aspects of the human condition, however, impoverishment often inspired compassion in the more fortunate.[15]

A second sense of the word was that poor persons were to be pitied because they suffered greatly in this life. Like "poor Job," an impoverished New Englander became "a necessitous or compassionable Object." In short, they became objects of pity. Benjamin Colman, pastor of Boston's Fourth Church, urged his hearers to exercise charity toward "the chosen *Objects*, poor *Saints* and Members of *Jesus Christ*." Also applied commonly to deceased persons, the term "poor" signified someone who was able to find comfort only in the afterlife. Whereas "poor" as an adjective highlighted a sense of want and the pity it often produced, the plural noun emphasized poor people as a class, the opposite of rich. Samuel Johnson defined the poor as those who "are in the lowest rank of the community" and "who cannot subsist but by the charity of others." Chief among these, noted the famed eighteenth-century wordsmith, were "widows and orphans." Johnson, like his religious contemporaries, did not associate poverty with social inequality, and his dictionaries expressed no clear understanding that persons of the "indigent" class were victims of inequitable social relations. Instead the poor were merely "oppressed with want."[16]

The idea that people were made poor through the oppression of others, an idea prominent in the writings of the Old Testament prophets, surfaced only occasionally among congregational religious leaders. Despite training in Hebrew exegesis at Harvard College and abundant lexical analysis in published sermons of the period, Puritan ministers rarely utilized that language's insights into social inequality in the ancient world. Two primary Hebrew words were translated by the English "poor" in Bibles used by congregationalist religious leaders: אֶבְיוֹן (*ebyon*), meaning in want, or needy; and דַּל (*dal*) meaning low, weak, or thin. But a third Hebrew term, עָנִי (*ani*), by far the most common one used in the Old Testament to describe the poor, translates as weak persons "oppressed by rich and powerful" others. The prophet Isaiah, for example, employed this word when he wrote: "'What do you mean by crushing My people, and grinding the face of the poor?' declares the Lord God of hosts."[17]

Yet the common Hebrew understanding of the oppressed poor was not altogether lost upon congregational clerics. Frequently between 1630 and

1775 they decried such merchant practices as the engrossing of wheat and other valuable commodities, the lending of money at usurious interest rates, and the sale of bread and other necessities at "unjust" prices. But such denunciations of merchant greed often amounted to a lament that traditional ethical standards were weakening; they rarely served as clear indictments of an increasingly unfair social order. Ministers traditionally stressed the plight and pitiable condition of poor persons, whereas the Hebrew language emphasized the social inequities that produced them. Influenced by their belief that God predetermined human impoverishment, Puritan clerics did not draw upon biblical traditions that highlighted oppression by the wealthy and powerful.[18]

Cosmological developments and worsening economic conditions in Massachusetts combined to cast doubt on religious explanations that God predestined human impoverishment. When widows and orphans were few, ministers plausibly could argue that God had ordained their condition. In the late seventeenth and early eighteenth centuries, however, the circle of the "godly poor" widened to include many visible saints who sought employment but, finding none, languished in poverty. The Anglo-French wars that began in 1689 claimed the lives of many New England men, leaving numerous widows and orphans, as well as conditions of near-famine, indebtedness, and "*Black Times.*" Sensitive to growing popular doubt that God ordained extensive earthly suffering and disinclined to believe that He intervened directly in human affairs, Mather and other ministers redefined religious explanations of divine providence in direct response to increasing human impoverishment.[19]

In common parlance of the day, providence referred to an event or events that God predestined. But Puritan doctrines of providence also explained divine provision for the material needs of humankind. Mather and other ministers during this second historical phase shifted their emphasis from the former to the latter. Beginning in the 1690s and continuing to the middle of the eighteenth century, Puritan ministers proposed a patchwork religious explanation of divine provision that shifted responsibility for suffering from God to humans and explained that spiritual laws or formulas could bring down divine provision from heaven to earth. Parishioners wanted to know if God would provide for their material needs in distressed times, but Puritan ministers were unwilling to teach that divine provision was freely available to all God's creatures. Instead, clerics maintained that God's provision for humankind was conditional and preferential. Many religious Bostonians, an increasing number of whom were experiencing poverty, consequently rejected these ministerial teachings as unbiblical and inequitable.

Mather also acted against the backdrop of significant developments in natural philosophy that undermined notions of divine intervention into human history and, with it, ideas that God impoverished people. The mature Isaac Newton, Nicholas Malebranche, and other natural philosophers labored to preserve a cosmology of divine agency within a universe they acknowledged was characterized by stability and fixed laws of nature. Enlightenment scientific ideas greatly influenced Increase and Cotton Mather and a generation of Puritan intellectuals, in part through the activities of Boston's Philosophical Society, founded by the elder Mather and loosely associated with the Royal Society of London. Its members included Cambridge minister and Harvard tutor William Brattle and "nearly all the principal ministers and magistrates of New England and New York." The scientific view of creation and God's relationship to it appealed to congregational ministers who believed in some type of divine mediation and dreaded the implications of a purely mechanistic universe. Malebranche's universe is "sustained in all its parts by the will of God," argues Norman Fiering, and its "operations are connected not by mechanical causation but by the constant exercise of God's conservatory will." In other words, "even the so-called laws of nature become immediate effects of special grace." Malebranche ruled out miracles in the day-to-day workings of the universe but maintained that the "continued existence of things as they are every moment is the one perpetual miracle." This one great miracle made unnecessary a plethora of smaller ones. Within Puritan clerical thought, God's hand became less like that of a puppeteer and more like that of a director in a complicated human drama.[20]

Mather modified religious explanations of divine providence in order to assign to human agency a greater role in the construction of reality. This expansion of human responsibility, in turn, loosened causal connections between the divine will and temporal suffering. He argued that God was the "true Original" or "*First Cause*" of human adversity primarily in the sense that he permitted it, but "*Second Causes*" (known also as "*Efficients*" or "*Instruments*") operated independently as causal agents. By shifting emphasis from the first proposition to the second, Mather helped shift the locus of accountability for temporal suffering from heaven to earth. Mather cited biblical Job as one who understood that "Sabeans & Chaldeans as well as more Natural Accidents" occasioned the loss of his "fair Estate." Job nevertheless looked beyond the "instruments" of his suffering to the divine "Hand from whence those losses" came. What religious teachings had assumed God *caused*, Mather now argued God *permitted*.[21]

By adjusting the balances that weighed the respective roles of heaven and earth in human suffering, Mather made a moral imperative to ameliorate misery. In his search to "both find the *Cause,* and obtain the *End,* of all the Calamitous *Losses,* which had overtaken" his parishioners and fellow Bostonians, Mather proposed a series of "Infallible Expedients for the Preventing, or the Repairing of these *Losses.*" To prevent "*Losses* which thus Creepled the Body of this People" at sea, he proposed the "great Use of *Guard Ships* and *Convoyes;* and the yet greater use of *Ensurance Offices,* . . . with Methods to stop *Fires.*" The historical significance of these "Infallible Expedients" lay in the knowledge that a fire at sea was attributable to human error as much as it was to God's judgment. Humankind's wounds, Puritan doctrine now began to emphasize, were as likely to be self-inflicted as to be divinely imposed.[22]

The means by which God provisioned His creation increasingly occupied the minds of clergy and laity after 1700. Two principal factors account for this change. First, less than five years after King William's War ended, Queen Anne's War worsened economic and social conditions considerably in New England. "The emergence of a serious poverty problem in Boston by the closing years of Queen Anne's War," Gary Nash has noted, "was clearly related to this series of calamitous campaigns, which not only claimed the lives of many single men of the laboring classes but also left many war widows and their children without means of support." Between 1705 and 1714 taxes rose astronomically to pay for the war and its fallout, and Boston's annual tax per capita in this ten-year period was second only to that of the French and Indian War years. In addition to war debt, increased numbers of widows and orphans, Boston's "Eighth Great Fire" in 1711, and a devalued currency plagued Massachusetts. Second, because most Puritan ministers believed that God superintended the universe through predictable laws and not directly, they searched for divinely appointed means through which God provisioned humankind. If Puritan clerics hoped to maintain their cultural authority in Massachusetts, they desperately needed to develop plausible explanations for worsening economic circumstances around them.[23]

Ministers sought to uncover divinely appointed instrumentalities or formulas through which God would provision his creatures. Their halting, experimental search to discover the acceptable means of divine provision was neither quick nor easy. Ministers in 1719 and again in 1740 thought they had uncovered two methods or instrumentalities through which New Englanders would be able to secure a share in God's material bounty: market participation and commercial revival. Each scheme was accompanied by a detailed theological rationale, but neither found popular acceptance.

Benjamin Colman, pastor of Boston's Brattle Street Church, argued that God's plan was for people in Massachusetts to find their daily bread by participating in the emerging market economy. In a 1719 tract designed to elicit support for establishment of a public market in Boston, Colman argued that public markets were necessary because God no longer provided food directly to his creatures. God now provisioned humankind through the instrumentality of the market economy. His reasoning, like that of Malebranche, deemphasized miracles and suggested that the laws of the market had become "immediate effects of special grace."[24]

Colman challenged the views of many Bostonians in 1719 that commercial values were immoral and that market mechanisms subverted faith. As late as 1734, despite the "usage of *Markets* as a point of wisdom and prudence" in New York and Philadelphia, Bostonians still resisted establishment of a public market in a fixed location with regular, stated hours, where people could freely negotiate sale and purchase prices. Religious scruples of town dwellers prevented the project from going forward. Many residents thought that by "setting up" a market they were conforming to "Vices and evil Customs" rampant in "the rest of the world." Although Colman's readers had long traded and bartered with one another, they looked in faith for God's blessing upon each neighborly exchange. Going to market was a matter of faith and morality to most Bostonians, and they hesitated to exchange belief in God's direct provision for their daily bread for faith in an impersonal market. Without a market and trusting that God would provide "a pig, or some poultry, or a little butter, or a few eggs," town residents preparing dinner "must Out for the supply, they know not whither," and "away they trapse toward the *Neck*, or half over to *Roxbury*." Searching daily for poultry or butter in this manner, while highly unpredictable and often inefficient, nevertheless afforded householders an opportunity to trust in God for their daily provision. Colman assured his readers that going to market was not necessarily a faithless activity, but he scorned their efforts to continue older ways. When Israel wandered in a wilderness (as Massachusetts once had been), Colman wrote, God sent "*Manna* and *Quails* for the meanest." But "we look now to live by the Blessing of God on our labour and frugality, and not by *Miracles*." God's miraculous interventions "ceas'd as soon as *Israel* came to Cities and Villages, to inhabit and till and Trade." Hence, God no longer provided for His people directly, but through the instrumentality of the market. By appealing to a biblical proof for his argument that God approved of markets, Colman thought he could persuade Bostonians that a public market was "biblical and therefore lawful" in God's eyes.[25]

Although Colman cited biblical precedent to encourage changes in popular economic behavior, he offended some people's sense of religious propriety by asking them not only to support but also to trust in the market. A boycott of Boston's public market when it opened in 1734 and its subsequent dismantling several years later reflect strong resistance to Colman's ideas. Colman argued not only that "*Markets* must be some time or other," but he ascribed to the market qualities often used to describe God and his loving provision for humankind. A market "once set up," Colman wrote, "is a *living* and certain supply that will outlive us, and provide for them that shall come after us." For people who "outed" each day in search of their daily provision, how could a public market be "a living and certain supply"? Even if Colman's readers granted his point that direct provision from heaven came only in the wilderness, they probably found it difficult to think of anything other than God himself as their "living and certain supply," especially when most knew from personal experience that livelihoods were so uncertain.[26]

Town dwellers also may have withheld their support for the market's establishment because Colman asked them to trust in a market that powerful merchants like Andrew Belcher so easily manipulated. Bostonians, in particular, remembered privations they had endured in 1710 when Belcher engrossed the town's supply of wheat and prepared to ship it abroad for a higher price than he could obtain in Boston. Only an outraged and hungry group of residents forcibly restrained its intended shipment when "the Rudder of Capt. Rose's Ship was cut." Community anger likewise erupted against Colman and his market proposal when a nighttime mob, "their faces blackened and some dressed as clergymen," destroyed the market house which Brattle Street Church's pastor strongly supported. People throughout Massachusetts welcomed material benefits they might derive from participation in a widened market but resented merchants who placed profit ahead of the public good. Colman's market proposal failed to address popular concerns that rich merchants could cut off God's divinely appointed means of provision. Most Bostonians, a growing number of whom faced impoverishment, trusted in God but did not necessarily trust some of their fellow men.[27]

In 1725 Colman believed he had uncovered in biblical texts a spiritual formula for bringing down divine blessing upon Boston's economy, an idea he implemented during Boston's Great Awakening in the early 1740s. Colman still maintained that the market was a divinely appointed method of human provision, but he no longer urged people to trust it for their daily bread. Instead, Colman theorized that Boston wealth, if it were devoted to godly purposes, would secure divine blessing on commercial life, enlarge the wealth and liberality of town benefactors, and expand poor donations substantially. Because Boston was the "Head" of Massachusetts in the minds of those who subscribed to an organic view of society, any spiritual and economic benefits it experienced would redound to Massachusetts as a whole. Colman further argued that corporate obedience in the matter of wealth sanctification secured divine favor upon the commerce of a people. Simply stated, the spiritual condition of Bostonians individually and corporately depended on the extent to which their wealth was "dedicated" to the Lord and His purposes. Personal wealth put to religious purposes secured God's blessing and increase. God-given prosperity to those who dedicated their wealth and economic life to Him, in turn, created a sense of gratitude and liberality in the heart. Consequently, thankful hearts donated generously to the Lord's work in the form of almsgiving to the poor and support of the ministry. The more people dedicated their wealth to God, the more they prospered and liberally supported the ministry and the poor. This escalating cycle of dedication and prosperity benefited both individual and community.[28]

Although Massachusetts experienced peace in the years between 1720 and 1740, cessation of warfare was a mixed economic blessing. As Gary Nash has argued, some conditions improved while others worsened during the peacetime years. Population, shipbuilding, trade, and construction increased throughout Massachusetts. Boston added 6,000 inhabitants over the two decades, from 11,000 to nearly 17,000. Yet a "General Small Pox" struck Boston especially hard in 1721 and 1730, killing 850 and 400 persons, respectively. Currency devaluation continued and five of the worst years ever for Boston seamen earning wages occurred between 1731 and 1740. Against this backdrop of worsening economic affairs, Colman discerned a biblical pattern for Boston's commercial prosperity.[29]

The most important medium for the dissemination of Colman's ideas, however, was the Great Awakening that began in Boston in 1740. By the time George Whitefield brought the Awakening message to Massachusetts during September and October of that year, Boston had begun to recover from its economic malaise. England had declared war against Spain, and wartime expenditures related to the conflict boosted economic activity in Boston and throughout the Bay Colony. Colman invited Whitefield to preach in Boston and grafted his own message of commercial revival onto that of the Great Awakener. The pastor of Brattle Street Church sought nothing less than a mighty revival of piety and prosperity.[30]

Colman never specified exactly how much wealth had to be dedicated to God in order to secure divine favor upon the town's economy. In practice, however, he gauged the extent of sanctified wealth by the amount of money affluent Bostonians contributed to the poor and the ministry. "One *natural Benefit* of Trade and Commerce to any People is that it *enlarges their Hearts to do generous Things*," Colman wrote. "This is most natural to Places of *Commerce; Something to give and a Heart to give.*" While Colman wanted all Boston residents—poor, rich, and the middling sort—to dedicate their "merchandise

TABLE 19. Monthly Poor Offerings in Brattle Street Church, Boston, 1740–1743

|      | Jan. | Feb. | Mar. | Apr. | May | June | July | Aug. | Sept. | Oct. | Nov. | Dec. |
|------|------|------|------|------|-----|------|------|------|-------|------|------|------|
| 1740 | £30  | £24  | £24  | £30  | £24 | £24  | £30  | £24  | £30   | £24  | £24  | £30  |
| 1741 | £24  | £24  | £24  | £30  | £24 | £30  | £24  | £24  | £30   | £24  | £24  | £30  |
| 1742 | £24  | £30  | £24  | £24  | £24 | £30  | £24  | £24  | £30   | £30  | £40  | £32  |
| 1743 | £32  | £40  | £32  | £32  | £32 | £40  | £32  | £40  | £32   | £32  | £40  | £24  |

Source: Brattle Street Church, Boston, Treasurer Records, Ms. Bos. Z. 15 (2), Department of Rare Books & Manuscripts, Boston Public Library, Boston, Mass.
Note: George Whitefield came to Boston in September 1740, and revival was over in Brattle Street Church by November 1741. Shaded months indicate the period of revival.

and hire" to God, the rich had considerably more of it to consecrate. Thus, Colman made a special effort to convince elite Bostonians to "render their merchandise holiness unto the Lord." His principal instrument for achieving this was the Quarterly Meeting for Collections for the Poor. Four times yearly to this "private meeting" Colman invited "the Gentlemen of the Town of Boston" whose duty it was "to pay the debts" of the poor. Wealthy benefactors who supplied necessities to the poor and the ministry were shielded from corrupting properties of unsanctified commerce. Colman warned wealthy auditors that when "Charities and Mercies" and "Works of Piety" diminish, "odious Vices grow up in their stead, offensive to God and Man." But, he assured them, "let our Merchandise and Hire be *holy to God,* and all this is prevented." Charitable contributions benefited not only poor persons but rich persons, by warding off mammon's corrupting influences.[31]

Boston experienced a powerful religious revival, but Colman's dream of commercial reawakening and greater giving to the impoverished never apparently materialized. Records for the Quarterly Meeting for Collections for the Poor have not survived, so benefactions from this society to Boston's poor cannot be measured. Conventional avenues of poor relief in which the wealthy did participate, such as monthly poor offerings within Brattle Street Church, remained static during the Awakening period. Financial records maintained by the deacons of the church show that monthly poor offerings did not reflect a surge in generosity. Unless we are to believe that wealthy benefactors sanctified their wealth in and through the Quarterly Meeting only, Boston's revival of piety did not loosen their purse strings significantly (see table 19).

Colman's plan to revive commerce through wealth sanctification foundered in part on controversies that discredited Boston revivalism as a whole. Colman and revivalist clerics from two other Boston churches promoted an enormously successful revival, but ministerial favoritism toward potential converts with family connections to the revivalist congregations created a widespread perception that the Awakening was inequitable and tainted by religious partiality. Bostonians passed over in the spiritual ministrations, including unchurched families, indentured servants, and enslaved blacks, fashioned a revival of their own, united in their belief that God was not a respecter of persons. Colman and the other revivalist ministers, weary from their monumental labors and eager to forestall further controversy, drew in their nets of clannish converts and brought revival in their three churches to an end. In all likelihood, Colman at this time relinquished any hopes he may have had for commercial revival.[32]

From this point forward, Colman's teachings on wealth underwent a subtle but important shift. He began to teach that prosperity redounded primarily to individuals instead of communities. Nor would economic prosperity come to Boston by a powerful divine intervention in the temporal world. "*Miracles* of *Mercy* and Compassion, Benignity and Bounty," Colman wrote, occur "gradually," albeit "in wondrous Manner brought about." Colman did not abandon the idea that the rich should give liberally to indigents, and he continued to encourage private giving to the city's needy. After the Great Awakening in Boston ended, however, Colman never again advocated his speculative plan to revive commerce through sanctified wealth.[33]

By mid-eighteenth century, Boston's ministers still had no viable religious explanation for the growing level of human impoverishment in their midst. The Puritan doctrine of providence, "too little Believed" early in the century still had not gained widespread acceptance among many churchgoing Bostonians. Ministerial formulations teaching that God provisioned humankind conditionally and preferentially, like so many trial balloons, were popularly disdained as lacking equity and biblical authority. In a 1752 sermon of monumental importance, Charles Chauncy propounded a religious explanation of human impoverishment that with peculiar force took hold in Massachusetts and throughout colonial society for many years thereafter. In *The Idle-Poor secluded from the Bread of Charity by the Christian Law*, the minister of Boston's First Congregational Church took as his sermon text: "This we commanded you, that if any would not work, neither should he eat." Many a sermon, of course, had flowed from this verse over the years, and clergy and laity alike were familiar with it. Chauncy, however, used it to forge a new and enduring religious explanation of poverty that joined divine providence with a moral theory of labor. In essence, he argued that God provisioned humankind through its willingness to work. This formulation had three important advantages that helped cement its grip upon the clerical imagination and much of the public's.[34]

First, Chauncy's theory of providence was impartial. God provisioned *all* persons who showed a willingness to work. Second, Chauncy's formulation derived significant cultural authority by appearing to rely upon a biblical text for its rationale. To many persons in the colonial era, if a practice was biblical it was "lawful." Third, and most important, Chauncy's argument elevated the divine-human provisional nexus to the level of a natural law like gravity. As the law of gravity upheld the planets (since God no longer interposed himself to uphold them directly), the law of labor provisioned humankind (since God no longer fed his creatures directly with manna and quail). The doctrine's first two features addressed long-standing popular objections to previous clerical teachings on the subject; its third facet persuaded ministers that they had uncovered the appointed means of divine provision. In labor or a person's willingness to work, Chauncy and other clerics found the provisional mechanism that had eluded them for more than a half century. Clerics who exchanged seventeenth-century interventionism for eighteenth-century instrumentalism perceived in Chauncy's new formulation a proper balance between divine grace and human responsibility, while poor persons found it difficult to gainsay its apparent equity and scripturalness. When phrases like "ungodly poor" disappeared from clerical explanations of poverty after the 1750s, it was no accident. Chauncy's teaching ratcheted up pressure on poor persons to demonstrate that their poverty did not result from idleness. Chauncy's sermons after 1752 increasingly include such descriptions as "Idle-Poor," "slothful poor," "Drones" who "doze away their Time and Senses over their Cups," and "Plagues to Society." Poor Bostonians did not passively accept what Chauncy's doctrine implied, but even clerics like Andrew Croswell who were critical of the teaching could not easily blunt its efficacy. Convinced they had discerned God's means of impartial provision to hmankind in Scripture, Chauncy and other clerics declared dogmatically after mid-century that free will—not fate—accounted for a person's poverty. Disarmingly simple, this clerical construct resonates to the present hour.

In *The Idle-Poor secluded from the Bread of Charity,* Chauncy reasoned that God provisioned humankind through labor. In labor, heaven and earth met and God gave daily bread to his creatures. "The *positive Will of God,*" he wrote, "has appointed *Labour* the *Means* in order to [secure] a Livelihood" in the temporal world. "Laborious Diligence," Chauncy continued, "is the *Means* by which he has *ordained* we should supply ourselves with Food, and other Necessaries of Life." Chauncy based his argument on God's command to Adam in Genesis 3:19: "In the sweat of thy face shalt thou eat bread, till thou return unto the ground." The divine precept, "tho' originally directed to Adam" was nevertheless "obligatory upon all his Posterity." Chauncy termed this command-in-perpetuity "the *Law of Labour*" and concluded that "Industrious Labour is therefore the Law of *Christianity*." Consequences for violating "the *Law of Labour*" were potentially costly. Persons who "Indulge to Idleness, who have Ability for Labour," Chauncy continued, "virtually set aside *the Method* God has been pleased to direct to, and enjoin, in order to be supported in Life." Such people "shall not be maintained at the Charge of others; shall not live upon the Charities of their Christian Friends and Brethren." Addressing as many as two hundred persons from Boston and surrounding towns who financially supported the Society for Encouraging Industry and Employing the Poor, Chauncy urged charity for "disabled Persons," those who "are *willing* to work, but can't get Employment," and those who are "incapable of Labour, by Reasons of Sickness, or Lameness, or the Decays of an infirm old Age." The rest should not eat.[35]

Chauncy's doctrine of providence, harsh as it was, had the appearance of fairness since all persons who were willing and able to work theoretically participated in the divine bounty. It also made allowances for those incapable of labor or of finding employment. Chauncy noted that the policy he urged was "far from being arbitrary and unreasonable" and "carries in it all the Marks of Fairness, Equity, and Goodness." In addition, Chauncy's unequivocal opposition to the Great Awakening insulated him from charges of religious partiality that tainted other Boston clergymen and enabled him to make the case for a new doctrine of impartial providence. Alone among Boston's congregational clerics, Chauncy had opposed the Great Awakening from start to finish, though he did not voice his opinions right away. Most of his clerical brethren praised the ministry of George Whitefield and condemned that of James Davenport in the revival's second phase; Chauncy supported neither. Because he was no friend of the revivals, he was no friend of the partiality that characterized them. At the time Chauncy presented his teaching, only one member of First Church served as an overseer of the poor in Boston, while eight overseers belonged to the three revivalist churches. In the popular mind, therefore, neither Chauncy nor his church was regarded as a respecter of persons in the way that ministers from the three revivalist churches were.[36]

Chauncy argued that charity for the idle poor exchanged human for divine wisdom in the conduct of earthly affairs. By "supporting the needy in Idleness, we constructively oppose the *Appointment* of God, and substitute a Method for their Maintenance of our own devising." Was "it fit," he continued, "if Men won't work, when they can, that a different Way, from what the Wisdom of God has instituted, should be taken for their Supply with Bread? . . . And this is reasonable? Can it be justified? Ought Persons to be maintained in plain Contempt of the Constitution of God?" Public charity to the idle poor, even if one was tempted to extend it, was not only an unsound basis for social policy, it was sinful. The appeal to Scripture that helped overturn proposals for a public market and smallpox inoculations invested with sacred authority Chauncy's plan to shear charity rolls of "Drones" who refused to work.[37]

While the apparent equity and scripturalness of Chauncy's providence shielded it from easy criticism, its supposed conformity to natural law cloaked the idea with an aura of scientific immutability. Ministers who abandoned interventionism in the late seventeenth century waited another half century for a viable alternative to the idea that God fated human impoverishment. Instrumentalism encouraged clerics to believe that God's relation to the world was mediated through various "methods" or formulas. Chauncy's discovery that God provisioned his creatures through "the *Law of Labour* given to Adam" paralleled Newton's idea that God upheld the universe through gravity. Conformity to nature's laws assured orderliness and safety in societies and individuals. Dire consequences attended their violation or alteration, however, just as gravity's sure results awaited persons who jumped off buildings. The "established Laws of Nature are such as render it impossible," Chauncy argued, "that Mankind should be supported, if they are generally lazy." One consequence of associating moral obligation with natural law was that the latter subsumed the former. Chauncy and other clerics still spoke in moral terms, but their morality increasingly was grounded in invisible laws instead of the divine character. Behavior, therefore, was not inherently wrong because it transgressed a divine precept; it was unworkable because it did not conform to an iron law. A year after Chauncy propounded his theory of free will poverty, Samuel Cooper of Boston's Brattle Street Church argued that "Universal Charity may very well be compared to the great Law of Gravitation, by which all Particles of Matter mutually operate upon, and attract each other. . . . Nor is Attraction more necessary in the natural, than Benevolence is in the moral World." Principles that governed the visible world governed the invisible, as well.[38]

Understanding this religious and philosophical context can lead us to a deeper, more nuanced comprehension of the charitable work schemes in Boston in the middle of the century. Gary Nash has shown that Boston's leading merchants were desperate to cut poor relief and in 1748 established a linen manufactory to employ widows and their children. By highlighting on a work scheme aimed primarily at women and children, Nash does not focus on the plight poor men suffered when ministers propounded new religious explanations of poverty. Official plans to curtail poor relief payments in

Boston, in fact, were two-pronged: reduce payments to women by giving them jobs, and limit payments to men by branding them as idle and unwilling to work. Clerics did not differentiate so sharply between men and women when they preached against sloth, but overseers of the poor armed with new ideas of providence did. Town officials no doubt thought they could coerce women and children to labor more easily than they could men, especially when it offered them "feminine" jobs in the manufactory like spinning. Moreover, long-standing charitable traditions ensured that widows and orphans would receive more gentle treatment when overseers and others called their industriousness into question. As Karin Wulf argues in an essay in this volume, ideas about gender shaped the types of relief designed by officials. And it should not surprise modern observers that plans to shear relief rolls treated poor women and their children more magnanimously. Women got harsh work while men got harsh words.[39]

Since ministers and other influential Bostonians looked more favorably upon widows and orphans, emerging explanations of human impoverishment probably were more severe than historians have argued. For example, Nash argues that "by the 1740s it had become clear that the problem in Boston was not one of able-bodied persons who refused work, but persons for whom no work was available." And in sermons, Nash continues, "the clergy castigated 'idleness' but they did not charge, as so frequently was the case in England, that it was voluntary." These observations are accurate, but only insofar as they describe sermon material aimed at widows and children. Clerical language aimed at the poor who were not widowed and orphaned goes beyond what Nash has claimed: it singles out able-bodied men who refused work, and it asserts that increasing numbers of poor Bostonians freely chose to be idle. Speaking before benefactors of the linen manufactory in 1752, Charles Chauncy acknowledged that "such among the Poor as are *willing* to work, but can't get Employment, are not the Persons secluded from the Bread of Charity. . . . [T]hey should be pitied and help'd." Chauncy and other influential Bostonians perceived that a threat was posed by "the other Sort of poor People, those who can work, but *won't*. . . . Concerning these Poor, it is the Command of an inspired Apostle, *that they shall not eat,* i.e., shall not be maintained at the Charge of others." Chauncy was urging that willingly idle persons be denied poor relief payments. Clerics did not believe that widows and orphans had idled themselves voluntarily, but they charged many other poor persons with doing just that. The scriptural command to withhold charity from persons willingly idle, Chauncy observed, was a "seasonable" admonition that applied to the situation in Boston. Chauncy compared voluntarily idle Bostonians to "*meer Drones,*" and "many such there have been among us." Due to "misplaced Charity," Chauncy continued, their numbers "have so increased upon us."⁴⁰

How many Bostonians preferred idleness to employment may never be known, but it is possible to discern the probable identity of "*meer Drones*" who clerics and town officials inveighed against. Chauncy's language suggests that impoverished males inspired trepidation in those responsible for maintaining social order in mid-eighteenth-century Boston. A drone is the male of the honeybee that does not help in honey gathering or care of the hive. It only helps the colony if a queen bee requires insemination. Chauncy's language implied that stout, able-bodied males refused to work and, as a result, did not care properly for their families. The adjective "meer" adds contempt, meaning that they are nothing more than drones. Similar to images of poor, especially black, males in our own time, Chauncy may have insinuated that sexual intercourse was the primary activity in which voluntarily idle males engaged. Such evidence is indirect, of course, but it seems likely that ministers purposely chose the male bee to describe poor men who, in their view, were willfully idle. Moreover, town fathers knew that "*meer Drones*" would resist any attempt to coerce their labor in a manufactory, possibly with violence; they mistakenly thought females would not.⁴¹

Religious explanations of human impoverishment exerted enormous psychic and social pressures upon impoverished males by forcing them to prove their industriousness or be denied poor relief. Like workers who have to look busy when the boss walks by, poor Bostonians—and males, in particular—had to endure sermons describing them as "*Drones* who are Burdens, without Profit, to the Community." When the linen manufactory closed in 1759, doctrines of an iron providence continued. In seventeenth-century Boston, poor persons had been regarded as objects of pity suffering under a divine fate. But as poverty mounted in the 1750s, Bostonians without daily bread increasingly came to be seen as responsible for failing to labor industriously for it.⁴²

So successfully did clerics propound the view that human impoverishment resulted from one's refusal to work that charitable contributions to Boston churches dried up. Chauncy's concern in 1752 had been to stop the steep rise in public taxes that went to poor relief, not to limit private charity. His warnings that almsgivers should bestow their money only upon poor persons who were willing "to feed and clothe themselves by their own Labour and Industry" fell upon receptive ears, especially in times of high taxation. Traditionally generous Bostonians heeded Chauncy's lesson so well that they found few recipients worthy of their benefactions in the years after 1752 and began to withhold their money even from church charities that supported widows and orphans. Alarmed at the drop in private charity, Chauncy tried to remove the scruples against almsgiving that his teachings had sown in the minds of churchgoers.

At a time when resistance leaders in Boston sought unity and popular support for American independence, Chauncy preached on the need for brotherly love. His sermon text, Acts 2:44, was very familiar to Bostonians, especially since Chauncy had alluded to it thirty years earlier in a famous sermon comparing Great Awakening participants to religious wife-swappers. Its recapitulation in 1773 helped capture public curiosity for a very different sort of message. In *Christian Love, as exemplified by the first christian church having all things in common,* delivered shortly before the Boston Tea Party, Chauncy urged imitation of primitive Christianity, especially "their example to do their utmost, that none of their brethren in Christ, especially of the same community with themselves, may be suffered to drag on life unrelieved under the straits, distresses, and miseries of unavoidable poverty." He reminded parishioners that the early church's "constant care" was "to provide, by their charitable distributions, for the relief of their brethren in Christ under distressing circumstances, whether through poverty, or the unjust treatment of a wicked and unbelieving world." Chauncy rebuked persons who "expend their money for that which profiteth not" while poor persons in the church "have so often been pinched with hunger, and cold, and suffered to groan under distress, through want, I do not say of the conveniences and comforts, but of even the necessaries of life." Others, like Reverend Andrew Croswell, had been warning for years that uncharitableness pervaded public life in Boston, citing as evidence cruel military punishments and prison conditions in Boston. Chauncy made a sincere effort to ameliorate the uncharitableness his teaching had inspired, but he never repudiated its central tenets that God helped only those who helped themselves. Instead he argued that a lack of charitable disbursements made mockery of the deacon's office, a divinely appointed institution. Putting the genie back in the bottle was more difficult than he imagined.[43]

In 1789, after states ratified the constitution of the new nation, Reverend Samuel Fish asserted that divine provision for humankind included daily bread for all, as well as written, legal protections to the poor. Fish, pastor of the congregational church in Lebanon, Connecticut, observed that God gave both food and a legal system to Israel in order that the latter might secure the former, especially for the poor. Thus, in Fish's mind, religious teachings should portray food and shelter as rights instead of as privileges obtained through hard work. Bread "rained down from heaven" in the wilderness, but in the promised land God "makes protection for them [Israel] by establishing laws to vindicate their rights." God "provided for the poor and for the stranger a residence in any part of his dominions." Moreover, God "has established a law to confirm this as their right" and "no man had a right to deprive them" of it. Fish singled out two ways that treatment of the New England poor violated biblical teaching: the "common practice" of "warning out" poor persons from communities to avoid municipal responsibility for their upkeep (as Ruth Herndon's essay in this volume discusses), and public slave auctions. The religious gloss on clerical support for such practices, Fish argued, was an unbiblical mask for immoral social constructs. "Custom hath a mighty influence on mankind," Fish urged, and "it is more forceable than any law whether of God or man."[44]

Thus, congregational clerics forged an enduring religious explanation of human impoverishment that, in the opinion of Fish, Croswell, and others, defied divine law and human reason. Its core proposition that God provisioned creation through the physical labor of His creatures took permanent form in the early 1750s after unworkable alternatives had been in existence for more than a century. New England clerics set in motion this process of doctrinal revision in the 1690s when they embraced Newtonian ideas of a self-regulating universe and subsequently abandoned teachings premised upon God's direct intervention in the physical world. Although they quickly retreated from the idea that God reached down from heaven to enrich or impoverish His earthly creatures, they could not so speedily find a suitable replacement to explain God's relation to the cosmos in a post-Newtonian world. When economic privations in early eighteenth-century Boston forced ministers to focus on specific ways that God provided daily bread for humankind, they thought they discerned in the Scriptures two spiritual formulas for bringing down from heaven God's material abundance. Many Bostonians did not share clerics' faith in the market and commercial revivalism, however, especially when powerful and unscrupulous individuals could so easily commandeer these divinely appointed mechanisms. Charles Chauncy proclaimed in 1752 that he had discovered a sacred law through which God provisioned humankind, and he placed this moral theory of labor on par with Newton's laws of motion and gravity. Invested with religious and scientific authority, this doctrine stated that God's appointed means for feeding humankind was labor and the sweat of one's brow. If one did not work, one did not eat. The hands that impoverished were no longer God's but our own. God helped only those who labored to help themselves. After this religious teaching had been in existence for nearly forty years, Samuel Fish argued that it too narrowly construed God's providence and that it had become a means of oppressing New England's poor. God provided the indigent with food, written legal protections, and many other things, Fish reasoned, and limited conceptions of God's bounty limited God Himself. Had members of the clergy forgotten that humans did not live by bread alone?

# Notes

1. Congregationalism was a movement of loosely affiliated churches throughout New England, each of which was independent in matters of church governance. Therefore, to distinguish it from a later denomination of a similar name, the lowercase is used throughout this essay (i.e., congregational, congregationalism, etc.). For Job's remarks, see Job 1:21; [Cotton Mather], *Some Seasonable advice unto the poor; To be annexed unto the kindnesses of God, that are dispensed unto them* [Boston, 1726], 7–8; idem, *Durable riches. Two brief discourses, occasioned by the impoverishing blast of heaven, which the undertakings of men, both by sea and land, have met withal* (Boston: John Allen, 1695), 1.

2. Simon J. Schaffer, "God's Relation to the Universe," in *Dictionary of the History of Science*, ed. W. F. Bynum, E. J. Browne, and Roy Porter (New York: Macmillan, 1981; repr., Princeton: Princeton University Press, 1984), 169–70. I am indebted to Schaeffer for his analysis of this controversy in the history of science. See also *The Oxford Classical Dictionary*, 2d ed., s.v. "Atlas."

3. Peter Burke, *Popular Culture in Early Modern Europe* (New York: New York University Press, 1978); David D. Hall, *Worlds of Wonder, Days of Judgment: Popular Religious Belief in Early New England* (New York: Alfred A. Knopf, 1989), 106–8. Although reform of European popular culture began before the Great Migration to New England in the 1630s was underway, it gained considerable headway among congregational clergy in this country in the 1690s.

4. Gary B. Nash, *The Urban Crucible: Social Change, Political Consciousness, and the Origins of the American Revolution* (Cambridge: Harvard University Press, 1979); Mather, *Durable riches*, 1.

5. Benjamin Colman, *Some Reasons and arguments offered to the good people of Boston and adjacent places, for the setting up [of] markets in Boston* (Boston: J. Franklin, 1719), 1–2, 4, 9–10, 12; Nash, *Urban Crucible*, 129–36, where Nash correctly sees the ideological challenge that Colman laid down to an older, conservative ethic of the market. On the commercial aspects of the Great Awakening in Boston, see J. Richard Olivas, "Great Awakenings: Time, Space, and the Varieties of Religious Revivalism in Massachusetts and Northern New England, 1740–1748" (Ph.D., diss., University of California, Los Angeles, 1997), 304–58.

6. Charles Chauncy, *The Idle Poor secluded from the Bread of Charity by the Christian Law. A sermon preached in Boston, before the society for encouraging Industry, and employing the Poor* (Boston: Thomas Fleet, 1752).

7. Schaffer, "God's Relation to the Universe," 169–70. Sir Isaac Newton in his later years (ca. 1680s) argued that God "subsumed gravity directly." See Betty Jo Teeter Dobbs and Margaret C. Jacobs, *Newton and the Culture of Newtonianism* (Atlantic Highlands, N.J.: Humanities Press International, 1995), 50. Also personal correspondence with Simon J. Schaffer, Cambridge University, London, September 8, 1998. Natural philosophy was synonymous with physics in the late seventeenth and early eighteenth centuries. See Samuel Eliot Morison, *Harvard College in the Seventeenth Century*, 2 vols. (Cambridge: Harvard University Press, 1936), 1:223–51, esp. 1:223n2; Norman Fiering, *Jonathan Edwards's Moral Thought and Its British Context* (Chapel Hill: University of North Carolina Press, 1981), 93–104. Fiering has written that most eighteenth-century clerics actually subscribed to a "post-Newtonian" cosmology that ruled out miracles in God's relationship to the world. The greatest and only miracle was that God upheld the "so-called laws of nature" (p. 95). The issue of God's ultimate superintendency distinguished this view from Cartesian, mechanistic conceptions of the universe.

8. This useful phrase I have borrowed from the excellent discussion of Increase and Cotton Mather found in Robert Middlekauff, *The Mathers: Three Generations of Puritan Intellectuals* (New York: Oxford University Press, 1971), 288. On the lore of wonders, see Hall, *Worlds of Wonder,* 71–116. Hall concludes that during most of the seventeenth century, "wonder stories" constituted a "mentality that united the learned and the unlearned" (p. 94). On shared worlds of clergy and laity, see Peter Burke, *Popular Culture in Early Modern Europe,* 23–64; and George Selement, "The Meeting of Elite and Popular Minds at Cambridge, New England, 1638–1645," *William and Mary Quarterly,* 3d ser., 41 (January 1984): 32–48; Increase Mather, *An Essay for the recording of illustrious providences: wherein an account is given of many remarkable and very memorable events which have happened this last age; especially in New England* (Boston: Samuel Green for Joseph Browning; 1684); Schaffer, "God's Relation to the Universe," 169; Thomas Burnet, *The Sacred theory of the earth: Containing an account of the original of the earth, and of all the general changes which it hath already undergone, or is to undergo till the consumation of all things,* 2d ed. (London: R. Norton for Walter Kettilby, 1691); William Whiston, *A new theory of the Earth from its original, to the consummation of all things; wherein the creation of the world in six days, the universal deluge, and the general conflagration, as laid down in the Holy Scriptures are shewn to be perfectly agreeable to reason and philosophy. With a large introduction concerning the genuine nature, style, and extent of the Mosaic history of the Creation* (London: J. Whiston, 1737).

9. Middlekauff, *Mathers,* 288; Mather, *Some Seasonable advice,* 7–8.

10. Mather, *Some Seasonable advice,* 7; idem, *Concio ad populum. A distressed people entertained with proposals for the relief of their distress* (Boston: B. Green for Benj. Eliot, 1719), 14.

11. Cotton Mather, *Marah spoken to. A brief essay to do good unto the widow: dispensing those lessons of piety, which are, the portion assigned for the widow, in the house and word of God,* 2d ed. (Boston: S. Kneeland, 1721), 5; idem, *Orphanotrophium. Or, orphans well-provided for. An essay on the care taken in divine providence for children when their parents forsake them* (Boston: B. Green, 1711), 18–19, 22, 37, 45–55 passim. On neglect of widows in New Testament period, see Acts 6:1–7. In chronological order, see Ignatius, *Epistle to Polycarp,* in J. B. Lightfoot, *The Apostolic Fathers* (Grand Rapids: Baker Book House, 1956), 87; Barnabas, *Epistle of Barnabas,* in Lightfoot, ibid., 155; Tertullian, *Apologeticum,* in Johannes Quasten, *Patrology,* vol. 2, *The Ante-Nicene Literature after Irenaeus* (Utrecht: Spectrum, 1950; repr., Westminster, Md.: Christian Classics, 1986), 259; Martin Luther, *Luther's Works,* ed. Helmut T. Lehman, vol. 46, *The Christian in Society* (Philadelphia: Fortress Press, 1967), 15, 42, 50, 78, 101; Steven Ozment, *Protestants: The Birth of a Revolution* (New York: Doubleday, 1992), 72–74. For biblical citations, see Exodus 22:22 and James 1:27.

12. Peter Richard Virgadamo, "Colonial Charity and the American Character: Boston, 1630–1775" (Ph.D. diss., University of Southern California, 1982), 26–42 and 46–83 passim, for the First Church of Boston's role in poor relief; Mather, *Some Seasonable advice,* 7.

13. Pastors, teachers, ruling elders, and deacons from Boston's nine congregational churches are listed in Harold Field Worthley, *An Inventory of the Records of the Particular (Congregational) Churches of Massachusetts Gathered 1620–1805,* Harvard Theological Studies, no. 25 (Cambridge: Harvard University Press, 1970), 51–87. Information on officers from Tenth Church and Eleventh Church does not exist. Depending on whether a list utilizes the date of decease or date of installation, religious leaders in Boston's congregational churches number between 110 and 142. See also Suffolk County Probate Records, 28:73 (Isaiah Tay), 32:259 (Zechariah Thayer), and 36:187 (Caleb Lyman), Suffolk County Courthouse, Boston.

14. George W. Harper, "Clericalism and Revival: The Great Awakening in Boston as a Pastoral Phenomenon," *New England Quarterly* 57 (December 1984): 561. Harper argues that Cotton Mather's model of pastoral ministry contrasted with older conceptions in which ministers "isolated themselves from their congregations in order to give their time to study and preaching." Mather's Second Church pastorate spanned the years 1685–1728. Cotton Mather, *Diary of Cotton Mather, 1681–1724,* 2 vols. (Boston: Massachusetts Historical Society, 1911–12), 2:187, 580–81.

15. Samuel Johnson, *A dictionary of the English language: in which the words are deduced from their originals; and illustrated in their different significations, by examples from the best writers: together with a*

*history of the language, and an English grammar,* 2d ed., s.v. "Poor." Johnson published the first edition of *DEL* in 1755. See also *OED*, 1971 ed., s.v. "Poor."

16. Benjamin Colman, *The Unspeakable gift of God; A right charitable and bountiful spirit to the poor and needy members of Jesus Christ* (Boston: J. Draper for H. Foster, 1739), 5; Johnson, *DEL*, 2d. ed., s.v. "Poor."

17. Morison, *Harvard College in the Seventeenth Century*, 1:200–207, 289–90. Morison noted that the "most distinctive feature of the Harvard curriculum was the emphasis on Hebrew and kindred languages" (1:200). Francis Brown, S. R. Driver, and Charles A. Briggs, eds., *A Hebrew and English Lexicon of the Old Testament* (Oxford: Clarendon Press, 1951), 2, 195 (hereafter BDB). See BDB, s.v. "עָנִי." The Hebrew עָנִי (*ani*) appears 63 times in the Old Testament, more than any other Hebrew word similarly translated "poor" in English versions. The Hebrew אֶבְיוֹן (*ebyon*) occurs 25 times; דַּל (*dal*) occurs 43 times. To establish occurrence of Hebrew words, see Robert Young, *Analytical Concordance to the Bible*, 22d ed. (Grand Rapids: William B. Eerdmans, 1980), 761–62. Isaiah 3:15, New American Standard Bible. No published sermon prior to 1775 used Isaiah 3:15 as its text. See www.library.Princeton.EDU/databases/earlyam_java.html for an online search of the *Early American Imprints* database on the Internet.

18. Cotton Mather, *Lex Mercatoria. Or, the just rules of commerce declared. And offences against the rules of justice in the dealing of men with one another, detected* (Boston: Timothy Green, 1705); idem, *Theopolis Americana. An essay on the golden street of the holy city: publishing, a testimony against the corruptions of the market place. With some good hopes of better things to be yet seen in the American world* (Boston: B. Green, 1710); Nathaniel Appleton, *The Cry of Oppression where judgment is looked for, and the sore calamities such a people may expect from a righteous God* (Boston: J. Draper, 1748).

19. Mather, *Durable riches*, 1. "Providence," an adaptation of a Latin word combining *pro* ("before") and *videre* ("to see"), means foresight. The phrase "providence of God" describes distinct but related theological ideas: (1) the "foresight, love, concern, and care God has for all his creatures"; (2) A "fate decreed by God. An event divinely ordained or preordained." See *OED*, 1971 ed., s.v. "Providence"; Peter A. Angeles, *Dictionary of Christian Theology* (San Francisco: Harper and Row, 1985), 167–68. Depending on its context, providence can mean either divine provision for humankind or heavenly arrangement of life's circumstances.

20. Raymond P. Stearns, *Science in the British Colonies of America* (Urbana: University of Illinois Press, 1970), 150–61; David Levin, *Cotton Mather: The Young Life of the Lord's Remembrancer, 1663–1703* (Cambridge: Harvard University Press, 1978), 26, 91, 92–94; Fiering, *Jonathan Edwards's Moral Thought*, 94–95.

21. Mather, *Durable riches*, 4–6.

22. Ibid., [i], 2–3.

23. Nash, *Urban Crucible*, 59–60. See also table 11, pp. 403–4.

24. Colman, *Some reasons and arguments*, 1–14 passim.

25. Nash, *Urban Crucible*, 129–36; Colman, *Some reasons and arguments*, 1, 2, 4, 12; Mather, *Orphanotrophium*, 38, where Mather wrote: "We see Things done for a Multitude of Poor Widows every day before our Eyes; They are not *Miracles;* But they are very little Short of *Miraculous*."

26. Colman, *Some reasons and arguments*, 10, 9.

27. Samuel Sewall, *Diary of Samuel Sewall, 1674–1729*, 3 vols. (Boston: Massachusetts Historical Society, 1878–82; repr. New York: Arno Press, 1972), entries for April 30 and May 1, 1710, p. 637; Nash, *Urban Crucible*, 76–80, 133. Nash has described this "enlarged mercantile world" as one "where economic decisions were made not with reference to local and public needs but according to laws of supply and demand that operated internationally. This wider market was indifferent to individuals and local communities; the flow and price of commodities, as well as labor and land, were dictated by invisible laws of the international marketplace" (p. 78).

28. Benjamin Colman, *The Merchandise of a people holiness to the Lord. A sermon, preached in part at the publick lecture in Boston, July 1, 1725. In part at a private meeting for charity to the poor, March 6. 1726. And now published as a thank-offering to God for repeated surprising bounties from London for uses of piety and charity* (Boston: J. Draper, 1736). Colman also assumed that Boston's economy, while connected by trade to domestic and foreign markets, operated somewhat autonomously.

29. Nash, *Urban Crucible*, 102–28; table 2, pp. 392–94. Colman's *Merchandise of a people,* preached in two parts during 1725 and 1726, was not published until 1736.

30. Nash, *Urban Crucible*, 165, 168–69.

31. Colman, *Merchandise of a people*, ii, 11, i, 24n3, vi, v, 33.

32. See J. Richard Olivas, "Partial Revival: The Limits of the Great Awakening in Boston, Massachusetts, 1740–1742," in *Inequality in Early America*, ed. Carla Gardina Pestana and Sharon V. Salinger (Hanover, N.H.: University Press of New England, 1999), 67–86.

33. Benjamin Colman, *The great God has magnified his word to the children of men. A sermon preach'd at the lecture in Boston, April 29. 1742* (Boston: T. Fleet for D. Henchman, 1742), 14.

34. Chauncy, *Idle-Poor secluded*. He preached the sermon August 12, 1752, using 2 Thessalonians 3:10 as his sermon text. The full passage reads: "For even when we were with you, this we commanded, that if any would not work, neither should he eat. For we hear that there are some which walk among you disorderly, working not at all, but are busybodies. Now them that are such we command and exhort by our Lord Jesus Christ, that with quietness they work, and eat their own bread. But ye, brethren, be not weary in well doing. And if any man obey not our word by this epistle, note that man, and have no company with him, that he may be ashamed. Yet count him not as an enemy, but admonish him as a brother" (2 Thessalonians 3:10–15).

35. Chauncy, *Idle-Poor secluded*, 7, 8, 9, 10, 12. As late as 1754, two hundred persons are named as "Gentlemen who continue to promote by their Subscriptions, the Society for encouraging Industry, and employing the Poor." See Society for Encouraging Industry and Employing the Poor, *Whereas it is found by experience that this province is not adapted for raising sheep . . . and inasmuch as considerable sums are yearly exported to purchase linens . . . which this province is very capable to produce and manufacture . . . a number of gentlemen have formed themselves into a voluntary society . . . The Society for Encouraging Industry and Employing the Poor* (Boston, 1754), 7–12.

36. Olivas, "Great Awakenings," 473. Between 1733 and 1767, John Hill was the only member of First Church who also served as an overseer of the poor in Boston. Hill served as an overseer from 1733 to 1756. Approximately twenty-five members from Third, Fourth, and Fifth churches served as overseers during the same period. I reviewed terms of service in Boston (Mass.), Registry Dept., *Report of the record commissioners of the city of Boston*, 28 vols. (Boston: Rockwell and Churchill, 1876–98), vols. 7, 8, and 12; and in Robert F. Seybolt, *The Town Officials of Colonial Boston, 1634–1775* (Cambridge: Harvard University Press, 1939).

37. Chauncy, *Idle-Poor secluded*, 11.

38. Samuel Cooper, *A Sermon preached in Boston, New England, before the Society for Encouraging Industry, and Employing the Poor* (Boston: J. Draper for D. Henchman, 1753), 12–13. In addition to securing the printing of this sermon, Daniel Henchman also belonged to the society and served as a deacon in Boston's Third Church and as an overseer of the poor between 1735 and 1755.

39. Gary B. Nash, "The Failure of Female Factory Labor in Colonial Boston," in *The Labor History Reader,* ed. Daniel J. Leab (Urbana: University of Illinois Press, 1985), 42–65.

40. Nash, "Failure of Female Factory Labor," 7–8, 45, 64.

41. Ibid., 63. Nash concludes the female factory labor scheme failed because "lower-class women stubbornly resisted the new ideology and institutions of poor relief."

42. Chauncy, *Idle-Poor secluded*, 22.

43. Charles Chauncy, *Enthusiasm described and caution'd against: A sermon preach'd at the Old Brick meeting-house in Boston, the Lord's Day after the commencement, 1742. With a letter to the Reverend Mr. James Davenport* (Boston: J. Draper, 1742), 15. Acts 2:44–45 reads: "And all that believed were together, and had all things common. And sold their possessions and goods, and parted them to all men, as every man had need." And idem, *Christian love, as exemplified by the first Christian church in their having all things in common, placed in its true and just point of light* (Boston: Kneeland and Davis for Thomas Leverett, 1773), 19–27. The sermon was delivered August 3, 1773. And Andrew Croswell, *Part of an exposition of Paul's journey to Damascus, Acts XXVI: In which the author having cautioned against shedding blood, shews that giving more than the forty stripes allowed Deuteronomy XXV. ver. 3. is breaking a moral law of God* (Boston: Kneeland and Adams), 1768.

44. Samuel Fish, *The Rights of the poor defended* (Norwich, Conn.: Trumbull, 1752), 8–9.

## *Eleven*

# The Delaware Indians and Poverty in Colonial New Jersey

JEAN R. SODERLUND

On January 22, 1777, in the aftermath of the battles of Trenton and Princeton, Quaker ministers John Hunt and Joshua Evans visited the Delaware Indians at the Brotherton reservation at Edgepelick, Burlington County, New Jersey, during very cold weather. "We found them in very low circumstances as to food and raiment," Hunt wrote. "Joshua took them a considerable parcel of old clothes, with which the poor naked children seemed exceedingly pleased." Evans also provided blankets and bought corn with money he obtained from the Indians. Hunt noted that "these poor creatures are too apt to lay out their money for strong drink." Nevertheless, he admitted that he discovered in the Brotherton visit "an instructive lesson. . . . Tho' they were poor, there seemed to be innocency, unity, quietude and peace amongst them, even at a time when it was so much otherwise with the white people." The faces of the elderly Delaware women "bespoke gravity, humility, innocence and tranquillity." A younger Indian woman, whose husband was "gone," had a three-week-old child: she was healthy and cheerful though her cabin was "very open, . . . with no bed but a little straw and a few blankets" and only a bushel of Indian corn. Their children were all very healthy.[1]

When Hunt and Evans visited Brotherton the following year, they found the Indians again "in a very poor, suffering condition as to food and raiment; but as to quietness and peace, they seemed much happier than many of the white people who were rich and abounded with plenty, yet were disquieted and afflicted in mind, because of the great destruction there was in the land." The Quaker ministers delivered "some blankets and old clothes . . . and the poor almost naked creatures seemed to receive them with abundance of thankfulness."[2] The Friends continued their visits to the Jersey Indians in subsequent years. As late as December 1795, Joshua Evans reported "paying a kind attention to the Situation of the Native Indians who dwell near us, by visiting them, and inspecting as well as helping their necessities, as winter is approaching, and we much indebted to them, as such who possess the Land which was theirs, and obtained from them at a cheap rate."[3]

No record exists of what the Delawares thought of these two Quaker men who visited the reservation once a year, in winter, bringing blankets and old clothes. Hunt mentioned that the children "seemed exceedingly pleased" with the clothing, but was silent on the women's reaction to the hand-me-downs and blankets. Hunt seemed faintly to recognize the inconsistency of his judgment that the Indians were poor because he noted that coincidentally they were healthy, exhibited good spirits, and could pay for the corn. Historian Daniel K. Richter found a similar disjuncture among Baltimore Quakers who in 1804 visited the Miamis near Fort Wayne and reported "that Many of the red people suffer much for the want of food and for the want of Clothing" despite significant evidence to the contrary.[4]

Scholars have used Hunt's and Evans's descriptions of Brotherton to chronicle the effective end of Indian existence in New Jersey, to suggest that the reservation's economic failure led to the Delawares' decision to sell their land and, in 1802, move to New Stockbridge, New York.[5] Hunt's and Evans's words matched the pattern of decline and extinction historians have assumed occurred in New Jersey as elsewhere "behind the frontier." Pushed off their land by sale, fraud, or indebtedness, the native people supposedly sank into despair, poverty, and drunkenness. "Praying towns" in Massachusetts and reservations in New Jersey and other colonies, according to these arguments, foreshadowed the disastrous policies of the United States government toward Native Americans in the nineteenth and twentieth centuries.[6]

In focusing on the Indians' poverty, Hunt and Evans sounded themes repeated by many other Euro-Americans before and after their time. In early New England, according to historian William Cronon, the original English settlers were surprised by the material simplicity of the natives' lifestyles, by their willingness to forgo riches in a land of plenty. In the words of settler Thomas Morton, the Indians lived "like to our Beggers in England."[7] Worse, to Europeans who believed civilization required fixed residence and private property, the native people moved around "to obtain their food wherever it was seasonably most concentrated in the New England ecosystem . . . their communities characteristically refused to stay put." To facilitate movement, the Indians built flexible housing and collected few possessions. They worked hard enough for subsistence and no more, and as a result sometimes they went hungry during the winter.[8] Karen Ordahl Kupperman has more recently demonstrated that English attitudes toward Native Americans were more complex in the early seventeenth century than other historians have suggested. Early writers, particularly some who visited North America, exhibited "mental dividedness," both "castigating the Americans as primitive savages" and praising their "vigor, simplicity, and primary virtue, contrasting that virtue with the luxurious degeneracy of England." Nevertheless, the negative view dominated the New England colonists' thinking.[9] Puritan missionaries, led by John Eliot, aimed to Christianize and "civilize" the Algonquians of eastern Massachusetts, settling them in "praying towns." As white settlement became dense and the Indians lost access to coastal shellfish beds and their hunting grounds, they adopted a more sedentary lifestyle in towns like Natick.[10] The Puritans spread their model to western Massachusetts, New York, and New Jersey during the eighteenth century; it became the basis of the new nation's Indian policy after the American Revolution. Focusing on traditional occupations of native men—rather than women who farmed—Anglo-Americans characterized Indians as "wandering hunters who refused to subdue and develop their land." Their substandard way of life, the whites thought, was morally deficient, leading to poverty, alcohol, and decline.[11]

In this essay I argue that the process by which New Jersey Indians came to be considered "poor" was complex, rooted in the choices native people made about their identity and economic pursuits, the perceptions of different groups of Euro-American settlers, and the quickening pace of economic development in the Delaware Valley after 1740. In central and southern New Jersey before the mid-eighteenth century, relations between the Lenape (called Delawares by Euro-Americans), the provincial government, and major religious groups were much different than between Indians and settlers in New England. Whereas native people such as the Natick of Massachusetts had become subject to the provincial government during the seventeenth century, the New Jersey Indians retained significant autonomy through the mid-eighteenth century. Despite frequent interaction and intermarriage in New Jersey, many of the Lenape kept their Indian identity and considered themselves separate from the Europeans. Except in cases of murder and debt, the Delawares were exempt from the settlers' government and law. Although living among European settlements, they continued to practice traditional ways of life. The Jersey Delawares situated their towns along streams that gave access to the Delaware River, the huge New Jersey Pine Barrens, and the Atlantic coast. They pursued a seasonal economy by hunting at the Forks of the Delaware (the Lehigh Valley) in Pennsylvania, gathering wood and cranberries in the Pine Barrens, and catching fish and shellfish along the coast. The Lenape required relatively little arable land, seeking their livelihood primarily by hunting, fishing, and collecting wood for baskets, brooms, and other articles they sold to settlers. Euro-Americans had little interest in the lands the Indians exploited—the sandy infertile New Jersey pinelands and, until the 1730s, the Pennsylvania northeastern frontier.

Before 1745, New Jersey settlers, unlike colonists in New England, apparently did not view the Indians as poor, nor did European settlement in central and southern New Jersey destroy the natives' traditional economy. The major churches of the region before the 1740s—Swedish Lutheran, Quaker, and Anglican—had little or no interest in converting the Lenape. Indians who married whites sometimes became part of the Euro-American community, including its religious congregations, but before the advent of the Moravian and Presbyterian missionaries, ministers took little notice of the native people. None of the Friends' monthly meetings mentioned Indians or offered them poor relief, nor did traveling Quaker ministers record visits to Lenape towns within the province. The Delawares sought no poverty relief from the local townships, nor did the colonists try to change their lives. The Indians, they thought, would take care of their own.

Relations among the Jersey Delawares and whites changed significantly after 1740 as commercial expansion led Euro-Americans to crave Indian lands in central New Jersey and northeastern Pennsylvania. Increasing demand for wheat and flour in Europe as a result of population growth, nascent industrialization, and poor harvests spurred the Mid-Atlantic region's already prosperous trade. In Pennsylvania and New Jersey, population soared with European immigration, stimulating demand for land. The Pennsylvania proprietors masterminded the eviction of Delawares from upper Bucks and Northampton counties with the Walking Purchase of 1737. In New Jersey, proprietary factions initiated suits to void land claims of both the Indians and settlers who had earlier purchased land from the Lenape rather than from the East Jersey Proprietors.[12]

The arrival of Connecticut missionary David Brainerd at Crossweeksung, the small Jersey Delaware town adjacent to the Quaker village of Crosswicks in northern Burlington County, coincided with this economic boom and land conflict and served as catalyst in changing relations between the Indians and the New Jersey government. Brainerd, concerned about the Delawares' indebtedness and "roving," tried to collect them into a mission he called Bethel, at Cranbury, modeled on the New England "praying towns." When he died and his brother John Brainerd took his place—and Robert Hunter Morris challenged the Indians' right to the Cranbury lands in court—the New Jersey assembly established the Brotherton reservation in southern Burlington County. In return, the Indians of central and southern Jersey ceded most of their extensive land claims south of the Raritan River.[13] Despite the Brainerds' best efforts, though, at Bethel and the reservation, the Delawares continued to "roam." They planted some corn but still collected wood for brooms and other articles they sold to whites, hunted in Pennsylvania, and fished along the coast. Living adjacent to the Pine Barrens, the huge wilderness "behind the frontier," the Indians at Brotherton and other places followed the economic pursuits that earlier Jersey residents—Quakers, Swedes, and Finns—had not questioned. But in post-1745 New Jersey, the Indians became "poor," even to Quakers such as Hunt and Evans, because of the influence of New Englanders like the Brainerds, the surrender of most Delaware land, and the increasing commercialization of colonial society.

When Dutch and English traders came to the Delaware Valley early in the seventeenth century, about forty Lenape villages were located along streams in what is now northern Delaware, eastern Pennsylvania, New Jersey, and southern New York. The villages had no unifying hierarchical political organization, but they allied with one another against common enemies. The Lenape of New Jersey divided geographically and linguistically into two groups: the Munsee-speaking people who lived north of the Delaware Water Gap and Raritan Valley, and the Unamis who lived to the south.[14]

The first Europeans to build farms along the Delaware were the Swedes and Finns of the short-lived colony of New Sweden. Although dealings between the colonial officials and Indians were sometimes difficult, relations among the settlers and Lenape were generally good. In West Jersey, peaceful coexistence resulted in part from common interests and customs among the Indians and Europeans and in part from the small size of the Swedish population.[15] According to a ninety-one-year-old Swede, Nils Gustafson, who spoke with Peter Kalm in the late 1740s, "the Indians were everywhere in the country" during his youth. "They lived among the Swedes." He knew of cases in which some Indians "stole children from the Swedes" and killed or scalped several adults. But, he said, "nobody could ever find out to what nation these savages belonged; for in general [the native people] lived very peaceably with the Swedes." The Lenape prized the turnips and livestock the Europeans brought to America, and the latter learned from the Lenape how to grow tobacco and Indian corn.[16] Similarities in the cultures of the Swedes, Finns, and Lenape helped them appreciate and learn from one another. The Finns in particular, like the Lenape, employed slash and burn agriculture and took steambaths in specially built huts (saunas). The Scandinavians, like the Delawares, came from a wooded environment in which they supported themselves economically by hunting, fishing, and agriculture. They used nets and spears in fishing, and crossbows and spears in the chase.[17]

Limited population growth before 1675 fostered continuing friendly relations among the Swedes and Finns and the Lenape, while at the same time warfare gripped the quickly expanding English colonies in New England and Virginia. Many Swedes and Finns, according to Thomas Paschall, who came with the Penn migration in the early 1680s, could speak "the Indian" (a simplified version of the Unami language) as well as English, Swedish, Finnish, and Dutch.[18] Evidence also exists of intermarriage (or less formal sexual relations) between the two groups. The earliest residents of New Sweden were all male, soldiers who surely sought sexual companionship from neighboring Lenape women. In the face of smallpox epidemics that decimated the Indian population throughout the seventeenth century, integration of Europeans into Delaware communities seems likely.[19] Settlers who arrived in the Delaware Valley after 1680 thought that Indians had intermarried with Swedes and Finns. "The savages and our Swedes are like one people," an observer noted, while another reported that "the Swedes themselves are accused, that they were already half Indians, when the English arrived in the year 1682." The Lenape called the Swedes and Finns "friend," "fellow tribesmen," or "those who are like us," while reserving the word *senaares* for other Europeans, whom they considered "alien." According to Terry G. Jordan and Matti Kaups, "certain southwestern New Jersey families still claim descent from a mixing of Swedes and Delaware Indians." The Swedish Moravian minister Abraham Reincke noted in 1745 that "we went to old John Hopmann's, who looks like an Indian" when visiting Swedes near the Maurice River in Salem County, New Jersey.[20]

When large numbers of English settlers arrived during the 1670s and 1680s, many with William Penn, the Delaware Valley landscape altered significantly. In West Jersey, the Unami sold their territory along the east bank of the Delaware to the Quakers and helped them adjust to the land. Mary Murfin Smith, who immigrated as a child in 1678, later recounted "that the Indians, very numerous but very civil, for the most part brought corn and venison and sold [them to] the English for such things as they needed." Soon after, many of the natives died of smallpox; in Mary Smith's account, "God's providence made room for us in a wonderful manner in taking away the Indians. There came a distemper among them so mortal that they could not bury all the dead. Others went away, leaving their town."[21]

The Lenape may have fled Smith's immediate neighborhood, but they did not leave West New Jersey or even Burlington County. Despite swelling English immigration, Quakers and Indians found ways to coexist. Though relatively few in number, references to Lenape in early Burlington court cases provide telling evidence of frequent interaction—settlers tried for selling rum to the Indians, a Lenape man finding a dead infant near a white family's house, a borrowed canoe, and disputes over trade.[22] Scattered evidence exists of continuing intermarriage among Indians and whites. In 1683, Richard Haines and his four brothers emigrated from Northampton, England, to settle in Evesham, Burlington County. He wed Mary Carlisle, an Indian, sometime before 1700. Three of their children, who numbered at least nine, married into the Matlack family, also English Quakers. William Aston, a poor weaver of Shrewsbury, Monmouth County, who described himself in his 1705 will as "antient and crasey," had a daughter Mary living near Crosswicks Creek, "maryed unto an Indian, who Calleth his name Peter Powell, as I am Informed." The parents of Elizabeth Morrey, wife of the African-American leader Cyrus Bustill, were an Englishman Richard Morrey and a Delaware woman, Satterthwait.[23]

Indians and Quakers also enjoyed cordial, if not so intimate, relationships, as they worked together and visited each other's homes. At Little Egg Harbor on the Atlantic coast, Native Americans welcomed Henry Jacobs Falkinburg, a Quaker and interpreter, as the first white settler in the area. The Indians sold land to Falkinburg, helped him pursue a livelihood as hunter, fisherman, and oysterman, and attended his wedding to an unnamed woman from Raccoon (now Swedesboro). Some years later, the Lenape leader Bathsheba Mullis stayed with white inhabitants at Little Egg Harbor rather than camp with the other Indians. According to tradition, a Quaker family near Crosswicks, who lived adjacent to the Indian trail known as the "Burlington Path," left their kitchen door open so that traveling Delawares could obtain shelter. The Presbyterian missionary David Brainerd, in the mid-1740s, noted that some Indians who lived with Quakers near Crossweeksung had accepted the Friends' doctrine of the inner light. He also complained that many Delawares reveled on Christmas with neighboring whites (though probably not Quakers). Such stories suggest that amicable relations between the Lenape and colonists continued from first settlement by the Swedes and Finns through English Quaker expansion in the early- and mid-eighteenth century.[24]

Despite advancing settlement and the treachery of some whites, the Delawares retained towns at Crossweeksung, Weekpink (also called Coaxen), and other places in West Jersey. In 1717, when an English settler John Wetherill attempted to defraud Mehemickwon (called King Charles by the English) of Weekpink lands, Quaker John Wills accompanied the Indians to obtain justice from Governor Robert Hunter. Wills knew the Unami language and had witnessed early land sales. Mehemickwon told the governor how "fraudulently and unjustly John Wetherill had obtained his hand to Deed for a parcel of land out of ye Tract he had reserved for the Indians to live upon out of

which he never Intended to Sell any having Sold all the rest to the English."
The Indian king rejected the notion that they should move away, questioning, "if [the land] be taken from us where must ye Indians go?" He argued
that they had lived among the English "since they came into the Country and
that they had lived lovingly and like Brothers together And that a little Land
would Serve the Indians And that there was Enough in the Country for
both."[25]

The Quakers respected Lenape rights to hunt, gather wood and cranberries in the Pine Barrens, and travel along Jersey streams, informal rules of
coexistence that the Indians had worked out with the Swedes and Finns
before the English arrived. Although the Lenape steadily lost land through
sale, debt, or trickery—and as a result some crossed the Delaware River in the
early eighteenth century to take up lands in northern Bucks County and the
Lehigh Valley—others found it possible to pursue traditional ways of life in
New Jersey, adjacent to Euro-American settlements and in the pinelands.
Most West Jersey Quaker settlers, their neighbors of other religions, and the
Lenape adhered to the principles that William Penn's deputies and the
Delaware sachems inscribed in a 1682 pact, but Europeans and Indians had
agreed upon much earlier. In the words of Penn's deputy, William Markham,
the Lenape and Quakers agreed "that wee may Freely pass Through any of
Their Lands as well that which is not purchased as that which is with out
molestio[n] as They doe quietly amongst us."[26] With minimal Lenape requirements for agricultural lands, access to the resources of the Pine Barrens and
shore, and respect for Indian land ownership and free passage across settlers'
lands, Jersey Delawares retained their identity and traditional economy.
Apparently no one thought their "roving" subsistence was a problem, that
their decision to live materially simple lives represented a poverty of moral
character or lifestyle. In fact, most early European settlers also lived materially simple lives, thereby minimizing cultural comparisons.

During the period before 1745, the Delawares chose from several strategies
of survival. Some, as discussed earlier, merged through cross-cultural unions
with Europeans and became part of Euro-American society. They acquired land
in fee simple and were accountable to English law. Adopting European names,
they became indistinguishable from whites to historians, and census takers identified them as white. Another group of Indians—some Delawares and some
imported into New Jersey as slaves early in the eighteenth century (probably
from South Carolina)—combined with whites and enslaved or free Africans to
become part of free black communities in northern cities or triracial groups in
the Jersey pines after the Revolution. Runaway advertisements for colonial New
Jersey reveal some mixing among African-American and Native American slaves.

The prominent Bustill family of Philadelphia descended from Cyrus Bustill, an emancipated slave from West Jersey, and his wife Elizabeth Morrey, who was part Delaware and part English.[27] Of those who retained their Indian identity, many settled across the Delaware River on Lenape territory in upper Bucks and Northampton counties, until the Walking Purchase of 1737 pushed them west to the Susquehanna and Ohio valleys.[28]

The fourth group, the Jersey Delawares, who did not move west but continued to consider themselves Indians, lived in small towns such as Crossweeksung and Weekpink in Burlington County, and several places farther south. Although some were descendants of Swedish, Finnish, or English settlers as well as Lenape, they held lands by Indian rights and retained many Delaware traditions.[29] Despite the proximity of Delaware and white settlements—and commingling of the two groups—they considered themselves, for the most part, politically and legally distinct. New Jersey courts are known to have tried several native people for murder, but none for other crimes.[30] And, more pertinent here, the settlers' local township and county governments did not include the Indian towns within their purview or extend poor relief to their residents.[31]

Indeed, before 1745, neither the Lenape themselves nor Euro-American commentators considered the Jersey Indians poor. They held extensive lands and pursued a traditional way of life. They purchased manufactured goods and rum from the Euro-Americans but maintained communal ownership of land. Because Indians shared food and other resources, everyone enjoyed abundance or suffered privation. One of William Penn's promotional letters described how the Lenape "kings" shared gifts equally among their people, remarking that the Indians "care for little, because they want but little; and the Reason is; a little contents them. . . . [T]hey are not disquieted with Bills of Lading and Exchange, nor perplexed with Chancery-Suits and Exchequer-Reckonings. We sweat and toil to live; their pleasure feeds them, I mean, their Hunting, Fishing and Fowling."[32] While Penn ignored the agricultural labor and artisanry of Indian women and men, his appreciation for their simplicity—a Quaker ideal, though not one he adhered to—was apparent.

In colonial New Jersey, white settlers provided poor relief through churches and the township governments. In northern Burlington County, Quakers distributed aid through the men's and women's meetings of Chesterfield Monthly Meeting and the township governments they dominated. None of the impoverished people to whom these agencies gave assistance were identified as Indians. The Chesterfield men's meeting took primary responsibility for helping distressed newcomers during the first years of Quaker settlement.

In 1685, for example, the meeting appointed Friends to look after the child of John Brown, who had died recently, and in 1686 checked on the circumstances of Robert Scholey, whose corn and hay had gone up in flames. They provided Andrew Smith with a coat and built a house and provided food for William Satterthwaite, who had lost his sight. After 1696, the meeting reported giving little aid, probably because the townships assumed that role and relatively few Friends in this rural area experienced need. The Chesterfield women's meeting seemed eager enough to provide relief in the period from 1707 to 1721, but most of the women to whom they offered help refused it.[33]

The Burlington County township governments for which minutes exist—Chesterfield, Nottingham, Northampton, and New Hanover—collected taxes for two main purposes: building and maintaining roads and bridges, and providing for the poor. The records make only brief mention of the Lenape—as creditors, not as recipients of aid. The township clerks failed to name every person who received assistance but did sometimes record the amount of taxes to be raised for the poor. As in many colonial areas, the level of funding remained relatively low until mid-century, when demands increased substantially. For example, Northampton Township (which included Bridgetown, later called Mount Holly) raised £20 (New Jersey currency) for the poor in 1741, £50 in 1754, £150 in 1762, and £180 in 1764. In 1762, Northampton empowered several residents to "treat" with neighboring townships "Concerning erecting a House for the Poor of said Towns." They apparently failed to reach agreement with Evesham, Chester, and Springfield because two years later the Northampton leaders resolved to "Rent a House and collect the Poor together therein and provide a Suitable Person to take care of them as they in their Discretion Shall think necessary." In 1773, Chesterfield Township also explored building "a Bettering house" in cooperation with adjacent towns.[34]

The townships provided aid to elderly infirm widows, women with young children, and disabled men. Because the towns did not list every recipient, it is impossible to determine the proportion of aid devoted to each of these groups. Most commonly, the townships paid a male resident "to Board wash Lodge and mend" for a needy person, as in the case of Nottingham's Joseph Daviss, "a Poor man." Obviously, women in the household provided most of these services for the poor. The same township paid to build a house for Jane Quicksall, while Northampton took responsibility for Samuel Reeve, "a Lunatick Pauper," and gave "a small pension" to Edward Fletcher, "he being an Object of pity and has not as yet thrown himself entirely on the Township." Chesterfield Township paid expenses when Mary Pen gave birth to a child out of wedlock and provided medical help to a number of poor men.[35] Although most township leaders of Burlington County knew each other through the Quaker meetings, they readily disputed responsibility for paupers. Townships sued each other in the provincial supreme court if they believed a poor person presently living in their jurisdiction was a legal resident elsewhere. Such cases became more prevalent after 1750, with the general increase in poor relief. From 1760 to 1762, for example, Nottingham and Chesterfield townships contested responsibility for English immigrant Samuel Barwell, "a poor man" who had succumbed to illness and other misfortunes around 1740. The court had difficulty finding evidence that he had established residency anywhere since his servitude in Chesterfield but ultimately directed Nottingham to pay his support.[36]

As in other parts of colonial British America, growing poverty accompanied increased consumerism and the boom in Atlantic trade. Historian T. H. Breen has documented the "exploding demand" for British manufactures, "rising 120 percent between 1750 and 1773. Throughout the colonies the crude, somewhat impoverished material culture of the seventeenth century—a pioneer world of homespun cloth and wooden dishes—was swept away by a flood of store-bought sundries."[37] In northern Burlington County, New Jersey, the area surrounding Crossweeksung, increasing probate estate values indicate that the wealth of white inhabitants grew substantially after 1740. West Jersey benefited from expanding markets for mid-Atlantic wheat and flour and participated fully in the demand for manufactured goods.[38]

Although native people lived at Crossweeksung (within the bounds of Nottingham Township) and Weekpink (in Northampton Township), no one identified as a Lenape participated in either township's governance or received poor relief. Early on, the clerks of Nottingham and Chesterfield mentioned native people, then all references dropped. The Nottingham clerk noted in January 1696 that the township would reimburse "the charges of our Neighbours of Chesterfield Towne touching on accommodation made with the Indians and for the better continuance of amity and Concord etc.," then in 1700 paid William Emley fifty-six shillings "by him formerly laid downe in moneys and goods for clearing off the Indians." Whether "clearing off" meant settling a debt (the clerk uses the phrase with that meaning in another case) or represented a land deal is unknown. The single reference in Chesterfield's town minutes to their Indian neighbors provides an example of the mundane nature of interaction with the Lenape, in this case paying them bounties for killing wolves. In 1694, the Chesterfield town meeting reimbursed Frances Davenport £1 and 18 shillings "for money hee has allreddy Layd out of his [own] for wolves to the Indeians."[39]

Local townships, the Burlington County court, and Friends meetings, at least officially, ignored the native people of Crossweeksung and Weekpink after the first thirty years of English settlement. The Jersey Indians who identified themselves by traditional landholding and way of life—who seasonally farmed small plots of land, hunted, gathered, and fished—remained formally separate from Euro-American communities, though individuals interacted on a regular basis through trade and neighborly encounter. The more sinister development during the period before 1745 was impingement by white settlers on native lands. Although deeds exist for many land sales by Indians to settlers, particularly for the period before 1720, by the mid-eighteenth century title of much New Jersey territory was hopelessly confused, contributing to the land riots by settlers in several parts of the province. In many places, the Lenape lost lands to squatters and speculators over the first half of the century, and by 1758, when Delaware representatives compiled a list of their lands for the New Jersey Indian commissioners, many whites lived on property the natives claimed, but could not prove, they had never sold.[40]

Despite their increasing marginalization in New Jersey, as some Delawares moved west and others merged with the white population, as late as 1745 the Jersey Indians had not become "poor," in their own estimation or that of local whites. With sufficient land for agriculture and continued access to fishing, gathering, and hunting grounds, they pursued customary ways of life. The silence of Quaker antislavery advocate John Woolman about the Delawares who lived in his vicinity suggests both the quotidian nature of Indian-white contact in colonial New Jersey and the respect settlers had for the right of the native people to determine their own lives. Throughout his life, Woolman lived in Northampton Township, downstream from Weekpink on Rancocas Creek. He never mentioned the local Indians in his journal or essays, despite his conscientious witness against injustice, particularly slavery, and his concern for the poor. Indeed, he failed to recognize the oppression of Native Americans through expropriation of land and decline in population until he visited Indian settlements on the northern branch of the Susquehanna River in 1763, during the conflict called Pontiac's War.[41] Woolman may have ignored the Jersey Delawares in part from a certain callousness toward people whose problems were familiar. In his first essay against slavery, published in 1754, he described the English domination of the Delaware Valley as a measure of God's benevolence, now imperiled if slavekeepers persisted in sin. "The wilderness and solitary deserts in which our fathers passed the days of their pilgrimage," he wrote, "are now turned into pleasant fields. The natives are gone from before us, and we establish peaceably in the possession of the land, enjoying our civil and religious liberties." He continued in a passage soon proved wrong by the outbreak of war on the Pennsylvania and New Jersey frontiers, that "while many parts of the world have groaned under the heavy calamities of war, our habitation remains quiet and our land fuitful."[42]

It seems more in keeping, however, with Woolman's deepening sensitivity toward injustice that he simply did not consider the people of Weekpink and Crossweeksung as oppressed. They lived in their own towns and enjoyed freedom to come and go as they pleased, whereas enslaved blacks, the focus of his concern, had little control over their lives—in work, place of residence, or creating families. Apparently Friends and their neighbors had little inclination to convert the Lenape or interrupt what Presbyterian missionary David Brainerd called their "roving" style of life, before Brainerd himself arrived in 1745.

The nature and vocabulary of white-Indian relations changed in central New Jersey with the appearance at Crossweeksung of Reverend David Brainerd, who was sponsored by the Society in Scotland for Propagating Christian Knowledge (SSPCK). A young, moderate New Light Presbyterian, he had been expelled from Yale College in 1742 for criticizing the tutor Chauncey Whittelsey for having "no more grace than a chair."[43] Brainerd ministered initially to Mahican Indians at Kaunaumeek, New York, then moved to the Forks of the Delaware, where he attempted to convert the Delawares, many of them originally from New Jersey. When Brainerd received little response among the Forks Indians, he transferred his mission across the Delaware River and south to Crossweeksung. There he met several Indian women who spread word to the native people at scattered settlements within thirty miles of the town of his desire to proselytize among them. Over the next several months, scores of Delawares gathered to hear Brainerd's preaching, as interpreted and explained by Moses Tatamy, the missionary's recent Indian convert. As numbers grew, a religious revival swept Crossweeksung and many joined Brainerd's flock of converted Presbyterians.[44]

The minister labeled the Delawares "poor," both those who became, in his words, "my people," and those who resisted his message. His brother, Reverend John Brainerd, who took over the mission when David died of tuberculosis in 1747, used the same language.[45] What they meant is not entirely clear; they may have referred solely to their perception of the Indians' economic condition but more likely they meant a more general assessment of the Delawares' moral, spiritual, and economic worth. This assessment helped justify the missionaries' efforts to "save" them.

David Brainerd came to New Jersey as an outsider, to both the native people of Crossweeksung and white Burlington County society. He found the

Indians more hospitable than the Quakers who dominated the region. In stirring an awakening among the Delawares and attempting to missionize them, Brainerd upset the modus vivendi by which the Indians and settlers had coexisted. The Brainerds' efforts, along with increasing land scarcity and the Seven Years' War, resulted in the liquidation of traditional Indian land titles and establishment of the three-thousand-acre reservation called Brotherton. Although the Jersey Indians resisted changing their seasonal work patterns, the substitution of the Puritan model of Indian-white relations for the Scandinavian and Quaker model, and the surrender of lands held by Indian title, challenged the Delawares' political autonomy in New Jersey. Now measured by Euro-American standards within the context of the mid-eighteenth-century consumer revolution, they became "poor" even in the minds of benevolent Quakers like John Hunt and Joshua Evans.

As the number of Indians increased at Crossweeksung in the months after David Brainerd's arrival—he reported 130 to 150 persons there in early 1746—he decided the site was impractical for a mission town. He had received training in the New England model of evangelizing native people from Reverend John Sergeant, the missionary at Stockbridge, Massachusetts. Thus, Brainerd established a school at Crossweeksung to teach the Delaware children Christian doctrine and morals; preached to the Indians on "the duty of labouring with faithfulness and industry"; taught them how to plant and operate farms on the English model (with men rather than women in the fields); and expected them to live in a single town instead of scattered settlements, as they had dwelled in their "Pagan state."[46] Brainerd did not encourage the Delawares to stop hunting and in fact obtained money from the SSPCK when "their hunting lands, in great part, were much endangered" by sale for debt. He believed that the natives could not live together near him "in order to their being a Christian congregation" without ability to supplement their diet with the chase. Still, as Crossweeksung expanded, Brainerd convinced the people to move to lands they owned at Cranbury, about fifteen miles northeast of their present site. There they would settle closer together, attend public worship, and send their children to the mission school. Brainerd described the Cranbury location as "the best and most convenient tract of their own lands." They would have much better acreage for planting, the Crossweeksung site "being of little or no value to that purpose." The Delawares, in Brainerd's estimation, had engaged in limited farming before their conversion and were generally "slothful in business." Adoption of English agriculture was important "to their religious interest, as well as worldly comfort."[47] Their "present method of living," the missionary thought, "greatly exposes them to temptations of various kinds."[48]

In April 1746, as the people at Crossweeksung prepared to move to the Bethel mission near Cranbury, Brainerd reported "a terrible clamour raised against the Indians in various places in the country, and insinuations as though I was training them up to cut people's throats." According to a report received by the New Jersey Provincial Council, only two Delawares had lived near Cranbury for the previous six years, "but now some 40 Men moved to live there, with talk of hundreds more." White settlers near Cranbury "were extremely Alarmed, at this number of Indians coming to Settle there, where its Esteemed impossible for such a Number to Live, without Stealing or killing their Neighbours' creatures." The uproar died quickly, however, when the Indians and Brainerd moved to Cranbury in May and built the mission town. In early June, the converted Indians worshipped with Reverend William Tennent's white congregation in Freehold. Brainerd observed that some Indians took communion "with other christians," which was, "I trust, for the honour of God and the interest of religion in these parts; as numbers I have reason to think, were quickened by means of it." It was a "comfortable season" to his congregation.[49]

Despite David Brainerd's success in converting some Jersey Indians—he reported baptism of thirty-eight adults and thirty-nine children by June 1746—and their move to better land at Cranbury, he seems not to have altered their economic lives significantly. They continued "wandering to and fro in order to procure the necessaries of life." This subjected them to temptation, Brainerd thought, either "among Pagans further remote where they have gone to hunt . . . or, among white people, more horribly wicked, who have often made them drunk; then got their commodities—such as skins, baskets, brooms, shovels, and the like, with which they designed to have bought corn, and other necessaries of life, for themselves and families." He noted that the Indians who had joined him in the mission were sued more frequently since he arrived than in the seven previous years. He assumed this occurred because they stopped going to tippling houses where they drank up most of what they gained by hunting and other means, and the tavern keepers now called in past debts.[50]

The Presbyterian Indians stayed at Cranbury until 1758, continuing to hunt, gather, and fish while also planting corn and attending worship and school. When David Brainerd died in 1747, his brother John took over the mission. In 1752, he reported that almost forty families belonged to the community, but some had "grievously backslidden." John Brainerd blamed the Indians' love of strong drink, the wickedness of some white people who "have endeavored to asperse my character to the Indians," and the natives' "indo-lent, wandering, unsteady disposition, which greatly prevails among them. In this manner they have been educated, and it seems to be so riveted into their natures that it is almost as difficult to reform them upon this point as to change their color."[51] Bethel also came under legal attack as Robert Hunter Morris, chief justice of the New Jersey Supreme Court and an extensive land-holder, claimed the Cranbury lands. In 1749, he sued Indians Thomas Store, Andrew Wooley, Philip Douty, and Stephen Calvin for trespass when they attempted to clear trees. Despite Morris's prominence, his suit seems to have been dropped.[52]

Nevertheless, Morris's pressure, along with John Brainerd's initiative and the outbreak of war in the Ohio country in 1754, which spread through Pennsylvania to the northwestern New Jersey frontier, resulted in the cession of the Delawares' lands. To prevent the Jersey Indians from joining their kin on the frontiers and to bring an end to attacks in Sussex County by Munsees, who had moved west but still had claims in the northern part of the colony, the New Jersey government requested negotiations with both the Delawares south of the Raritan River and the Munsees. At the first Crosswicks confer-ence, in 1756, the government's representatives asked the Delawares for a list of lands they had never sold to whites. In 1758, the Indians submitted exten-sive claims, including territory on which Euro-Americans were living. Because the native people could prove title to few of these lands, they agreed to exchange most of their tracts south of the Raritan River for the three-thou-sand-acre reservation in central Burlington County. The Delawares retained the rights to hunt on uncultivated lands throughout the province and to fish in the rivers and bays, as well as title to lands they held in fee simple: the Weekpink site and several tracts held by Moses Tatamy and Thomas Store (the latter probably at Cranbury). In accepting Brotherton in exchange for their traditional lands, they potentially lost considerable autonomy, for they now would need permission from the New Jersey assembly to lease or sell reservation land, and the legislators could appoint a superintendent for the community. Nevertheless, the proximity of Brotherton to the pinelands and water passage to the sea allowed the Indians to pursue their seasonal rotation of hunting, fishing, small-scale agriculture, and gathering of cranberries and wood for baskets and brooms. Protecting claims to extensive agricultural acreage was less important to the Delawares than rights for hunting, fishing, and gathering. In return for remaining land claims north of the Raritan River, the provincial government paid the Munsees, who now lived in Penn-sylvania and New York, one thousand Spanish pieces of eight.[53]

According to John Brainerd, in 1761 "something upward of an hundred, old and young" Indians moved to Brotherton, while about forty still lived at Weekpink, another forty remained at Cranbury, and there were "yet some few scattering ones still about Crossweeksung." In all, about two hundred Delawares lived in central New Jersey out of a total of three to four hundred in the entire colony.[54] Just one-quarter to one-third of Indians in New Jersey settled at Brotherton. Some stayed on their traditional lands whether they retained rights under the 1758 deed, as at Weekpink and Cranbury, or had yielded those rights, as at Crossweeksung. Others joined the provincial forces to fight against the French and their native allies; about twenty men never returned, according to John Brainerd, to their families in New Jersey. And at least several prominent Jersey Indians, including interpreter Joseph Peepy, headed west to the Ohio Valley instead of Brotherton.[55]

The supposed decline of the Jersey Delawares into "poverty" resulted from the New Jersey government's adoption of the New England "praying town" model, the cession of traditional Indian land rights, and changing Euro-American perceptions with increasing commercialization. Affluent whites expected the Delawares to turn Brotherton into a thriving agricultural complex. But with access to the Pine Barrens and the sea, they kept their traditional ways. In the midst of rising consumerism among whites, the Jersey Delawares retained their Indian identity in part by resisting efforts to force them into the European economic mold. Like his deceased brother, Reverend John Brainerd encouraged the Brotherton Indians to plant corn and lectured them "upon Industry: Pointing out the great Evil of Idleness, and exhorting them to honest, diligent Industry as being friendly both to their temporal and Spiritual good."[56] He held worship services at Weekpink and at a settlement of Indians across the Delaware River at Pennsbury as well as at Brotherton, preaching in the Indian language. At Weekpink he officiated to "a mixt Congregation of Indians and white People."[57] Earlier, while still at Cranbury, he had purchased spinning wheels for the native women but could find no one to instruct them in their use. He thought that if the women could make their own clothing "which they have hitherto bought at a dear rate by brooming, basketry, and the like," they could stay home and send their children to school."[58]

Try as he might, John Brainerd failed to convince the people at Brotherton to become more sedentary. In August 1762, the missionary canceled his Sunday evening service because the "Indians have been much abroad of late, providing Fodder against Winter etc.," which probably included materials they foraged in the pinelands for baskets, brooms, and other home manufactures.[59] Further evidence that the Delawares continued gathering wood comes from scattered sources. In 1767, two Indian women, Hannah Hughes and Catherine, were murdered with their own axe when they refused to submit to rape by two white men (who were subsequently hanged for the crimes). James Still, the noted African-American doctor of the pines, reminisced that in the early nineteenth century, during his childhood in Indian Mills, Burlington County (where the Brotherton reservation had stood), scores of Indians could be seen "traveling through the wood, and the marks of whose axes were left on many a white oak, trying its quality for basket stuff." Still's closest neighbors were an Indian family.[60]

Brotherton's population declined after the early 1760s, and in 1771 its residents requested the provincial government's permission to lease some of their land to white farmers (which was denied). Three years later, only fifty to sixty residents remained there, while the population at Weekpink, Crossweeksung, and Cranbury was still one hundred.[61]

The Delaware women and children John Hunt and Joshua Evans visited at Brotherton in 1777 were poor by affluent Euro-American standards, yet, as the Quaker ministers reported, they were healthy and cheerful, with "innocency, unity, quietude and peace." Arriving in winter, Hunt and Evans—like Quaker committees in Philadelphia and elsewhere—provided aid to people they thought were living on marginal resources. They returned only in winter with blankets and used clothing, and they charged the Indians for corn. But the Delawares had money, presumably from selling their products in a market economy, and supported themselves and their families in ways they had pursued since before the Europeans arrived.[62] The New England experiment to missionize the "poor" Indians of central New Jersey failed; John Brainerd mourned his inability to convert more native people and left the reservation in 1768. Despite his efforts, even the Presbyterian Delawares refused to become proper farmers and spinsters in the European tradition. Women continued to move about the countryside gathering wood instead of staying home to spin and knit. Men hunted and fished. Proximity to the Pine Barrens, with plentiful fish, game, cranberries, lumber, and streams leading to the sea, but without the rich farmland white settlers prized, permitted Jersey Indians to follow their seasonal occupations for years to come.[63]

While increasing consumerism among prosperous Euro-Americans and their dispossession of most of the Indians' land led them to define the Delawares as poor, the Indians viewed their situation differently. They retained the legal right to hunt and fish throughout New Jersey and continued to use land that the whites considered marginal at Crossweeksung, Cranbury, Weekpink, the Pine Barrens, and Atlantic coast. The Jersey Delawares employed these lands as had their ancestors and thereby retained their Indian identity despite economic exchange and (by some) acceptance of Christianity and intermarriage with Europeans. They retained substantial political autonomy by refusing to stay on the reservation. If they had become "poor" by the standards of affluent Euro-Americans, they had remained Indians by their own.

# Notes

1. John Hunt's Journal, published in *Friends' Miscellany*, vol. 10: *Containing Journals of the Lives, Religious Exercises, and Labours in the Work of the Ministry of Joshua Evans and John Hunt, Late of New Jersey* (Philadelphia: J. Richards, 1837), 226–27.

2. Ibid., 228.

3. Ibid., 229–30; Joshua Evans, Journal, vol. 2, p. 144, Joshua Evans Papers, Friends Historical Library of Swarthmore College, Swarthmore, Pa.

4. Daniel K. Richter, "'Believing That Many of the Red People Suffer Much for the Want of Food': Hunting, Agriculture, and a Quaker Construction of Indianness in the Early Republic," *Journal of the Early Republic* 19 (1999): 601–2.

5. Edward McM. Larrabee, "Recurrent Themes and Sequences in North American Indian-European Culture Contact," *Transactions of the American Philosophical Society*, n.s., 66, pt. 7 (1976): 14–17; C. A. Weslager, *The Delaware Indians: A History* (New Brunswick, N.J.: Rutgers University Press, 1972), 271–78; Ives Goddard, "Delaware," in *Handbook of North American Indians*, vol. 15, Northeast, ed. Bruce G. Trigger (Washington, D.C.: Smithsonian Institution, 1978), 222. Other work on the Jersey Delawares includes Herbert C. Kraft, ed., *A Delaware Indian Symposium* (Harrisburg: Pennsylvania Historical and Museum Commission, 1974); Robert Steven Grumet, "'We Are Not So Great Fools': Changes in Upper Delawarean Socio-Political Life, 1630–1758" (Ph.D. diss., Rutgers University, 1979).

6. Recent studies reveal a complex and enduring history of native people behind the frontier in other British colonies; see, e.g., Jean M. O'Brien, *Dispossession by Degrees: Indian Land and Identity in Natick, Massachusetts, 1650–1790* (Cambridge: Cambridge University Press, 1997; Daniel R. Mandell, *Behind the Frontier: Indians in Eighteenth-Century Eastern Massachusetts* (Lincoln: University of Nebraska Press, 1996); James H. Merrell, "'The Customes of Our Countrey': Indians and Colonists in Early America," in *Strangers Within the Realm: Cultural Margins of the First British Empire*, ed. Bernard Bailyn and Philip D. Morgan (Chapel Hill: University of North Carolina Press, 1991), 117–56; Daniel H. Usner Jr., "American Indians in Colonial New Orleans," in *Powhatan's Mantle: Indians in the Colonial Southeast*, ed. Peter H. Wood et al. (Lincoln: University of Nebraska Press, 1989), 104–27; Usner, *American Indians in the Lower Mississippi Valley: Social and Economic Histories* (Lincoln: University of Nebraska Press, 1998); Helen C. Rountree and Thomas E. Davidson, *Eastern Shore Indians of Virginia and Maryland* (Charlottesville: University Press of Virginia, 1997); Donna Keith Baron et al., "They Were Here All Along: The Native American Presence in Lower Central New England in the Eighteenth and Nineteenth Centuries," *William and Mary Quarterly*, 3d ser., 53 (1996): 561–86; Ruth Wallis Herndon and Ella Wilcox Sekatau, "The Right to a Name: The Narragansett People and Rhode Island Officials in the Revolutionary Era," *Ethnohistory* 44 (1997): 433–62. Despite the recent plethora of distinguished scholarship on the Delawares who moved west to the Lehigh, Susquehanna, and Ohio valleys, the Lenape who remained in New Jersey have received relatively little attention from historians. On the Delawares of Pennsylvania and Ohio, see, e.g., Gregory Evans Dowd, *A Spirited Resistance: The North American Indian Struggle for Unity 1745–1815* (Baltimore: Johns Hopkins University Press, 1992); Richard White, *The Middle Ground: Indians, Empires, and Republics in the Great Lakes Region, 1650–1815* (Cambridge: Cambridge University Press, 1991); James H. Merrell, *Into the American Woods: Negotiators on the Pennsylvania Frontier* (New York: W. W. Norton, 1999); Jane T. Merritt,

"Dreaming of the Savior's Blood: Moravians and the Indian Great Awakening in Pennsylvania," *William and Mary Quarterly*, 3d ser., 54 (1997): 723–46; Francis Jennings, "'Pennsylvania Indians' and the Iroquois," and Michael N. McConnell, "Peoples 'In Between': The Iroquois and the Ohio Indians, 1720–1768," in *Beyond the Covenant Chain: The Iroquois and Their Neighbors in Indian North America, 1600–1800*, ed. Daniel K. Richter and James H. Merrell (Syracuse, N.Y.: Syracuse University Press, 1987); Daniel K. Richter, *Facing East from Indian Country: A Native History of Early America* (Cambridge: Harvard University Press, 2001).

7. Quoted in William Cronon, *Changes in the Land: Indians, Colonists, and the Ecology of New England* (New York: Hill and Wang, 1983), 33.

8. Ibid., 37–41 (quote on p. 37).

9. Karen Ordahl Kupperman, *Indians and English: Facing Off in Early America* (Ithaca: Cornell University Press, 2000), 19–20, 23, 27 (quote on p. 20).

10. Mandell, *Behind the Frontier*, 13–17.

11. Michael D. Green, "The Expansion of European Colonization to the Mississippi Valley, 1780–1880," in *The Cambridge History of the Native Peoples of the Americas*, ed. Bruce G. Trigger and Wilcomb E. Washburn, vol. 1, North America, pt. 1 (Cambridge: Cambridge University Press, 1996), 488; Dowd, *Spirited Resistance*, 134–36; Richter, "Believing," 601–28.

12. John J. McCusker and Russell R. Menard, *The Economy of British America, 1607–1789: With Supplementary Bibliography* (Chapel Hill: University of North Carolina Press, 1991), 194; Marianne Sophia Wokeck, *Trade in Strangers: The Beginnings of Mass Migration to North America* (University Park: The Pennsylvania State University Press, 1999); Francis Jennings, "'Pennsylvania Indians' and the Iroquois," in *Beyond the Covenant Chain*, ed. Richter and Merrell, 75–91; Brendan McConville, *These Daring Disturbers of the Public Peace: The Struggle for Property and Power in Early New Jersey* (Ithaca: Cornell University Press, 1999).

13. Samuel Smith, *The History of New-Jersey*, 2d ed. (Trenton: Wm. S. Sharp, 1877), 440–46; N.J. Secretary of State Deeds, book I-2, 85–88, New Jersey State Archives, Trenton; Larrabee, "Recurrent Themes," 7–10; Peter O. Wacker, *Land and People: A Cultural Geography of Preindustrial New Jersey: Origins and Settlement Patterns* (New Brunswick, N.J.: Rutgers University Press, 1975), 90–91; Thomas Store et al. to Israel Pemberton, March 8, 1758, Philadelphia Yearly Meeting Indian Committee records, AA1:427, Quaker Collection, Haverford College, Haverford, Pa.

14. Scholars disagree on this division, with some suggesting that the Unamis were further divided into northern and southern groups. Others minimize differences between even the Munsees and Unamis. By the mid-eighteenth century, colonial officials often distinguished between the Munsees and Unamis but generally referred to both groups as Delawares. Goddard, "Delaware," 213–16; Grumet, "We Are Not So Great Fools," 5–7; Jane T. Merritt, "Kinship, Community, and Practicing Culture: Indians and the Colonial Encounter in Pennsylvania, 1700–1763" (Ph.D. diss., University of Washington, 1995), 10–11; Smith, *History of New-Jersey*, 29; Weslager, *Delaware Indians*, 35–47; William W. Newcomb Jr., *The Culture and Acculturation of the Delaware Indians* (Ann Arbor: University of Michigan), 5–9.

15. Wacker, *Land and People*, 72–88; Weslager, *Delaware Indians*, 98–154; Smith, *History of New-Jersey*, 92–125; Frank J. Esposito, "The Lenape and the Swede: Indian and White Relations in the Delaware River Region, 1638–55," *New Jersey History* 112 (1994): 1–14.

16. Adolph B. Benson, ed., *Peter Kalm's Travels in North America* (New York: Wilson-Erickson, 1937), 1:268.

17. Lorraine E. Williams, "Indians and Europeans in the Delaware Valley, 1620–1655," in *New Sweden in America*, ed. Carol E. Hoffecker et al. (Newark: University of Delaware Press, 1995), 118–19; Terry G. Jordan and Matti Kaups, *The American Backwoods Frontier: An Ethnic and Ecological Interpretation* (Baltimore: Johns Hopkins University Press, 1989), 87–92; Goddard, "Delaware," 219; Paul A. W. Wallace, *Indians in Pennsylvania*, rev. ed. (Harrisburg: Pennsylvania Historical and Museum Commission, 1991), 30.

18. "Letter of Thomas Paschall, 1683," in Albert Cook Myers, ed., *Narratives of Early Pennsylvania West New Jersey and Delaware 1630–1707* (New York: Charles Scribner's Sons, 1912), 252;

Ives Goddard, "The Delaware Jargon," 137–49.

19. As in the case of the Iroquois (Daniel K. Richter, "War and Culture: The Iroquois Experience," *William and Mary Quarterly*, 3d ser., 40 [1983]: 528–59) and the Catawbas (James H. Merrell, "The Indians' New World: The Catawba Experience," *William and Mary Quarterly*, 3d ser., 41 [1984]: 537–65).

20. Jordan and Kaups, *American Backwoods*, 88–89, 92; "Reincke's Journal of a Visit Among the Swedes of West Jersey, 1745," *Pennsylvania Magazine of History and Biography* 33 (1909): 101.

21. Ewan M. Woodward and John F. Hageman, *History of Burlington and Mercer Counties, New Jersey* (Philadelphia: Everts and Peck, 1883), 9–11.

22. H. Clay Reed and George J. Miller, eds., *The Burlington Court Book: A Record of Quaker Jurisprudence in West New Jersey, 1680–1709* (Washington, D.C.: American Historical Association, 1944), 34, 47, 62, 125, 166, 218, 294.

23. Franklin W. Earl to Samuel Allinson, January 11, 1875, in Allinson Family Papers, box 8, "Indians," Quaker Collection, Haverford College; *New Jersey Archives* (hereafter *NJA*), 1st ser., 30:210; *NJA*, 1st ser., 23:17; Anna Bustill Smith, "A Communication," *Journal of Negro History* 10 (1925): 645.

24. Woodward and Hageman, *Burlington and Mercer Counties*, 333, 336; George DeCou, *Historical Sketches of Crosswicks and Neighborhood* (Burlington, N.J.: Burlington County Historical Society, 1956), 14; Jonathan Edwards, ed., *Memoirs of the Rev. David Brainerd; Missionary to the Indians on the Borders of New-York, New Jersey, and Pennsylvania*, rev. ed. Sereno Edwards Dwight (New Haven: Sherman Converse, 1822), 260, 262. See also Robert Daiutolo Jr., "The Early Quaker Perception of the Indian," *Quaker History* 72 (1983): 103–19.

25. *NJA*, 1st ser., 4:276–81.

26. Mary Maples Dunn and Richard S. Dunn et al., eds., *The Papers of William Penn*, 5 vols. (Philadelphia: University of Pennsylvania Press, 1981–1987), 2:264–65.

27. Billy G. Smith and Richard Wojtowicz, *Blacks Who Stole Themselves: Advertisements for Runaways in the Pennsylvania Gazette, 1728–1790* (Philadelphia: University of Pennsylvania Press, 1989); Graham Russell Hodges and Alan Edward Brown, eds., *"Pretends to Be Free": Runaway Slave Advertisements from Colonial and Revolutionary New York and New Jersey* (New York: Garland, 1994); *NJA*, 1st ser., vols. 11–12, 19–20, 24–29, 31; Anna Bustill Smith, "The Bustill Family," *Journal of Negro History* 10 (1925): 638–44; Julie Winch, *Philadelphia's Black Elite: Activism, Accommodation, and the Struggle for Autonomy, 1787–1848* (Philadelphia: Temple University Press, 1988), 5–8, 173, 184, 191; Philip S. Foner, ed., *The Voice of Black America*, vol. 1 (New York: Capricorn Books, 1975), 13. See also Weslager, *Delaware Indians*, 277–78. For the incorporation of Indians and blacks in African-American communities elsewhere in North America, see Daniel R. Mandell, "Shifting Boundaries of Race and Ethnicity: Indian-Black Intermarriage in Southern New England, 1760–1880," *Journal of American History* 85 (1998): 466–501; and Usner, "American Indians," 109.

28. Anthony F. C. Wallace, *King of the Delawares: Teedyuscung, 1700–1763* (Syracuse, N.Y.: Syracuse University Press, 1990), 1–30; Jennings, "Pennsylvania Indians," 75–91.

29. The Delaware representatives to the 1758 Crosswicks conference, listed in Smith, *History of New-Jersey*, 442, had "Christian" names and surnames, as well as Indian names. Some had last names like Swedes and Finns: Claus (Classon); Stille (Stille); Cuish (Quist); Loques (Lock); and Swanelac (Swanson). Quite a few had surnames that were common among the English or other European settlers: Wheelwright, Evans, Gosling, Store, Calvin, and Wooley. Teedyuscung, who claimed to be "king" of the Delawares during the Seven Years' War, was the son of a Delaware woman and probably a white man; he had ties to both the white and Indian communities.

30. This generalization is based on my reading of Burlington County court records and New Jersey Supreme Court records. Indians were sometimes sued for debt or for trespass in the supreme court. New Jersey Supreme Court records, New Jersey Archives, Trenton; Reed and Miller, eds., *Burlington Court Book*; Burlington County court minutes, 1709–17, and Indictments, 1731–68, Burlington County Historical Society, Burlington, N.J.

31. Northampton Towne Book, 1697–1768, New Jersey Archives; New Hanover Township Minute Book, 1729–74, New Jersey Archives; Chesterfield Town Book, 1692–1712, New Jersey Archives; Chesterfield Town Book, 1712–74, Burlington County Historical Society; Nottingham Township Minute Book, 1692–1710, 1752–72, published in *Proceedings of the New Jersey Historical Society* 58 (1940): 22–44, 74, 124–38, 179–92.

32. Myers, ed., *Narratives*, 233.

33. Chesterfield Monthly Meeting men's minutes, 11M/1685, 7M/1686, 10M/1687, 10M/1689, 2M/1691, 2M/1694; Chesterfield Monthly Meeting women's minutes, 1700–1760, both at the Friends Historical Library of Swarthmore College. See also, Jean R. Soderlund, "Women's Authority in Pennsylvania and New Jersey Quaker Meetings, 1680–1760," *William and Mary Quarterly*, 3d ser., 44 (1987): 736–39.

34. Northampton Towne Book, 72, 93, 124, 132; Chesterfield Town Book (1712–74), 63.

35. Nottingham Township Minute Book, 37, 185; Northampton Towne Book, 101, 102, 120; Chesterfield Town Book (1712–74), 34, 38, 42, 54.

36. Chesterfield Town Book (1712–74), 58; Nottingham Township Minute Book, 132; New Jersey Supreme Court case #41839.

37. T. H. Breen, "'Baubles from Britain': The American and Consumer Revolutions of the Eighteenth Century," in *Of Consuming Interests: The Style of Life in the Eighteenth Century*, ed. Cary Carson et al. (Charlottesville: University Press of Virginia, 1994), 450–51; see also in the same volume, Lois Green Carr and Lorena S. Walsh, "Changing Lifestyles and Consumer Behavior in the Colonial Chesapeake," and Cary Carson, "The Consumer Revolution in Colonial British America: Why Demand?"

38. Average inventory values (in £ sterling) increased by decade from £120.6 in 1721–30 and £139.1 in 1731–40, to £170.1 in 1741–50, £240.6 in 1751–60, and £353.8 in 1761–70. Evidence from inventories, of course, is skewed toward the more affluent segment of society because the estates of the poor were less often inventoried. Jean Ruth Soderlund, "Conscience, Interest, and Power: The Development of Quaker Opposition to Slavery in the Delaware Valley, 1688–1780" (Ph.D. diss., Temple University, 1982), 199. See also, Peter O. Wacker and Paul G. E. Clemens, *Land Use in Early New Jersey: A Historical Geography* (Newark: New Jersey Historical Society, 1995), 273.

39. Nottingham Township Minute Book, 25, 29; Chesterfield Town Book (1692–1712), 2.

40. Smith, *History of New-Jersey*, 442–46; Thomas Store et al. to Israel Pemberton, March 8, 1758, Philadelphia Yearly Meeting Indian Committee Papers, AA1:427, Quaker Collection, Haverford College.

41. Phillips P. Moulton, ed., *The Journal and Major Essays of John Woolman* (New York: Oxford University Press, 1971); John Woolman Papers, Historical Society of Pennsylvania, Philadelphia.

42. Moulton, ed., *Woolman*, 207.

43. Richard W. Pointer, "'Poor Indians' and the 'Poor in Spirit': The Indian Impact on David Brainerd," *New England Quarterly* 67 (1994): 403–7.

44. Edwards, ed., *Memoirs of David Brainerd*, 3–5, 203–24.

45. Ibid., 226; David Brainerd's Journal 1745 (MS), American Philosophical Society, Philadelphia, 7; Thomas Brainerd, *The Life of John Brainerd* (Philadelphia: Presbyterian Publication Committee, 1865), 243, 254, 259; Pointer, "Poor Indians," 407–8.

46. Pointer, "Poor Indians," 408–9; Edwards, ed., *Memoirs of David Brainerd*, 274–75, 290–91.

47. Edwards, ed., *Memoirs of David Brainerd*, 274, 290–91, 298.

48. Ibid., 303.

49. Ibid., 298, 316–18; *NJA*, 1st ser., 6:406–7.

50. Edwards, ed., *Memoirs of David Brainerd*, 328, 360, 362–63.

51. Brainerd, *Life of John Brainerd*, 253–59.

52. New Jersey Supreme Court cases #24262, #26476, #26886, #26888; New Jersey Supreme Court Minute Book, 1749–52, pp. 11, 37, 43, 49, 62, 75, and 87, New Jersey State Archives, Trenton. In 1750, the Society in Scotland for Propagating Christian Knowledge, upon hearing of

Morris's suit, asked its London correspondents and "the Most Honourable The Marquis of Lothian, The Earl of Marchmont, The Lord Advocate for Scotland, requesting they may interpose for procuring a Recommendation from his Majestys Secretarys of State to the Governour of Jersey for supporting the right of the Indians there to their lands." The SSPCK records include no report of their success, but Morris's suit does disappear from the New Jersey Supreme Court minutes. SSPCK records, minutes of General Meetings (GD95/1), vol. 4, pp. 450–51, National Archives of Scotland, Edinburgh.

53. Smith, *History of New-Jersey*, 440–46; Larrabee, "Recurrent Themes," 9–17; N.J. Secretary of State Deeds, book I-2, 85–88, 89–92, New Jersey State Archives, Trenton.

54. Brainerd, *Life of John Brainerd*, 317; Larrabee, "Recurrent Themes," 15.

55. Brainerd, *Life of John Brainerd*, 314, 316; Merrell, *Into the American Woods*, 288–89; Paul A. W. Wallace, ed., *Thirty Thousand Miles with John Heckewelder* (Pittsburgh: University of Pittsburgh Press, 1958), 198–99.

56. John Brainerd, Journal: 1761–62 (MS), Department of Rare Books and Special Collections, Princeton University Libraries (Firestone Library), 6, 9, 32–33.

57. Ibid., 19, 25, 27, 58.

58. Brainerd, *Life of John Brainerd*, 248–49.

59. John Brainerd, Journal: 1761–62, 49; Larrabee, "Recurrent Themes," 14.

60. New Jersey Supreme Court case #20358, New Jersey State Archives, Trenton; *Early Recollections and Life of Dr. James Still, 1812–1885* (New Brunswick, N.J.: Rutgers University Press, 1973), 19–20, 22.

61. Larrabee, "Recurrent Themes," 15; Brainerd, *Life of John Brainerd*, 405.

62. Hunt's Journal, 226; Richter, "Believing," 601–28.

63. In *The Pine Barrens* (New York: Farrar, Straus and Giroux, 1981), 38–43, John McPhee described a seasonal economy of residents of the pinelands that is reminiscent of the Lenape way of life.

# CONTRIBUTORS

MONIQUE BOURQUE is Fellowships and Prizes Advisor at Swarthmore College. She received her Ph.D. in American history and museum studies from the Hagley Program in the History of Industrialization at the University of Delaware. Her dissertation analyzed the social and economic relations between poorhouses and their communities in the antebellum Delaware Valley. Her current research interests include the promotion of sericulture and antebellum women's moral education, and women's participation as writers and scientists in the nature study movement of the late nineteenth century.

RUTH WALLIS HERNDON is a member of the history faculty at the University of Toledo. Her research focuses on groups of people marginalized socially, economically, and culturally in early America. She is the author of *Unwelcome Americans: Living on the Margin in Early New England* (2001). With Narragansett Indian elder Ella Wilcox Sekatau, she has written several collaborative essays on Native and European interactions, including the prize-winning essay "The Right to a Name: The Narragansett People and Rhode Island Officials, 1750–1800," published in the journal *Ethnohistory* (1997). She is presently working with economic historian John E. Murray on a collection of essays on servant apprenticeship, "'Proper and Instructive Education': Children Bound to Labor in Early America."

THOMAS HUMPHREY, assistant professor of history at Cleveland State University, has published several articles on landlords and tenants in the Hudson River Valley, including "William Prendergast and the Revolution in the Hudson River Valley" in *The Human Tradition in the American Revolution*, edited by Nancy L. Rhoden and Ian K. Steele (2000). His book on this topic is forthcoming.

SUSAN E. KLEPP is professor of colonial American and American women's history at Temple University. Much of her work has focused on the demographic history of early America. Her article "Revolutionary Bodies: Women and the Fertility Transition in the Mid-Atlantic Region, 1760–1830" appeared in the *Journal of American History* (1998). Among her books are *The Swift Progress of Population: A Documentary and Bibliographic Study of Philadelphia's Growth, 1642–1859* (1991) and *Philadelphia in Transition: A Demographic History of the City and Its Occupational Groups, 1720–1830* (1990). She also coedited *The Infortunate: The Voyage and Adventures of William Moraley, an Indentured Servant* (1992).

PHILIP D. MORGAN is Harry C. Black Professor of History, Johns Hopkins University. He is the author of *Slave Counterpoint: Black Culture in the Eighteenth-Century Chesapeake and Lowcountry* (1998). He is currently completing a book on the early Caribbean, ca. 1500–1800.

JOHN E. MURRAY is associate professor of economics at the University of Toledo. His current project is a book with the working title "The Poor Children of Antebellum Charleston." Preliminary essays on this subject have appeared in *Journal of Interdisciplinary History* and *Journal of Economic History*. The latter article (coauthored with Ruth Wallis Herndon), "Markets for Children in Early America: A Political Economy of Pauper Apprenticeship," won the 2002 Program in Early American Economy and Society prize for best article in early American economic history. Previous research concerned demographic and religious history in nineteenth-century America and appeared in *Demography, Population Studies, Bulletin of the History of Medicine,* and *Agricultural History*.

GARY B. NASH is professor of history at UCLA and director of the National Center for History in the Schools. He served as president of the Organization of American Historians in 1994–95 and won its Distinguished Service Award in 2003. His latest book is *First City: Philadelphia and the Forging of Historical Memory* (2002). Among his many other books are *Red, White, and Black: The Peoples of Early North America,* now in its fourth edition, and *The Urban Crucible: Social Change, Political Consciousness, and the Origins of the American Revolution* (1979).

SIMON NEWMAN has degrees in American studies and history from the University of Nottingham, the University of Wisconsin, and Princeton University. He is the Sir Denis Brogan Professor of American Studies at the University of Glasgow and is the author of *Parades and the Politics of the Street: Festive Culture in the Early American Republic* (1997) and *Embodied History: The Lives of the Poor in Early Philadelphia* (2003).

J. RICHARD OLIVAS is a member of the faculty in the History Department at West Los Angeles College, one of nine campuses in the Los Angeles Community College District. He earned his Ph.D. in early American history from UCLA, where he studied with Gary Nash. At WLAC, Olivas teaches a variety of courses in American history and is currently writing a book on the religious revivals of the 1740s in New England.

BILLY G. SMITH is the Michael P. Malone Professor of History at Montana State University. His research has focused primarily on reconstructing the history of the "inarticulate" in early America, including laboring people, African Americans, and women. He is the author of numerous articles and books, including *The "Lower Sort": Philadelphia's Laboring People, 1750–1800* (1990), and coeditor of *The Infortunate: The Voyage and Adventures of William Moraley, an Indentured Servant* (1992). Currently he is working on creating a computerized virtual walking tour of late eighteenth-century Philadelphia.

JEAN R. SODERLUND is professor and chair of the Department of History at Lehigh University in Bethlehem, Pennsylvania, and codirector of the Lawrence Henry Gipson Institute for Eighteenth-Century Studies. She is the author of *Quakers and Slavery: A Divided Spirit* (1985) and coauthored *Freedom by Degrees: Emancipation in Pennsylvania and Its Aftermath* (1991) with Gary B. Nash. She is currently working on a study of the Lenape Indians within mid-Atlantic colonial society.

KARIN WULF is associate professor of history at American University and Book Review Editor of *The William and Mary Quarterly*. She is the author of *Not All Wives: Women of Colonial Philadelphia* (2000) and the coeditor, with Catherine Blecki, of *Milcah Martha Moore's Book: A Commonplace Book from Revolutionary America* (1997), and, with Susan Klepp, *The Diary of Hannah Callender Sansom, 1758–1788* (forthcoming).

# INDEX

accidents, 9, 12, 22, 43, 45, 52–54, 55, 72, 74, 80, 84, 87, 139, 172–75, 181, 193–95, 204, 223, 236, 239, 242, 278

Adams, John, 26

Adams, Martha, 170

Adams, Samuel, 23

Africa, 13, 108, 119, 120; Africans, xv, 104, 108, 115–17, 290; Bight of Benin, 108

African Americans, 7, 18, 24, 49, 65, 94, 103–12, 135, 145–48, 204, 216, 226, 229, 277, 282, 295, 296, 301, 306; free, 5, 24; mulattos, 146, 148

agriculture, xv, 6, 9, 66, 194, 195, 205, 240, 293–97, 300–305. *See also* farmers

Albany County, New York, 235, 236, 244

Albro, Alice, 140

Albro, John, 149

alcohol, xviii, 17, 19, 21, 56–58, 80, 83, 87, 165, 191, 195, 198, 290, 291, 303

Aldrich, Doctor William, 149

Aldrich, Stephen, 149

Allen, Phebe, 144

almshouse, xvi, xviii, 2–5, 8, 10, 11, 15–21, 42, 55, 76, 86, 112, 116, 136, 140, 144, 150, 151, 157, 163–82, 189–206, 213, 218, 227, 266; managers, 3, 179, 196–204, 228. *See also* Chester County Poorhouse; Overseers of the Poor

American Philosophical Society, 44

American Revolution, 3–13, 17, 22–28, 41, 55, 74, 94–99, 104–11, 148, 150–57, 164, 181, 238–55, 264, 291. *See also* wars

Ames, William, 267

Anderson, Hanna, 205

Andover, Massachusetts, 24

Andrew, John, xviii

Anthony, Tent, 141

Anti-Federalists, 252–53

apprentices, 4, 51, 52, 58, 101, 117, 141, 143, 163, 165, 178, 193, 202, 204, 214–15, 225–27. *See also* artisans; indentured servants; orphans

Arendt, Hannah, 94

Ariès, Philippe, 59

Armstrong, Andrew, 56

Armstrong, James, 171

Arnold, John, 252

Arnold, Josiah, 141

artisans, xv, 8, 11–14, 17, 23–24, 27, 51, 67, 71, 81, 86, 107–20, 196, 205, 216, 226. *See also* apprentices; journeymen

Aston, William, 295

Atkinson, John, 205

Atlantic World, 6, 7, 103, 291, 295, 299, 306

Australia, 103

Babcock, George, 145

badges, for poor, 143

Bahamas, 104, 106

Bailey, John, 52

Bailyn, Bernard, xiii, 239

Baitzel, Debbie Ann, 202

Baker, Thomas, 202

Baltimore, Maryland, 194, 290

Barker, Elizabeth, 138

Barwell, Samuel, 299

Bates, John, 225

Baumgarten, Linda, 110

beggars, xvi, 2, 3, 11, 13, 17, 21, 24, 28, 42, 95, 121, 176

Belcher, Andrew, 274

Bennan, Mary, 165

Bennett, John, 144

Bentley, Rev. William, 13

Berkeley County, South Carolina, 215, 217

Bernard, Governor Francis, 23

Besely, Sarah, 202

Bethel Mission, 292, 303–4. *See also* Brainerd, David

Bethesda (orphanage), 215. *See also* orphans

Bethlehem, Pennsylvania, 65

Bickerdite, Jane, 20

Birch, William Russell, 44

births, 49, 52, 54, 63–86, 103–4, 121, 138, 147, 266, 298; stillbirths, 45, 52, 59, 68, 70, 77, 81–82, 87. *See also* fertility; midwives

Blackmar, Priscilla, 143